COLERIDGE
THE VISIONARY

COLERIDGE
THE VISIONARY

By

J. B. BEER

Sometime Fellow of St. John's College,
Cambridge

1959

CHATTO & WINDUS

LONDON

Published by
Chatto and Windus Ltd
42 William IV Street
London WC 2

*

Clarke, Irwin and Co Ltd
Toronto

Printed in Great Britain by
T. and A. Constable Ltd
Edinburgh

To the author of THE ANCIENT MARINER

Your poem must eternal be,
Dear sir! it cannot fail,
For 'tis incomprehensible,
And without head or tail.

COLERIDGE'S ANONYMOUS POEM OF 1800, AS QUOTED
IN *Biographia Literaria*

The principle of the imagination resembles the emblem of
the serpent, by which the ancients typified wisdom and
the universe, with undulating folds, for ever varying and
for ever flowing into itself,—circular, and without
beginning or end.

A TYPICAL SAMPLE OF COLERIDGE'S CONVERSATION
Hazlitt, *London Magazine*, 1820

CONTENTS

ACKNOWLEDGMENTS

I wish to thank the publishers and authors concerned for permission to include extracts from the following works:

Bollingen Foundation Inc. and Routledge & Kegan Paul Ltd.: *The Notebooks of Samuel Taylor Coleridge*, Volume I, edited by Kathleen Coburn.

Bowes & Bowes Ltd.: *The Disinherited Mind* by Erich Heller.

Jonathan Cape Ltd.: *Between Two Worlds* by John Middleton Murry.

The Clarendon Press, Oxford: *The Poetical Works of S. T. Coleridge* (edited by E. H. Coleridge); *Coleridge's Biographia Literaria* (edited by J. Shawcross); *Collected Letters of Samuel Taylor Coleridge* (edited by E. L. Griggs).

Constable & Co. Ltd. and Houghton Mifflin Company: *The Road to Xanadu* by J. L. Lowes.

Constable & Co. Ltd.: *Unpublished Letters of Samuel Taylor Coleridge* (edited by E. L. Griggs); *Coleridge's Miscellaneous Criticism* and *Coleridge's Shakespearean Criticism* (edited by T. M. Raysor).

Rupert Hart-Davis Ltd.: *Coleridge* by Humphry House.

The Hogarth Press Ltd.: *The Death of the Moth* by Virginia Woolf; *The Notebook of Malte Laurids Brigge* by R. M. Rilke (translated by John Linton); *Sonnets to Orpheus* and *Duino Elegies* by R. M. Rilke (translated by J. B. Leishman).

Longmans, Green & Co. Ltd.: *Psychoanalytic Method and the Doctrine of Freud* by R. Dalbiez.

Oxford University Press: *The Letters of John Keats* (edited by H. B. Forman).

Routledge & Kegan Paul Ltd.: *Inquiring Spirit* (edited by Kathleen Coburn); *Philosophical Lectures of Samuel Taylor Coleridge* (edited by Kathleen Coburn); *The Condemned Playground* by Cyril Connolly.

University of Chicago Press: *Coleridge, Opium and Kubla Khan* by E. Schneider.

I am also grateful to Mr. A. H. B. Coleridge, holder of the copyrights, and to Miss Kathleen Coburn, Professor D. J. Gordon, The Bollingen Foundation, and the Syndics of the Fitzwilliam Museum, Cambridge: for permission to quote from the unpublished notebooks of Coleridge and other manuscript materials; and to the late Mr L. A. G. Strong for permission to quote from his broadcast talk, *Reminiscences of W. B. Yeats*.

PREFACE

For over a century, the myriad-mindedness of Samuel Taylor Coleridge has steadfastly refused to be contained within the bounds of a single volume, and this book is no exception to that rule. It does not set out to provide either a complete account of Coleridge's thought or a detailed appreciation of his poetry. It does attempt, however, to explore some of the fields where poet and thinker met, and thus to throw light on both the intellectual organization of the poetry and the imaginative qualities implicit in the philosophy. Although the argument finds its natural point of focus in the great poems, therefore, it also includes many quotations from and references to Coleridge's writings as a whole. In addition, I have quoted from a large number of contemporary works, in order that the reader may see for himself the elements in them which set fire to Coleridge's imagination. It should be pointed out that such passages are often representative of a much wider hinterland of speculation and imagery.

In quoting from Coleridge's manuscript writings, current editorial practice has been followed in reproducing the text, idiosyncrasies included, as faithfully as possible: experience shows that when he is writing at speed even the most trifling abbreviation may give some clue to the organization of his thought. On one or two occasions where an obvious mistake might distract the reader unduly however, the text has been corrected. In the case of other quotations, the edition most likely to have been known to Coleridge is given and a similar editorial policy followed.

I wish to acknowledge a particularly large debt to Professor Basil Willey, who has read this work at several stages and made many valuable comments. I would also like to express appreciation to Mr Hugh Sykes Davies and Dr R. T. H. Redpath for their constant encouragement; to Dr David Daiches and Professor John Danby for many helpful criticisms and suggestions; and to Dr George Whalley, whose fund of knowledge about Coleridge and his reading has been made constantly available to me. The first two volumes of Miss Kathleen Coburn's monumental edition of the notebooks arrived just in time for me to make a few last-minute additions and alterations to the text: on the very rare occasions where I have ventured to differ from her, it has only been after careful consideration of a doubtful passage. She too has been constantly willing to answer my various inquiries. No one can write on Coleridge now without constant awareness of the debt due to her

PREFACE

and to the other recent scholars whose work has made whole ranges of Coleridge's thought readily accessible for the first time. Like them, I am conscious that what seems difficult in Coleridge can often be explained by further reference to his omnivorous reading and writing: and I shall always be glad to hear of points which I may have overlooked so far.

The librarians and staff of St John's College, Jesus College and the University Library in Cambridge, and of the British Museum, also deserve my thanks for many varied services. I must finally express my deep gratitude to St John's College, Cambridge, for a series of research awards which made this work possible in practical terms.

J. B. B.

Cambridge, April 1959

Chapter I

COLERIDGE AND ROMANTICISM

THE term 'Romantic Movement' is less fashionable than it used to be with critics, and understandably so. Nowadays, movements involve the paraphernalia of manifestos, slogans, action committees and party lines: and it is hard to find anything of the sort among poets and artists of the late eighteenth century. The Preface to the *Lyrical Ballads* is sometimes regarded as a manifesto, admittedly, but a comparison of its precepts with the published work of Wordsworth and Coleridge shows how small its influence was. Perhaps there was the desire for a movement, a groping for it even, but the individual differences between the artists involved were too great to admit of anything more. The critic finds himself on firm ground only when he turns from common beliefs to common problems, and common problems do not constitute a movement.

The word 'romantic' ought not to be allowed to pass out of usage, however. Even if some of its early protagonists did not think that they were doing anything more than introducing a new fashion, or criticizing some particular aspect of eighteenth-century practice, we can now see that romanticism, in all its many ramifications, was a distinct departure in the human mind, significant in fields outside literature and possessed of characteristics that can be recognized and described. Even when it reverted to the art of earlier periods, the very manner of its reversion bore witness to its own essential originality.

Some years ago, in an article 'On the Discrimination of Romanticisms'. A. O. Lovejoy argued that we ought to learn to use the word 'romanticism' in the plural.[1] If a common denominator of romanticisms existed, he said, it had never been clearly exhibited, and its presence ought not to be assumed *a priori*. A good deal of confusion would be avoided by speaking separately of the various romanticisms which are commonly lumped together under the one simple

heading. Replying to his arguments, René Wellek maintained that in spite of their wide range, all forms of romanticism had certain central principles in common, and he proposed a threefold formulation to comprise them: namely,
imagination for the view of poetry, nature for the view of the
world, and symbol and myth for poetic style.[2]

One may agree with Wellek that there is likely to be some
underlying coherence in a term that has been found useful
for so long by so many eminent critics, but it is less easy to
accept the formula which he offers. Not only are the terms
vague, but they remain isolated in the mind. The reason why
they should have been drawn together into a single stream is
not made clear. In such circumstances, it is better to examine
the question historically, by way of a point which Wellek
examines in the course of his discussion. How did the artists
of early romanticism regard the events in which they found
themselves involved?

The evidence which Wellek brings forward is rather
surprising. It suggests that many poets of the time realized
that something important and new was happening, but that
they were unwilling to use the word 'romantic' in describing
it. Even when they were familiar with the word as a description of the new poetic schools on the continent of Europe,
they still tended not to apply the term to their own activities.

Wellek suggests no explanation for this phenomenon, but
it is possible that it should be sought in the history of the
word in English. At the time of which we are speaking, the
word 'romantic' already had a distinctive sense which linked
it closely with the eighteenth century. It had then been used
to describe certain fashions in taste, such as the liking for
Gothic and, more specifically, the old romances. The artists
of the new generation may well have felt that it described
something which had happened before their time, and which
they themselves were in process of superseding.

At this point it is profitable to look at the contents of a
philosophical lecture delivered by Coleridge in 1818, which
opened with a discussion of the Middle Ages.[3] The medieval
mind, he maintained, had been two-sided. On the one hand
it was scholastic, connecting without combining and prefer-
ring the federal in art and society—yet contriving by virtue

of the discipline thus imposed on it to fashion tools for the human mind finer than any hitherto known. On the other hand, there also existed the 'other part of the Gothic mind', which he characterized as 'inward', 'striking' and 'romantic'. It might be described, he said, as the 'genius' of the Gothic mind, but if so, it was a genius bearing the marks of its birthplace—a world of nature untouched by human mark and of men still in the grip of superstition.

Miss Kathleen Coburn has pointed out that this may have been the first time that romanticism was characterized publicly in such detail and with so many of the concepts that we still associate with it.[4] The point may be accepted, but it does not follow, of course, that Coleridge himself would have thought it an adequate description of the aims of himself and his contemporaries. The fact that he describes it as a 'part' of the Gothic mind suggests otherwise, for it was foreign to his nature to give whole-hearted approval to anything which satisfied only a part of human nature. I think it more likely that in deliberately contrasting Gothic genius with Scholastic precision, he was pointing to a 'dissociation of sensibility' which he felt to have existed in the medieval mind and to have been paralleled in the literary scene of his own youth.[5] Medieval scholasticism had had its counterpart in eighteenth-century rationalism, just as its rude 'genius' had been matched by the current taste for Pindaric odes, graveyard meditations and the 'sublime'. The latter had been important, but as a necessary reaction against a sterile rationalism: they had been a protest, not a solution. 'The horrible and the preternatural have usually seized on the popular taste, at the rise and decline of literature,' he wrote in 1797; and shortly afterwards, describing his projected play, *Osorio*, as ' "romantic & wild & somewhat terrible",' he commented, 'but indeed I am almost weary of the Terrible'.[6] For him, it seems, the value of the 'romantic' lay in its function as a complementary force in the contemporary mind. By bringing to the light factors which the age's narrow rationalism ignored, it helped to undermine the autarchy of that rationalism.

Coleridge did not wish to destroy rationalism: his aim was simply to set the current idea of rationalism in a broader interpretation of the universe. In medieval art, the problem hardly arises at all, for there symbolism relates to an agreed metaphysical universe; in Renaissance art it has a high status as point of reference for a humanity that shares common ideals and aspirations; but after that its history is one of a decline first into the portrayal of separate, esoteric, social universes and then into the expression of private, individual worlds. In the last stage, there is danger of a complete breakdown in communication—a danger which has been well pictured recently by Erich Heller.[8]

The predicament of the symbol in our age is caused by a split between 'reality' and what it signifies. There is no more any commonly accepted symbolic or transcendent order of things. What the modern mind perceives as order is established through the tidy relationship between things themselves. In one word: the only conceivable order is positivist-scientific. If there still is a—no doubt, diminishing—demand for the fuller reality of the symbol, then it must be provided for by the unsolicited gifts of art. But in the sphere of art the symbolic substance, dismissed from its disciplined commitments to 'reality', dissolves into incoherence, ready to attach itself to any fragment of experience, invading it with irresistible power, so that a pair of boots, or a chair in the painter's attic, or a single tree on a slope which the poet passes, or an obscure inscription in a Venetian church, may suddenly become the precariously unstable centre of an otherwise unfocused universe. Since 'the great words from the time when what *really* happened was still visible, are no longer for us' (as Rilke once put it in a Requiem for a young poet), the 'little words' have to carry an excessive freight of symbolic significance. No wonder that they are slow in delivering it. They are all but incommunicable private symbols, established beyond any doubt as symbols by the quality and intensity of artistic experience behind them, but lacking in any representative properties. Such is the economy of human consciousness that the positivist impoverishment of the one region produces anarchy in the other. In the end, atomic lawlessness is bound to prevail in both.

The romantic artist, faced with an unstable universe, works under strain. As an artist, it is his task to wrestle with his materials, both physically and intellectually, but it is not his task to create those materials in the first place. If the poet is to achieve a work of some magnitude, it is not enough that he should wrestle with the structure of language and adapt it to his thought: that thought must also be part of a large and widely accepted universe of thinking in which he feels at home. It is necessary both that his imaginative powers should be called out and exercised fully, and that they should work in a sphere which has points of unquestioned security. Small works of art, embodying isolated insights, may be achieved with effect in an unstable imaginative universe, but an extended work needs the mythology which comes only from a stable one.

T. E. Hulme once described romanticism as 'spilt religion',[9] and thus drew attention to some of the broader implications of this situation. Religion represents, among other things, stability: and the artist who can no longer find a metaphysical stability in the universe at large will come to seek it in the common human nature of mankind: and if that fails him (for his fellows are themselves a part of the external universe) he may be driven to set up himself as the stable point in a universe that seems otherwise devoid of stability.

One can trace a development of this sort in English literature from the Renaissance onwards. At the beginning of the seventeenth century, both the medieval world-picture and the implications of the new discoveries were present with such equal imaginative force that writers were able to delight in the dramatic contrast between them. As the empirical attitude began to dominate, however, literature fell back upon common humanity. Pope's assertion that 'the proper study of mankind is man', a fair summing-up of the Augustan attitude, succeeds in excluding individual man at one extreme and any metaphysical reference at the other ('Presume not God to scan'). Johnson had a more limited view of the possibilities of human culture, but still felt himself able to appeal to 'the good sense of the common reader'. It was Wordsworth who first took as a central theme the significance of man in solitude, cut off from the influences

17

of society at large, and Coleridge who first gave the most important place to the inward life and perceptions of man, as opposed to his outward behaviour.

It is in Wordsworth and Coleridge, therefore, that the peculiar strains associated with romanticism first show themselves strongly. The artist's insecurity is not necessarily a handicap in the realization of small works—indeed the sudden release of pent-up energy may result in short works of great power. In extended creation, however, the romantic predicament becomes evident. The lack of a mythology makes the creation of a sustained work such as an epic extremely difficult: and ironically, it is one symptom of the romantic that the epic is highly attractive to him. But the projection of a complete universe demands from him nothing short of complete self-sufficiency of imagination. The romantic artist, in his human weakness, has not the power to achieve this, though his struggles towards it may provide the materials of a memorable autobiography. It is no accident that Wordsworth's *Prelude* and Coleridge's *Biographia Literaria* remain to us as the chief products of their extended powers.

Autobiography is no substitute for epic, however; moreover, the autobiographic phase of poetic thought carries with it peculiar dangers of its own. As we have already suggested, the artist who sets up individual man as the stable point of reference in his poetic universe is only one step away from setting himself up in that position. When that happens, when creator and subject-matter are one and the same, there is danger of unlimited self-involution. If the artist is to steer a course between the Scylla of incomprehensibility and the Charybdis of insanity, he must establish within himself a peculiarly delicate poise—a poise which will enable him to remain, as it were, constantly at one remove from himself.

It is a testimony to the capabilities of human nature that this difficult poise has at times been achieved and maintained. At its best it has even been held effortlessly and almost unconsciously. Keats maintained that a poet should seek for a knowledge which is at one and the same time universal and spontaneous within his own mind[10]; and his own success in that search is enshrined in the *Odes*.

The balance is always a precarious one, however. The

18

precariousness is everywhere apparent in the transitoriness of most romantic inspiration, and may be found boldly depicted in Scott Fitzgerald's novel *The Great Gatsby*. Jay Gatsby, the hero, embodies many qualities of romantic man in a blatant form. He is described by the narrator as a man who[11]

> ... sprang from his Platonic conception of himself. He was a son of God—a phrase which, if it means anything, means just that—and he must be about his Father's business, the service of a vast, vulgar, and meretricious beauty.

As the novel unfolds, it becomes evident that the glory of a man who, like Gatsby, springs from his Platonic conception of himself, involves a tragic flaw. In Gatsby's case, the flaw is symbolized by a green light across the bay, near which lives a woman whom he has loved for many years, and still desires desperately to possess. The disillusionment of actually meeting her, the destruction of the external strut that supports his inward vision, precipitates his tragedy.

The glorious, yet tragic careers of such heroes epitomize the glory and tragedy of romanticism. Even the most self-sufficient of artists cannot avoid making certain assumptions about the external world, and the point where these assumptions are made is the point of his weakness. It is at this point that the stability of his beliefs about man may be upset by some intractability of the world or of society.

This precariousness of vision goes back long before the Romantics, of course. To achieve writing of epic stature, as we have said, a writer must be describing a universe, the ultimate structure and ordering of which lie beyond the field of his critical analysis. As soon as this ceases to be true, to however limited an extent, a certain unsatisfactoriness begins to creep in. Even in the last great epic to be achieved in the English language, the difficulties of the form for a post-Renaissance mind are already apparent. *Paradise Lost* does contrive to raise such an objective structuring before the reader, but its author is often driven to the very walls and bulwarks of his citadel. A concentration of pressure, one feels, might send him hurtling, like his own Satan, into the abyss. Even Milton, in other words, is more the shrewd secretary of a hardly-held republic than the bard of an established, irreversible order. We admire his vision, and even more the strength of intellect that can maintain it against such odds; but the steady assurance of the classical epic-writers is necessarily lacking.

The romantic artist does not even possess Milton's beleaguered citizenship. He is a lonely, diminished figure. In the seventeenth century, when the ultimate battlefield lay outside the human being, Adam and Eve could be allowed to take their sad and solitary way from Eden still in possession of a certain human dignity. But a struggle which takes place inside the individual man can have little to do with human dignity. For such a concept, the romantic thinker is forced to substitute the more limited one of moral stature.

Romantic achievement of any magnitude must accept this state of affairs as a starting-point: and once this precariousness is allowed for, achievement becomes possible within its limitations. A new world begins to be built from the materials of the old. From the old order, the romantic author may extrapolate, for example, the conceptions of the 'fallen angel' and the 'pilgrim of eternity': and if so, these can become for him new archetypal figures. Most romantic artists see themselves in both rôles: but the proportions involved vary considerably from one individual to another. The romantic artists who have achieved most have tended to accept one or other mould as dominant and have accordingly allowed their work to reflect either their pride or their predicament.

The 'pilgrim of eternity' creates an art which pivots upon the very perplexity of the individual in engagement with a universe whose meaning is hidden from him. His art is likely to be an art of struggle and perplexity. The scope of the rôle is by no means narrow, for it can include the achievements of men as diverse in temperament and upbringing as Wordsworth and Kafka.

These two writers may well stand, indeed, for the two poles of the 'pilgrim' artist, and the diversity between them rests upon a diversity of attitude towards the human imagination. It might be thought that the power of imagination is the one fact which no artist could doubt without losing his artistic nature altogether, but this is not so. Wordsworth stands as the supreme example of an artist who lost faith in the imagination as an ultimate value, and created a poetry which avoids reliance upon it. The result necessarily lacks the easy elegance of art which is the straightforward outflowing of an unchecked imagination, but that does not destroy its status as art. On the contrary, it becomes a supreme example of the poetry of struggle and alienation. The human being may often be helped by his visionary powers in dealing with the universe, but it is a source upon which he may not rely. He may accept the help and healing of nature, but he must also wrestle with her physical, palpable intractability. Wordsworth's passages on the tenderness of nature are those which find their way into the anthologies, but equally characteristic of the man are his descriptions of the fearfulness of nature, and even more important, of the drabness, hardness and bleakness beneath her tender surface. This combination of art-forms which presuppose imaginative experience with a deep distrust of that experience results in an art which is memorable, yet strangely divided against itself. It is perhaps best summed up in the well-known passage in *The Prelude*, where the imaginative child lost in the hills is terrified to come upon a place where a murderer was once hanged in chains, and where his name is still to be seen carved in the turf[12]:

> A casual glance had shown them, and I fled,
> Faltering and faint, and ignorant of the road:
> Then, reascending the bare common, saw
> A naked pool that lay beneath the hills,
> The beacon on the summit, and, more near,
> A girl, who bore a pitcher on her head,
> And seemed with difficult steps to force her way
> Against the blowing wind. It was, in truth,
> An ordinary sight; but I should need
> Colours and words that are unknown to man,
> To paint the visionary dreariness
> Which, while I looked all round for my lost guide,
> Invested moorland waste, and naked pool,
> The beacon crowning the lone eminence,
> The female and her garments vexed and tossed
> By the strong wind.

The peculiar poise of the Wordsworthian attitude is enshrined in that phrase, 'visionary dreariness'. It is equally enshrined in his vision of the moon from the summit of Snowdon, as recorded in the last book of *The Prelude*.[13] The description there of the moon as an emblem of the mighty mind remains the best allegory of Wordsworth's attitude to his own powers. At its highest, the human mind may be possessed of a strange radiance as it broods over the dark abyss of human affairs—it may even be enabled to detect a harmony within the still sad music of humanity's many voices: but this vision is only likely to be granted after long periods of struggling ascent.

To the Wordsworthian, therefore, it follows that force of character is as important as power of imagination. For this reason, many Victorian moralists found in him their mainstay when the light of their faith in Christianity died. For this reason, also, many of the great Victorian artists excelled in the portrayal of moments of 'visionary dreariness'. Tennyson's *In Memoriam*, the novels of George Eliot, and the novels and poems of Hardy all contain passages which witness to the fact that there has been a Wordsworth in the world.

Wordsworth's was a form of romanticism peculiar to certain types of English character, however. In general, romantic artists retain their faith in the imagination, and in so doing achieve a higher degree of elegance. Kafka, for example, has such a faith, even though his universe yields little meaning to the questing human being. Whether he is a traveller, trying to reach the castle, or a prisoner, unable to discover what is going on at his trial, man is doomed to disappointment, yet his experience contains a certain aesthetic satisfaction. As in Wordsworth's poetry, the picture of an isolated man endeavouring to reach some settlement with a mysterious universe is great and memorable: and his endurance against forces outside himself assures him of a certain stature. But the techniques of the two writers are different. Wordsworth's poetry at its most characteristic is a struggle with the intractability of language; Kafka, on the other hand, induces a dream-like fluidity in his writing which Wordsworth rarely achieved or aspired to outside the 'Lucy' poems.

Artists such as Kafka and Wordsworth succeed in dealing with the romantic predicament to the extent that they produce lasting works of art: but their particular course does not satisfy the deepest urge of most artists, which is to present, not a search for significance, but significance achieved. And this 'achieved significance' must be something which expresses the personality as a whole. It is this demand, and the consciousness that on rare occasions in his past it has been fulfilled, which makes the romantic artist a 'fallen angel'.

The 'fall' is not simply a metaphysical supposition: it is to many artists a fact in time, for the state to which they aspire is one which they are conscious of having possessed in childhood. Cyril Connolly has made precisely this point in an essay on Rimbaud[14]:

> Romantic poetry is the poetry of the Fall, poetry in which childhood represents a state of grace, a period of innocence, of the apprehension of beauty, and hence maturity a period of disillusion, when the sense of guilt, the knowledge of good and evil, of the conflict between soul and body, poisons everything. . . . Romanticism is a state of mind which has been suggested to humanity by Christian morality and which is tragic when not supported by Christian belief, for it is the idea of Eden and the Fall, without Paradise to round it off.

This is only true of some artists, however. For them, as Connolly points out in his essay, it is a rejection of maturity, and therefore an attempt to run away from human experience. But for others, this consciousness may continue to exist as an essential part of their developed art. Rilke, for example, gives mature expression to this conception in his figure of the 'angel'.[15]

> The 'Angel' of the Elegies has nothing to do with the Angel of the Christian heaven (rather with the angelic figures of Islam) . . . the Angel of the Elegies is the creature in whom that transformation of the visible into the invisible we are performing already appears completed. For the Angel of the Elegies all bygone Towers

23

and Palaces are existent, *because* they have long been invisible, and the still surviving Towers and Bridges of our existence *already* invisible, although still (for us) remaining corporeal. The Angel of the Elegies is the being who vouches for the recognition of a higher degree of reality in the invisible.—Therefore 'terrible' to us, because we, its lovers and transformers, still cling to the visible.

Elsewhere Rilke describes the 'angel' in action. In the Spanish landscape, 'the last', he says, 'that I illimitably experienced',[16]

. . . everywhere appearance and vision came, as it were, together in the object, in every one of them a whole inner world was exhibited, as though an angel, in whom space was contained, were blind and looking into himself.

Rilke's path is another that is open to the romantic artist, then. He may dedicate himself to the moments of revealed harmony and ignore the rest of his experience.

Such moments are likely to be rare, however: at other times, the artist's vision will inevitably be fragmentary, or will involve the deliberate imposition of an interpretation which is known to be, in some respects, purely subjective. If he is to produce works of art with any regularity, he must find some way of coming to terms with this situation.

Keats had not yet recognized this when he allowed himself to 'remain Content with half knowledge'[17]:—he was willing to set his course by the inspiration of the moment, and to let it lead him to an immediate destination. Such a willingness was adequate for the time being, but it depended upon his continuing to have this type of insight. For the developing poet, the time will come when he wishes to produce work of greater magnitude: and this, as we have said, calls for a more dependable subject-matter—one with which he himself is less personally involved. The evidence of the Letters suggests that Keats would gradually have come to 'mask' his identity, as Yeats did, and thus to save it from submersion. The adoption of a 'mask' in such circumstances is not an act of hypocrisy: it is simply the adoption of one interpretation of the universe as a framework for art, the poet accepting the structuring of vision with which, for the time being, he will look at the world, and continuing to live within these self-imposed limitations until he finds that he has worked his way beyond them. The whole process is much less conscious and deliberate than this, of course, and it is probably the most successful method which has been devised for dealing with the romantic predicament. Yet it is always known to be a second best. We have only to read Yeats's late poem *The Circus Animals' Desertion*[18] to see, in the poet's final dissatisfaction, that even here the problem has not been solved.

Nevertheless, the existence of these two moulds, and the flexibility with which they offer opportunity for creative activity of many, varied types, should warn us against taking too pessimistic a view of romanticism. It is not, in the last analysis, a disease but a faith: and one misunderstands it if one ignores this fact. The faith in man which dominated the Renaissance has always been active within it, and was particularly marked at the time when it first sprang up. It was still so marked a century later, indeed, that T. E. Hulme could contrast it with the previous restraint of classicism by means of his well-known image of the bucket and the well.[19] The classicist, he said, saw man as a bucket lowered into a well, whereas the romantic identified him with the well itself. The relevance of this analysis to both early and late romanticism is emphasized by the fact that Lowes found an appropriate motto for Book One of *The Road to Xanadu* in a quotation from Hofmannsthal: 'The deep well knows it certainly.'

Coleridge does not fit naturally into any of the types which we have noticed above. He has elements of most of them, but woven together in a complicated form. He is both fallen angel and pilgrim of eternity, but in a form which makes for inhibition of his creative faculties except on rare occasions. Nor will the traditional and obvious grouping of him with Wordsworth stand in this context, for the theme of man's lonely struggle, physically and intellectually, with the universe is not one which attracted him or elicited his best work. The few notable exceptions, such as *Dejection: an Ode*, contain other preoccupations, point in a different direction, and owe their existence in the first place to his intercourse with Wordsworth.

There is a closer affinity with Keats, but it is not close enough to make a grouping of the two poets profitable. Keats himself was aware of the essential difference between their attitudes, and observed with his customary insight[20]:

> Coleridge ... would let go by a fine isolated verisimilitude caught from the Penetralium of mystery, from being incapable of remaining Content with half knowledge.

This is the heart of the difference: it is expressed independently and in surprisingly similar terms by Coleridge's daughter Sara, who was conscious of the same trait in herself[21]:

> ... whatever subject I commence I feel discontent unless I could pursue it in every direction to the farthest bounds of thought. .... This was the reason that my father wrote by snatches. He could not bear to complete incompletely, which everybody else does.

As usual, Coleridge himself was aware of the existence of this trait: and as usual he saw more deeply into its causes. A particularly good account appears in a notebook of about 1804.[22]

> [I] go on from circle to circle till I break against the shore of my Hearers' patience, or have my concentricals dashed to nothing by a Snore.—that is my ordinary mishap.

Just before this, he offers an explanation:

> My illustrations swallow up my thesis. I feel too intensely the omnipresence of all in each, platonically speaking; or psychologically my brain-fibres, or the spiritual light which abides in the brain marrow, as visible Light appears to do in sundry rotten mackerel and other *smashy* matters, is of too general an affinity with all things/and tho' it perceives the *difference* of things, yet is eternally pursuing the likenesses, or rather that which is common.

It will be noticed, nevertheless, that Keats did not deny to

Coleridge the possession of Negative Capability, or feel that his mind was 'a select party'. His complaint lay elsewhere— that Coleridge would not allow his negative capability to fall into solution, because he was always following the trail still further. Certainly, Coleridge himself would have been the first to agree that the mind should be a thoroughfare for all thoughts: he described Shakespeare as 'myriad-minded'[23] and evidently regarded his own mind in similar terms. In later years, he once discussed the difference between Dr Johnson and himself as conversationalists, comparing Johnson to a 'single drum', and himself to a timeless Aeolian harp.[24] And the Aeolian harp is, after all, the perfect image of negative capability.

So marked is the diversity within his mind, indeed, that some of his critics have been moved to formulate their interpretations around it. Stephen Potter has suggested that one may speak of two Coleridges: 'Coleridge' and 'S. T. C.'[25] The productions of 'Coleridge', on the one hand, spring from the spontaneous, imaginative poet: those of 'S. T. C.', on the other, from the theologian, the self-conscious, moralizing pedagogue—identifiable, presumably, with the pathetic snuffler of Carlyle's description and the table-talking bore of Max Beerbohm's cartoon.

To make a Jekyll and Hyde of Coleridge, however, is to under-rate his sensitivity and range—and Potter himself half acknowledges this in an appendix to his book.[26] In particular, it leads to a dichotomy between Coleridge the poet and Coleridge the religious thinker which involves a total misunderstanding of his position, and which has yet been encouraged in the work of some of his most sympathetic commentators.[27]

It is true of course that there is an unsatisfactory element in Coleridge. When reading his letters, we must occasionally find ourselves agreeing with Virginia Woolf that we are listening to 'the very voice . . . of Micawber himself'. Yet the *caveat* which she enters immediately afterwards discourages the reader from judging too hastily.[28]

But there is a difference. For this Micawber knows that he is Micawber. He holds a looking-glass in his hand. He is a man of exaggerated self-consciousness, endowed with an astonishing power of self-analysis. Dickens would need to be doubled with Henry James, to be trebled with Proust, in order to convey the complexity and the conflict of a Pecksniff who despises his own hypocrisy, of a Micawber who is humiliated by his own humiliation.

This is true; and we have already glimpsed one reason for Coleridge's apparent hypocrisy, which helps to explain much of it. His powers of negative capability, coupled with his desire for friendship, led him to sympathize with people of the most diverse attitudes, and to speak to them in the language of their own opinions. In consequence he could be betrayed into making statements which appear to be mutually contradictory. He once remarked to Hazlitt that lack of consistency is often due to excess of sympathy,[29] and this was clearly true of himself.

Nowhere is Coleridge's 'excess of sympathy' more evident than in his attitude towards the two major metaphysical theories which have been in conflict since the Renaissance. There are few writers who have not been touched by the conflict in some way: a recent example of its use as a theme is to be found in Lionel Trilling's novel, *The Middle of the Journey*.[30] It hinges ultimately upon the dilemma about the nature of man which is implicit in the romantic dilemma. Is man truly made in the image of his Creator, and hindered only by the ruthless conditions of his environment from realizing the glory of his true identity? Or is he, after all, in the clutches of a spiritual disease, stained by an eternal guilt? So wide is the gulf between the two views that it is no exaggeration to say that their respective protagonists speak different languages. Those who put their faith in the divinity of mankind talk of building the new Jerusalem, of striving towards the ideal, of choosing right courses of action, of responsibility; while those who hold the other speak of sin and redemption, of man's insufficiency and God's mercy, of necessary evils and the protection of innocence.

In the course of human life, few people succeed in adhering completely to one belief or the other, and the path of moral thought is scattered with compromises between the two. Yet it is clear that in terms of pure logic at least, each attitude is ultimately exclusive of the other, and admits of no compromise. Coleridge was one of those who find themselves torn between an awareness of this and an unwillingness to choose. The reason, for him as for many of the others, was that commitment to one view or the other would necessarily have involved the falsification of part of his experience. The dilemma is present, openly and clearly stated, in his early poem, *The Eolian Harp*[31]; it can be traced in several of his early letters on theological subjects[32]; while in later years he was to represent his life as having been one long struggle to reconcile Greek and Hebrew forms of thought.[33]

The conflict was pressingly conscious to him, for the two sides of it represented varying phases in his own personality. When he was most aware of the working of his imagination, his powers seemed little short of angelic. The poet in him seemed to be not merely made in the image of God, but invested with some of the divine creative powers. When illness or unhappiness robbed him of his creativity, on the other hand, he felt himself helpless and weak, infinitely dependent on the divine mercy.

Coleridge at his most creative periods, moreover, was not merely the poet. At such times, his questing self also came to the fore. His 'disquisitive mind' was devoted to the pursuit of knowledge—knowledge sought, not merely for the sake of writing poetry, but in the conviction that ultimate truth was itself a poetic harmony. It is this dialectic within him between the angelic creator and the pilgrim scholar which sets him beyond the attitudes represented by Wordsworth and Keats respectively.

It is interesting to notice that even in his own day there was a tendency to find a classification for him outside the familiar 'Lake school'. An anonymous contributor to the *London University Magazine* wrote in 1830[34]:

... we have a confident hope that Coleridge, Blake, and Flaxman are the forerunners of a more elevated and purer system, which has even now begun to take root in the breast of the English nation; they have laid a foundation for future minds—Coleridge, for the development of a more internal philosophy—Blake and Flaxman, for a purer and more ennobling sentiment in works of art.

Jakob Götzenburger, the German artist, who visited England between 1824 and 1826, said, 'I saw in England many men of talent, but only three men of genius—Coleridge, Flaxman, and Blake; and of these Blake was the greatest.''[35]

There may be a Swedenborgian bias in these judgments, since an interest in the sect was shared by all three artists, but this is not likely. Coleridge did not consider himself a Swedenborgian, and was thought heretical by some members of the sect. On the whole, it seems more likely that it was their preoccupation with the spiritual significance of material phenomena—their 'theories of correspondences'—which set these men apart from other English artists, in the eyes of some observers.

To say this is not to deny that there was a deep difference between Coleridge and Blake. In this case, the difference was governed by their varying attitudes to science. For all his antipathy towards narrow rationalisms (an antipathy which can be traced even in his days of Hartley-worship), Coleridge had a wish to bring scientific truths within the orbit of his poetic vision which was quite uncharacteristic of Blake. Except for a brief period, which he swiftly regretted,[36] Coleridge thought of Newton as a genius of the first order—even a divine intellect.[37] Blake agreed that Newton was a genius, but thought him mistaken in his narrowness of vision—the best that could be said of him was that he was asleep.[38] Blake, with his radical and total condemnation of the scientific attitude, set his course by the star of the imagination and succeeded, in spite of many lapses, in achieving a series of homogeneous works in art and poetry. Coleridge could not limit himself in this way. The Reason which Blake despised was to be the sun of his universe. To fail in achieving a synthesis of Reason and Imagination was preferable in his eyes to success in vindicating the Imagination alone.

Yet in spite of this difference, Blake and Coleridge probably understood one another better than did any of their contemporaries. Coleridge was filled with enthusiastic admiration on reading the *Songs of Innocence and of Experience*, and after visiting Blake 'talked finely' of him.[39] Both poets were one in their conviction that a spiritual reality lay behind the world of everyday: the only difference between them lay in their varying readiness to be influenced by rigorous scientific analysis. Apart from this, they were such kindred spirits that the anonymous writer mentioned above could describe them as being like 'congenial beings of another sphere, breathing for a while on our earth',[40] while Walter Pater was to detect a similarity, despite superficial differences of detail, between the 'vision' in *The Ancient Mariner* and Blake's engraving, *When the Morning Stars sang Together*.[41]

At this point of sympathy with Blake, Coleridge stands apart from most other English Romantics. In the end, he was not content with a poetry based purely on individual experience: he looked, on the contrary, for an all-embracing vision which should encompass all things in heaven and earth, reconciling the truths of science with those of religion. He envisaged this interpretation in three dimensions: the plane of relationship between an individual and his fellow human beings, the plane of relationship between man and nature, and the plane of relationship between man and the spiritual order. The pattern which he sought would be valid in all three dimensions.

This search led him to a lifelong interest in allegory and symbolisms of all types, ranging from the stiff personifications of moral qualities which could be found in late Renaissance art to mystical theories of 'correspondences' between the physical world and the spiritual. In an autobiographical passage, he describes how in childhood he apprehended the universe as one vast whole, and how even then the shapings of his inward mind dominated his preceptions. One evening, his father, walking home with him to Ottery, told him of the vastness and grandeur of the universe[42]:

I heard him with a profound delight & admiration; but without the least mixture of wonder or incredulity. For from my early reading of Faery Tales, & Genii &c &c——

31

my mind had been habituated *to the Vast*—& I never regarded *my senses* in any way as the criteria of my belief. I regulated all my creeds by my conceptions not by my *sight* —even at that age. Should children be permitted to read Romances, & Relations of Giants & Magicians, & Genii?—I know all that has been said against it; but I have formed my faith in the affirmative.—I know no other way of giving the mind a love of 'the Great', & 'the Whole.' —Those who have been led to the same truths step by step thro' the constant testimony of their senses, seem to me to want a sense which I possess—They contemplate nothing but *parts*—and all *parts* are necessarily little— and the Universe to them is but a mass of *little things*.

Two days before writing this reminiscence for Poole, he had set down a developed form of the same sentiment in a letter to Thelwall[43]:

I can *at times* feel strongly the beauties, you describe, in themselves, & for themselves—but more frequently *all things* appear little—all the knowlege, that can be acquired, child's play—the universe itself—what but an immense heap of *little* things?—I can contemplate nothing but parts, & parts are all *little*—!—My mind feels as if it ached to behold & know something *great*—something *one* & *indivisible*—and it is only in the faith of this that rocks or waterfalls, mountains or caverns give me the sense of sublimity or majesty!—But in this faith *all things* counterfeit infinity!

In these two extracts, a delicate relationship between the human mind, the physical universe and the spiritual universe is shadowed, the connecting link between them being the sense of the Vast and Infinite. To see how such conceptions, together with that of the One and the Many, came to take their part in his mature conception of poetry we may turn directly to a letter written nearly twenty years later, in which he criticized Cottle's *Messiah*, and set forth his own ideal of epic poetry[44]:

I have read about one half; and tho' I myself see your

plan, yet I find it difficult to explain it, to the Public so as to make it consistent with the received conception of a Poem, call it epic, heroic, divine or what you like. The common end of all *narrative*, nay of *all*, Poems is to convert a *series* into a *Whole*: to make those events, which in real or in imagined History move on in a *strait* line, assume to our Understandings a *circular* motion—the snake with it's Tail in it's mouth. Hence indeed the almost flattering and yet appropriate Term, Poesy—i.e., poiēsis = *making*. Doubtless to *his* eye, which alone comprehends all Past and all Future in one eternal Present, what to our short sight appears strait is but a part of the great Cycle—just as the calm Sea to us *appears* level, tho' it be indeed only part of a *globe*. Now what the Globe is in Geography, *miniaturing* in order to *manifest* the Truth, such is a Poem to that Image of God, which we were created with, and which still seeks that Unity, or Revelation of the *One* in and by the *Many*, which reminds it, that tho' in order to be an individual Being it must go forth *from* God, yet as the *receding* from *him* is to *pro*ceed towards Nothingness and Privation, it must still at every step turn back toward him in order to *be* at all—Now, a straight Line, continuously retracted forms of necessity a circular orbit. Now God's Will and Word *cannot* be frustrated. His aweful *Fiat* was with ineffable awefulness applied to Man, when all things and all living Things, himself (as a mere animal) included, were called forth by the Universal—*Let there be*—and then the Breath of the Eternal superadded to make an *immortal* Spirit—immortality being, as the author of the 'Wisdom of Solomon' profoundly expresses it, the only possible Reflex or Image of Eternity. The Immortal Finite is the contracted Shadow of the Eternal Infinite. There nothingness or *Death*, to which we move as we recede from God and the Word, *cannot* be nothing; but that tremendous medium between nothing and true Being, which Scripture and inmost Reason present most, most horrible! I have said this to show you the connection between things in themselves comparatively trifling, and things the most important, by their derivation from common sources.

This account of the poetic process gives us an important account of Coleridge's ideal in poetry: and the most revealing aspect of it is the constant analogy which he draws between poetic creation and the Divine Creation of the Universe—an analogy which suggests that his well-known statement concerning the primary Imagination in *Biographia Literaria* is no idle piece of high-flown rhetoric[45]:

> The primary IMAGINATION I hold to be the living Power and prime Agent of all human Perception, and as a repetition in the finite mind of the eternal act of creation in the infinite I AM...

These statements, in fact, point us to the heart of Coleridge's romanticism. We spoke earlier of the typical Romantic as fallen angel or pilgrim of eternity, and of the existence of both characters in the great Romantics, among whom Coleridge is to be numbered. When Coleridge was aware mainly of his imaginative powers, 'his genius had angel's wings and fed on manna'[46]; when he looked outside himself he saw a 'World' from which he must keep himself separate —a world consisting of the 'poor loveless ever-anxious crowd'.[47] Yet his yearning for the truth meant that he must not seek to escape from it—and such is the mark of the great romantic pilgrim, even if it is not that of Bunyan's Christian.

We cannot, nevertheless, regard his career as that of a beautiful and ineffectual angel, beating in the void his luminous wings in vain[48]: nor can we see it purely as a modern *Pilgrim's Progress*. These elements within him only fall into place when seen against the background of his view of the imagination, his claim that the true poet is, within his finite limitations, a type of God the Creator. Instead of working out his destiny in one or other of the romantic characters, Coleridge was willing to stake everything on achieving the absolute knowledge, the high creative ecstasy, which would inhere in the making of a great epic.

When we think of the 'angelic' in connection with Coleridge, then, we are not to picture the characteristics of gentle, ministering spirits, but of Miltonic angels, filled with power and shining in the radiance of their divine knowledge. His own idea of poetic sublimity at its highest was contained in the biblical description of[49]

> the mighty Angel that came down from Heaven, whose face was as it were the Sun, and his feet as pillars of fire: Who set his right foot on the sea, and his left upon the earth. And he sent forth a loud voice; and when he had sent it forth, seven Thunders uttered their Voices: and when the seven Thunders had uttered their Voices, the mighty Angel lifted up his hand to Heaven, & sware by Him that liveth for ever & ever, that TIME was no more.

Such qualities were not merely poetic sublimities, moreover: he felt them as potencies within himself. When Hazlitt and Lamb knew him as a young man, he impressed them by his power. Lamb, in his satiric 'Theses', accepted Coleridge's intellectual powers, begging leave only to question whether he had the *moral* qualities necessary to the angelic nature.[50] Hazlitt, who wished in later years to 'rouse him up once more into an archangel's shape'[51] was obsessed by this early impression of power: ' "With mighty wings outspread, his imagination might brood over the void, and make it pregnant." '[52] He remembered him preaching at Shrewsbury, launching into his subject 'like an eagle dallying with the wind', and ' "fluttering the *proud Salopians* like an eagle in a dove-cote" '.[53]

Even in later years, when he was a changed man, the impression of surviving power still tempered all accounts of his decay. Hazlitt at his most venomous, says that his genius 'has angel's wings; but neither hands nor feet', but declares immediately afterwards that he is still hardly[54]

> 'Less than arch-angel ruined, and the excess Of glory obscur'd.'

Lamb, equally typically, describes him a year or two later as 'an Archangel a little damaged'.[55] Byron, satirizing his metaphysical speculations, speaks of him as 'like a hawk encumbered with his hood',[56] while Shelley's well-known description in the *Letter to Maria Gisburne* employs the image yet again[57]:

> You will see Coleridge—he who sits obscure
> In the exceeding lustre and the pure
> Intense irradiation of a mind,
> Which, with its own internal lightning blind,
> Flags wearily through darkness and despair—
> A cloud-encircled meteor of the air,
> A hooded eagle among blinking owls.

Although aware of such powers within himself, Coleridge was naturally wary of speaking of them in such arrogant terms. When he does employ the image it is usually to describe future hopes in youth, or consciousness of lost powers in age. A variant passage to the early *Destiny of Nations* reads,[58]

> Know thyself my Soul!
> Confirm'd thy strength, thy pinions fledged for flight
> Bursting this shell and leaving next thy nest
> Soon upward soaring shalt thou fix intense
> Thine eaglet eye on Heaven's Eternal Sun!

Ten years later he wrote,[59]

> Let Eagle bid the Tortoise sunward soar—
> As vainly Strength speaks to a broken Mind.

In the intervening period, an unhappy decline in his powers had taken place: but even before this he had been aware at times of the finite limitations to human capability, and their constricting effects. He was always conscious of the imperfections of the human spirit, and the inadequate grasp of the human mind; in his more optimistic moments, however, he had felt that a great enough artist could overcome them. 'Observe the march of Milton,' he wrote in 1797,[60] '—his severe application, his laborious polish, his deep metaphysical researches, his prayers to God before he began his great poem, all that could lift and swell his intellect, became his daily food.' He planned a similar course of intellectual discipline for himself, in spite of the great increase of material in his day—and in tracing the course of his reading and study throughout life, one can see this aim hovering constantly before him.

In time of trouble, on the other hand, he would sometimes become so conscious of human limitations as to swing from this optimism to a sense of humility and unworthiness[61]:

> My philosophical refinements, & metaphysical Theories lay by me in the hour of anguish, as toys by the bedside of a Child deadly-sick.

In youth, such troubles merely suspended his optimism temporarily, without permanently destroying the creative powers on which it was based: a new crisis emerged when repeated illness and further unhappiness came to sap the strength from the imaginative powers themselves. *Dejection: an Ode* is a heart-felt poem at the side of which the conclusion of *The Eolian Harp* falls into place as an improving exercise in humility. On the reverse side of the illuminated Coleridge, optimistic, aquiline, angelic, is the 'sinful and most miserable man,/ Wilder'd and dark', of the early poetry, who eventually becomes the 'S. T. C.' of the *Epitaph*.[62]

Which was the true Coleridge? Did he most nearly approach his true nature in the state of creative ecstasy? Or was that ecstasy an exalted dream-state, from which the dreamer must waken to a cold, hard world of reality, like the knight-at-arms of Keats's poem? This is our dilemma as much as it was Coleridge's. It is the counterpart to his metaphysical dilemma, and is indeed partly responsible for the form which that dilemma took. Upon it rested many of the problems which interested him most, such as the nature of dreams, and the relationship between imagination and reality or between the visionary and the man of action. It explains, too, his deep interest in transcendental philosophy, and in the studies by German psychologists of the place of the shaping mind in human behaviour. Most important of all, it helps to explain his growing distrust of his own vision-ary powers, until, towards the end of his life, he deleted from a copy of the *Biographia Literaria* the passage describ-ing the Imagination as 'a repetition in the finite mind of the eternal act of creation',[63] and wrote a bitter recantation of his once-held faith in the 'Heaven-descended Know Thyself'.[64]

In this book, naturally, we are concerned mainly with the speculations of Coleridge the optimistic visionary, the Coleridge of the great poems. It is necessary to bear in mind his later, more pessimistic attitude, however, not simply as a contrast to this, but also because it vitally affects the evaluation of evidence drawn from his later writings. He seems to have become shy of mentioning his early speculations except in terms which tended to obscure their optimistic nature; and sometimes to have attacked opinions which he had formerly held. It also seems as though he continued to hold some of these views in a private and esoteric form.

Since this 'esoteric' attitude will sometimes emerge in the course of the present study, it will be worth while to examine some examples of it. It is half-suggested in his reminiscences of the days when he was canvassing subscribers for *The Watchman*[65]:

O! never can I remember those days with either shame or regret. For I was most sincere, most disinterested! My opinions were indeed in many and most important points erroneous; but my heart was single. Wealth, rank, life itself then seemed cheap to me, compared with the interests of (what I believed to be) the truth, and the will of my maker.

Even at this stage, however, his beliefs were not as simple as his heart. A few pages later, we come across this account of his religious opinions[66]:

These principles I held, *philosophically*, while in respect of revealed religion I remained a zealous Unitarian. I considered the *idea* of the Trinity a fair scholastic inference from the being of God, as a creative intelligence; and that it was therefore entitled to the rank of an *esoteric* doctrine of natural religion. But seeing in the same no practical or moral bearing, I confined it to the schools of philosophy.

The use of the word 'esoteric' is significant, and in a later chapter it will be suggested that Coleridge's philosophic interest in the Trinity was, as always with his philosophy, something more than a mere academic exercise.

It was during his residence in Malta, however, that he

seems first to have been overwhelmed by the realization that
he had reached manhood, and must change his attitude to
other men. He recalled this moment some years later when
Stoddart was saying that there was [67]

> ... a period in a man's Life, varying in various men, from
> 35 to 45—& operating most strongly in Batchelors,
> Widowers, or those worst and miserablest of Widowers,
> unhappy Husbands, in which a man finds himself at the
> *Top of the Hill*—and having attained perhaps what he
> wishes begins to ask himself—What is all this for?—
> begins to feel the *vanity* of his pursuits—becomes half-
> melancholy, gives in to wild dissipation, or self-regardless
> Drinking—and some not content with these—not slow
> —poisons, destroy themselves ...

He commented:

> I had *felt* this Truth; but never saw it before clearly; it
> came upon me at Malta, under the melancholy dreadful
> feeling of finding myself to be *Man*, by a distinct division
> from Boyhood, Youth '*Young Man*'—Dreadful was the
> feeling—before that life had flown on so that I had
> always been *a Boy*, as it were—and this sensation had
> blended in all my conduct, my willing acknowledgement
> of superiority, & *in truth*, my meeting every person, as a
> superior, at the first moment. ... Yet if men survive this
> period, they commonly become chearful again—that is a
> comfort for mankind, *not for me*!'

The last sentence points to a darker discovery. Coleridge
was awakening to the fact that his personal ideals were
unlikely now ever to be achieved. For he, unlike Wordsworth, had not aspired to the egotistical sublime: his personal
ideal, like his philosophical, lay in the achievement of a
communion of true spirits. Faced with the prospect that this
ideal (the original inspiration of Pantisocracy) was likely to
be fulfilled neither with his wife nor with the Wordsworths,
he was forced to seek it elsewhere.

This, I think, is one reason for his later devotion to the
seventeenth century, and to the Anglican church of that
period. When he had reached the point of being able to

accept a trinitarian position in theology, he was enabled by his sympathy with the divines of that century to make an existential commitment of his personality to Anglicanism, thus interpreted. From that time forward, he could seek his community of minds with a few friends, and with a large company of kindred spirits of previous generations.

This form of commitment could not possess more than a limited validity, however, and it is difficult to account for Coleridge's statements and expressions of opinion in later life, taken as a body, without supposing that during this period he was liable to assume various masks in order to deal satisfactorily with people of varying beliefs and attitudes. The supposition may be supported by reference to other notes written at Malta. In a 'Serious memorandum', for example, he determined never to dissent from anyone as to the *merits* of another, especially in his own department, but to content himself with praising in his turn; reserving his true opinions for books, where he could evolve the whole of his thought and feeling. He concluded[68]:

> Coleridge! Coleridge! will you never never learn to appropriate your conversation to your company? Is it not desacration, indelicacy, a proof of great weakness & [even vanity] to talk to (?) etc., etc., as if you [were talking to] Wordsworth or Sir G. Beaumont?

A week later he renewed the theme in the form of an exhortation to youth[69]:

> O young man, who hast seen, felt, & known the Truth, to whom reality is a phantom, & virtue & mind the sole actual & permanent Being, do not degrade the Truth in thee by disputing.

Instead, he felt, it was better to say—

> . . . if I felt this to *be* that Day or that moment, a sacred Sympathy would at once compel and inspire me to the Task of uttering the very Truth/ Till then, I am right willing to bear the character of a mystic, a visionary, or self-important Juggler who nods his Head & says, *I could if I would*; but I cannot, I *may* not bear the reproach of

profaning the Truth which is *very Life*, in moments when all passions heterogeneous to it are eclipsing it to the exclusion of its dimmest ray . . .

More revealing still is a little-known anecdote by an anonymous Swedenborgian, who was later to recall how, just before the publication of *Aids to Reflection* in 1825, the 'London Coffee Meeting' received a communication to the effect that Coleridge was willing to write a *Life of the Mind of Swedenborg* if £200 were raised for him. He continues,[70]

> Mr Arbouin having doubts of Mr Coleridge's doctrinal fitness, and knowing the gentleman with whom Mr Coleridge was stopping at Highgate, went there just before the dinner hour, and was invited to stay dinner. After dinner, he determined to satisfy his doubts by directly and openly asking Mr C. his opinion of Swedenborg, when he received a guarded but unfavourable reply. This was conveyed to the Coffee Meeting, and put an end to the proposal to subscribe £200. Mr Tulk, no doubt mortified somewhat, asked Mr Coleridge for an explanation, when he said that, being, as he judged, rudely questioned before a mixed company, he was not prepared unreservedly to give his opinion, and so he replied accordingly.

From the nature of the case, one would not expect many statements on the subject to have come down to us from Coleridge himself, but those cited show that, for a variety of reasons, he would sometimes mask his basic opinions for what he conceived to be a greater good.

The picture that we are tracing is a complicated one, then. It is the picture of a man who seeks to devote himself completely to the realization of a single vision, and who yet finds that that vision must be largely hidden from the world. Nevertheless, the complications are chiefly of importance in dealing with his later writings, and in using his later thought as a means of interpreting the earlier. The more one concentrates attention on the earlier period, the clearer the picture becomes. Indeed, if the theory to be advanced in these pages is correct, the *annus mirabilis* is the centre not only of his poetry but of his thought. During this brief period, the creative ecstasy which he enjoyed embraced his thinking as well as his emotions.

Various reasons have been adduced for the achievements of this period, but none of them are entirely convincing. He may have been happier than usual, but if so it was hardly the result of outward circumstances. Ill-health dogged him at this time, and misfortunes befell those around him.[71] The stimulating company of William and Dorothy Wordsworth no doubt had its effect—but he was to go on enjoying it for ten more years. I think, in fact, that one can only fully explain his happiness at this time by invoking a more strictly intellectual factor. He had in no way achieved the grand, embracing myth which would have been necessary for the forming of a true epic; but for the time being his imagination had seized upon a limited myth which was vivid enough to be an organizing framework for poetry. It was a myth that had the advantage of linking truths of the various levels mentioned above: those, namely, of human society, of the universe in general, and of the ultimate spiritual order. It also provided a possible interpretation of the subjects which interested him most deeply—religion, politics, history, philosophy and artistic creation.

This is a large claim to make for any myth, and it can only be made good by a lengthy examination of certain strains in Coleridge's developing thought. Such an examination must occupy us in the chapters that follow. In the meantime, however, it may be pointed out that such a theory would go a long way towards explaining the apparent decline of quality in Coleridge's productions after 1798. The decline has been associated with Coleridge's ill-health after his return from Germany: but it was not until seven years later when he returned from Malta that his friends noticed a striking change for the worse.[72] His notebooks in the meantime contain some of his finest and most subtle thinking and observation. Opium has been blamed, but this he had been taking since his schooldays. Metaphysics has been blamed, but Coleridge had too much of the poet in him to allow abstruse speculations to swamp his creative gifts permanently, had their presence been marked. Each of these theories has a limited validity, of course—and, even more interestingly, each of them can be supported by statements of Coleridge himself. It is also true that the hopeless division which he tried to make between conjugal love for his wife and spiritual love for Sara Hutchinson was an important factor in precipitating his decline. Yet it seems as though, in the last analysis, the logic of that decline was the logic not of external events but of internal intellectual development. For the myth which excited him at this time, whatever its relation to the contemporary intellectual world, was highly attractive to him personally. It also demanded to be fulfilled in some way, and the metaphysics, the opium and the hopeless love for Sara Hutchinson, together with the unhappiness and ill-health which they fostered between them, marked different attempts to fulfil it and different sorts of failure.

The myth may demonstrate the link between Coleridge's poetry and philosophy: and it is to be hoped that it will be an aid towards an understanding of the man himself. It is easy to despise Coleridge at his weakest, but it is only fair that even then he should be seen as a man far removed from spineless sensualism. Both in his poetic explorations and his intellectual inquiries, he was a pilgrim dedicated to a vision, possessing something of the heroic in his enduring devotion to that vision, something of the Quixotic in his refusal to be turned from his course, right or wrong.

And since the vision which he pursued was a vision that had at times been revealed to him, and had even possessed him, this pilgrim sometimes had a strange radiance about him. 'His face when he repeats his verses hath its ancient glory, an Archangel a little damaged,' said Lamb twenty years later.[73] 'When in the poetic state,' said Washington Allston, 'no face I ever saw was like to his; it seemed almost spirit made visible, without a shadow of the visible upon it.'[74] And since then T. S. Eliot has found it necessary, in accounting for his puzzling personality, to say that 'for a few years he had been visited by the Muse . . . and thenceforth was a haunted man'.[75]

Chapter II

THE SENSE OF GLORY

MENTION of the eighteenth century brings to mind the cultured life of the fashionable. Alexander Pope in his grotto at Twickenham, Samuel Johnson in coffee-house or club, polished gentlemen who write with ease: these are the dominant images. The occasional extravaganzas—Walpole's Strawberry Hill or Beckford's Fonthill—serve to emphasize the normality of the age, an age, above all, of polish, urbanity and wit.

If these characteristics are the main current in eighteenth-century civilization, however, it is a current to be associated primarily with London and with the aristocracy. Many gentlemen of the time, particularly in the provinces, had other interests and other ideals. If the Royalism of the seventeenth century traced its spiritual heirs in the elegant wits of the time, Puritanism also had its descendants, who often combined an enthusiasm for the scientific and industrial developments of the age with a concern for the impact of the new ideas on traditional Christian doctrines. Many of them could find no logical answer to the problems raised except in strict Deism: others by-passed the intellectual problem by making religion a matter not of the head but of the heart, and became Methodists. In between them, striving for a compromise, were the Unitarians.

This last strain has been partly hidden from view in succeeding years, perhaps because it produced no major artistic genius. The geniuses which it did produce were primarily men of science: Newton, Hartley, Priestley. The emotional element in this culture does not begin to be apparent until we turn to some little-known work such as Thomas Amory's *Life of John Buncle, Esq.*, which gives glimpses of the wide range of interests possessed by many Unitarians of the time. John Buncle, in the course of his wanderings, has long, technical discussions with people whom he meets, on subjects which range from sea-shells to the Tower of Babel, from mathematics to muscular motion. Such catholicity of interests might be no more than the amiable eccentricity of a single character if it were an isolated phenomenon; but a glance at the pages of Unitarian magazines such as the *Analytical Review* or the *Monthly Magazine* reveals an equally bewildering variety of subjects. The same width of range is to be found in the syllabuses of the dissenting academies (which took the place of the older universities for the sons of Unitarians)[1] and in the published transactions of the 'societies of gentlemen' which sprang up in most provincial centres at this time, for the presentation of learned papers by individual members.

The emotional accompaniment of this intellectual exuberance is, as one might expect, a steady delight in the physical universe created by God, with all its wonders: John Buncle, for example, setting off one morning at sun-rise, was filled with delight at the scene[2]:

> The sun was rising as we mounted the horses, and struck me so powerfully with the surpassing splendor and majesty of its appearance, so cheered me by the gladsome influences, and intimate refreshment of its all-enlivening beams, that I was contriving as I rid on an apology for the first adorers of the solar orb, and imagined that they intended nothing more than the worship of the transcendent majesty of the invisible Creator, under the symbol of his most *excellent* and nearly resembling creature; and this according to some *imperfect* tradition, that man, as a *compound Being*, had, in the beginning, a *visible glorious presence* of *Jehovah Elohim*—a visible exhibition of a more distinguished presence by an inexpressible brightness or glory: this is some excuse for the first worshippers of the solar orb. . . .

Delight in the universe was a logical conclusion from many features of eighteenth-century thought. It is not surprising, then, to find that Coleridge as a young man was attracted to this sort of society. During one of his vacations from Cambridge, he helped to prepare a contribution for the Society of Gentlemen at Exeter.[3] At the time when he was planning the Pantisocratic scheme, he had a circle of

Unitarian friends in London.[4] In 1796, having already established himself among the 'Unitarians and Liberals of Bristol',[5] he set off in search of subscribers for *The Watchman* and called on several similar groups of people in cities of the Midlands and North.[6]

The influence of these societies is apparent in Coleridge's writing and thinking,[7] but they did not form him. They provided an anvil on which he could hammer out his developing opinions, and stimulated him to further efforts; and they also satisfied a side of his personality which is often neglected: his underlying desire that his speculations should achieve practical results.

Practical results, however, could not ultimately blind him to the fact that he was not finding true satisfaction in them. In spite of his adherence to the mechanistic philosophy of Locke and Hartley, he was aware of elements in his experience which did not fit into so limited an explanation of the universe. The workings of his creative imagination seemed to involve something more mysterious than an ordered mechanism; and there was little place for the human heart in the 'head-work' of the Unitarians. A more wide-ranging philosophy was required, that would find a place for such phenomena.

To find the native cast of Coleridge's mind, in fact, one needs to go to a period preceding his allegiance to Unitarian-ism. Long before this time, even in his schooldays, he was reading and dreaming and thinking with strength and vivid-ness. Lamb's account of him, in his essay, *Christ's Hospital Five and Thirty Years Ago*, gives striking evidence of this[8]:

Come back into memory, like as thou wert in the day-spring of thy fancies, with hope like a fiery column before thee——the dark pillar not yet turned——Samuel Taylor Coleridge——Logician, Metaphysician, Bard! How have I seen the casual passer through the Cloisters stand still, intranced with admiration (while he weighed the disproportion between the *speech* and the *garb* of the young Mirandula), to hear thee unfold, in thy deep and sweet intonations, the mysteries of Jamblichus, or Plotinus (for even in those years thou waxedst not pale at such philo-sophic draughts), or reciting Homer in his Greek, or

Pindar——while the walls of the old Grey Friars re-echoed to the accents of the *inspired charity-boy*!

Part of the glory which surrounded Coleridge in Lamb's eyes was no doubt due to his position as a Grecian. John Middleton Murry, who knew Christ's Hospital in its old Newgate Street buildings, commented on the life-long persistence of this relationship between Coleridge the Grecian and Lamb the Deputy Grecian and explained its significance.[9]

... the Grecians in those old days were visibly the lords of the school. When the masters were not actually teaching they disappeared from the school precincts. The domestic authority in the Hall was the Warden, in the wards the Matron—a being far inferior to the august Grecian, who listened to her conversation and her complaints with a *distrait* and preoccupied air. With his velvet cuffs, his multitudinous buttons (which all small boys firmly believed to be stamped out of pure silver), with his coat of superfine cloth and his gracefully drooping girdle, he sat on the polished granite stones, plumb in the middle of the Grecians' cloister, itself plumb in the centre of the school. He was, indeed, the cynosure of every eye, the observed of all observers: he was more, he was the navel and centre of the life of the school.

Between the days when he cowered beneath the magisterial authority of James Boyer and his entry to Cambridge, Coleridge had a short period of glory, which no doubt left its permanent mark upon him[10]:

In person he was a tall, dark, handsome young man, with long black flowing hair; eyes, not merely dark, but black and keenly penetrating; a fine forehead, a deep-toned harmonious voice; a manner never to be forgotten, full of life, vivacity and kindness; dignified in his person and, added to all these, exhibiting the elements of his future greatness. Yet there was something awful about him, for all his equals in age and rank quailed before him. No wonder, therefore, if I did, who was selected to be his 'boy' or attendant; he was to me the very impersonation of majesty, and stern indeed he could be when offended.

This glimpse of glory is relevant to our theme: and the intellectual element in it points us further. Coleridge's enthusiasm for Homer and Pindar is understandable: he was being true to the gods of Gothic poets such as Gray and Collins; but his taste for 'Jamblichus and Plotinus' is more arresting. Why should neoplatonic philosophy have attracted him at so early a stage? He could have known Plotinus in English, for part of his treatise *Concerning the Beautiful* had been translated by Thomas Taylor in 1787, but unless his knowledge of Iamblichus derived from some secondary source, he must have read him in the original Greek. The motive for such interest is not at first clear.

There is some evidence to suggest that neoplatonism was one of the interests of the age, taking its place in a panorama vividly described by Livingston Lowes[11]:

> Ancient cults . . . and primitive religions, Neoplatonic speculations, ethnology and oxygen and electricity were all seething together in men's minds. And with the new wonders of the air which science was disclosing merged the immemorial beliefs in its invisible inhabitants, whether vouched for by Iamblichus, or Hermes Trismegistus, or Captain Cook.

The effect presented is kaleidoscopic, a whirl of colourful images, each ousting the one before; and no doubt there were many people who read butterfly-fashion, occupying themselves with one fascinating subject after another, in the way that Lowes suggests. Nevertheless, there are many minds, and Coleridge's was certainly one of them, for which a kaleidoscope has only a limited appeal. Such minds are primarily interested in interpreting phenomena and finding the patterns which explain them.

The Unitarian scholars mentioned above were often of this order, but the pattern for which they looked was essentially rationalistic and mechanical. They studied books of travel, scientific theories and history, but it is not clear that they were interested in neoplatonism. The appeal of this last was to a slightly different group of people whom, for the sake of convenience, I propose to call the 'visionaries'— though they did not form a close-knit body of any kind.

The visionaries are a real but somewhat intangible presence in the late eighteenth century. At their simplest, they represent simply a harmless indulgence in the pleasures of the imagination. In a poem called *The Visionary*, for example Charles Jenner writes that it is his task[12]

> To bid groves, hills, and lucid streams appear,
>   The gilded spire, arch'd dome and fretted vault;
> With sweet society for ever near,
>   Love ever young, and friends without a fault.

A poem such as this expresses no more than a mild dissatisfaction with the rationalism of the time, but the more vehement visionaries sounded a sharper note. 'Imagination is the Divine Body in Every Man,' said Blake, and, elsewhere,[13]

> The Nature of Visionary Fancy, or Imagination, is very little known, & the Eternal nature & permanence of its ever Existent Images is considered as less permanent than the things of Vegetative & Generative Nature; yet the Oak dies as well as the Lettuce, but Its Eternal Image & Individuality never dies, but renews by its seed; just so the Imaginative Image returns by the seed of Contemplative Thought. . . .

"Did Jesus . . . /Charge Visionaries with decieving?" he inquired in *The Everlasting Gospel*.[14] At a more complicated level, moreover, not unrelated to the primary one, the visionaries were continuing a tradition which had risen to importance in the seventeenth century and had emerged fitfully since then. Certain of the Cambridge Platonists, concerned at the widening gulf between traditional religion and the new scientific outlook, had tried to build a bridge which should link the empiricism of Bacon and Descartes with Platonic speculation. Henry More, for example, hoped that 'Plato should provide the soul, Descartes the body', of this new philosophy, and looked to the cabbalistic writings for help in the task. Robert Fludd, some years earlier, had sought aid from the 'excellent philosopher Hermes' and other 'ethnick philosophers' in interpreting Mosaic science.[15]

The late eighteenth century had one important belief in

common with the seventeenth century which it does not share with our own. The world-picture of the day was still largely shaped by the traditions recorded in the Bible. Specialization in knowledge was limited by the strongly surviving hope that all human knowledge might yet be harmonized into one universal pattern, which would be reconcilable with that laid down in the Bible and ancient classical authorities. Milton's fascination for writers of the time has already been mentioned, and the 'sublimity' with which they invested him was due to his subject-matter as well as to his poetic gifts. To justify the works of God to man was the supreme task, and one which they hoped might be repeated in their own generation. Indeed, the dead hand which science seemed to be laying on the world rendered the task more urgent than in Milton's day.

Interest in cabbalistic and other occult ways of thought was not, then, simply a dilettante delight in fascinating but useless lore. Like Cambridge Platonism, it related directly to a disquiet concerning the trends of scientific thought which led even young progressives of the time to look backwards as well as forwards for their ideals. Shelley has been described as a 'Newton among poets'; nevertheless, the young Poet of his *Alastor*[16] did not spend his days in a laboratory, but in 'dark Ethiopia'.

> Among the ruined temples there,
> Stupendous columns, and wild images
> Of more than man, where marble dæmons watch
> The Zodiac's brazen mystery, and dead men
> Hang their mute thoughts on the mute walls around,
> He lingered, poring on memorials
> Of the world's youth, through the long burning day
> Gazed on those speechless shapes, nor, when the moon
> Filled the mysterious halls with floating shades
> Suspended he that task, but ever gazed
> And gazed, till meaning on his vacant mind
> Flashed like strong inspiration, and he saw
> The thrilling secrets of the birth of time.

Coleridge's attitude was a similar one. He was eager to learn about new scientific discoveries and theories, but his deepest enthusiasm was reserved for 'all out of the way books, whether of the monkish times, or of the puritanical aera . . . Metaphysics, & Poetry, & 'Facts of Mind'—(i.e. Accounts of all the strange phantasms that ever possessed your philosophy-dreamers from Tauth the Egyptian to Taylor, the English Pagan) . . .'[17]

Nevertheless, he was in a difficult position. In his more scientific moods, he could not but accept the age's contempt for 'visionaries' and their idle dreams. To his rationalist friends such as John Thelwall, he felt obliged to justify his interests as part of an objective investigation into certain psychological phenomena. His imagination, on the other hand, insisted on becoming more deeply engaged. Was it possible that the extreme visionaries were right after all, and that the sweep of scientific investigation would ultimately come full circle to confirm them? This was a question which haunted him, to a greater or lesser extent, all his life.

Because of this dilemma, he was always particularly interested in any occult phenomena for which a scientific basis was claimed. I have already mentioned his ambiguous attitude towards Swedenborg, and shall shortly return to it. A more immediate claim to link the physical and metaphysical lay in the contemporary cult of hypnotism, known at the time as 'animal magnetism'. The discovery of electricity and magnetism had disturbed traditional concepts of the nature of matter, and now gave new significance to the idea that living bodies, as well as inanimate objects, attract and repel each other by a form of magnetic power. The controversy and its implications constantly fascinated Coleridge, and his early interest in the subject has been discussed by Lane Cooper in an article entitled 'The Power of the Eye in Coleridge'. He draws attention to the fact that the popular craze for animal magnetism was at its height during the years when Coleridge was a schoolboy in London, and describes the success of such magnetizers as John Holloway, or the Loutherbourgs (whose Hammersmith house was once besieged by over three thousand people unable to gain admission) or Dr Mainaduc, who set up in Bristol in 1788 with an extraordinary fashionable success.[18]

The discovery of electricity was followed by new investi- • gations in chemistry, in which Humphry Davy was to play an outstanding part. Coleridge showed great interest in his experiments, especially those which concerned the effect of certain chemicals upon emotional states, and at one time thought that Davy was destined to be the greatest philosopher of his age.

Light, however, was the scientific phenomenon which fascinated him most of all. In this, again, he was true to his time. It was natural that an age which was dominated by the discoveries of Isaac Newton should take light as its central symbol in many fields; Swift's appeal to 'sweetness and light' was echoed everywhere. Even in religious architecture, the dim religious light of Gothic churches had been superseded by the large plain windows of the typical Unitarian chapel. 'Enlightenment' was the watchword of the age.

Light became for Coleridge a central symbol, second only to love in its power to bind together disparate strands of his thinking. His constant preoccupation with the divine and its relation to human reason becomes more comprehensible when one realizes that, for him, both concepts were invested with a luminous quality which linked them together in his imagination. Wherever he sees light, in fact, he sees potential symbolism. At one point he is noting that the light from two candles held together is greater than the light from two candles held separately, and storing this up as a symbol for marriage.[19] The flash which is said to be observed in certain plants after dusk finds its way into a love-poem.[20] And above all, he is fascinated by the light of the great heavenly bodies— sun, moon and stars.

Love of the heavenly elements had been fostered by the conditions of his childhood. In *Frost at Midnight*, he recalled how he[21]

<blockquote>
was reared
In the great city, pent 'mid cloisters dim,
And saw nought lovely but the sky and stars.
</blockquote>

In the first version of *Dejection* he developed this theme more fully.[22]

> Feebly! O feebly!—Yet
> (I well remember it)
> In my first Dawn of Youth that Fancy stole
> With many secret Yearnings on my Soul.
> At eve, sky-gazing in 'ecstatic fit'
> (Alas! for cloister'd in a city School
> The Sky was all, I knew, of Beautiful)
> At the barr'd window often did I sit,
> And oft upon the leaded School-roof lay,
>   And to myself would say—
> There does not live the Man so stripp'd of good
>   affections
> As not to love to see a Maiden's quiet Eyes
> Uprais'd, and linking on sweet Dreams by dim
>   Connections
> To Moon, or Evening Star, or glorious western Skies—
> While yet a Boy, this Thought would so pursue me,
> That often it became a kind of Vision to me!

Already, the heavenly elements held symbolical significance for him—and indeed symbolizing and allegorizing was one of his favourite pursuits at this time, as he records in the first version of *Hope and Time*[23]:

> In the great City rear'd, my fancy rude
> By natural Forms unnurs'd & unsubdued
> An Alien from the Rivers & the Fields
> And all the Charms, that Hill or Woodland yield[s],
> It was the pride & passion of my Youth
> T'impersonate & color moral Truth
> Rare Allegories in those Days I spun,
> That oft had mystic senses oft'ner none.
> Of all Resemblances however faint,
> So dear a Lover was I, that with quaint
> Figures fantastically grouped I made
> Of commonest Thoughts a moving Masquerade.

There are many other evidences of this lifelong fascination. Before his fifteenth birthday, he tells us, he had translated the eighth hymn of Synesius, and when he was discharged from the army, one of his first actions was to redeem a copy of the bishop's works which he had been obliged to sell.[24] These hymns were addressed to God, symbolized in the elements; and it is relevant to recall that to the end of his life Coleridge cherished among his many projects the desire to write his own series of hymns to the Sun, Moon, and other Elements.

Perhaps it was the same fascination that led him to buy his 'curious Walking-Stick' from a countryman in Cambridge, since it displayed on one side 'the head of an Eagle, the Eyes of which represent rising Suns, and the Ears Turkish Crescents'.[25] Certainly, the idea of an eagle gazing at the sun had the force of a personal symbol for him at times—an ideal which he may have taken over from his hero Jacob Boehme, part of whose memorial emblem is described as follows[26]:

> To the right Hand, from the South Side, a black Eagle, perched on the Summit of a high Hill, was painted on the Cross. He trod with his left Shank or Foot upon the Head of a large enfolded Serpent. In the right Foot he held a Palm-Branch, and with his Beak he received a Lily-Stalk, reached to him out of the Sun: under which, with no Impropriety, stood the word VIDI.

Further evidence of Coleridge's tendency to find symbolism in the heavenly elements may be sought in a work which has received little attention as a potential source of information concerning his early life: Charles Lloyd's novel, *Edmund Oliver*, first published in 1798. Admittedly, it is not easy to decide which passages in it are founded on fact, but some reference to Coleridge was clearly intended in the chief character. Coleridge himself pointed out that if it was not impossible, it was at least difficult not to see in Edmund's 'love-fit, debaucheries, leaving college & going into the army' a reference to his own love-fit, debaucheries, leaving college, and going into the army.[27] His bitterness was expressed with less restraint in a poem *To One who Published in Print what had been entrusted to him by my Fireside*.[28]

The passages in which Edmund describes his taking of laudanum have often been quoted; on reading through the book, however, one is impressed by other Coleridgean touches. Indeed, there are times when the book reads almost like a dialogue within Coleridge's own mind. Edmund is described by the author as 'a character of excessive sensibility and impetuous desires, tamed down by disappointment to that evenness of temper, and subduedness of will, which may ensure all the comforts this state of existence is capable of affording'. The novel is the story of his 'reformation, and gradual return from the slavery of passion to reason and manly fortitude'.[29] In order to achieve this, Edmund's friend, Charles Maurice, impresses upon him the existence of many material injustices in the world, and the insignificance of one's own introspective ills by comparison. As it happens, precisely the same arguments had been used by Coleridge in a poem which he addressed to Lloyd himself: the lines *To a Young Man of Fortune who abandoned himself to an indolent and causeless Melancholy.*[30]

Coleridge's influence in the novel ran deep—deeper, perhaps than Lloyd himself realized. One suspects that there are, embedded in the novel, fragments of Coleridge's conversation which his hearer had only partly understood. Some parts of Edmund's description of his own passionate nature, for example, display a peculiar depth, considering their context.[31]

> I passed my infancy and youth in solitude; my feelings were ever more than commensurate with the objects which acted upon them! I combined and recombined. I panted for happiness which I had not heard of! from this circumstance may be traced my dissatisfaction with the state of society in which I was educated; and my subsequent ardour for the introduction of more generous and impartial principles among men.

> . . . My mind was active, but slow to receive impressions from others: it felt its own shapings more interesting than any ideas suggested from foreign sources: it was too full of itself to be passive to the mouldings of authority or experience. From this restlessness of spirit, supported by a warm and impetuous temperament, and connected with solitariness of habits, I soon acquired imagination; or the

faculty of ever combining the moral with the physical world; or on the other hand, of embodying intellectual conceptions in the borrowed shapes of the visible elements.

Feelings more than commensurate with the objects that acted upon them, 'combining and recombining' (not unlike the function of the secondary imagination in *Biographia Literaria*), dissatisfaction with society, the mind possessed by the interest of its own shapings—all these ideas are familiar to us from Coleridge's own writings: and it is interesting to compare them with a letter written by him to Lloyd's own father in 1796, in which he expresses his dissatisfaction with social humanity, and declares that in his rural cottage he will have several companions, two of which are his own 'shaping and disquisitive mind', and Nature, with its 'thousand looks of Beauty' and its 'thousand melodies of Love'.[32] As for 'the faculty of ever combining the moral with the physical world; or on the other hand, of embodying intellectual conceptions in the borrowed shapes of the visible elements', if ever a phrase shouted aloud its Coleridgean origin, surely this one does.

All this, I think, throws light on Coleridge's early enthusiasm for certain mystical writers, and various mythological traditions. Most of them embody, in various forms, attempts to make the phenomena of nature symbolize ultimate truths, and it is hardly surprising that the young Coleridge should have turned eagerly to them in the hope of finding food for his own speculations.

Among Coleridge's contemporaries, a taste for the writings of Mesmer was often accompanied by an interest in the teachings of Swedenborg, and this reflects with some accuracy the complementary position occupied by the latter. For if Mesmer's observations on hypnotism seem to bear metaphysical implications, Swedenborg's metaphysical speculations are stamped by references to the physical universe which demonstrate the scientific disposition of their originator. In them the physical world is constantly used as a guide to the heavenly. The sun, for example, is treated as a type of the 'heavenly sun', and one of Swedenborg's favourite texts is from Isaiah[33]:

. . . the light of the moon shall be as the light of the sun,
and the light of the sun shall be sevenfold, as the light of
seven days . . .

Swedenborg's interest in the angelic also points forward
to the great romantics, and no doubt accounts for his popu-
larity with some of them. For these elements in Swedenborg's teaching conflicted with orthodox Christian doctrine
in a way which appealed to the age. If man has an angelical
quality within his nature, it seems that he must necessarily
be, in however limited a fashion, still in communion with the
divine. Under the traditional doctrine of the Fall, on the
other hand, man is completely cut off from communion with
God—only to be restored by God's own act and God's own
mercy. And it was precisely this element in traditional
theology which was least attractive to many minds. Human
perfectibility was the current theme. Radical political thought
was occupying itself with the possibility of evolving forms of
society which would actively encourage virtue in their
members and make towards the equality and fraternity of
mankind. Advances in the physical sciences offered the hope
that the physical universe was on the point of surrendering
its most tantalizing secrets. In such circumstances, the
traditional doctrine of the Fall seemed an unnecessary
encumbrance in theology.

To minds which were working on these lines, the doctrines of Swedenborg offered an attractive alternative. The
doctrine of the Atonement as normally formulated was, he
maintained, incorrect. The Fall had consisted not in 'Guilt
and Offence', but in 'a Departure from God and his Laws of
Order and Uprightness, and a consequent Fall into Disorder
and Unrighteousness, whence came Disease and Death, to
the human Soul or Spirit'. Atonement, therefore, was to be
brought about by what had 'a Tendency to lead Man out of
the Disease and Disorder thereby occasioned, and restore
him to Health, Order and Uprightness through a Return to,
and Conjunction again with his God'.[34]

In view of this favourable audience, it is not surprising to
learn that the period from 1780 to 1790 was the time when
Swedenborgianism expanded most rapidly in this country,

and particularly in London.[35] It is difficult to believe that Coleridge, who was then at Christ's Hospital, did not come into contact with the doctrines in some form.

Not all the visionaries were Christians, of course. One of the most influential figures among them was Thomas Taylor, the 'English pagan', whose primary enthusiasm was for the religion of the Greek mysteries and the philosophy of the Platonists. Nevertheless, even here we are not as far from theological questions as might at first be imagined. In the ancient mysteries of Bacchus, just as in orthodox Christianity, man was portrayed as fallen from an ideal state. In some primeval catastrophe the ideal Bacchus, or Dionysus, had been broken, and man was condemned to live in the world shorn of the indwelling power and happiness which he had possessed, unless he could by some means be re-integrated into the heavenly Bacchus.

Most of the treatises which Taylor translated attempted in various ways to associate the teachings of Plato and the content of the mysteries. A typical example, and one which seems later to have impressed Coleridge deeply, was his translation of the myth of Cupid and Psyche, published in 1795 together with a treatise interpreting it as the search of the soul for its lost lover.

Running through both Swedenborgianism and neoplatonism, in fact, there is the sense of lost glory; and it is this sense which appealed to the Romantics. It occurs again, even more vividly, in yet another branch of the occult: the cabbalistic lore. When Lamb called Coleridge 'the young Mirandula',[36] he was probably thinking particularly of his precocious oratorical powers, and his extraordinary memory.[37] But I suspect that he may also have intended a reference to Mirandola's interest in 'magic and Kabbalah', and his endeavours to blend cabbalistic lore with the doctrines of neoplatonism.[38]

As in the case of Swedenborgianism, Coleridge's early knowledge of the Cabbala is a matter of probability rather than of definite fact. Hazlitt, whose intimacy with him lasted from 1798 to 1804, spoke of his interest in necromancy and Cabbala, and in Coleridge's later notebooks, his familiarity with some technical terms of the art suggests long acquaintance. It seems likely that his adolescent taste for the occult had led him either to the Latin writings of Mirandola, or to some seventeenth-century work such as Henry More's *Conjectura Cabbalistica*.[39]

The main point which distinguishes the cabbalistic doctrines from the others which we have examined is its greater emphasis on the relationship between the sexual and the divine. In other words, the divine creative activity, like that of human beings in procreation, is thought of as a joyful dialectic between male and female elements. Their coming together, known as the marriage of the King and the Matrona, irradiates a divine light, called the 'Shechinah'. Wherever the divine creative forces are at work, there also is the Shechinah.

The cabbalistic doctrine, like the others, carries certain implications concerning the Fall of Man. At the Fall, man was deprived of the Shechinah which had hitherto surrounded him, and the creative principles fell apart into male and female. Whether this was a physical disjunction from one body into two, or whether Adam and Eve lost the Shechinah which they had hitherto jointly possessed is a matter for dispute; but in either version, the Shechinah is lost, and can only be regained at rare moments of exaltation —one of them being when complete love and harmony exist between a man and woman. And so closely are the human and the divine creativity linked that if the Shechinah is recovered between human beings, God himself is affected. He is given a joy which he would not otherwise possess.[40]

In Coleridge's writings this concept is used several times. In the notebooks, he refers to the 'Shechinah of the Conscience', and to the Scriptures as the '*Shechinah* or Epiphany of Reason'. Elsewhere he writes,[41]

> I fall asleep night after night watching that perpetual feeling, to which Imagination . . . has given a place and seat of manifestation, a Shechinah in the heart . . .

It has to be acknowledged that his references to cabbalistic doctrines are not always approving. On occasion, he can speak of 'Superstition and cabalistic Frippery', for example.[42] A careful examination of his various scattered statements suggests that he gave them an important position in intellectual history, while withholding from them unqualified acceptance. He was at great pains to assign to them an origin before the days of Christ, on the grounds that the Jews would hardly have invented a doctrine so close to the central mysteries of Christianity once they had rejected Christianity itself.[43] And elsewhere he argued that while within Judah the expectation of a political leader as Messiah could explain the interest in Christ's teaching, it was much more difficult to explain that interest in the Gentile world, unless one supposed that the Cabbala, with their expectation of the Shechinah in the form of the Messiah, had acted as a guide, to bring pantheism to the verge of Christianity.[44] The Cabbala alone had soared to the idea of a Spiritual Redeemer, and a mystic reconciliation and remarriage of the repudiated Spouse to her celestial Lover.[45]

Whatever Coleridge's acquaintance may have been with the cabbalistic doctrines at this time, there was one source where he certainly found them: namely, in the writings of Jacob Boehme. The exact nature of his debt to this German mystic forms a particularly thorny problem, and one which can only be touched on here. At first sight there might even appear to be flat self-contradiction, when we turn from his handsome tribute to Boehme and other mystical writers in the *Biographia Literaria*, and find him writing to Lady Beaumont, '. . . for myself, I must confess I never brought away from his works anything I did not bring to them'.[46] The position is not clarified by his reported assertion elsewhere that all Schelling had said, he had 'either thought himself, or found in Jacob Boehme'.[47] Nevertheless, I think that the contradiction is superficial only, and can be reconciled with the aid of another passage, where he speaks of the days when he 'conjured' over Boehme's *Aurora* at Christ's Hospital.[48] In other words, where an image or a sentiment in Boehme found an echo in the shapings of his own imagination, it was eagerly taken up into the pattern, and valued for the hint of external confirmation which it offered.

He is recalling an example of such 'conjuring', in fact, in the passage from the *Biographia* which has just been mentioned. In his tribute to the mystics, he says,[49]

They contributed to keep alive the *heart* in the *head*; gave me an indistinct, yet stirring and working presentiment, that all the products of the mere *reflective* faculty partook of DEATH and were as the rattling twigs and sprays in winter, into which a sap was yet to be propelled from some root to which I had not penetrated, if they were to afford my soul either food or shelter.

The distinction between the workings of the head and the heart is such a commonplace one, that it is easy to overlook the great importance which it held in Coleridge's thinking, and still more its place in his image-making. And I suspect that Boehme's *Aurora* was one of the chief sources for the hold of this distinction on his imagination[50]:

First there is the *Power*, and in the Power is the Tone or *Tune*, which rises up in the Spirit, into the Head, into the *Mind*, as in Man in the Brain; and in the Mind it *has its open Doors or Gates*; but in the *Heart* it has its *Seat*, Residence and Original, where it exists out of all Powers.

For the Fountain of all Powers floweth in the Heart, as it does also in Man and in the Head it has its *Princely* seat, where it sees all, smells all, and feels all.

In the angelic nature, Boehme is saying, head and heart are one, and there is an interplay of powers between them, creating a deep harmony. And when Coleridge says that head and heart are joined in the true philosopher, or that the beauty of woman's character arises from the more exquisite harmony of all the parts of the moral being, constituting one living total of head and heart; or when he greets the initial enthusiasm for the Pantisocratic plan with the triumphant exclamation, 'My head, my heart are all alive,' one senses in the background Boehme's image of the angelic.[51] Awareness of the image also illuminates other remarks of his: it throws into sharper relief his distinction between 'the *head* and fancy of Akenside, and the *heart* and fancy of Bowles',[52] and adds tragic point to his description, in 1806, of 'such a wreck as my head and heart'.[53]

Another example of the deep influence of Boehme's

visionary images may be found in a series of jottings in the Gutch notebook[54]:

> throned angels—upboyling anguish
> Leader of a Kingdom of Angels.
> Love-fires—a gentle bitterness—
> Well-spring—*total God.*

Boehme constantly speaks in cabbalistic terms of physical love, and one expression from the *Aurora* seems to have attracted Coleridge particularly—no doubt because of its scientific associations. Again and again in that work, the various phenomena of love are described with the use of the word 'flash'. Coleridge's *Lines written at Shurton Bars* end[55]:

> 'Tis said, in Summer's evening hour
> Flashes the golden-colour'd flower
> A fair electric flame:
> And so shall flash my love-charg'd eye
> When all the heart's big ecstasy
> Shoots rapid through the frame!

This is accompanied by a note on the flashing light from flowers at dusk.[56] And many years later, in a letter to Crabb Robinson, he argued that, just as, at sunrise, the sun appears to start up from the horizon, so it is with love[57]:

> . . . and this I many years ago planned as the subject-matter of a poem, viz.—long and deep affection suddenly, in one moment, flash-transmuted into *Love.*

If it is clear that isolated images and ideas in Boehme were taken up into Coleridge's visionary speculations, is there any evidence to support the further claim that he also habitually connected Jacob Boehme's doctrines with those of cabbalism and the esoteric Greek mysteries as all offering a doctrine of the Fall of Man different from the normally accepted one? As it happens there is. A passage in one of his notebooks contrives to mingle the decisive concepts of all three traditions.[58]

> Man in the savage state as a water-drinker or rather Man before the Fall possessed of the Heavenly Bacchus

(as Jac. Boehmen's Sophia or celestial Bride) his fall—forsaken by the $\Delta\iota o\nu\nu\sigma o\varsigma$—the savage state—and dreadful consequences of the interspersed vacancies left in his mind by the absence of Dionysus—the Bastard Bacchus comes to his Relief, or rather the Gemini, the one $o\iota\nu o\varsigma$ permitted by the Dionysus—the other a *Gnome*—this pursues, in the mix'd effects of the first—the accursed thing of the letters $\overline{To\upsilon\rho\kappa o\iota}$, an hour of productive Fancy required, to invent the Birth or origin of these.

.   .   .   .   .

The concept of the 'lost glory' was not only to be traced in the lost Dionysus or lost Shechinah of the mystic writers. Coleridge's age was an age when travel-books were eagerly read, not only for their descriptions of peoples and customs, but for their accounts of the mythologies of various countries. Scholars and others had noted the many similarities between mythologies of widely separated communities, and it was not long before they were offering their theories to explain the common origins of all myths, whether in sun-worship or distortion of the biblical tradition. George Eliot's Mr Casaubon, with his projected *Key to all Mythologies*, had a long line of devoted scholars behind him.[59]
It is against the background of this sort of interest that one has to view the extraordinary success of such a work as James Bruce's *Travels to Discover the Source of the Nile*, first published in 1790. Coleridge later spoke of Bruce as the 'Prince of Travellers',[60] and the description seems to be justified. Possessing all the excitement of an adventure-story, his book was calculated to fire the imagination of the young: so that even the sensitive Charles Lamb was inspired, as a boy, to emulate Bruce's exploits and search for the source of the River Lea.[61] Moreover, the book seemed to settle, once and for all, the classic question of whether the Nile had a normal source at all. Over and above this again, Bruce's accounts threw light on the mysterious, glamorous race of Abyssinians—particularly on their language and religious beliefs. The tradition still survived that the Abyssinians might represent the oldest civilization of all, and Mount Amara 'true paradise'. The elusive Troglodytes of Abyssinia might be guardians of traditions which were otherwise lost:

63

perhaps somewhere in the temples of Abyssinia one might decipher among the hieroglyphics 'the thrilling secrets of the birth of time'.[62]

Nearer home lay a similar set of traditions, which made the investigation all the more fascinating. The eighteenth century showed great interest in Celtic and Druidic lore: an interest which was quickened by the possibility that such a mythology might both replace the Greek and Roman for English poets,[63] and give guidance towards the religion of nature which an age of reason required.[64] The Druids themselves were men with mysterious powers of divination and prophecy: they included the Bards, who united the functions of poet and prophet in a single, awe-inspiring ecstasy.[65] They were sometimes identified, moreover, with a race as elusive as the troglodytes: the[66]

> Borealis race
> That flit ere you can point their place.

Hecateus' description of the 'happy Hyperboreans', which had been quoted by Diodorus Siculus, was commonly thought to refer to Britain.[67]

Amongst them that have written old Stories much like Fables, *Hecateus* and some others say, that there is an Island in the Ocean over against *Gall*, (as big as *Sicily*) under the *Artick* Pole, where the *Hyperboreans* inhabit, so call'd, because they lye beyond the Breezes of the *North* wind. That the Soyl here is very rich, and very fruitful; and the Climate temperate, insomuch as there are Two Crops in the Year.

They say that *Latona* was born here, and therefore that they worship *Apollo* above all other Gods; and because they are daily saying Songs in praise of this God, and ascribing to him the highest Honours, they say that these Inhabitants demean themselves, as if they were *Apollo's* Priests, who has there a stately Grove, and renown'd Temple of a round Form, beautify'd with many rich Gifts. That there is a City likewise consecrated to this God, whose Citizens are most of them Harpers, who playing on the Harp, chant Sacred Hymns to *Apollo* in the Temple, setting forth his glorious Acts. . . .

They say, moreover, . . . that *Apollo* once in Nineteen
Years comes into the Island. . . . At this time of his
appearance (they say) that he plays upon the Harps, and
sings and daunces all the Night from the Vernal Equinox,
to the rising of the *Pleiades*, solacing himself with the
Praises of his own successful Adventures. . . .

Coleridge must have known Diodorus Siculus well, and
when among his friends at Stowey he used to be known as
'the Bard', and to call his house 'Apollo's Temple',[68] and
when in *Fears in Solitude* he wrote,[69]

> O divine
> And beauteous island! thou hast been my sole
> And most magnificent temple, in the which
> I walk with awe, and sing my stately songs,
> Loving the God that made me!

one suspects more than a hint of Hecateus' idyllic account.
Whether to be taken seriously or not, the idea of the Druids
as guardians of the ancient tradition, descended in a direct
line from Noah (who in his turn had received the traditions
which he taught them from Adam and thus from God),
with all that this suggested concerning the antiquity of
English civilization, was bound to fascinate an imaginative, idealistic young poet.[70]

Other works on English mythology were studied at the
time. Leigh Hunt speaks of reading Mallet's *Northern
Antiquities* at Christ's Hospital[71] and enthusiasm for the
Druids was probably also stimulated when, in 1791, George
Richards, an old Blue, won the coveted Newdigate Prize
at Oxford, with a poem on *The Aboriginal Britons*.[72] Mason's
Druid play *Caractacus* was another great favourite. And
apart from this, Coleridge and his school-friends were
great lovers of all mythology. He himself pored over Tooke's
Pantheon, and vividly remembered for the rest of his life
some of the pictures which he saw there.[73] His enthusiasm
was later shared by Leigh Hunt[74]:

Tooke was a prodigious favourite with us at [Christ's
Hospital]. I see before me, as vividly now as ever,
his Mars and Apollo, his Venus and Aurora . . . the Mars,

c   65

coming on furiously in his car; Apollo, with his radiant head in the midst of shades and fountains; Aurora with hers, a golden dawn; and Venus, very handsome, we thought and not looking too modest in "a slight cymar'.

The glamour of mythology was at work everywhere, from the school-room to the lonely country vicarage where some old clergyman would pore over accounts of mythology in search of the key that would unlock them all. Perhaps the most notable of all English mythologists was Jacob Bryant, one-time secretary to the Duke of Marlborough, who produced, among a host of works on the subject, his *Analysis of Ancient Mythology* (1774). In this book he attempted to prove, largely by verbal resemblances, that the world's great myths could all be traced back to sun-cults, and that the sun-cults all eventually sprang from Noah's son, Ham, and his descendants, The method of the work, which now seems ludicrous, did not seem so impossible to an age which believed that all languages sprang from a single original, and Bryant's work enjoyed a considerable vogue. It was quoted by most writers on mythology in the subsequent period, and a complete mythological dictionary was produced from its contents.[75] Among the illustrations to the first edition was an engraving, now attributed to Blake, showing the Ark as a crescent moon resting on the waters.[76] Coleridge later wrote a clever parody[77] of such methods of interpretation, but it is likely that he was deeply impressed by them in youth.

At this point, it may be mentioned that Coleridge at some point of his life seems to have evolved an interpretation of the development of ancient religion and mythology. It is not possible to say with certainty that he drew it up as early as this, but the changing pattern of his interests suggests that it is more likely to have been a youthful theory than one worked out later in life. I do not know of any place where he has presented his theories in a fully worked out form: but working through his lecture on the Prometheus of Aeschylus, and comparing it with a number of scattered comments and remarks, it is possible to perceive

a consistent theory. A few years before he died, he wrote,
that the more he read the Old and New Testament,[78]

> the more confirmed does my persuasion become of the
> truth of an oral and traditional, but from its spirituality,
> esoteric Faith, from the Patriarchs to Moses & from
> Moses to the last of the Prophets—& then continued,
> tho' by refraction, bedimmed & refracted, yet continued
> in the earliest *Cabbala/*

This is his most explicit statement of a theory which
emerges in many places. He speaks, for example, of the
possibility of law handed down from the patriarchs having
been preserved in the Temple of Isis[79]—which he would
presumably have located in Abyssinia. Apart from this, his
speculations are concentrated upon two major themes. The
first is the method by which the mysteries and certain other
elements in Greek religion reached Greece. He is emphatic
that Greek philosophy did not come from Egypt. Such
claims, he maintains, are groundless[80]: the scientific knowledge of the Egyptian priesthood was trivial.[81] On the
contrary, almost everything intellectually great in Egypt
seems to him of Grecian origin.[82] On the other hand, he
thought that Dionysus, or Bacchus, was brought at least
from Egypt,[83] and that the Greek mysteries derived ultimately from patriarchal traditions, probably by way of the
Phoenicians.[84]

He felt that pantheism had been taught in the mysteries,[85]
and seems to have associated this with the cult of Isis, which
he felt to have been the first departure from the patriarchal
tradition.[86]

> . . . the sacerdotal religion of Egypt had, during the
> interval from Abimelech to Moses, degenerated from the
> patriarchal or arkite monotheism into a pantheism,
> cosmotheism, or worship of the world as God.
> . . . the cow, the Isis, and the Io of the Greeks, truly
> represented, in the first instance, the earth or productive
> nature, and afterwards the mundane religion grounded
> on the worship of nature, or the τὸ πᾶν, as God. In after
> times, the ox or bull was added, representing the sun, or

generative force of nature, according to the habit of male and female deities, which spread almost over the whole world,—the positive and negative forces in the science of superstition. . . .

During this period of Egypt's religious development, two things happened. Moses, an alumnus of the temple of Isis, or On,[87] led out the people of Israel, restoring to them the patriarchal tradition. Meanwhile the Egyptians had worked out a philosophy based upon their observation of the heavenly bodies.[88]

Wherever the powers of nature had found a cycle for themselves, in which the power still reproduced the same phenomenon during a given period, whether in the motions of the heavenly orbs, or in the smallest living organic body, there the Egyptian sages predicted life and mind:—TIME, cyclical time, was their abstraction of the Deity, and their holydays were their gods.

In a notebook he mentions that the Egyptians made the crab the symbol of the cyclical motion of the planets round the sun. 'At every point the strait line falls back on itself, whence of course a circle.'[89] This pantheism was taken over by the Greeks:[90]

The Homeridæ (so I interpret the famous passage in Herodotus) first united or identified the Egyptian Symbols of Time, Jupiter & their Dei majores with the Heroic traditions of the Asiatic & Javanic Greeks—and Jupiter, = the Year, became one with a Hero of Crete— &c &c.

By uniting the religious conceptions of Isis and Osiris which they gained from Egypt with the doctrines of the mysteries which they gained from Phoenicia, the Greeks were able to evolve the myth of Prometheus and Io,[91] which Coleridge felt to be one of the great pre-Christian enunciations of truth. In spite of this, however, their religion, like that of the Egyptians, gradually declined into fertility-cults,[92] and their pantheism inevitably led to polytheism.[93]

This appears to be Coleridge's theory, so far as it can be

pieced together. The fact that it is never stated in an ordered fashion in itself suggests that his mind was playing over ideas which had first been formulated long before. In Coleridge's youth, moreover, speculations about Egyptian symbols were common. One of the people to stimulate this interest was William Stukeley, the archaeologist, who, being fascinated, like many of his contemporaries, by the Druids and the possible relationship between their culture and other ancient civilizations, examined the remains at Stonehenge and Avebury (or Abury) and sought, in two treatises, to establish their significance in Druid-worship. Avebury, he decided, had originally been designed as a serpent-temple, with a circular area in the middle, and wavy serpentine avenues leading off in either direction. This he took to be a reproduction of the ancient Egyptian hieroglyphic of the serpent proceeding from a circle, which, he asserted, had a significance not only in solar worship, but also as an esoteric representation of the Trinity. The latter interpretation he expounded, not in his book, but in a letter to Roger Gale[94]:

As you are a druid and a fellow-labourer at Aubury, I shall open to you part of the secret of it, desiring you not to communicate it to any but druids. The form of that stupendous work is . . . the picture of the Deity, more particularly of the Trinity, but most particularly what they anciently called *The Father and the Word*, who created all things; this figure you find on the tops of all the obelisks, &c. being equivalent to the Hebrew *Tetra Grammaton*. A snake proceeding from a circle, is the eternal procession of the Son, from the first cause. The Egyptians frequently added wings to it, then it was the trinity properly; but our ancestors judged, I suppose, that they could not represent the wings well in stonework, so omitted them. The Aegyptians call this figure *Hemptha*, the Greeks in abbreviated writing used it for *Daimon*, or the good Genius. . . .

The figure of the sun, the serpent and the wings had been discussed by other writers of the time, including Bryant and Bruce.[95] That it was known to Coleridge is more or less

certain: and I am inclined to think that it formed a basis for
his speculations concerning the Egyptian veneration for the
cyclical, and thence became one of the most important
paradigms in his thinking. Again and again in his writings
there are descriptions of the creative energy of the universe
which suggest that this pattern of imagery is at work in his
mind.

Sometimes it was the serpent that was uppermost in his
mind. He likened the motion of poetry to 'the motion of a
serpent, which the Egyptians made the emblem of intellectual power',[96] and compared Shakespeare's versification
to 'the sinuous and ever-varied lapses of a serpent, writhing
in every direction, but still progressive, and in every posture
beautiful'.[97] Making the same point in a notebook, he
quoted Milton's description of the serpent in Paradise[98]:

> erect
> Amidst the circling spires that on the Grass
> Floted Redundant—
> So varied he & of his tortuous train
> Curls many a wanton wreath;
>
> yet still he proceeds & is proceeding.—

Hazlitt later quoted, as a subject for ridicule, his assertion
that 'the principle of the imagination resembles the emblem
of the serpent, by which the ancients typified wisdom and
the universe, with undulating folds, for ever varying and for
ever flowing into itself,—circular, and without beginning or
end'.[99] And in a passage on artistic creation which has
already been quoted, he declared, 'The common end of all
narrative, nay, of *all*, Poems is to convert a *series* into a
Whole: to make those events, which in real or imagined
History move on in a *strait* Line, assume to our Understandings a *circular* motion—the snake with it's Tail in it's
mouth . . ."[100] Elsewhere he uses the image more widely: in
sensibility, he says, 'we see a power that in every instant *goes
out* of itself, and in the same instant retracts and falls back on
itself: which the great fountains of pure *Mathesis*, the
Pythagorean and Platonic Geometricians, illustrated in the
production, or self-evolution, of the point into the circle'.[101]
He was fond of depicting the serpentine orbit of the moon,

and described the creative Logos as 'A bodiless Substance, an unborrow'd Self—God in God immanent, the eternal Word, That goes forth yet remains, Crescent, and Full, and Wane, Yet ever entire and one. . . .'[102]

.   .   .   .   .

By now the relevance of Coleridge's mythological studies to his mysticism and his romantic sense of lost glory is no doubt evident. If the snake with its tail in its mouth represents the ideal of creative activity, it can also be used to represent the restored Shechinah. Similarly, the figure of the Uraeon, with the snakes proceeding from the sun, and the wings around all, can represent the harmony of head and heart which enables humanity to soar. If the pattern is broken, the wings will disappear, and the other components lose their glory. The sun will become wrathful and unbearably hot, the serpent loathsome, stinging its own head. Nevertheless, they still remain, indispensably, the elements of reconciliation. If harmony is to be re-created, it will be done not by destroying the serpent, but by raising it up to its former glory.[103]

One of the interesting features about this figure is that it could be brought forward to help interpret some puzzling passages in the Bible. It could be related, for example, to the cursing of the serpent after the Fall, and to the terms of that curse[104]:

I will put enmity between thee and the woman, and between thy seed and her seed; it shall bruise thy head, and thou shalt bruise his heel.

It could be thought of as throwing light, also, on the lifting up of the serpent in the wilderness by Moses, and on Christ's use of that action as a symbol to describe the redemption of man. Coleridge was certainly familiar with some elements, at least, of this tradition, since he later dwelt on the tradition that Eve had expected Cain to be the new man who would vanquish the serpent; and he also mentioned more than once the expectation among the nations that the Messiah would be the Serpent-treader.[105]

Further discussion of this theme can be left until later;

and we may turn to the author who exercised a more potent sway over eighteenth-century visionaries than any other— John Milton. Milton's influence on eighteenth-century poetic diction has often been noticed, and Eliot's picture of it as a great Chinese Wall across English poetry has been widely approved. It is important to recognize, however, that this influence was achieved and maintained largely because of Milton's extraordinary hold upon the imagination of young writers, a hold which was strengthened with the rise of romanticism. Geoffrey Grigson has called Milton 'the great goldfield, the Klondike of the Romantic Miners'.[106] And to the great Romantics he was even more than a quarrying-ground, or static source of colourful poetic imagery: it was the poet himself who engaged their attention, as the ideal poet, with a vision to be sought after and shared. Gray saw him riding sublime 'upon the seraph-wings of Extasy'. Collins cried despairingly that

> Such bliss to one alone,
> Of all the sons of soul was known.

To be Milton, in fact, was to achieve the true sublime.[107]

Coleridge once described his devotion to Milton as second only to his devotion to the Bible.[108] A note of 1800 records an apparent conception of bliss: 'To have a continued Dream, representing visually & audibly all Milton's Paradise Lost.'[109] And no one can read through his early poetical works without being constantly aware of this devotion and delight.

There can be little doubt that his enthusiasm for Milton acted as a strong organizing force for the imagery that has been discussed in this chapter. Above all, it gave Coleridge a vision of the angelic which haunted him throughout life. It is one thing to read some of the long discourses on the importance of the Reason in *The Friend* at their face-value; it is another to read them with some knowledge of the way in which he constantly associated the intellectual with the angelic. Lamb, who shared his enthusiasm for Milton, was fully aware of this trait in his friend, as is clear from some of the bitingly ironic 'Theses' which he sent to him on the occasion of their quarrel in 1798[110]:

IV

Whether the seraphim ardentes do not manifest their virtues by the way of vision and theory? and whether practice be not a sub-celestial, and merely human virtue?

V

Whether the higher order of seraphim illuminati ever sneer?

VI

Whether pure intelligences can *love*, or whether they can love anything besides pure intellect?

Nor can there be any doubt of the part of *Paradise Lost* which furnished Coleridge with his central idea of angelic intelligence. As a motto to the vital thirteenth chapter of *Biographia Literaria*, 'On the Imagination', he prefixed the following lines from Raphael's discourse to Adam[111]:

> . . . Flowers and their fruit,
> Man's nourishment, by gradual scale sublim'd
> To *vital* spirits aspire: to *animal*:
> To *intellectual!*—give both life and sense,
> Fancy and understanding; whence the soul
> REASON receives, and reason is her *being*,
> Discursive or intuitive.

This is a key-passage, the importance of which for Coleridge cannot be over-estimated. He used it as a central point of reference for his view of the imagination and the reason: and was even to describe it in a marginal note as an almost perfect 'enunciation of the only true system of physics'.[112]

This sense of an acute relationship between the intellectual and the divine was never to leave him; but in his early years it had an obsessive hold on him. For the young romantic poet, steeped in Gray and Collins, it was even more difficult to separate the idea of Milton from that of the angelic. His picture of the ideal genius embraced them both. If we want to see this vision at its purest in Coleridge, therefore, we have to turn to a time when he was as yet innocent of army-life, of marriage and of political journalism—to the time when, as never before or after, he was able to live the life of a visionary poet, untroubled by any sense of the world and its demands. This Coleridge, his imagination as yet unviolated, is the Coleridge of Christ's Hospital and of Cambridge. His dizzy flights reached their climax in the *Greek Ode on Astronomy* which he submitted unsuccessfully for the Browne Gold Medal in 1793. His failure to win the prize was a severe blow, particularly as he thought it better than the ode with which he had actually won it the previous year, and his later comment that it 'was so *sublime* that nobody could understand it', reveals rather than conceals his sense of disappointment.[113] The Greek version has not survived, but an English translation of it survives in Southey's collected poetical works.[114] It is reproduced as an appendix to the present volume: the translation, of course, is Southey's, but there is no reason to doubt its faithfulness to the original.

One or two points in the poem call for particular attention. A Miltonic note, observable throughout, is particularly evident in the references to Urania and to Wisdom, which echo Book Seven of *Paradise Lost*.[115] Here, however, Wisdom is described as the 'Creatrix', a concept derived, not from Milton but from the cabbalistic writings. Similarly, the identification of the sun with the human mind leads him to speak of the stars which

> Around the ever-living Mind
> In jubilee their mystic dance begun.

In the last three stanzas, Coleridge the visionary comes into his own. Here neoplatonic touches abound, as in the phrase 'when comes again the natal hour', and in the lines, addressed to his own soul,

> Love of thy native home inflames thee now,
> With pious madness wise.

It is perhaps surprising to discover that the 'divine man' of this poem is Newton. Besides representing astronomy, however, Newton stands for the universality of genius in Coleridge's eyes. For him the genius is the 'seer', in whatever field of art or science he may show his powers. Newton is priest of nature: and, even more appropriately, he is priest of light.

74

In this way, the concluding stanzas become not only a eulogy of Newton, but a hymn to genius. In all fields, the genius rules 'by harmony's mild force': and receives its powers from the 'spring ebullient with creative energy'. And when, in the last stanza, Coleridge addresses his own soul as a potential genius of this sort, he expresses the ideal of romantic man: the belief in self-knowledge; the desire to soar into the empyrean; and, most daring of all, the belief that when this ideal is achieved, the genius is in a state of equality with the divine—'A God the Gods among'.

Never again was Coleridge to express his hopes and ideals with such openness, but they remained, none the less, liable to emerge at times of exceptional imaginative activity. It would be irrelevant to accuse him, on this count, of arrogance or presumption. His view sprang, not from any lust after power, or imagined superiority to his fellows, but from his enthusiasm for creative activity—whether artistic creation, the love of man and woman, or, on an infinite scale, God making the universe. Such was his manifest delight in all these forms of creativeness that it is impossible to feel distaste. Mary Evans was nearer the mark when she wrote to him, 'There is an Eagerness in your Nature, which is ever hurrying you into the sad Extreme.'[116] The danger of his belief in human perfectibility lay, indeed, not in any application to himself, but in his tendency to feel that it could be applied to all mankind, under favourable conditions. It was thus that his early visionary speculations came to produce not megalomania, but the 'visionary scheme' of Pantisocracy.

Chapter III

'SCIENCE, FREEDOM AND THE TRUTH IN CHRIST'

COLERIDGE'S arrival in Cambridge is often taken to mark the first flowering of his intellectual powers. The raw young freshman, one is led to believe, was brought under the influence of William Frend at Jesus College, and it was not long before he duly became a liberal in politics and a unitarian in religion.

We have little detailed evidence of Coleridge's opinions during his residence at Cambridge, but what there is suggests a more complex picture. To begin with, he was already well developed, intellectually, when he arrived. A good deal of the visionary speculation described in the last chapter should apparently be dated to his schooldays, and there is evidence to suggest that it was still a dominating interest at the university. In one of the few contemporary records of him as an undergraduate, Christopher Wordsworth wrote that, after a long literary discussion, 'Coleridge talked Greek, Max. Tyrius he told us, and spouted out of Bowles.'[1] Clearly then, his enthusiasm for the neoplatonists was undiminished, and one may look at a passage in Tyrius' *Dissertations*, as later translated by Thomas Taylor, for some clue as to the reason[2]:

> Consider all this as a certain harmony of a musical instrument, and that the artist is divinity, from whom the harmony originates, and proceeding through the air, the earth, and the sea, through animals and plants, and after this descending into many and dissimilar natures, composes the war which they wage with each other; just as a coryphæan harmony descending into the garrulity of a choir composes its tumult.

If we are looking for the 'essential' Coleridge of this period, it is impossible to ignore the neoplatonic and visionary enthusiasms which were to figure so strongly in the *Greek Ode on Astronomy*.

A complete examination of Coleridge's early political and theological views falls outside the scope of this book, but they are sufficiently bound up with his visionary themes for some sort of consideration of them to be necessary. Most readers of Hazlitt's essay *My First Acquaintance with Poets* must have been surprised to find the author of *The Ancient Mariner* occupying a Unitarian pulpit; and the Unitarian congregations themselves were often surprised when their poet-preacher delivered a sermon which turned out to be little more than a political speech.[3] What was the relationship, if any, between these various activities?

Let us begin with his Unitarianism. Here the situation is in any case complicated by the fact that the sect was still not respectable, and its allegiants were liable to serious civil disabilities. In consequence, Unitarians were not inclined to make a parade of their faith, and it might be ignored even by their biographers.[4] Coleridge, who had gone up to Cambridge in order to prepare for the Church, would be less likely than most people to announce his conversion publicly.

Nevertheless, I find it difficult to agree with his biographers in assigning his conversion to the early part of his Cambridge career.[5] That he was unorthodox in some of his religious views while at Cambridge is indubitable, and according to his later account of the matter he did not attend the communion service after his first year.[6] He seems to have dallied briefly with Quakerism,[7] and was sufficiently fashionable intellectually to feel the pull of Unitarianism, which often went hand-in-hand with political liberalism. But it is not until the autumn of 1794 that we find positive evidence of his association with members of the latter sect. From this time onwards, his allegiance is clear, his association with the London Unitarians being followed by residence in Bristol, friendship with Estlin the Unitarian minister there, and his first sermons, probably delivered before November, 1795. As late as July, 1794, however, he was attending church while on a walking-tour,[9] and his marriage, on October 4, 1795, took place at the church of St Mary Redcliffe, Bristol.[10]

Evidence as to the state of his mind while at Cambridge is scanty but suggestive. In 1827, when news came that his brother George was dying, he meditated on their lifelong relationship and their various quarrels. Among the causes of these last, he mentioned 'My Cambridge Eccentric Movements, with my connection with the Unitarians and Liberals of Bristol & imprudent marriage . . .'[11] He seems here to associate his Unitarianism with Bristol, and only 'eccentricity' with Cambridge. In another notebook he gave in outline the plan for a novel, the first chapters of which were to be autobiographical; one section of the outline reads,[12]

4. University—platonizing Socinianism/&c.

Here, I think, lies the key to the puzzle. If it was not until after his final departure from Cambridge that Coleridge became an avowed Unitarian, this entry suggests that he had developed Socinian sympathies before this, but thought that he could reconcile them with allegiance to the Anglican Church. The use of the adjective 'Platonizing' is particularly significant. In the *Biographia Literaria* he describes his religious views in 1796, and declares that they combined an exoteric, practical Unitarianism with an esoteric, Platonic Trinitarianism.[13] It is not easy to see why he should have developed the two beliefs concurrently as a Unitarian; but they would have been of great use to him if he was trying to reconcile Socinian sympathies with membership of the Anglican Church. He would then be able to declare his belief in the Trinity with a quiet mind.

There is some evidence that Trinitarian speculations had occupied him while he was still at Christ's Hospital. In the course of an autobiographical note concerning this period of his life, he says,[14]

My infidel vanity (it never touched my heart) was but of a month or two—. Afterwards, I became Sabellian, then Arian, then (tho' much later) Socinian, even to my 25th year—But only in these few months, in the enjoyment of the supposed new light given me by Voltaire, and the pride of courage in *wounding* (?) them, have I ever ever with my lips (with my heart I never did) abandon the name of Christ/—.

The most interesting ingredient in this list is the mention of Sabellianism, since one would hardly have expected even so wide-ranging a reader as Coleridge to have come across it at so early a stage. It seems as though his knowledge of this third-century heresy must have been derived, either at first or second hand, from the writings of Epiphanius. What was it that the young disciple of Voltaire found to attract him in so obscure a source?

According to Epiphanius,[15] the Sabellians thought of the Trinity as consisting of three modes in one hypostasis, and illustrated this by the example of the sun, which combines in a single entity its light-giving power, its heat-giving power, and its orbicular form. They went on to relate the sun's orbicular form to God the Father, its light to the Son, and its heat and power to the Holy Spirit. The rays of the sun resembled the activity of the Son: like him they were poured forth into the world, and having enlightened it returned to their source. Likewise, the Holy Spirit, acting in harmony and power, was despatched into the world to enter successively, and singly, into all those who were worthy of the gift, and to cherish life and heat within them.

It was this element of allegory from the universe which probably attracted Coleridge, since it promised a conception of the Trinity based on the laws of nature. And I suspect that this image of the Trinity remained at the back of his mind throughout life, but especially in the days of his Platonic Trinitarianism, which he described as follows[16]:

> ... I was at that time and long after, though a Trinitarian (i.e. ad normam Platonis) in philosophy, yet a zealous Unitarian in Religion.

It has been suggested in a recent study that this Trinitarianism 'ad normam Platonis' refers to Plato's trinity of values—beauty, truth and goodness.[17] That this is not the case, however, seems clear from a later passage in the *Biographia*, which amplifies the first statement considerably[18]:

> These principles I held, *philosophically*, while in respect of revealed religion, I remained a zealous Unitarian. I

79

considered the *idea* of the Trinity a fair scholastic inference from the being of God, as a creative intelligence;
and that it was therefore entitled to the rank of an
esoteric doctrine of natural religion. But seeing in the same
no practical or moral bearing, I confined it to the schools
of philosophy. The admission of the Logos, as *hypostasized*
(i.e. neither a mere attribute, or a personification) in no
respect removed my doubts concerning the incarnation
and the redemption by the cross . . .

This clarifies the situation, but the reader may still be left
wondering where in the writings of Plato he could find a
Trinitarian doctrine of this sort. Further elucidation of
Coleridge's meaning, however, is provided by a passage in
the *Philosophical Lectures* of 1818, where he declares his
conviction that the Dialogues of Plato were intended by the
author merely as a preparatory discipline before the revelation of his more esoteric doctrines. These 'unwritten dog-
mata . . . which he would not publish and which were
peculiarly, and which alone were, his own', had been
preserved in a fragment by Stobaeus.[19]

I refer to the passage in which we are told that the
intelligential powers, by the Pythagoreans and Anaxa-
goras called the *Nous*, (the *Logos* or the *Word* of Philo and
St John) is indeed indivisibly united with, but yet not the
same as the absolute principle of causation, the paternal
One, the super-essential Will; nor yet, though indivisibly
One with, is it the same as the energy of Love, the
sanctifying spirit so sublimely described in the Apocrypha
under the name of the Wisdom of Solomon, remembering
that Σοφια, Wisdom, is the term which the Fathers of the
Church made peculiar to the Holy Ghost.

From all this it appears that beneath the innocent
Platonic Trinitarianism of Coleridge's early days there lay a
wealth of speculation. The sun, under its various aspects of
orb, light and heat, had become the emblem not only of the
divine Trinity, but also of creative activity within the human
being—particularly the poet. In order to understand the link
between Coleridge's theological and aesthetical doctrines, it

is vital to grasp this limited identification of the word of the poet with the Word of God. A passage in one of the note-books shows how his thinking in the one sphere inter-penetrates his thinking in the other.[20]

> ... the redeemed & sanctified become finally themselves Words of the *Word*—even as articulate sounds are made by the Reason to represent Forms, in the Mind, and Forms are a language of the Notions—Verba significant phaenomena, phaenomena sunt quasi verba poematum (τῶν νουμενων) As he in the Father, even so we in him!

The manner in which words come to have a life of their own—to be *things*, in fact, was always one of the mysteries which fascinated Coleridge, and in the sphere of religion, he was equally possessed by the idea that men, through the operation of the Word, themselves becomes 'Words of the Word'.

It is all very well, of course, for Coleridge to speak of 'platonizing Socinianism', or of holding a philosophical, esoteric Trinitarianism alongside his Unitarianism, but the matter is not so simple as it is made to sound. For this sort of speculation marks a point of departure from the common Unitarianism of his day. If God not only creates through his Word, but makes the redeemed of mankind 'Words of the Word', this presupposes divine intervention in the day-to-day affairs of the world—which was precisely the point which most Unitarians, with their belief in a mechanistic universe, had difficulty in accepting.

That this was Coleridge's view, and that he identified Christ with the Logos in this sense, seems clear from various of his statements. We may turn, for example, to his picture of Christ in *Religious Musings*[21]:

> Holy with power
> He on the thought-benighted Sceptic beamed
> Manifest Godhead, melting into day
> What floating mists of dark idolatry
> Broke and misshaped the omnipresent Sire . . .

This power, he goes on to say, awakened a kindred sensation in the human soul,

Till of its nobler nature it 'gan feel
Dim recollections

and finally soared to the ideal state,

> God only to behold, and know, and feel,
> Till by exclusive consciousness of God
> All self-annihilated it shall make
> God its Identity: God all in all!
> We and our Father one!

This is followed by a description of 'the elect of Heaven', in other words the truly wise and good, which culminates in the following passage[22]:

> There is one Mind, one omnipresent Mind,
> Omnific. His most holy name is Love.
> Truth of subliming import! with the which
> Who feeds and saturates his constant soul,
> He from his small particular orbit flies
> With blest outstarting! From himself he flies,
> Stands in the sun, and with no partial gaze
> Views all creation; and he loves it all,
> And blesses it, and calls it very good!

God, the sun, the divine man,—even in his Unitarian days, these three are set together by Coleridge. 'You are a temporary sharer in human miseries,' he wrote to Lamb, 'that you may be an eternal partaker of the Divine nature.'[23] And Lamb, who was a more orthodox Unitarian, replied, 'What more than this do those men say, who are for exalting the man Christ Jesus into the second person of an unknown Trinity,—men, whom you or I scruple not to call idolaters?'[24]

If it is true that Coleridge erred from Unitarian orthodoxy in this respect, it is easier to understand an incident which took place many years later. Lecturing at Bristol in 1814, he made a light-hearted observation, which cost him the friendship of Estlin, the Unitarian minister there.[25] In *Paradise Regained*, he said, Milton had represented Satan as a sceptical Socinian: and he later justified this remark by citing two speeches from the fourth book—one which begins,[26]

> Be not so sore offended, Son of God;
> Though Sons of God both Angels are and men . . .

and another which includes the following lines:

> . . . I thought thee worth my nearer view
> And narrower Scrutiny, that I might learn
> In what degree or meaning thou art call'd
> The Son of God, which bears no single sense;
> The Son of God I also am, or was,
> And if I was, I am; relation stands;
> All men are Sons of God . . .

It is very understandable that Estlin should be offended if he heard Coleridge satirizing, not orthodox Unitarianism, but the views which he himself had held, heretically, in youth.

In saying all this, however, it is necessary also to stress the fact that speculations such as these were the products of Coleridge's more visionary moods. At such times, all visionaries were 'sons of God'. He concluded a letter to Davy in 1802 with the words, 'May God & all his Sons love you as I do.'[27] Carlyon records his opinion in Germany that Christ was inspired—but not more than, say, Newton or any other great philosopher.[28] 'I am fully persuaded', he wrote in a notebook of 1803, 'that all the Dogmas of the Trinity & Incarnation arose from Jesus asserting them of himself, as man in genere.'[29] In his philosophical lectures of 1818-19, he pointed out that the neoplatonists had not been lacking in reverence for Christ—they had simply claimed that Plotinus and Pythagoras were of the same type[30]: and his sympathetic presentation of their case suggests that this is an opinion which he himself had formerly supported.

At other times, however, and in other contexts, he could be as rationalist and mechanist as any of his fellow Unitarians. This is even more true of his early political opinions which, at one stage, seemed indistinguishable from those held by most radicals of the time. We may therefore turn to the development of this element in his thinking for further light on his youthful views.

· · · · ·

At Cambridge, Coleridge's political opinions seem to have run in the same current as his religious beliefs. There can be no doubt of his liberal bias: his behaviour at the trial of William Frend,[31] and his plan for blazing the words 'Liberty' and 'Equality' across the lawns of St John's and Trinity[32] are sufficient demonstration. On the other hand, it would be unwise to draw extreme conclusions from such evidence. In *The Friend*, he categorically denies that he ever hoped for improvements from a violent change of Government, or that he became a Jacobin.[33] He also denies the story that he had been dishonoured at Cambridge for preaching Deism. On the contrary, he says, '. . . for my youthful ardour in defence of Christianity, I was decried as a bigot by the proselytes of French Phi- (or to speak more truly, Psi-) losophy'.[34] Liberalism, in all its forms, was his chief passion: and one of his most characteristic undergraduate achievements was to win the Browne Medal with a Greek ode on the slave trade.[35]

Two factors steered him into a sterner course. The first was his enlistment, which woke him to a sense of the world about him and its demands. The second was his meeting with Robert Southey, shortly after his discharge from the army. Of the latter encounter, he later wrote,[36]

I dwell with unabated pleasure on the strong and sudden, yet I trust not fleeting, influence, which my normal being underwent on my first acquaintance with him at Oxford. . . . Not indeed upon my moral and religious principles, for *they* had never been contaminated; but in awakening the sense of the duty and dignity of making my actions accord with those principles, both in word and deed.

In the company of Southey during the next few months, Coleridge passed through a period when practical action and moral virtue dominated his thinking. Together the two poets worked towards the realization of a perfect society in America. Nevertheless, to follow the progress of the scheme is to see them gradually diverging as the natural cast of each mind asserted itself. Southey's enthusiasm for the scheme took the form of a passion for political justice, engendered by his reading of Godwin. The streak of stoicism in his character responded readily to Godwin's subordination of emotion to logic. Godwin argued, simply and lucidly, that men of disinterested feelings could reorganize society towards a scheme of material justice for all. Southey 'read, and all but worshipped'.[37]

From the first, Coleridge responded to the scheme in much more enthusiastic and imaginative terms. The words with which he describes it, harking back to his visionary speculations concerning the head and the heart, illustrate his emotional approach[38]:

> Pantisocracy—O I shall have such a scheme of it! My head, my heart are all alive—I have drawn up my arguments in battle array—they shall have the *Tactician* Excellence of the Mathematician with the Enthusiasm of the Poet—The Head shall be the Mass—the Heart the fiery Spirit that fills, informs, and agitates the whole. . . .

Pantisocracy was, for him, not simply a scheme in which principles of abstract justice should be realized, but a society in which all the members, including himself, would find the harmony of reason and imagination which they sought. Thus he was able to reject with contempt the cynical comments of his Cambridge friends[39]:

> [Caldwell] told me, that the Strength of my Imagination had intoxicated my Reason—and that the acuteness of my Reason had given a directing Influence to my Imagination.—Four months ago the Remark would not have been more elegant than Just—. Now it is Nothing.

Soon he could show why it was 'nothing' in a sonnet on the venture.[40]

> No more my visionary soul shall dwell
> On joys that were;

he begins, and paints a picture of the idyllic life that awaits the settlers,

Where Virtue calm with careless step may stray,
And dancing to the moonlight roundelay,
The wizard Passions weave an holy spell.

If Coleridge's approach was more emotional and idealistic, however, the extent of his thinking about human
nature also led him, in moments of doubt, to see difficulties
in the scheme which were more radical than those perceived
by Southey. Southey was alive to the practical difficulties of
beginning a colony in America, but does not seem to have
doubted the general idea that greater happiness would be
found in such a scheme, once the practical difficulties were
surmounted. Coleridge, on the other hand, felt that the
important difficulties lay elsewhere. A month after his return
to Cambridge, in October 1794, he spent an evening discussing the scheme with two intellectual friends, Lushington
and Edwards, who finally admitted that the scheme was
impregnable—supposing the assigned quantum of virtue
and genius in the first individuals.[41] Coleridge, having
achieved this result, returned home triumphantly at one
o'clock in the morning; but soon doubts beset him. Lushington had argued that the women of the expedition would not
be able to develop sufficient strength of mind, liberality of
heart or vigilance of attention, and the doubts, once sown,
stuck. Had the women of the party been sufficiently edu-
cated, morally and intellectually? Had they been taught to
cultivate 'the generous enthusiasm of Benevolence'? And
would not the children of the party, who had already learnt
fear and selfishness, infect the children who would be born
later?[42]

So far, Coleridge's doubts on the subject of the scheme
lay well within the ultimate theory on which it was based—
the theory, based on the teachings of Locke and Rousseau,
that man was born innocent and spoilt by his environment.
He was simply doubting whether the ideal environment
could be obtained, with the party as it was then constituted.

In the event, of course, Pantisocracy foundered not on
such doubts as these but on the defection of Southey, and
for the rest of his life Coleridge apparently continued to
believe that the scheme was a workable one.[43] Nevertheless,

the discussions had posed another problem, which was not
to be resolved by varying the composition of the party. How
far was it true that human beings were fundamentally innocent in the way suggested? It is interesting to watch Coleridge half-grappling with the question, though not properly
aware of its existence.[44]

> All necessary knowlege in the Branch of Ethics is com-
> prised in the Word Justice—that the Good of the whole is
> the Good of each Individual. Of course it is each Indivi-
> dual's *duty* to be Just, *because* it is his *Interest*. To perceive
> this and to assent to it as an abstract proposition—is easy
> —but it requires the most wakeful attentions of the most
> reflective minds in all moments to bring it into practice—
> It is not enough, that we have once swallowed it—The
> *Heart* should have *fed* upon the *truth*, as Insects on a Leaf
> —till it be tinged with the colour, and shew it's food in
> every the minutest fibre.

On this occasion, the problem floats across the page as
lightly and transiently as a cloud-shadow, but it is none the
less there, in that requiring of 'the most wakeful attentions
of the most reflective mind'. In some way, it seems, one has
to be *actively* passive in order to acquire virtue—but is that
not a contradiction in terms?

The dilemma is so fundamental in romanticism that it is
rare to find any romantic writer managing to deal with it
squarely. He is more likely to be brought up against it
obliquely, skirmish with it briefly, and then leave it. Coleridge, more conscious of the problem than most of his
contemporaries, did not have any greater success. It can be
said, however, that he dealt with it more patiently, more
subtly, and at greater length.

To some of his associates, of course, there was no problem
in the first place. George Dyer, for example, with whom he
corresponded during the period of planning Pantisocracy,
and who was a great enthusiast for the scheme, might well
stand for necessitarianism at its purest. On the one hand,
his beliefs led him to orthodox Unitarianism, and a passion
for social justice which was expressed in his *Complaints of the
Poor People of England*.[45] On the other, he cultivated a 'wise

passiveness' to the extent of composing poetry by its means. On returning to his lodgings in the evening, he relates, he would endeavour to work himself up into a kind of poetic frenzy, purifying his affections by thinking about the most amiable person that he knew. He would then smoke a pipe, thinking over the events of the day, until he fell into a sleep of three hours or so. During this period he would often dream, and on waking would smoke another pipe, setting down on paper anything that he wished to preserve. His dreams were all in verse.[46]

George Dyer may have been an eccentric, but he was an eccentric in tune with his age. He seems to have influenced Lamb, who became 'a Unitarian Christian, and an Advocate for the Automatism of Man'.[47] And Coleridge became for a time so strong a believer in Philosophical Necessity that he deplored petitionary prayer as 'Impotence of Mind',[48]—adopting instead, presumably, Priestley's substitute: 'the deepest *humility*, the most intire *resignation* to the will of God, and the most unreserved *confidence* in his goodness and providential care'.[49]

Coleridge's exploration of the twin doctrines of Necessity and Passiveness can be traced in his employment and development of certain symbols: notably that of the breeze and the harp.[50]

> And what if all of animated nature
> Be but organic Harps diversely fram'd
> That tremble into thought, as o'er them sweeps
> Plastic and vast, one intellectual breeze,
> At once the Soul of each, and God of all?

By means of this concept, he was able to reconcile necessitarianism with a benevolent theism. The universe could be imagined as a set of instruments, God being the supreme harmonist. And once again, it was possible to draw some sort of parallel between the 'creative activity' of the human mind and the harmonizing creation of God[51]:

> While shadowy PLEASURE, with mysterious wings,
> Brooded the wavy and tumultuous mind,
> Like that great Spirit, who with plastic sweep
> Mov'd on the darkness of the formless Deep!

By the time he came to write *The Friend*, his utterance on this, as on many matters, was more cautious:[52]

> The Intelligence, which produces or controls human actions and occurrences, is often represented by the Mystics under the name and notion of the supreme Harmonist. I do not myself approve of these metaphors: they seem to imply a restlessness to understand that which is not among the appointed objects of our comprehension or discursive faculty. . . .

There had, nevertheless, been a time when he approved strongly of such metaphors: as, for example, when he wrote his *Ode to the Departing Year* in 1796:[53]

> SPIRIT who sweepest the wild harp of time!
> It is most hard, with an untroubled ear
> Thy dark inwoven harmonies to hear.
> But, mine eye fix'd on Heaven's unchanged clime,
> Long had I listen'd, free from mortal fear . . .

According to the 'argument' prefixed to the poem shortly afterwards, the ode begins with an 'address to the Divine Providence that regulates into one vast harmony all the events of time, however calamitous some of them may appear to mortals'. In view of this declared belief, it is not surprising that he should have been jocularly known to some of his more intimate friends as a puzzling Pangloss.[54] He was sufficiently Leibnitzian to cherish hopes of discovering the pre-established harmony, at least in his more daring flights.

But given the 'breeze-harp' concept of human nature, was there anything that the human being could do to put himself in touch with the hidden harmony of the universe? Often, Coleridge simply ignores the problem. For example, he speaks of the poetry of Bowles simply as follows[55]:

> To Mr Bowles's poetry I have always thought the following remarks from Maximus Tyrius peculiarly applicable:—'I am not now treating of that poetry which is estimated by the pleasure it affords to the ear—the ear having been corrupted, and the judgment-seat of the

89

perceptions; but of that which proceeds from the intellectual Helicon, that which is *dignified*, and appertaining to *human* feelings, and entering into the soul.'

Here there is direct communication between the intellect and the divine: but there is no indication of the means. The only hint lies in the supposed corruption of the ear—which might suggest the need for purification of some sort: and this idea may be supported by the fact that Coleridge twice in his poems speaks of the 'purgéd eye' of his heroes.[56] It is always difficult in such cases, however, to discover just how seriously he expects his images to be taken, and the purification often seems to be no more than departure from error. On the whole, the communication seems to be something granted directly in certain favourable circumstances, and the means by which those circumstances can be manipulated is not discussed.

At times, for example, the harp image is dropped in favour of the statue of Memnon, which sent forth a musical note when touched by the rays of the sun[57]:

> The finely-fibred Heart, that like the statue of Memnon, trembles into melody on the sun-beam touch of Benevolence, is most easily jarred into the dissonance of Misanthropy. But you will never suffer your feelings to be benumbed by the torpedo Touch of that Fiend—/I know you—and know that you will drink of every Mourner's sorrows, even while your own Cup is trembling over it's Brink!—

Here one senses a certain fatalism: and at the height of his necessitarianism he even seems to play with the image of the wind-harp as though it could be treated with strict literalness. 'I go farther than Hartley,' he says, 'and believe the corporeality of *thought*—namely, that it is motion.'[58]

By the time that he came to write *Dejection: an Ode*, he was less optimistic in outlook. When he uses the Aeolian harp image in this poem, it is to describe not a soft summer breeze, but a mournful evening wind. It is difficult not to read this as a deliberate change, or to see in the description of the sound a subtle reflection of the dull, jarring state of his own nerves.[59]

This Night, so tranquil now, will not go hence
Unrous'd by winds, that ply a busier trade
Than that, which moulds yon clouds in lazy flakes,
Or the dull sobbing Draft, that drones & rakes
Upon the Strings of this Eolian Lute,
    Which better far were mute.

Geoffrey Grigson has said that this change in Coleridge's
use of one of his favourite images marks the end of the
innocent time when he had been (to quote his own remark)
'intoxicated with the vernal fragrance & effluvia from the
flowers and first-fruits of Pantheism, unaware of it's bitter
root'.[60] There is, at all events, a remarkable change of
emphasis: and it is noticeable that in this poem he comes out
explicitly with the view that one of the necessary conditions
of the joy that flows from a soul in perfect harmony with the
universe is a state of purity[61]:

Joy, innocent Sara! Joy, that ne'er was given
Save to the Pure, & in their purest Hour,
Joy, Sara! is the Spirit & the Power
That wedding Nature to us gives in Dower
    A new Earth & new Heaven
Undreamt of by the Sensual & the Proud!

With the decline of his optimism, however, the Aeolian
Harp did not entirely lose its place as an important image in
his thought. In one of his Philosophical Lectures, for
example, he mentions it in connection with religious thinking
and devotion[62]:

I was led to Teresa [*of Avila*] by a letter of hers in
which she gives serious advice to her friend Lorenzo to
keep holy water by him, to sprinkle about when he felt
any inward confusion, sudden aridity, or any under-
whispers of temptation, all which she assures him proceed
from the pressure of some evil spirit felt by the soul,
though not evidenced by the senses. This led me to
reflect on the importance of any act in strengthening and
enlivening the will, and I could not but think, what if a mind
like hers had attached anything like a religious meaning
to the Aeolian harp, as she did to the crucifix and the holy

water? What endless religious applications and accommodations all its irregular tones would produce!

In a note of later years he uses the harp as a personal symbol, in comparing himself with Dr Johnson.[63]

| Timeless | ⚹[1] | All Time. |
| Eolian Harp | | Single Drum. |

Hence the E.H. pours forth delicious tones, and surges of Tone but which can be neither measured nor retained —the faintest of all memories, the memory not *of*, but *about* a past sensation, broadly *particularized* by the wide *general*, delightful, sweet, tender, aerial, &c. &c.—

Query. As Conversationists is not S. T. C. ⚹[2] Dr J. as Eol[ian] Harp to Single Drum. Hence the stores of remembered Sayings of the latter—while S. T. C. sparks

> Sparks that fall upon a River,
> A moment bright, then lost for ever.

In these, and the many other places where he uses the image, however, it has lost its dominating position as a primary symbol, and remains only as a useful symbol for certain permanent elements in human experience. In the meantime, Coleridge had found another image, which helped to avoid some of the difficulties encountered when using the Wind Harp as a symbol of the intellect in relation to the divine. This image I suspect that he derived ultimately from his reading of the neoplatonists, for the pith of it can be found in a passage from Plotinus which he printed in the *Biographia Literaria*[64]:

> For in order to direct the view aright, it behoves that the beholder should have made himself congenerous and similar to the object beheld. Never could the eye have beheld the sun, had not its own essence been soliform.

As the eye must have something of the sun within itself in order that the sun may be perceived, so the human soul must have something of the divine within itself in order to achieve communion with the divine. This use of the 'sol intelligibilis'[65] to depict the 'translucence' of the human

---

[1] Contrasted to   [2] Compared with   (*Coleridge's notes*)

intellect at its highest is one of his most important images. It lies at the heart of his theories of Reason, of Imagination and of Genius; each of which is conceived as being, in its own way, a reproduction in little of the divine light. It underlies his idea that the symbol actually *contains* that which it symbolizes (and can thus be described paradoxically, as a part that is greater than the whole it represents).[66] More important still, it brings into his necessitarianism a strong dynamic element. The drawback of the Aeolian image was that, if interpreted literally, the divine activity in the universe was made to seem, like the breeze blowing on the harp, a mechanical process. The new concept, however, gave the passive element in the process an importance of its own: the divine creativity and harmony were now made to pass through certain individuals in a way which made them, in their turn, creators and harmonizers.

This might seem to involve the supposition that these favoured individuals become gods, but there is an important reservation in Coleridge's symbolism. When he conceives of the visionary, the transmitter of divine light, it is normally not as a sun but as a moon. The visionary, in other words, may be able to reveal the truth, to show forth the light, but he cannot normally transmit heat—the transfusion of power is beyond his capabilities.

It is interesting that both Coleridge and Wordsworth use this image of the moon to describe the visionary. No reader of *The Prelude* is likely to forget easily the passage in the last book in which Wordsworth describes how, in the company of a friend and a guide, he once made a night-ascent of Snowdon: and how they finally climbed through a belt of mist and cloud to find themselves suddenly at the summit, with the moon shining out of a clear sky upon the clouds and mountain peaks around them. He continued,[67]

> When into air had partially dissolved
> That vision, given to spirits of the night
> And three chance human wanderers, in calm thought
> Reflected, it appeared to me the type
> Of a majestic intellect, its acts
> And its possessions, what it has and craves,

What in itself it is, and would become.
There I beheld the emblem of a mind
That feeds upon infinity, that broods
Over the dark abyss, intent to hear
Its voices issuing forth to silent light
In one continuous stream; a mind sustained
By recognitions of transcendent power,
In sense conducting to ideal form,
In soul of more than mortal privilege.

There is nevertheless, a certain sombreness about Words-worth's visionary eye, a sense of brooding without power to help.[68]

The Clouds that gather round the setting sun
Do take a sober colouring from an eye
That hath kept watch o'er man's mortality.

For Coleridge, on the other hand, if the visionary cannot immediately help mankind, he does not remain in complete detachment from them, either. The artist has power over the imaginations of men, at least, and can fascinate their emotions as by a spell. He seems to have recognized this difference between himself and Wordsworth when they divided their functions in writing the *Lyrical Ballads*: he himself was to act like moonlight, actively awakening the supernatural, and at the same time procuring 'for these shadows of imagination that willing suspension of disbelief for the moment, which constitutes poetic faith'. Wordsworth, on the other hand, was to imitate the sunset in giving 'the charm of novelty to things of every day'.[69]

Coleridge, for his part, went on to develop the 'moon-visionary' idea. He seems, for example, to have applied it to his son, Hartley[70]:

An utter Visionary! like the Moon among thin Clouds, he moves in a circle of Light of his own making—he alone, in a Light of his own.

At about the same time, Wordsworth also used the image to describe Hartley:

Thou faery voyager! that dost float
In such clear water, that thy boat

94

May rather seem
To brood on air than on an earthly stream.

This passage, if taken in conjunction with Wordsworth's
fantasy of the moon as a 'sky-canoe',[71] suggests a clear
image. There is a further link in this particular chain, moreover. Hartley Coleridge, as a child, used to bear the nickname, 'Moses',[72] and this name is apparently connected with
his character as 'an utter Visionary'. On Good Friday, 1802,
Coleridge wrote in his notebook, 'A Great Man making a
circle like the Moon, in a white cloud.'[73] Moses, whom he
called "veil of the Light",[74] would be another example of
such greatness. He would be fully cognizant of the various
traditions that spoke of Moses as endowed at times with a
strange, glorious light. In his childhood, he was supposed
to have been distinguished by a 'singular beauty in his face'[75]
and the tradition was invoked by Coleridge's friend Humphry
Davy in planning a poem on Moses. The second book was
to have begun with a festival of the God of Nature, and to
have included a 'Moonlight Scene' and Jethro's reflections
on the System of the Universe. In book three, Miriam was
to tell him of a 'Light of Glory surrounding his Body'—
after which he believed himself under the immediate
inspiration of the Deity. The scheme, which was not carried
out, seems to have been drawn up at a time when Davy was
intimate with Coleridge.[76]

There were other traditions which would have made
Moses attractive to Coleridge's visionary moods. In Tooke's
Pantheon, for example, he would have come across the theory
that Bacchus was really Moses the many resemblances
between their careers including their beauty, their striking
water from a rock, their passage into lands flowing with milk
and honey, and their horns of glory.[77] The 'pagan' element
in Moses came vividly to Coleridge's mind some years
later, when he stood in the church of San Pietro in Vinculis
at Rome and discussed with a companion the powerful
effect of Michelangelo's 'Moses'.[78]

> . . . our conversation turned on the horns and beard of
> that stupendous statue; of the necessity of each to support
> the other; of the super-human effect of the former, and

the necessity of the existence of both to give a harmony and *integrity* both to the image and the feeling excited by it. Conceive them removed, and the statue would become *un*-natural, without being *super*-natural. We called to mind the horns of the rising sun, and I repeated the noble passage from Taylor's Holy Dying. That horns were the emblem of power and sovereignty among the Eastern nations, and are still retained as such in Abyssinia; the Achelous of the ancient Greeks; and the probable ideas and feelings, that originally suggested the mixture of the human and the brute form in the figure, by which they realized the idea of their mysterious Pan, as representing intelligence blended with a darker power, deeper, mightier, and more universal than the conscious intellect of man; than intelligence; —all these thoughts passed in procession through our minds.

This is one of Coleridge's rare references to the 'darker powers' of nature. When he makes them elsewhere, it is usually with an explicit mention of Bacchus. 'In his earthly character,' he says in a lecture, '[Bacchus was] the conqueror and civilizer of India, and allegorically the Symbol . . . of festivity, but worshipped in the mysteries as representative of the organic energies of the Universe, that work by passion and joy without apparent distinct consciousness, and rather as the cause or condition of skill and contrivance, than the result; and thus [he was] distinguished from Apollo and Minerva, under which they personified the causative and pre-ordaining intellect manifested throughout nature.'[79] Moses in his eyes represented both Bacchus and Apollo: he was the perfect image of the restored Dionysus. 'The first man, on whom the Light of an IDEA dawned, did in that same moment receive the spirit and the credentials of a Law-giver,' he once wrote[80]; and in another place he wrote a meditation on the theme of Mount Sinai, aflame at the presence of the Lord,[81] concluding, '. . . the darkness explodes into *Light*, the Dionysus from *Semele*, of *Jove*/— the *Ground*-Lightning'. Elsewhere, he spoke of the moment when the theory of natural philosophy would be completed: —'when all nature was demonstrated to be identical in essence with that, which in its highest known power exists in man as intelligence and self-consciousness; when the heavens and the earth shall declare not only the power of their maker, but the glory and the presence of their God, even as he appeared to the great prophet during the vision of the mount in the skirts of his divinity.'[82]

In Moses, Coleridge saw his ideal of humanity: the political leader uniting with the inspired writer and prophet. He even identified himself with his hero sometimes. It will be remembered that Lamb saw him in retrospect 'in the dayspring of thy fancies, with hope like a fiery column before thee—the dark pillar not yet turned . . .'[83] and Coleridge was equally fond of the metaphor. On one occasion he noted of his youthful liking for the writings of the mystics, 'If they were too often a moving cloud of smoke to me by day, yet they were always a pillar of fire throughout the night, during my wanderings through the wilderness of doubt, and enabled me to skirt, without crossing, the sandy deserts of utter unbelief.'[84] More than once, he used the metaphor for his personal pilgrimage.[85] In 1796, he wrote to Poole,[86] 'Thou hast been "*the Cloud*" before me from the day that I left the flesh-pots of Egypt & was led thro' the way of a wilderness—the *cloud*, that hast been guiding me to a land flowing with milk & honey—the milk of Innocence, the honey of Friendship!'

Always he saw himself as the wandering visionary, giving light, if lacking in the fullness of power. But there can be little doubt that, for himself and others, he dreamed of a state where light and power might combine, as in the transfigured Moses. 'Socinianism Moonlight—Methodism &c. A Stove! O for some Sun that shall unite Light & Warmth.'[87] He felt this to be true not only of religion but also of himself and all men who were looking for the truth[88]:

Will you find any pretence to light in that which has really no warmth? There is nothing in it that can be called tangible—nothing which presents motives or shapes itself to human imperfections. Allow the light: it is moonlight and moths float about in it! Again, those who reject all knowledge, who have wonderful incommunicable we-know-not-what, in the recesses of we-know-not-where, and who scorn all knowledge and all the means of attaining it, we will say here again, you have warmth; this may be a stove of life, and crickets and other insects sing their inarticulate songs in it!

But you must be as the lark and enjoy the [*light as well as the*] warmth, and therein your own being will be made fit for its appointed happiness and the extension of power which will come when the spring has been given.

Then only will true philosophy be existing when from philosophy it is passed into that wisdom which no man has but by the earnest aspirations to be united with the Only Wise, in that moment when the Father shall be all in all.

In evolving this strain of imagery, it will be observed, the Aeolian image had been gradually superseded as an interpretation of human behaviour. It remained in his mind as a subtle way of describing certain important truths, and as such was never relinquished.[89] It could also be used to describe certain important manifestations of genius. But as a central image of human nature, it was rejected in favour of an imagery which promised closer identification between the active, shaping mind and divine inspiration.

Thus the rise and decline of the Aeolian imagery marks out accurately an important phase in Coleridge's intellectual development. In tracing it, we are able to see how what had seemed at its height to be an unshakable necessitarianism and materialism in religion and politics could move, as if carried by a noiseless but irresistible current, back to the visionary philosophy in which he was always most at home.

Chapter IV

THE DAEMONIC SUBLIME

THE events of the French Revolution inevitably heralded a period of crisis for English liberal thinkers. The idealism of the early days, followed by the savage excesses of the later, raised problems which demanded an answer. Must it after all be acknowledged that human nature was not worthy of liberty? For those who answered in the affirmative, the effect of the events was to plunge them back into another form of conservatism, based on a pessimistic view of humanity. Others opposed any such idea vigorously, and held that the violence would prove to have been no more than birthpangs of the new order, which was about to emerge in all its glory.

Coleridge found himself unable to agree with either of these extreme viewpoints. His idealism was strong enough to prohibit the view that human nature must necessarily be bad, while he was sufficiently realistic in outlook to see that the excesses of the Revolution must be regarded, not as temporary excrescences, but as part of a chain of violence which must inevitably follow attempts to achieve the ends of liberty by force. 'The Temple of Despotism, like that of the Mexican God, would be rebuilt with human skulls, and more firmly, though in a different architecture.'[1] He applauded this metaphor of Southey's: and when, some years later, he came to write *France: An Ode*, he expressed the idea again in equally vigorous language[2]:

> The Sensual and the Dark rebel in vain,
> Slaves by their own compulsion! In mad game
> They burst their manacles and wear the name
> Of Freedom, graven on a heavier chain!

By now, however, with his emphasis upon the 'sensual and the dark', he had made his own ideas more precise, following a long period of thought concerning the nature of man. His own reaction to the political events in France had, in fact,

99

passed through two phases. In the first, he had proposed, by the Pantisocratic scheme, to succeed where they had failed: to create a miniature libertarian state which, by avoiding violence, and by including only the virtuous, would avoid the rocks on which the French Revolution had foundered. While carrying on this intensive experiment, he was to have exerted himself, by means of poetry and journalism, in favour of the principles of true liberty—and thus to have served society at large.

The obstacles with which he met in both these fields and the final abandonment of the scheme led him to a period of frustration, during which he reconsidered his view of human nature. By July, 1797, he was writing to Estlin,[3]

> ... I am wearied with politics, even to soreness.—I never knew a passion for politics exist for a long time without swallowing up, or absolutely excluding, a passion for Religion—. Perhaps I am wrong: but so I think.

And to his brother George he wrote in the following year,[4]

> I have for some time past withdrawn myself almost totally from the consideration of *immediate* causes, which are infinitely complex & uncertain, to muse on funda-mental & general causes—the 'causae causarum.'—I devote myself to such works as encroach not on the anti-social passions—in poetry, to elevate the imagination & set the affections in right tune by the beauty of the inani-mate impregnated, as with a living soul, by the presence of Life—in prose, to the seeking with patience & a slow, very slow mind 'Quid sumus, et quidnam victuri gigni-mur'—What our faculties are & what they are capable of becoming.

It is important to recognize the existence of this second phase, and the nature of Coleridge's interests during it, because it not only marked an important stage in his intel-lectual development, but was also the phase in which his greatest poetry was written. And it will therefore be in order to consider something of his studies during this period, and their bearing upon the problems just outlined.

It is impossible to embark on the latter task without

making some reference to the work of John Livingston Lowes, whose book, *The Road to Xanadu*, is recognized as the great pioneer work on Coleridge's poetic art and its relation to his reading. Within its own field, the majority of the points made in the book are likely to remain undisputed. Lowes's feats of research in tracking Coleridge's reading by means of the Gutch notebook, and in showing how widely scattered pieces of material were brought together in his imagination to compose a new, magical image, have a permanent place in the annals of literary research.

At the same time, some later writers have felt that Lowes had not told the whole story.[5] In his book, emphasis is laid upon the Romantic Movement as a movement of wonder, and on Coleridge as a leading magician within it. The poems of the *annus mirabilis* are represented as the work of a poet who found his true voice once, for a short period, and then lost it for ever. And there is more than a hint that he found his true voice mainly because, for a short period, he managed to forget metaphysics. Lowes's (not entirely unjustified) comments on Coleridge's plan to 'introduce a dissection of Atheism' into the *Hymns*[6] are followed by this sort of praise for *The Ancient Mariner*[7]:

> ... Sun, Moon, Air, Fire, and Water—no longer hid in a mist of Godwinian and Berkeleyian speculations, but in visible, tangible, trenchantly concrete reality—weave the very fabric of the poem.

There is a similarly scornful note in his description of the rise of neoplatonism[8]:

> With the nebulous and grandiose conceptions which resulted, we have nothing whatever to do. The one thing which does come into our reckoning is the fact that into this metaphysical cloudland there drifted strange waifs and strays from those obscure fastnesses of the supernatural, the rites and mysteries of the ancient cults.

Is this, then, to be the final word on our picture of the young Coleridge unfolding, in his deep and sweet intonations, the mysteries of Iamblichus and Plotinus?

One important result of Lowes's initial assumptions is

that he is led to examine Coleridge's reading purely for the poetic material which it contained. 'Coleridge', he declares, '. . . was reading with a falcon's eye for details in which lurked the spark of poetry.'[9] But surely, the reader may ask, Coleridge did not read books *only* for that purpose?

It must be acknowledged that if he did, he certainly lighted upon some extraordinarily unpromising works. Let us take, for example, the book which occasioned this remark —Maurice's *History of Hindostan*. This, it turns out, is not a book abounding in highly poetic descriptions of India. Its main concern is with the mythological lore of Hindustan, and its connections with other mythologies. Even a casual glance at the book will convince most people that whatever Coleridge may have found in the book, he must have gone to it in the first place with some other purpose in mind.

There is another assumption of Lowes's that ought to be questioned. In his second chapter he points out that on one or two occasions in his reading, Coleridge either went on to examine passages given as references in a book, or made a note to do so. By the end of the chapter, he is describing this practice as a habit[10]:

> . . . Coleridge not only read books with minute attention, *but he also habitually passed from any given book he read to the books to which that book referred*. And that, in turn, makes it possible to follow him into the most remote and unsuspected fields.

A moment's reflection will show the ridiculous results which would follow the literal pursuit of such a course—a point which could be demonstrated effectively by compiling the formidable and cumulative reading-list which would await Coleridge on completing only one book. Lowes himself does not make illegitimate use of his theory, but it has occasionally been used by other writers to justify Coleridge's knowledge of out-of-the-way sources.[11]

This point leads us to a more central one in Lowes's work: his assumption that all the images which Coleridge had ever come across entered his imagination, unsubjected to any organizing principle, and lay there waiting to re-emerge from their sleep in new and unexpected beauty. The idea is attractive, but it strikes one as an inadequate account of what went on in a mind as active and intelligent as Coleridge's; and it is at variance with Coleridge's own criticism of the theory of limitless association[12]:

In practice it would indeed be mere lawlessness. Consider, how immense must be the sphere of a total impression from the top of St Paul's church; and how rapid and continuous the series of such total impressions. If therefore we suppose the absence of all interference of the will, reason, and judgement, one or other of two consequences must result. Either the ideas, (or relics of such impression,) will exactly imitate the order of the impression itself, which would be absolute *delirium*: or any one part of that impression might recall any other part, and (as from the law of continuity, there must exist in every total impression, some one or more parts, which are components of some other following total impression, and so on ad infinitum) *any* part of *any* impression might recall *any* part of any *other*, without a cause present to determine *what* it should be.

Many phrases, no doubt, entered Coleridge's mind by virtue of their beauty and vividness, but there is evidence that other selecting principles were also at work. In the Gutch notebook, for example, he recorded Franklin's observation that two candles held together give more light than when they are held separately, and wrote underneath, 'Picture of Hymen'.[13] Lowes comments,[14]

He had . . . seen in Franklin's two candles which gave more light together than when separate what certainly, on the occasion of a pair of candles, never entered the heart of Benjamin Franklin to conceive—to wit, the emblem of a happy marriage. But the touch of sentiment is incidental. . . .

Is it? Are we not seeing here a principle of selection different from that which takes up a poetic image simply because it is vivid? The question becomes more important when one turns to Coleridge's interest in daemons and daemonology, a subject to which Lowes devotes several pages. His whole account is touched with ridicule, which takes the form of a patronizing irony. He speaks of 'two colossally learned' German monographs on the subject, 'for anyone who cares to track his daemons from the egg'. Michael Psellus writes of daemons, he says, 'with the conviction of one who has himself hobnobbed with them on occasion'. He mentions the theory that daemons speak the language of the country 'of which they are (as it were) "nationals" '. 'It is, accordingly, perfectly good form, daemoniacally speaking, that in the poem the Polar Spirit's fellow-daemons should speak English.'[15] Throughout, daemons are regarded as amusing, quaint beings which captured Coleridge's fancy for that reason. But the romantic writers were interested in daemons for other than dilettante reasons. They were led to them mainly by their interest in genius and the 'daemonic urge', and the idea that some men, such as Socrates, were guided by a personal daemon. They were interested in the possibility of describing some of the more mysterious energies of mind and spirit by such a symbolism. Shelley's writings are full of the idea. He associated daemons, 'good bad or indifferent', with animal magnetism as a source of knowledge of the supernatural.[16] His revision and abridgement of *Queen Mab* was entitled *The Daemon of the World*. The title of his poem *Alastor* is not, as is sometimes supposed, the name of the hero, but a word meaning evil genius or cacodaemon.[17]

Coleridge hardly used the concept in his poetry outside *The Ancient Mariner* and *Kubla Khan*, but it appears with some frequency in his notes and other writings. At various times, he discussed the daemons of Socrates and other philosophers, cited a description of poetry as a 'vinum Dæmonum' and wrote a lengthy disquisition on cacodaemons in one of his notebooks.[18] He spoke of opium as the 'avenging Daemon' of his life and of events in 1830-1 as the 'punishing Daemon of Civilized Europe'.[19] It is improbable that a man who constantly used the image with such thought and precision went to books on daemon lore simply to find quaint poetic images: it is more likely that this study of his was an important element in his study of the nature of evil. The contrast between the angelic and the daemonic was a favourite one with him, from the simple concept of the

Angel of Light changing suddenly into the Dæmon of Destruction[20] to more subtle versions of the idea. 'When the people speak loudly and unanimously, it is from their being strongly impressed by the godhead or the demon'.[21] 'Only fiends or angels could order their lives on the principles of the abstract reason.'[22] These two sentences, taken together, provide a neat summary of his views on the French Revolution; and further light is thrown on his conception of the nature of these forces by a comment in the *Table Talk*: 'If a man's conduct cannot be ascribed to the angelic, nor to the bestial within him, what is there left for us to refer it to, but the fiendish? Passion without any appetite is fiendish.'[23]

Coleridge's conception of the daemonic probably derives ultimately from his early reading of Boehme, which would have set his mind working on the idea of the devil as a twisted angelic nature, still possessing all the materials of the true angelic but in distorted form. He refers somewhere to the Devil as an Angel of Light, who chose the Darkness within him[24]: in another note, he says, 'Let only the Will of Hades detach itself from the Divine Will within us . . . the Fiend is revealed—the Enthusiasts, the Heroes in Evil'. He goes on to name Napoleon and Cæsar Borgia as examples of this unnatural heroism.[25] A later note on the theme throws light on his theories of dialectic[26]:

> . . . a *Devil*, an *evil* Power striving against, yet controlled by the Great Spirit—in this there is the chiaro-oscuro, the working of the modifying Energy in the dim combination of contraries.

This 'dim combination of contraries' is often worked out in the image of an association between lustful daemons. He uses this image, which may have been originally prompted by Milton's account of the unnatural copulation between Sin and Death, and by the account of the great Whore in Revelation, in several widely scattered places. In *Religious Musings*, he describes the religion of Mystery[27]—

> She that worked whoredom with the Daemon Power,
> And from the dark embrace all evil things
> Brought forth and nurtured: mitred Atheism! . . .

The daemons who dice for the Ancient Mariner are male and female: and in a notebook he speaks of the age as being possessed by two spirits—the fiend Mammon, and the fiend-hag, Anxiety.[28] He also writes of the connection between superstitious terror and sensual lust: 'gloomy Daemons both & that love the Dark'.[29]

If his study of the daemonic formed part of his thinking about evil, it was also closely involved with that study of the human faculties and their meaning which occupied him throughout life and was particularly important to him during the period after the collapse of Pantisocracy. This might be described as the scientific counterpart to his mystical speculations on the nature of evil—it was an attempt to give an account of human nature which would be at variance with both the completely mechanical view of Deism and the view of the orthodox, who regarded it as hopelessly corrupted.

While this tendency was still struggling into his consciousness, however, the political aspirations which had been awakened by Southey and Pantisocracy carried him on with their momentum. This is evident from his reading of the period. Up to the end of 1795, the books which he borrowed from the Bristol Library were not books on 'visionary' themes. They were mainly concerned with that loyalty to contemporary Unitarianism and Liberalism which fully engaged his energies for some time. After this, gradual signs of a change in interests begin to appear. The quickest way of describing the change is to say that metaphysics becomes dominant, although such a statement requires immediate clarification. 'Metaphysics and Poetry and "facts of mind" ' is Coleridge's own phrase to describe his interests, and this puts the metaphysics of the period in its proper context. Certainly the 'mist of Godwinian and Berkeleyian speculations' to which Lowes refers is a serious misnomer. It clouds the fact that Berkeley had ousted Godwin from Coleridge's mind and that the two philosophies could not have existed there together. By May, 1796, he was writing, 'I was once and only once in Company with Godwin—He appeared to me to possess neither the strength of intellect that discovers truth, or the powers of imagination that decorate falsehood— he talked futile sophisms in jejune language.'[30] Two months before writing this, he had borrowed the second volume of Berkeley's works at Bristol,[31] and this had marked the beginning of a period of enthusiasm for his philosophy which lasted at least until his departure for Germany in September, 1798.[32]

Muirhead, noticing this enthusiasm, says that Coleridge's admiration was evidently for the later Berkeley—the Platonic philosopher.[33] Yeats went further and suggested that he was particularly influenced at this time by Berkeley's Platonic treatise, *Siris*.[34] In the volume which he borrowed, Coleridge seems to have been particularly interested in the *Maxims*:[35] but it is noticeable that *Siris* is the only work of first-rate importance in it. A reading of that treatise, which as he later put it, 'beginning with Tar ends with the Trinity, the omne scibile forming the interspace',[36] probably took place at that time, therefore.

If so, this helps to explain a trend in his reading-tastes which is observable by the autumn. In November, 1796, he wrote to Thelwall, asking him to obtain some books which he had selected from a bookseller's catalogue, which contained works by several neoplatonic philosophers.[37] The two which he mentioned with most urgency were Iamblichus and Julianus. Berkeley's exposition of their doctrines in *Siris* may well have sparked off this interest[38]:

Julianus, the Platonic philosopher, as cited by Ficinus, saith it was a doctrine in the theology of the Phœnicians, that there is diffused throughout the universe, a pellucid and shining nature pure and impassive, the act of a pure intelligence.

Although the Ægyptians did most symbolically represent the supreme divinity sitting on a lotus, and that gesture has been interpreted to signify, the most holy and venerable being to be utterly at rest reposing within himself; yet, for any thing that appears, this gesture might denote dignity as well as repose. And it cannot be denied, that Jamblichus, so knowing in the Ægyptian notions, taught there was an intellect that proceeded to generation, drawing forth the latent powers into light in the formation of things . . .

As we have seen earlier, the idea of God as a pure intelligence was highly attractive to Coleridge, while the idea of the creator God sitting on a lotus, which he would also have found in Maurice's *Hindostan*, was used by him more than once. He employed it in a letter of October, 1797, going on to quote some lines from his recently completed play, *Osorio*[39]: ·

> . . . I should much wish, like the Indian Vishna, to float about along an infinite ocean cradled in the flower of the Lotos, & wake once in a million years for a few minutes— just to know that I was going to sleep a million years more. I have put this in the mouth of Alhadra my Moorish Woman . . .

> . . . It were a lot divine in some small skiff
> Along some Ocean's boundless solitude
> To float for ever with a careless course,
> And think myself the only Being alive!

Coleridge would also have been fascinated by Berkeley's theory that the mysterious substance known as aether was in fact the vital spirit of the world. Aether was a great subject for discussion among eighteenth-century scientists.[40]

Whether or not stimulated by *Siris*, Coleridge's interest in topics of this sort was very marked at this time, and was not a sideline. In schemes of study which he drew up at this time, 'ancient metaphysics' had an important place.[41] When, in the *Aids to Reflection*, he declared that in all countries of civilized men metaphysics had outrun common sense, he was speaking of mythological traditions[42]: and a similar identification is evident in the period which we are discussing. Between 1796 and 1798, he asked Lamb to obtain Plutarch and Porphyry for him[43]; borrowed Hyde's Latin treatise on ancient Persian religion[44]; read the first volume of Maurice's *History of Hindostan*[45]; borrowed a Latin volume of Apuleius which included the myth of Cupid and Psyche and much neoplatonic philosophy[46]; and grappled with Brucker's *Historia Critica Philosophiae*.[47] He also sent off the request for neoplatonic texts mentioned above, in which he spoke of his 'darling Studies': 'Metaphysics, & Poetry, & "Facts of mind"—(i.e. Accounts of all the strange phantasms that ever possessed your philosophy-dreamers from Tauth, the Egyptian to Taylor, the English Pagan,).' In the same letter he reported, 'I am just about to read Dupuis' 12 octavos, which I have got from London. I shall read only one Octavo a week—for I cannot *speak* French at all, & I read it slowly.'[48] This work, the *Origine de Tous les Cultes, ou Religion Univer-selle*, was yet another of the eighteenth-century works which made an encyclopaedic effort to explain all mythologic lore in terms of a single theory. The theory of Dupuis was (to quote Coleridge's own description some years later) 'that Jesus Christ was the sun, and all the Christians worshippers of Mithra'.[49]

From the evidence available, it is clear that Coleridge was so fascinated by ancient metaphysics and mythology at this time that he would go to great lengths to obtain works on the subject. He was quite prepared to read them in Latin or French, and to spend money which he could ill afford. What was it about them that engaged his attention so strongly?

The answer, I think, is to be found in his current pre-occupation with the nature of God and the problem of evil. In the neoplatonic writings, and more particularly in Berkeley's interpretation of them, he could find passages like those quoted above, which pictured God as a pure intelli-gence: he could also find the groundwork of a theory of evil and redemption. To develop the point, we may turn to a passage in *Siris* which is even more closely packed with mythologic lore than most of the works which Coleridge consulted: Berkeley's discussion of Isis and Osiris.[50]

The difference of Isis from Osiris resembles that of the moon from the sun, of the female from the male, of *natura naturata* (as the schoolmen speak) from *natura naturans*. But Isis, though mostly taken for nature, yet . . . it some-times signified τὸ πᾶν. And we find in Montfaucon an Isis of the ordinary form with this inscription, Θεοῦ παντός. And in the mensa Isiaca, which seem to exhibit a general system of the religion and superstition of the Ægyptians, Isis on her throne possesseth the center of the table. Which may seem to signify, that the universe or τὸ πᾶν was the center of the ancient secret religion of the Ægyptians; their Isis or τὸ πᾶν comprehending both Osiris the author of nature and his work.

A fourfold allegory lies implicit in this brief paragraph: it embraces Isis and Osiris, moon and sun, female and male, and the two creative principles, *natura naturata* and *natura naturans*. One might therefore suppose that Coleridge, with his constant interest in the symbolism of the elements would be arrested and fascinated by it. In dealing with his early interests, we have already noticed his fondness for the idea of a 'male-female' dialectic in creative processes, and for the sun as an emblem of the divine. Clearly, then, this passage by Berkeley would provide a neat schematism of his ideas. But is there any definite evidence that he did notice this paragraph, tucked away in an obscure corner of the treatise? As it happens, there is. In one of his philosophical lectures of 1818, the following observation appears[51]:

. . . the idealist concedes a real existence to one of the two terms only—to the *natura naturans*, in Berkeley's language, to God, and to the finite minds on which it acts, the *natura naturata*, or the bodily world, being the result, even as the tune between the wind and the Aeolian harp.

The terms 'natura naturans' and 'natura naturata' were not, of course, originated by Berkeley. Coleridge himself pointed out elsewhere in the lecture that they were used in the writings of the schoolmen, and he must have met with them in other philosophers also.[52] The specific point which he is assigning to Berkeley here is the identification of the *natura naturans* with God; and there could be no stronger testimony to the impression which the passage in *Siris* must have made upon him than this casual reference to a doctrine which is only to be extracted with some subtlety from it.

Isis and Osiris are, of course, familiar figures in English literature. In Milton's *Areopagitica*, for example, Isis seeking for the pieces of her lost Osiris symbolizes the search for lost Truth.[53] And it would seem likely, as we have said before, that Coleridge had long since made his first researches into Egyptian lore. His neoplatonic interests would have led him to it naturally enough: and there are occasional casual references to Egypt in his early works that suggest familiarity with the subject. In his essay on the National Fast, for example, he writes,[54]

> We collect from Herodotus and Porphyry, that before their annual sacrifice of a cow to Isis, the Ægyptians fasted forty days . . . .

A rather puzzling note to *Religious Musings*, first inserted in the edition of 1797, refers to 'Damas. De Myst. Aegypt.'[55] Bruce's *Travels to Discover the Source of the Nile*, and earlier, Warburton's *Divine Legation of Moses*, were other famous books of the time which had stimulated interest in Egyptology.[56]

It is true that in his public statements later in life, Coleridge occasionally spoke with some scepticism on the subject. In a lecture of 1818, he declared his opinion that the hieroglyphics had excited much more attention than anything but their antiquity could call for, and went on to suggest that they had originated simply in visual representations of material objects. Elsewhere in the same lecture he pointed out that the Egyptian worshippers of nature did not take the further step by which they would have seen nature as an allegory or revelation of God.[57]

> Take Egypt. Did it follow that the Egyptian people, from observing and worshipping a deity, according to their account, in [the] Ibises, in crocodiles, and in the Nile and so forth, rose lastly to consider the whole world as a kind of language—as the painted veil of Isis in which the Almighty was speaking to them? History shews to us the contrary. Juvenal tells us of the wars between the [Ombites'] Gods and the [Tentyrites'] Gods and shews us, as the Bible indeed has done with higher authority, all the sensuality that followed. Need we wonder that sensuality should follow from directly appealing to the senses, and instead of weaning man from that which was his fall, gradually strengthened it . . .?

Nevertheless, the detailed knowledge which Coleridge displays in support of the argument which he is attacking, suggests that there had been a time when he had toyed with it himself: and this is not surprising when we remember that in *The Destiny of Nations* he had described 'all that meet the bodily sense' as[58]

> Symbolical, one mighty alphabet
> For infant minds.

His reference to 'the painted veil of Isis', moreover, reminds us that in his copy of Tooke's *Pantheon* at school, and in other places, he would have read of[59]

> the Inscription which was heretofore to be seen in the Temples of *Minerva*, written in golden Letters, amongst the *Egyptians; I am what is, what shall be, what hath been; my Veil hath been unveil'd by none: the Fruit which I have brought forth is this, the Sun is born.*

In later years, he sometimes attacked the idea that the Egyptians had contributed anything to European philosophy but there remained some sort of reservation or even contradictory sentiment in his mind, for the *Aids to Reflection* includes a note which presupposes a different view of Egyptian hieroglyphics. The note, which is a discursion on the subject of the allegorical element in the first chapters of Genesis, is important enough to be reproduced in full.[60]

> In the temple-language of Egypt the Serpent was the Symbol of the Understanding in its twofold function, namely, as the faculty of *means* to *proximate* or medial ends, analogous to the *instinct* of the more intelligent Animals, Ant, Bee, Beaver, &c. and opposed to the practical Reason, as the Determinant of the *ultimate* End; and again, as the discursive and logical Faculty possessed individually by each Individual—the Logos ἐν ἑκάστῳ in distinction from the Nous, *i.e.* Intuitive Reason, the Source of Ideas and ABSOLUTE Truths, and the Principle of the Necessary and the Universal in our Affirmations and Conclusions. Without or in contravention to the Reason (*i.e.* 'the *spiritual* mind' of St Paul, and '*the Light that lighteth every* man' of St John) this Understanding (φρονημα σαρκος or carnal mind) becomes the *sophistic* Principle, the

wily Tempter to Evil by counterfeit Good; the Pander and Advocate of the Passions and Appetites; ever in league with, and always first applying to, the *Desire*, as the inferior nature in Man, the *Woman* in our Humanity; and through the DESIRE prevailing on the WILL (the *Man*hood, *Vir*tus) against the command of the Universal Reason, and against the Light of Reason in the WILL itself. (N.B. This essential inherence of an intelligential Principle (φῶς νοερὸν) in the Will (ἀρχὴ θελητικὴ), or rather the Will itself thus considered, the Greeks expressed by an appropriate word (βουλὴ)). This, but little differing from Origen's interpretation or hypothesis, is supported and confirmed by the very old Tradition of the *Homo androgynus, i.e.* that the original Man, the Individual first created, was bi-sexual: a chimæra, of which and of many other mythological traditions the most probable explanation is, that they were originally symbolical *Glyphs* or Sculptures, and afterwards translated into *words*, yet *literally, i.e.* into the common names of the several Figures and Images composing the Symbol, while the symbolic *meaning* was left to be decyphered as before, and sacred to the Initiate. As to the abstruseness and subtlety of the Conceptions, this is so far from being an objection to this oldest *Gloss* on this venerable Relic of Semitic, not impossibly ante-diluvian, Philosophy, that to those who have carried their researches farthest back into Greek, Egyptian, Persian, and Indian Antiquity, it will seem a strong confirmation. Or if I chose to address the Sceptic in the language of the Day, I might remind him, that as Alchemy went before Chemistry, and Astrology before Astronomy, so in all countries of civilized Man have Metaphysics outrun Common Sense.

The passage has a threefold importance. By its reference to 'Semitic, not impossibly ante-diluvian philosophy', it reveals that even as late as 1825 he was still ready to believe in a pure tradition of knowledge that had existed before the Flood, and had survived in Egyptian lore. The appeal to those 'who have carried their researches farthest back into Greek, Egyptian, Persian, and Indian Antiquity', is equally interesting, for we know that Coleridge himself had carried out such researches during the period which we are discussing. Finally, the whole passage gives an important clue as to the chief reason for such researches, for its subject is the Fall of Man and the origin of evil.

These questions, as we have seen, were crucial for Coleridge in the Bristol years. From a letter of Lamb's it appears that he had contemplated writing a long poem on the Origin of Evil as early as 1794[61]; and it seems likely that his intercourse with Wordsworth had revived the project in his mind. During that period, certainly, the writing of a joint poem on *The Wanderings of Cain* was planned, while Coleridge's *Osorio*, and Wordsworth's *Guilt and Sorrow*, together with his psychological essay on guilt, prefixed to *The Borderers*, all reflected a preoccupation with the subject.[62] When, many years later, Coleridge wrote to Wordsworth, pointing out that *The Recluse* did not fulfil his expectations of it, he said,[63]

I understood that you would . . . have affirmed a Fall in some sense, as a fact, the possibility of which cannot be understood from the nature of the will, but the reality of which is attested by experience and conscience. . . .

This was presumably the plan which had emerged from their discussions on the subject, and it reflects accurately Coleridge's beliefs at the time. In March, 1798, he wrote to his brother,[64]

Of GUILT I say nothing; but I believe most stedfastly in original Sin; that from our mothers' wombs our understandings are darkened; and even where our understandings are in the Light, that our organization is depraved, & our volitions imperfect; and we sometimes see the good without *wishing* to attain it, and oftener *wish* it without the energy that wills & performs.

Now it is clear that his desire to affirm a 'Fall in some sense' must have affected his visionary speculations in important ways. So far, we have mentioned his use of sun-imagery to express this perfectionist ideals, and his interest in the 'lost Shechinah' as a way of expressing the discrepancy between the world of mankind and the ideal order. He had come to see original sin not as an inherited guilt, but as a lack of enlightenment and a powerlessness to perform the good. His theory of redemption was equally heretical: he was inclined, he tells us, to 'lay the main stress on the resurrection rather than on the crucifixion'[65] and to attack any theory of redemption which involved a substitutionary sacrifice or the paying of a debt.

In this situation, the groundwork of an appropriate doctrine lay ready to his hand, in the shape of the myth of Isis and Osiris. This myth included not only Isis, the healing principle of nature, but also Typhon, the evil destructive principle in nature. Plutarch's treatise on Isis and Osiris describes them as follows[66]:

> ... Isis, according to the Greek interpretation of the word, signifies *knowledge*; as does the name of her professed adversary *Typho, Insolence* and *Pride*, a name therefore extremely well adapted to one, who, full of ignorance and error, tears in pieces and conceals that *holy doctrine*, which the Goddess collects, compiles and delivers to those, who aspire after the most perfect participation of the divine nature. . . .

Typhon has destroyed Osiris, hewn his body in pieces and usurped his kingdom; Isis is constantly and patiently seeking to find the pieces and restore her lost husband.

Plutarch discussed several possible interpretations of the myth. One view would make moisture the key: in which case Osiris is to be identified with the Nile, Isis with the part of the country which the Nile overflows, and Typho with the sea which finally dissipates and destroys it, and perhaps also with everything that is dusty, fiery and generally destructive of moisture.[67] Typho's alliance with Aso, queen of Ethiopia, would refer to the southern winds that blow from that country.[68]

Another interpretation would make Typho the orb of the sun, and Osiris that of the moon, in view of the moistening and prolific nature of the latter, compared with the violent, destructive heat of the sun.[69] Under this interpretation, the moon would be androgynous, uniting Isis and Osiris: female in receiving the influence of the sun and male in dispersing

the principles of fecundity. Plutarch rejected this interpretation, pointing out that in the sacred hymn to Osiris he
was described as one '*who lies concealed in the arms of the sun*',
and declaring that 'nothing which is bright and shining,
nothing which is salutiferous' ought to be attributed to
Typho.[70]

It is clear from his account, however, that he had missed
one possible interpretation of the myths with which he was
dealing. Under this interpretation, Osiris would represent
the ideal fertility, with Typhon its enemy and Isis its friend.
Consequently when Osiris is made to stand for the Nile,
Typhon would stand for the various enemies of the Nile:
the sea, which dissipates it, and the heat of the sun and
scorching winds that dry it up. Isis, on the other hand,
would represent the friends of the Nile: the moon and the
fountains which produce it, and the soil of the Nile valley
which it fertilizes.

The same interpretation could be carried out in terms of
the heavenly elements. The Egyptians perceived that the sun
in their climate sometimes favoured fertility, sometimes
destroyed it. It was light-giving and powerful, but its heat
and power were often so strong as to wither rather than
nourish. The moon was a more unambiguous friend, its
light-giving unaccompanied by destructive qualities. In
consequence, they came to represent the phases of the moon
as a regular attempt to re-create the ideal sun. Slowly and
patiently Isis does her work, until at the full moon she brings
together the whole of Osiris except the *membrum virile*: but
this one failure means that he must subsequently be lost
again. In consequence, the usurping Typhon remains in
possession of the sun, hiding its true glory, and Osiris only
'lies concealed in the arms of the Sun'. The world must
continue to endure the endless dialectic between the life-
renewing forces of Isis and the sterilizing forces of Typhon,
for the ideal sun and the ideal sacred river are alike lost.

We have already discussed Coleridge's receptiveness to
imagery which used the sun as a symbol of creative energy
and the lost Shechinah: and we have seen the importance
which he attached to Egyptian mythology as a source of the
Greek.[71] We have also seen him toying with the separation of

heat and light as elements of a lost ideal: 'Socinianism moonlight—Methodism a Stove! O for some sun to unite heat & Light!'[72] This he derived from Swedenborg, according to whom there is a Sun in the spiritual world, which is 'pure Love from Jehovah God', and from which 'proceedeth Heat, which in it's Essence is Love; and Light, which in its Essence is Wisdom'.[73] Coleridge used the Swedenborgian dichotomy in a new way however, treating all forms of fanaticism as heat and all intellectualism as light—sterile poles so long as they remain separate. He also used it of his love for Sara Hutchinson[74]:

> If Love be the genial Sun of human Nature, unkindly has he divided his rays in acting on me and [Asra]—on her poured all his Light and Splendor, & permeated my Being with his invisible Rays of Heat alone.

He was also fond of relating this polarity to another favourite distinction: that between the activities of the head and the heart. Thus he took over the old Puritan term 'heart-work' as a description of both the virtues and limitations of enthusiasm, and used the parallel term, 'head-work', to describe the corresponding virtues and limitations of Unitarianism.[75]

Elsewhere he brought the two images, sun and moon, heart and head, into closer parallel. His description of his ideal self will be remembered—'The Head shall be the Mass —the Heart the fiery Spirit, that fills, informs, and agitates the whole . . .'[76] It is interesting to turn from this, which appears to be sun-imagery, to a passage in his translation of Schiller's *Wallenstein*, made just after his return from Germany. Wallenstein, in *The Piccolomini*, is considering the results of his astronomical observations[77]:

> And sun and moon, too, in the Sextile aspect,
> The soft light with the vehement—so I love it.
> Sol is the heart, Luna the head of heaven,
> Bold be the plan, fiery the execution.

This passage seems to be in a line of organic development from the previous one, and it is not surprising to find that it has no place in the original German. A piece of Coleridge's visionary speculation has found its way into his rendering of Schiller.

In a later note, Coleridge showed that he interpreted the Isis-Osiris cult in the terms which Berkeley had used. The ceremonial burning of a heifer by the Israelites, he said, was a rejection of the Egyptian Isis-worship, which had become the cult of a World-God, the worship of *Nature* as the natura Gemina, naturans et naturata. '(Mem. Osiris represented the *active* or masculine, Isis the passive, recipient, feminine Nature.)' All this was an apostasy from the conception of God as I AM, and therefore the true *natura naturans*.[78]

An example of his treatment of Isis as an image of this sort may be found in a note which he made in Grew's *Cosmologia Sacra*[79]:

... such must be the sophistic results of every pretence to understand God by the World, instead of the World by God. It is an attempt to see the Sun by Moonlight.

Generally speaking, though not always, he tends to speak of 'moonlight' when he is showing some sympathy with the idea of natural revelation, and 'moonshine' to display his contempt for the concept when held only in isolation. His final position in relation to the symbol is to be found in his conclusion to the *Aids to Reflection*, where he limits the moonlight image to describe the natural mystic within a religious faith. The natural mystic outside religion, on the other hand, is merely a man with a lantern: he illuminates the scene but is totally incapable of interpreting it to others.[80]

During the period which we are discussing, however, it seems as though Coleridge not only made moonlight a symbol for the revelation of God through nature, but valued this type of revelation highly. His regard for it is shown in his portrayal of Enos, son of Cain, as a 'child of nature', in his projected poem, *The Wanderings of Cain*. At the beginning of the fragment of the poem which was actually composed, Enos is discovered picking fruits 'by moonlight, in a wilderness'.[81]

The destructive Typhon also had a place in his speculations. In one of his late notebooks, for example, where he was fond of speculating on racial theories, there appears the entry, 'Typhon—*Seth*! the terrible in the void, the blasting wind, the all-dreaded God that makest desert . . ."[82] And as in the case of moonlight, the drafts for *The Wanderings of Cain* throw considerable light on his early speculations. While Enos represents the redeeming principle in the poem, Cain is the destructive character, who might be supposed to be under the domination of the 'Typhonian' principle. If Coleridge was urged on by the success of Gessner's *Death of Abel*, on the one hand,[83] it is also reasonable to suppose that he saw in the story ample scope for working out his theories of evil and redemption. And here, as elsewhere, he may well have been impressed by a passage from Berkeley. A passage in *Siris* on the traditions connecting God with fire and light contains an interesting reference to Cain and his descendants[84]:

At the transfiguration, the apostles saw our Saviour's face shining as the sun, and his raiment white as light, also a lucid cloud or body of light, out of which the voice came; which visible light and splendor was, not many centuries ago, maintained by the Greek church to have been divine, and uncreated, and the very glory of God; as may be seen in the history wrote by the emperor John Cantacuzene. And of late years bishop Patrick gives it as his opinion, that in the beginning of the world the Shecinah, or divine presence, which was then frequent and ordinary, appeared by light or fire. In commenting on that passage, where Cain is said to have gone out from the presence of the Lord, the bishop observes that if Cain after this turned a downright idolater, as many think, it is very likely he introduced the worship of the sun, as the best resemblance he could find of the glory of the Lord, which was wont to appear in a flaming light. It would be endless to enumerate all the passages of holy scripture which confirm and illustrate this notion, or represent the Deity as appearing and operating by fire. The misconstruction of which might possibly have misled the Gnostics, Basilidians, and other ancient heretics into an opinion that Jesus Christ was the visible corporeal sun.

It is quite easy to see how the Isis-Osiris mythology could be interpreted in terms of this tradition. Cain, having lost the Shechinah, becomes afraid of the heat of the sun, because it reminds him of his guilt: in consequence his religion, and that of his descendants, comes to take the form of propitiating the fiery sun, who is regarded as an angry and violent being. From this it is a short step to the use of Typhon to represent this wrathful, destructive principle. Yet on the other hand, the moon, with its light, stands in the heavens as a reminder of the lost Shechinah and its glory, and a constant symbol of the vision of God which fallen man secretly longs to regain.

A theory of the origin and nature of evil is thus produced, which is both comprehensive and psychological. God has not changed; but man, under the curse of Cain, has deprived himself of the true vision of God, and thus entangled himself in a situation which constantly defeats his hardest efforts to do good. His inability to understand the true nature of the world in which he lives is responsible both for his evil-doing, and for his fear of the very forces which, rightly understood, would lead him to good.

The probability that Coleridge developed this sort of theory is strengthened by the fact that similar speculations can be found in several of his favourite mystical authors. Philo, the Jewish allegorizer, suggested in *The Sacrifice of Abel and Cain* that Abel figured 'the God-loving principle', and Cain 'the self-loving principle'; and that both principles 'lie in the womb of the single soul'.[85] Jacob Boehme, who employs a similar 'Cain-principle' and 'Abel-principle' in his writings, was fond of maintaining that God's true nature is one of light and sweetness; and that the fire and wrath which are the necessary basis of such a nature only become noxious to man because, by his sin, he cuts himself off from the light and exposes himself to the heat alone. In his own nature, also, he loses the light of his own soul, and becomes a prey to the heat which, rightly ordered, is a necessary basis of his being. The following quotations from Boehme make his views clear[86]:

> God is angry and destructive according to His eternal fire-ground, not according to what He is in Himself.

> In God there is no anger, there is pure love alone. But

in the foundation, through which the love becomes mobile, there is the fire of anger, though in God it is a cause of joy and of power. On the other hand, in the centre of the wrath-fire it is the greatest and most terrible darkness, pain, and torment.

God calls Himself a consuming Fire, and also a God of love; and his name GOD has its original in the love. . . . We all in the originality of our life have the source of the anger and of the fierceness, or else we should not be alive; but we must go out of it, with God, and generate the love in us.

All this throws light on the various symbols used in *The Wanderings of Cain*. Cain is walking in the darkness, and only the guidance of his child Enos can lead him into the moonlight. The first of the prose drafts begins as follows[87]:

He falls down in a trance—when he awakes he sees a luminous body coming before him. It stands before him an orb of fire. . . . The Fire gradually shapes itself, retaining its luminous appearance, into the lineaments of a man. A dialogue between the fiery shape and Cain, in which the being presses upon him the enormity of his guilt and that he must make some expiation to the true deity, who is a severe God, and persuades him to burn out his eyes. Cain opposes this idea, and says that God himself who had inflicted this punishment upon him, had done it because he neglected to make a proper use of his senses, etc. The evil spirit answers him that God is indeed a God of mercy, and that an example must be given to mankind, that this end will be answered by his terrible appearance, at the same time he will be gratified with the most delicious sights and feelings. . . .

In the second draft, the evil spirit appears to Cain in the shape of Abel, and, as in the prose version of Canto II, tells him of a God of the dead, who is different from the God of the living, the Lord. In the prose version, Cain enquires what sacrifices he can make to this God of the Dead; the story continues as follows in the draft[88]:

Abel offers sacrifice from the blood of his arm. A gleam of light illumines the meadow—the countenance of Abel becomes more beautiful, and his arms glistering—he then persuades Cain to offer sacrifice, for himself and his son Enoch by cutting his child's arm and letting the blood fall from it. Cain is about to do it when Abel himself in his angelic appearance, attended by Michael, is seen in the heavens, whence they sail slowly down. Abel addresses Cain with terror, warning him not to offer up his innocent child. The evil spirit throws off the countenance of Abel, assumes its own shape, flies off pursuing a flying battle with Michael. Abel carries off the child.

Cain is a haunted figure. In the prose version he longs for 'darkness, and blackness, and an empty space'. The idea that there is need for an atoning sacrifice, placed in the mouth of an evil spirit, is probably a projection from his own guilt-ridden soul. Like Boehme's unredeemed man, he is not only afraid of the sun, but burnt up from within by untempered fire.[89]

> For the mighty limbs of Cain were wasted as by fire; his hair was as the matted curls on the bison's forehead, and so glared his fierce and sullen eye beneath: and the black abundant locks on either side ... were stained and scorched, as though the grasp of a burning iron hand had striven to rend them; and his countenance told in a strange and terrible language of agonies that had been, and were, and were still to continue to be.

Cain is his own punisher. As Coleridge put it in *Religious Musings*,[90]

> ... no Cain
> Injures uninjured (in her best-aimed blow
> Victorious Murder a blind Suicide) ...

And so with the sons of Cain. The vicious circle of crime, remorse and fresh crime is inevitable: the fire must remain untempered unless there is a restoration of the light which alone can bridle it.

The pattern emerges, the paradigm which Coleridge was imposing upon mythology and metaphysics. The Fall, implicit in the withdrawal of the Shechinah from Adam and Eve, becomes explicit in the relationship between Cain,

Abel and Enos. And this in its turn is refracted into other mythologies. The lost Abel becomes the lost Osiris, the fierce Cain becomes the destructive Typhon, the redeeming Enos becomes Isis.

This is the pattern of guilt, however. It is interlocked with a different pattern, which involves the persistence of the unfallen in mankind. Within the first paradigm, the lost Paradise is dimly remembered; within the second, it is still active. This second pattern, however, is best approached by way of the first. In the ordinary human condition, which is the condition of Cain, the Shechinah is lost, but it is still remembered. In consequence, all objects which are associated with it are emotionally ambivalent to mankind. They are feared, and yet they are also subtly attractive.

This ambivalence of fear and fascination is particularly active in phenomena which are close to the lost Shechinah. Thus the sons of Cain become worshippers of the sun, according to Bishop Patrick, because its glory elicits worship and propitiation from them. And glory in all its forms takes on a numinous quality. This fact, I think, has its place in Coleridge's interest in the natural phenomenon known as the 'glory', which dates from an early period of his reading. In the Gutch notebook, he transcribed a long description of a glory from the Manchester Transactions.[91]

Lowes has drawn attention to this entry, and to Coleridge's interest in the poetic possibilities of this natural phenomenon, by which a person standing on the summit of a mountain sees his own figure projected and magnified on a nearby cloud, and surrounded by a glorious light.[92] But it is clear that Coleridge was fascinated by the idea not simply because of its vividness as a poetic image, but also because of its symbolic aptness. In *Constancy to an Ideal Object*, he uses it to illustrate the idealization of a beloved object, and in his criticism applies it to Shakespeare.[93] Even more significant is his reference to it in a passage on genius in *Aids to Reflection*[94]:

In application to the present case, it is sufficient to say that Pindar's remark on sweet Music holds equally true of Genius: as many as are not delighted by it are disturbed, perplexed, irritated. The Beholder either recognizes it as a projected Form of his own Being, that moves before him with a Glory round its head, or recoils from it as from a Spectre.

The fact that one and the same phenomenon could be called either a 'glory', as in Haygarth's description, or a 'spectre', as at the Brocken, had not escaped Coleridge's allegorizing observation.[95]

.　　　.　　　.　　　.　　　.

Two other objects which had the same psychological ambivalence as the sun and the glory seem to have attracted Coleridge's attention: they were the daemon and the serpent.

Daemons appear constantly in the literature of the supernatural, but it is not always made clear whether their influence is good or bad. They can be, it seems, either guiding spirits, as in the case of Socrates, or 'demons' in the popular modern sense, inciting to evil. Indeed, they are often distinguished as good and bad—agathodaemons and cacodaemons.

The ambiguity can be resolved, however, if one thinks of daemons in terms, not of their influence on human beings but of their inward power. For good or evil, they are characterized by their peculiar supernatural energies, like Milton's Satan—and may indeed be equated with fallen angels. Like Boehme's fire, they have lost an essential part of their angelic nature, and the residue, which should normally be the basis of that nature, is now available as energy for either good or evil.

I have already spoken of this idea as an alternative fall-theory, and it is worth while to remember at this point that there is in the Old Testament itself a story which has sometimes been regarded by theologians as another attempt to describe the Fall of Man. In the sixth chapter of Genesis, it is related that 'the sons of God saw the daughters of men that they were fair; and they took them wives of all that they chose'. The incident, according to the subsequent text, precipitated the Deluge; but that is not the important point for our purposes. What is important is that this account, unlike the story of Adam and Eve as normally interpreted, gives the Fall-doctrine a Promethean touch. In the orthodox story, it is true, man ate of the Tree of Knowledge and acquired knowledge of good and evil: but the story of the 'sons of God' suggests that man actually became half-divine. Being invested with daemonic power, he was henceforth not truly at home in the fallen universe because he was also pulled towards the divine.

As it happens, this alternative tradition of the Fall was brought into prominence by an author who has already been mentioned: James Bruce, explorer of the Nile and Abyssinia. Among his discoveries, particular interest and discussion was excited by a number of hitherto unknown manuscripts, which he brought back from Abyssinia, and presented to various European libraries. The most important of these was an apocryphal book which had till then been presumed lost, and is now known as the Ethiopic book of Enoch. The book was not translated into English for some years[96]: but Bruce gave a brief account of its contents, and made it clear that the book consisted mainly of an amplified version of the tradition under discussion and long accounts of the relations between the giants and this world.[97]

There are several indications that Coleridge was familiar with this tradition in its various forms. One of the most important is an entry in the Gutch notebook, made probably in 1799. It reads as follows.[98]

> Dioclesian King of Syria
> fifty Daughters in a ship unmann'd
> same as Danaides—land in England—commix
> with Devils.

Lowes traces the source of this story to Milton's *History of Britain*: and if we turn up the relevant passage we find that the result of these unions was, as in the Ethiopic book of Enoch, a race of giants.[99] Southey, also, mentions the tradition of this giant-race in trying to explain the arrival of the giant stones in the Valley of Rocks.[100]

These entries probably reflect a long-standing interest. During the earlier Bristol years, Coleridge was interested in another story which contained a similar tradition. It was probably in the autumn of 1796 that he copied a quotation from the apocryphal Book of Tobit into the Gutch notebook; and a list of projected works overleaf was headed by 'An Essay on Tobit'.[101] His first acquaintance with this book would no doubt have been the reference in *Paradise Lost* to Asmodeus, and [102]

> the fishie fume
> That drove him, though enamourd, from the Spouse
> Of *Tobits* son . . .

If one may hazard a guess as to the nature of the proposed *Essay*, it is that it would have been an allegorical interpretation of the Asmodeus incident. Asmodeus slew all the husbands of Sarah until, finally vanquished by the combined efforts of Tobias and Raphael, he was forced to flee into 'the outmost parts of Egypt'.[103] Tobias's subsequent declaration, 'I take not this my sister for lust, but uprightly', would open the way for an interpretation which may be supported by quoting a passage from one of Coleridge's late notebooks. It takes the form of an 'avowal of the admiration & psychological interest' with which he first read and now meditates on 'Jacob Behmen's assertion respecting the nature of the guilty Act by which the Adam with his Eve fell—. More than happy that Man who has never had occasion or an opportunity for noticing in himself a transition of pure tender affection for a lovely object into a movement of concupiscence. . . .'[104] This is a clear statement of a belief which is implicit in many other parts of Coleridge's thought —the idea of the Fall as a fall of *nature* from the higher to the lower, from love to lust. It is likely that he wished to interpret Tobit, and other stories which involved daemon-lovers, as allegories of what he took to be a psychological fact.

The common connection between daemons and lust serves to remind us that the figure of the daemon is rarely far removed from that of the serpent. No reader of *Paradise Lost* easily forgets the scene where Satan exultantly proclaims news of the Fall of Man to his fellow daemons, to be greeted with a universal hiss as they all find themselves turned into serpents.[105] This transformation, as Milton makes clear, fulfils the curse pronounced in the Garden of Eden[106]: 'Upon thy belly shalt thou go, and dust shalt thou eat all the days of thy life.' Thus the serpents of this world lose the plumed glory which they possessed in Eden,[107] and the fallen angels lose the glory which up till now they had retained. Coleridge later discussed the curse in his note in the *Aids to Reflection*, where he identifies the serpent with the wisdom of the flesh.[108]

This 'daemonic ambivalence' can be traced in a good deal of the mythology concerning serpents, where the serpent appears sometimes as a good figure, sometimes as a bad. The mythologists of Coleridge's day were fond of pointing out that the Hebrew word s'r'ph could signify either a serpent or an angelic being. Two passages in Maurice's *Hindostan*, which Coleridge read, develop the point at some length[109]:

> I ought not to omit mentioning, that some writers from the Hebrew word SARAPH, signifying at once a serpent and a seraph, have conceived the fable of the dragon vomiting flames, and guarding the golden apples of the Hesperides, to be founded upon the circumstance related in the same divine book, that on the expulsion of Adam from Paradise, God placed a flaming band of cherubim, or seraphim, for they seem to be the same order of celestial beings, at the eastern gate, whose bodies moving every way, and glittering like the vibrations of a *flaming sword*, guarded the approach to that lovely but forbidden retreat, Dragons, fiery or vomiting flames, are always ready, upon occasions like these, to execute similar offices of guardian vigilance in the Pagan theology. . . .

> Subjoined is a literal translation from Sanscrit, by Mr Wilkins, describing this luxuriant paradise of Eendra, so remarkable for being guarded by serpents breathing fire, the flaming seraphim of Scripture, for *saraph* means a serpent. The commentator just cited is of opinion that Satan, when he tempted Eve, assumed the body of one of those beautiful serpents of the East, whose bodies are of the colour of flame, or gold; and thus Rabbi Bechai . . .

observes:—'this is the mystery of our holy language (Devinagara) that a serpent is called saraph, as an angel is called seraph'. Serpents are indeed in India an order of angels, but in general, as before observed, they are of a malignant character: some, however, like the Cneph of Egypt, are benevolent beings, and we have shown them to be symbolically used in the Elephanta caverns, as the emblems of immortality. 'There is a fair and stately mountain,' says Mr Wilkins, translating an episode of the Mahabbarat, 'and its name is MERU, a most exalted mass of glory, reflecting the sunny rays from the splendid surface of its gilded horns. It is clothed in gold, and is the respected haunt of Devas and Gandharves. It is beyond conception beautiful, is not to be encompassed by *sinful man, and is guarded by dreadful serpents*. Many celestial medicinal plants adorn its sides, and it stands piercing the heavens with its aspiring summit; a mighty hill, inaccessible even to the human mind: it is adorned *with trees and pleasant streams*, and resounds with the delightful songs of various birds.'

Among the papers read to the Society of Gentlemen at Exeter[110] was an essay on the Mythology and Worship of the Serpent by Hugh Downman, whom Coleridge knew as a member. Like Maurice, Downman dwells upon the ambiguous position of the serpent in Egyptian mythology, pointing out that under the name of 'Cneph' it signified the 'good principle', but under the name of 'Typhon' the 'destructive principle', in the universe.[111] And whether or not Coleridge knew this passage, he certainly knew the sources from which such deductions were made.

In these sources, it is also stated that the 'agathodaemon' Cneph was often pictured as a winged serpent, and this is a reminder of the way in which serpent and wings are continually found together in various attempts to figure the daemonic ideal. For yet another example of this we may turn to a Greek myth, the tale of Cupid and Psyche. Coleridge borrowed the volume of Apuleius containing the *Metamorphoses* from the Bristol Library in November, 1796, and it seems likely that this tale, which appears in it, was the object of his interest. It was one of the myths most discussed in Coleridge's day: Thomas Taylor had published a translation of it, complete with neoplatonic interpretation, in 1795, and a few years earlier Sir William Jones, the well-known authority on Oriental literature and mythology had commented on it as follows[112]:

> The metaphors and allegories of moralists and meta physicians have been also very fertile in Deities; of which a thousand examples might be adduced from PLATO, CICERO, and the inventive commentators on HOMER . . . the richest and noblest stream from this abundant fountain is the charming philosophical tale of PSYCHE, or the *Progress of the Soul*; than which, to my taste, a more beautiful, sublime, and wellsupported allegory was never produced by the wisdom and ingenuity of man.

The story of Cupid and Psyche is well known. Psyche, a woman of this earth, was visited every night by an unknown husband, who never revealed himself to her gaze. At last her sisters, who thought that he must be a serpent, persuaded her to look at him one night while he was asleep. As she shone the light upon him, she saw that he was in fact the winged and beautiful Cupid: but at the same moment she dropped some wax upon him, and he started up in fright and flew away. In order to regain him, she was bound to undertake a long series of arduous labours at the instance of Venus.

This gives the myth of Isis and Osiris a new twist. In this story, the Isis-figure is sinner as well as redeemer. By the act of suspecting her husband to be a serpent (and so becoming preoccupied with the flesh and the material world) she destroyed the relationship which had existed between them and 'fell in love with love'.[113]

Coleridge used the myth several times. He projected an allegory to follow it in a notebook, and in *The Friend* quoted Milton's reference to Psyche.[114] In a passage which he used both for *The Friend* and his philosophical lectures, he spoke of the vast labours which must await the true scientist before he could reach 'the law which was to reward the toils of the over-tasked PSYCHE'.[115] He was also interested in the fact that the Greek word 'psyche' meant both soul and butterfly, writing a poem on the subject and then quoting the poem in his discussion of the evolution of the poetic psyche in *Biographia Literaria*.[116] He also used the image to describe Derwent's phase of free-thinking opinions at the university. ("I felt sure that it was not the true *Image* of the *Psyche*, but only one of the Larvae that he would soon *slough*. . . .")[117]

In later life, his attitude towards the myth was to change together with his attitude towards Platonism. The literary lectures of 1818 contain several references to it: he called it 'the most beautiful allegory ever composed . . . written by one of those philosophers who attempted to Christianize a sort of Oriental and Egyptian Platonism enough to set it up against Christianity,' and a 'philosophical attempt to parry Christianity with a *quasi*-Platonic account of the fall and redemption of the soul'.[118] It is in the *Aids to Reflection*, however, that the most developed version of his later views appears. Here he maintains that Greek mythology began with an attempt to unite the Patriarchal Tradition with Pantheism, in the myths of Prometheus ('that truly wonderful Fable, in which the characters of the rebellious Spirit and of the Divine Friend of Mankind ($\Theta\acute{\epsilon}os$ $\Phi\iota\lambda\acute{a}\nu\theta\rho\omega\pi os$) are united in the same Person') and of Io ('which is but the sequel of the Prometheus'). Then, some centuries later, when Christianity had presented Greek philosophy with a moral challenge, 'the beautiful Parable of Cupid and Psyche was brought forward as a *rival* FALL OF MAN: and the fact of a moral corruption connatural with the human race was again recognized. In the assertion of ORIGINAL SIN the Greek Mythology rose and set.'[119]

Thus, in later years, the myth was 'placed' in relation to the Christian orthodoxy which he had come to accept; but all the indications suggest that in earlier years, when his ideas were more vague—comprehending a 'Fall in some sense'— 'that from our mother's wombs our understandings are darkened'[120]—he saw the myths of Prometheus and of Cupid and Psyche with an even more sympathetic eye, just as Platonism then had a more central place in his religion.

In previous chapters, we have discussed Coleridge's idealism, and his attempts to find an allegory of the ideal in various phenomena of the material universe. It may be that his interest in the daemonic, and in the various myths which involve daemonology dates, with so much else, from the days when, at Christ's Hospital, [121]

> It was the pride & passion of my Youth
> T'impersonate & color moral Truth . . .

If so, however, it seems that this particular range of his speculations sprang into new prominence in the years when the failure of the Pantisocratic scheme had thrown him back to meditations on human nature. From boyhood, he must have been fired by Akenside's picture of the forms of genius in *Pleasures of Imagination*: ranging from the scientists who explore the secrets of the world and the heavens to those, 'temper'd with a purer flame', for whom [122]

> the sirc omnipotent unfolds
> The world's harmonious volume, there to read
> The transcript of himself . . .

and who thus

> see portray'd
> That uncreated beauty, which delights
> The mind supreme.

He must also have followed Akenside in connecting genius with love.

> . . . from Heaven descends
> The flame of genius to the human breast,
> And love and beauty, and poetic joy
> And inspiration.

In his speculations, however, he had now developed these ideas and carried them to heights which would probably have surprised the earlier poet. In the workings of creative genius and in love, he had traced the same daemonic power, the same recreation of the divine. And this interest in the daemonic meant that a new, dynamic force was introduced into his thinking. Not only virtue, but also sin might be accounted for by man's reaction to the daemonic: 'as many as are not delighted by it are disturbed, perplexed, irritated. The Beholder either recognizes it as a projected Form of his own Being, that moves before him with a Glory round its head, or recoils from it as from a Spectre.'[123] In this fear, and in the active misuse of his daemonic powers by the genius himself, lay the twin sources of the evils that beset the world. The problem confronting the good genius, therefore, was to find some way of countering these two forces: to temper power with light and to resolve discord in harmony.

It was while pursuing this vein of speculation that Coleridge came to write his greatest poems.

Chapter V

THE GLORIOUS SUN

'**B**UT why so violent against *metaphysics* in poetry?'
Coleridge's question to Thelwall, in a letter of
1796,[1] does not at once arouse the reader's sympathy.
It calls to mind too readily the Miltonizing verse of *Religious
Musings*—the poem which he was defending—and the 'rage,
& affectation of double Epithets' for which he had at that
moment been apologizing. And if the reader turns instead
to *The Ancient Mariner* or *Christabel*, the immediate impression is so vividly sensuous that he is likely to say, with
Muirhead, 'It would be pedantry to look for philosophical
doctrines in their magical lines.'[2]

So it would be, indeed, if Coleridge were a normal
metaphysician. If the preceding chapters have made one
thing clear, however, it is that Coleridge at this time was not
a 'normal metaphysician'. Rather, he resembled the young
bard of Akenside's poem, who could not separate poetry
from the pursuit of truth. In the same way the studies which
he delighted in were those where intellectual rigour combined with sensuous delight. Ancient metaphysics to him
meant ancient mythology: and he looked for the crown of
his own metaphysical researches in the writing of an epic
poem. The human reason could not rise to its full stature
without the ministry of the human imagination: and 'metaphysics' must therefore find a place for both.

It was largely at the instance of Wordsworth[3] that
Coleridge later sub-titled *The Ancient Mariner* 'a Poet's
Reverie', and from the time of the poem's composition there
have been several attempts to interpret it as something more
than a racy ballad with a conventional moral. Leslie Stephen's
judicious comments are particularly relevant[4]:

> The germ of all Coleridge's utterances may be found—by
> a little ingenuity—in the 'Ancient Mariner'. For what is
> the secret of the strange charm of that unique achieve-
> ment? I do not speak of what may be called its purely

literary merits—the melody of versification, the command of language, the vividness of the descriptive passages, and so forth—I leave such points to critics of finer perception and a greater command of superlatives. But part, at least, of the secret is the ease with which Coleridge moves in a world of which the machinery (as the old critics called it) is supplied by the mystic philosopher.

After throwing out this seminal hint, Stephen goes on to deal with the poem in a way which leads us away from the 'mystic philosopher', at any rate as he has been portrayed in these pages. That is quite understandable, for the Victorian thinker could hardly think of mysticism without thinking of dreaminess, and when the mysticism was Coleridge's, the step was almost unavoidable. Robert Graves has recently distinguished between the poems of 'Coleridge entranced', and those of 'Coleridge unentranced'.[5] and the distinction must crystallize the impression of many readers. There is a strange dreamlike quality in his greatest poetry, a combination of vivid impression and fluid movement, which stamps them as products of the imagination at its purest and most untrammelled.[6]

Nevertheless, the modified conception of Coleridge the metaphysician which has been built up in these pages may enable us to consider the intellectual structure of his poetry without for a moment discounting the atmosphere of wonder which remains their supreme quality. And to do so may help not only to increase our respect for Coleridge the thinker, but even to deepen the sensuous impression which we receive in reading the poem, by illuminating the background of some of the images. Lowes's concentration upon the 'texture' of the poem has thrown a good deal of light on Coleridge's creative processes; but it has also helped to confirm a situation in which many readers enjoy the poem without ever noticing that anything more than a simple, overt moral is intended; and this has led in turn to a conception of Coleridge as the naïve poet of wonder. We find Irving Babbitt sneering at[7]

the Ancient Mariner, who, it will be remembered, is relieved of the burden of his transgression by admiring the color of water-snakes!

while Leslie Stephen observes pointedly that[8]

> ... the moral, which would apparently be that people who sympathise with a man who shoots an albatross will die in prolonged torture of thirst, is open to obvious objections.

The critical reader may well make these objections, and others as well. The 'moral' at the end of the poem may strike him as not only trite, but also singularly unrelated to the rest of the poem. The Mariner urges the wedding-guest to love 'all creatures great and small', and yet apparently disapproves of his attending the wedding-feast—where such love might be expected to find high expression. And although the act which precipitates the Mariner's ordeal is clear, the relationship between the various tortures and visions which ensue is not.

These problems have not received a great deal of attention in recent criticism, but this does not mean that critics have ignored the 'meaning' of the poem. They have rather tended to approach it from a different angle, attempting first and foremost to discover symbolic patterns of imagery in various of the major poems. Robert Graves and Maud Bodkin, for example, have treated the poetry in psycho-analytic terms. Graves, on the one hand, tried to extract a purely personal analysis from *Kubla Khan*, while Miss Bodkin saw that poem and *The Ancient Mariner* as particularly fine examples of poetry which awakens racial archetypes in the reader's unconscious.[9] Other critics have simply dwelt on the symbolic meaning of the poem, without considering very deeply whether the meaning was intentional or not in the poet's mind. Particular mention must be made of the work of critics such as George Whalley, George Wilson Knight, Kenneth Burke and Robert Penn Warren.[10] A good deal of what they had to say was summarized and considered by Humphry House in his Clark Lectures of 1951-2, which also included further important contributions to the interpretation of the major poems.[11]

This line of approach has not passed unchallenged, however. E. E. Stoll,[12] and, more recently, Elisabeth Schneider, have attacked vigorously, and at length, all attempts to trace strains of symbolism in the poems. Their attack, in both cases, is massed around the contention that Coleridge himself betrays little sign of symbolist intent either at the period of composition or in later discussions.

Most of Stoll's points are paralleled in Miss Schneider's book, and we may therefore concentrate our attention upon that. The tone of her attack is to some extent set by her opening remark[13]:

> Not until the present century, apparently, has *Kubla Khan* been found to mean more than it says, though when symbolic criticism once seized upon the poem it made up for lost time.

The tendentiousness of this opening, however, is followed by arguments which deserve more serious consideration. Discussing Wilson Knight's interpretation of the poem, she says,[14]

> I think it will have to be agreed that this mode of thought was never in accord with Coleridge's conscious practice, and probably not with his theory either. . . . Often enough he conferred upon images of nature some deep significance, but he regularly made that explicit. . . .

As examples of this explicitness in his early poems, she cites *A Wish*, *The Eolian Harp*, and *To a Young Friend*; where explicitness of this sort is lacking, she continues, it is always present in some form: 'The snake images in *Christabel* are patently evil; the reader does not have to guess.'

Already, one notices, the argument is becoming a little twisted. Nevertheless, part of it is to be accepted: Coleridge's symbolism, in his minor poetry, is usually perfectly explicit. But can we legitimately draw deductions about Coleridge's major poetry from his minor? I do not think so: on precisely such grounds we might argue against Coleridge's authorship of the three major poems, for it is generally felt that they are distinguished from the others by a division which is qualitative.

Schneider's argument can only be allowed to carry negative force, therefore; the important issue concerns that symbolism, the existence of which she admits. For is it not possible, indeed likely, that when Coleridge's poetic powers rose to their greatest intensity, one result should be the emergence of a symbolism more subtle and more concentrated than that which he normally employed? Admirers of the great poems dwell on the economy of language and images. May this economy not extend to the symbolism also?

Returning to Miss Schneider's argument, we have to acknowledge that there is a little force in the irony of her attack on those critics who, she says, imagine that Coleridge departed from his normal practice, 'yet at the same time departed so invisibly that posterity has required a hundred and some years to uncover the meaning'. Yet the position is not as clear-cut as that. Even among the Victorians, occasional attempts were made to interpret all three poems[15]; and this in an age when symbolist interpretations were not normally looked for—the choice lying between explicit moral teaching and indirect sensuous communication. If Coleridge made no vehement claims for symbolism in his poetry, it was not likely that his Victorian critics would go out of their way to look for it. There was a perfectly good meaning at the narrative level, and why should they probe deeper?

But what of Coleridge's own intentions? This is the more important issue. Here Miss Schneider is able to quote Coleridge's criticism of allegorizers, which she labels triumphantly as his 'derisive comment on his unborn symbolic interpreters'[16]:

> The most decisive verdict against narrative allegory is to be found in Tasso's own account of what he would have the reader understand by the persons and events of his Jerusalem. Apollo be praised! not a thought like it would ever enter of its own accord into any mortal mind; and what is an additional good feature, when put there, it will not stay, having the very opposite quality that snakes have—they come out of their holes into open view at the sound of sweet music, while the allegoric meaning slinks off at the very first notes, and lurks in murkiest oblivion —and utter invisibility.

It is, of course, impossible to generalize as to Coleridge's views on allegory from this passage. We know that in the case of Cupid and Psyche, for example, he approved the form.[17] Moreover, as Miss Schneider herself points out, he drew a sharp distinction between allegory and symbol: and it is what he has to say about the symbol that is of prime importance. His central discussion of the subject is well known[18]:

It is among the miseries of the present age that it recognizes no medium between *Literal* and *Metaphorical*. Faith is either to be buried in the dead letter, or its name and honors usurped by a counterfeit product of the mechanical understanding, which in the blindness of self-complacency confounds SYMBOLS with ALLEGORIES. Now an Allegory is but a translation of abstract notions into a picture-language which is itself nothing but an abstraction from objects of the senses; the principal being more worthless even than its phantom proxy, both alike unsubstantial, and the former shapeless to boot. On the other hand a Symbol (ὅ ἐστιν ἀεὶ ταυτηγόρικον) is characterized by a translucence of the Special in the Individual or of the General in the Especial or of the Universal in the General. Above all by the translucence of the Eternal through and in the Temporal. It always partakes of the Reality which it renders intelligible; and while it enunciates the whole, abides itself as a living part in that Unity, of which it is the representative. The other are but empty echoes which the fancy arbitrarily associates with apparitions of matter, less beautiful but not less shadowy than the sloping orchard or hill-side pasture-field seen in the transparent lake below.

The concept which runs through Coleridge's description of the symbol is that of translucence: and that image relates his discussion directly to his other speculations about light—particularly his idea that the visionary eye partakes of the light which it perceives. Whenever Coleridge speaks of Reason, or Imagination, or Ideas, this concept of light as not merely transmitted, but actively awakened in the transmitting agent, is always present. The poise of forces thus supposed to exist in the symbol, which at one and the same time abides as a living part and yet enunciates the whole, is quite inadequately represented in Miss Schneider's attempt at exposition[19]:

. . . he appears to confine symbolism to passages in which an expression of a specific love, for example, or fear, or power, becomes symbolic of the same feeling generally or universally.

In the same way, it is difficult to accept another passage cited by her as the argument against symbolism and allegory which she maintains it to be. Discussing Bowles's poetry in a letter of 1802, Coleridge wrote,[20]

> There reigns thro' all the blank verse poems such a perpetual trick of *moralizing* every thing—which is very well, occasionally—but never to see or describe any interesting appearance in nature, without connecting it by dim analogies with the moral world, proves faintness of Impression. Nature has her proper interest; & he will know what it is, who believes & feels, that every Thing has a Life of it's own, & that we are all *one Life*.

That this is intended as an argument against all allegorizing is belied by Coleridge's specific use of the word 'moralizing', and by the fact that later in the same letter he praises Milton's allegorizing in the highest terms. In any case, it has to be recognized that he is here attacking Bowles for qualities which he had praised in earlier years. In his preface to the *Sheet of Sonnets*, written in 1796, he had stated with approval that in Bowles's sonnets, 'moral Sentiments, Affections or Feelings, are deduced from, and associated with, the scenery of Nature'.[21] His attitude to Bowles had changed in the intervening period, because his attitude to Nature had changed. He had in no way departed from the view that a symbolic significance existed in Nature, but he had come to insist that this symbolism could be discovered only by patient and exclusive devotion to Nature herself—and certainly not by using her as a series of pegs on which to hang disparate moral thoughts. This later view of symbolism in nature is stated clearly in a note of 1805.[22]

> In looking at objects of Nature, while I am thinking, as at yonder moon dim-glimmering through the dewy window-pane, I seem rather to be seeking, as it were *asking*, a symbolical language for something within me

that already and for ever exists, than observing anything new. Even when that latter is the case, yet still I have always an obscure feeling as if that new phænomenon were the dim awaking of a forgotten or hidden Truth of my inner Nature/ It is still interesting as a Word, a Symbol! It is Λoyos, the Creator! and the Evolver!

Even when Coleridge had moved from his poetic phase into a phase of perfect fidelity to nature, therefore, his search for symbolism was in no way relaxed. But it is time to return from the pursuit of Miss Schneider's argument to the period which concerns us, and examine a little-known contemporary source which suggests that Coleridge not only wrote *The Ancient Mariner* and *Christabel* with symbolic intent, but was fond of expounding the meaning of the poems to his friends. This is Clement Carlyon's account of his conversation when he joined a tour undertaken by several young Englishmen in Germany, during his stay there in 1798-9. Carlyon's account runs as follows[23]:

> Coleridge was in good spirits, very amusing, and as talkative as ever, throughout this little excursion. He frequently recited his own poetry, and not unfrequently led us rather farther into the labyrinth of his metaphysical elucidations, either of particular passages, or of the original conception of any of his productions, than we were able to follow him.

> ' 'Tis the middle of night by the castle clock,
>   And the owls have awakened the crowing cock;
>   Tu-whit!—Tu-whoo!
>   And hark again! The crowing cock,
>   How drowsily it crew.'

At the conclusion of this, the first stanza of *Christabel*, he would perhaps comment at full length upon such a line as

Tu whit!—Tu whoo!

that we might not fall into the mistake of supposing originality to be its sole merit. In fact, he very seldom went right on to the end of any piece of poetry—to pause and analyze was his delight.

What he told his fellow-travellers respecting *Christabel*, he has since repeated in print, in words which, if not the very same, are equally Coleridgian.

'In my very first conception of the tale,' he says, 'I had the whole present to my mind, with the wholeness no less than the loveliness of a vision', all of which he trusted he should some day be able to 'embody in verse;' but this day, I believe, came not, for it does not appear that he got beyond two, out of the four parts which he contemplated.

After quoting Coleridge's account, in *Biographia Literaria*, of the genesis of the two poems and the *Lyrical Ballads*, Carlyon continues,[24]

... I must candidly confess, that in discussing the merits of the 'Rime of the Ancient Mariner,' it did happen that

'There pass'd a weary time,'

or something very like it, for I was unable to follow him to my certain satisfaction either in the verse or the accompanying colloquy, and yet

'Day after day—Day after day,'

he was at one time fond of returning to it, but either my mind was not 'in the right temper,' or from some defect or other, I could not fully appreciate the mysteries of the Albatross.

I have often read it since, and I think I may venture to say, that the pleasure with which its re-perusals have been attended, was not the less from my being able to enter, unattended by the author and his bewildering metaphysics

'Into that silent sea.'

I do not remember that he ever dwelt upon his 'Religious Musings,' which he has termed 'A desultory Poem' ...

Coleridge, of course, was not above pulling the legs of his friends at times, but the insistence with which he returned to this particular theme suggests that on this occasion he was serious. One can only wish that Carlyon had been able to record something, at least, of the explanations which he offered. In lieu of them, we must make our own attempt at a reconstruction.

The first point that needs examination is also, as it happens, the most obvious. Both *The Ancient Mariner* and *Christabel* were evidently intended as essays in the supernatural—but what did Coleridge mean by that term?

It seems clear that he did not simply intend to write a pair of Gothic tales, in spite of the current fashion for them, for he was not in sympathy with the vogue. In February, 1797, he had begun his review of Lewis's *The Monk* by declaring, 'The horrible and the preternatural have usually seized on the popular taste, at the rise and decline of literature.'[25] It seems unlikely that he would have gone back on so uncompromising a statement so soon unless he had had some further purpose in mind.

Nethercot has suggested that Coleridge's use of two separate words, 'preternatural' and 'supernatural' may indicate some distinction in his mind between separate literary genres.[26] Besides the usage just quoted, he recalls that in March, 1801, Coleridge was planning to publish *Christabel* with two essays, one on the Praeternatural and the other on Metre.[27] In 1817, his eleventh lecture (never published) was entitled 'On the Arabian Nights Entertainments, and on the *romantic* use of the supernatural in Poetry and in works of fiction not poetical',[28] and in *Biographia Literaria*, he promised to prefix an essay 'on the uses of the Supernatural in poetry', to some future edition of *The Ancient Mariner*.[29] On the basis of these statements, Nethercot suggests that *Christabel* was intended to represent the preternatural in poetry, and *The Ancient Mariner* the supernatural. This may be so, but it has to be pointed out that the distinction may simply be one in time. The word 'preternatural' was used in 1797-1801, the word 'supernatural' round about 1817; and the difference may result from a distinction between the two words which Coleridge wished to draw in the earlier period, but no longer thought important in later years. On the whole, the word 'preternatural' seems with him to carry a certain pejorative force, from which the word 'supernatural' is exempt, and it is not unlikely that he intended, when he wrote his poems, to distinguish between literature which simply made use of supernatural 'machinery' for the sake of sensationalism, and that which was concerned with the possible significance of extra-sensory phenomena as a revelation of the metaphysical.

Such a distinction would certainly fit in with Coleridge's views of both poetry and philosophy. In his essay 'On Poesy or Art', he maintains that it is the artist's task to represent, not *natura naturata* merely, but *natura naturans*.[30] And this statement may legitimately be taken in conjunction with another, in the *Aids to Reflection*, where he defines [31] 'Natura', as 'that which is *about to be* born, that which is always *becoming*. It follows, therefore, that whatever originates its own acts, or in any sense contains in itself the cause of its own state, must be *spiritual*, and consequently *super-natural*: yet not on that account necessarily *miraculous*. And such must the responsible WILL in us be, if it be at all.'

By the time that he came to write the *Aids*, Coleridge was inclined to identify the organ of the supernatural with the human will: but his earlier remarks on art point us back to a time when he thought of 'super-nature' as identified with *natura naturans*—which it was the poet's task to imitate. In this view, the supernatural was not separate from the natural, but the inner essence of it[32]:

> And blest are they,
> Who, in this fleshly World, the elect of Heaven,
> Their strong eye darting through the deeds of men,
> Adore with steadfast unpresuming gaze
> Him Nature's essence, mind, and energy!

It is this sense of the link between the natural world and the metaphysical, apprehended by the visionary, which is the key to Coleridge's major poetry; and it is this sense also which lies at the heart of his Berkeleyanism. I have already mentioned Yeats's suggestion that Berkeley's *Siris* was an important influence upon Coleridge the poet,[33] and his point may be accepted. Once the language of Berkeley's treatise is familiar, the reader is impressed by the strangely sensuous, physical force of his ideas. Words such as 'intelligence', 'intellectual', 'Trinity', even, each carry a latent charge of nervous energy, generated by Berkeley's central theme of the divine substance that penetrates, mysteriously, all things in heaven and earth.

In *The Ancient Mariner*, on the other hand, the reverse process takes place. Here, the flashing lights, the fires, the darting water-snakes all suggest the permeating presence of the divine Intellect in nature. To make the point clearer, we may quote two passages from *Siris*[34]:

Fire or light mixeth with all bodies, even with water; witness the flashing lights in the sea, whose waves seem frequently all on fire.

. . . this vital flame, being extremely subtile, might not be seen any more than shining flies or *ignes fatui* by daylight.

With these, we may compare three excerpts from *The Ancient Mariner*[35]:

> The western wave was all a flame
> The day was well nigh done!
> Almost upon the western wave
> Rested the broad bright Sun;
> When that strange shape drove suddenly
> Betwixt us and the Sun

> . . . But where the ship's huge shadow lay,
> The charmed water burnt alway
> A still and awful red.

> Beyond the shadow of the ship
> I watch'd the water-snakes . . .

> The upper air bursts into life,
> And a hundred fire-flags sheen
> To and fro they are hurried about;
> And to and fro, and in and out
> The stars dance on between.

Each of these passages comes at a point in the poem when the reader is intended to be aware of supernatural forces at work; but Berkeley's treatise takes him a stage further, and connects the lights and fires with the inward energies of the divine. Whether hostile or friendly, they have this common source. Lowes has pointed out how Coleridge picked up many images of flashing lights, water-snakes and so on from his reading: but it is Berkeley who gives us one of the most important reasons for their ultimate emergence into the pattern of the poem.

If Berkeley helps us to see Coleridge's supernatural forces as rooted in the divine energies, however, we still have to consider the other elements in the poem, and their relation to the supernatural. And here the figure of the Mariner himself naturally engages our attention.

Lowes pointed out that by Coleridge's own testimony, the poem was written instead of *The Wanderings of Cain*, and suggested that some of Cain's qualities were transferred to the Mariner.[36] Reminding us of the traditional relationship between Cain and the Wandering Jew, he pointed out that[37]

Wandering Jew/a romance

was apparently one of Coleridge's literary projects at this time. 'The Wandering Jew' is also the title of a poem in Percy's *Reliques* (source of so much in the Lyrical Ballads), and a character in Lewis's *Monk*. When Coleridge reviewed this in February, 1797, he singled out the portrayal of the Jew as displaying 'great vigour of fancy', and suggested a source in Schiller's 'incomprehensible Armenian'—who, as Lowes pointed out, enters a wedding-feast in the guise of a monk and there, 'motionless and silent, . . . holds the wedding-guests spell-bound by his look'.[38] Lowes then pointed out that the Wandering Jew of tradition also 'passes like night from land to land' and even has 'strange powers of speech'; but warned the reader against any closer identification. 'The Mariner', he says, 'is *not* the Wandering Jew.'[39] Since he wrote this, manuscript evidence has come to light confirming that the Wandering Jew was in fact in Coleridge's mind when he wrote *The Ancient Mariner*.[40] Nevertheless, Lowes is right: there are important differences. For example the Wandering Jew is rarely, if ever, associated with the sea.

There is in the contemporary literature of the period, however, a passage which may help to explain how the Wandering Jew and the Ancient Mariner came to be linked in Coleridge's mind. Richard Hole's *Remarks on the Arabian*

Nights' Entertainments was first published in 1797, the year when *The Ancient Mariner* was begun. Hole himself was a member of the Society of Gentlemen at Exeter, for which Coleridge had helped prepare a paper in 1793,[41] and was one of the people whom Coleridge had specifically mentioned as being a member.[42] The likelihood that he and Wordsworth would have made special efforts to acquire the book is increased by the fact that both poets had been particularly fond of the *Arabian Nights' Entertainments* in their childhood,[43] and by Hole's treatment of Romantic themes, which was in harmony with their own views.

The book deals mainly with the adventures of Sinbad in the *Arabian Nights* and their connection with other legends. This leads, naturally, to a discussion of the Old Man of the Sea, and similar figures, in the course of which he states,[44]

> An Arabian writer mentions, among other ideal inhabitants of the ocean, one styled 'senex judaeus, cuius facies instar humanæ est, barbâ canâ, corpus ut corpus ranæ, pili ut pili bovis, statura vituli'. He introduces another, under the designation of 'homo aquaticus'. 'Quando conspici dicitur in mari Damasceno animal huius speciei, cui scilicet est hominis species & barba cana, unde vocant *senem marinum*, & eo viso magnam annonæ vilitatem præsagiunt.'

It seems likely that these two strange beings, with their grey beards, provided the connecting link between the Wandering Jew (*senex judaeus*) and the Ancient Mariner (*senex marinus*) as the poem took shape in Coleridge's mind. Another, less important link in the chain may be found in one of the drafts for *The Wanderings of Cain* which were apparently made immediately before *The Ancient Mariner* was begun[45]:

> . . . Cain wonders what kind of beings dwell in that place —whether any created since man or whether this world had any beings rescued from the Chaos, wandering like shipwrecked beings from another world, etc.

We have still not arrived at the spark which actually touched off the poem, however. The situation we know:

William, Dorothy and Coleridge set off on a tour to Linton and the Valley of Stones and 'agreed to defray the expense of the tour by writing a Poem'.[46] But why did they choose a long ballad as the most likely form for a saleable poem? Presumably because they had at least one notable example before them, which they felt that they were capable of emulating.

There is one further clue to identifying this ballad which was their pattern. Southey described *The Ancient Mariner* as 'the clumsiest attempt at German sublimity I ever saw', and (when he had had time to polish his phraseology) a 'Dutch attempt at German sublimity'.[47] From this it seems clear that he thought Coleridge to be trying to copy Bürger's *Lenore*, which had recently had great success in this country. This possibility has of course been discussed before, and there is no need to repeat the discussion here, except to remark that everyone who has taken part in it has assumed that it was Taylor's translation alone that he knew.[48] In 1796, however, a translation by Sir Walter Scott had appeared, together with one of Bürger's *Wilde Jäger*, under the title of *The Chase* and *William and Helen*. Coleridge may have taken the idea of his antiquated spelling from Taylor, but it was Scott who put the rhythms of *The Ancient Mariner* to work[49]:

XLVII

Tramp! tramp! along the land they rode;
 Splash! splash! along the sea;
The steed is wight, the spur is bright,
 The flashing pebbles flee.

LXIV

The furious Barb snorts fire and foam;
 And with a fearful bound
Dissolves at once in empty air,
 And leaves her on the ground.

Anyone who cares to read through *William and Helen* will find many echoes of this sort. It is clear that both Bürger's daemonic hunter, who, heeding not the laws of God or man, was forced to hunt eternally, and the exciting rhythms of Scott's version of *Lenore* had intoxicated Coleridge's imagination. His own version of such a ballad would be not an imitation but a development, nevertheless. One finds oneself drawing nearer to it when one reads in Hole's *Arabian Nights* of the incident where Sinbad's companions kill a sacred bird[50]:

> . . . after a long navigation he touched at a desart island, in which his companions perceived an egg equal to that he had seen in his second voyage. A young roc was in it, just on the point of being hatched, and its bill began to appear. His brother merchants, in spite of his remonstrances, break the egg with hatchets, and pull out the young bird piece by piece, and roast it; but the banquet proves no less fatal to them, than that did to the companions of Ulysses which they made on the oxen sacred to Apollo. Sindbad, whose oratory was equally inefficacious with that of the Grecian chieftain, has merely, like him, the melancholy satisfaction of surviving his voracious companions.

Sinbad, like the Mariner, has the 'melancholy satisfaction' of surviving his companions; but differs from him in one very important respect: for he has no part in the killing of the bird and actively tries to dissuade his companions from it. This difference serves to throw into relief the peculiarity of Coleridge's poem which Leslie Stephen noticed—the fact that the Mariner's companions, who did no more than approve the killing of the albatross (and then only belatedly), all die, while the Mariner himself, who actually committed the crime, is spared. The anomaly can be partly explained by the simple truth, which Coleridge intended to exploit in *Christabel*, that in this world the innocent do often suffer for the crimes of the guilty[51]; but it is worth asking whether this provides a complete explanation. Perhaps we ought to examine the Mariner's act in killing the bird in greater detail.

The figure of the albatross, in spite of its superficial derivation from Shelvocke's *Voyage*,[52] has already excited some attention among critics. This is partly due to the importance which attaches to its death in the poem. If the killing is not to be thought of simply as a violation of a superstition, or of the laws of hospitality (and the fate of the Mariner's shipmates suggests a deeper significance) it looks as though the bird must stand for an important hidden force: and this interpretation is reinforced by the fact that Coleridge relates it explicitly to daemonology——[53] thus involving it in symbolic implications which we have already touched upon.

If the albatross is notable for the very force which it seems to conceal, however, the Mariner's actions are distinguished by their lack of positive motivation. His shooting of the bird is a negative action. The whole weight of the poem suggests that if he had had any idea of the significance of his action, he would have refrained. It is because he has not seen the albatross's place in that inner harmony of the universe which later haunts his vision that he can shoot it with such unconcern.

Yet even this unconcern is strange. It is not the unconcern of the devil-may-care sailor in a moment of abandon, for the Mariner was bound to be aware not only of the rigid taboo which forbade his action but also of the impending anger of his mates when they knew. On the contrary, then, he is revealed by his action as a man notably lacking in any sense of social ties. Throughout the poem he becomes more and more detached from his companions, until his anomalous survival completes his isolation. There is evidence from Coleridge's neoplatonic authors which suggests that this is not an accident, and that the Mariner is intentionally cast in a different mould from his companions. According to this interpretation, his survival after their deaths is due to the fact that he was not, like them, a slave to the immediate testimony of his senses. They reveal their enslavement both by their initial condemnation and their subsequent approval of the Mariner's action. They are prevented from shooting the bird largely by superstition; when bad luck follows the Mariner's action they obey their superstition and blame him: but when this is followed by fair weather they at once tack about and accept this new fact as a basis for approving the deed. 'That man is indeed a slave, who is a slave to his own senses, and whose mind and imagination cannot carry him beyond the distance which his hand can touch, or even his eye can reach,'[54] to quote from one of Coleridge's later lectures. The Mariner demonstrates his freedom from such slavery by ignoring both his shipmates and superstition. This independence is something apart from moral virtue, however. His action in shooting the albatross is existentially right, but morally it cannot be justified.

In support of this interpretation, attention may be drawn to a neoplatonic writing which Coleridge almost certainly knew: Proclus' commentary on Euclid, translated by Thomas Taylor. In the appendix to this work, there is an interpretation of the wanderings of Ulysses in terms of neoplatonic allegory. The prolongation of Ulysses' exile from his native country after his blinding of the Cyclops is accounted for on the grounds that the latter represented his natal daemon.[55]

> . . . Ulysses after a voluntary submission to his natal dæmon, by indulging the irrational appetites and desires of his soul, flies from his base servitude; and adds irritations to his flight. He is, however, pursued by the anger of the marine and material dæmons, and punished for his escape. For he who blinds the eye of sense, and extinguishes its light, after his will has profoundly assented to its use, must expect punishment for the attempt; as necessary to his own private good, and the general order of the universe. Indeed, troubles and misfortunes resulting from such undertakings, not only contribute to appease the anger of their malevolent authors, but likewise purify and benefit the subjects of their revenge.

The mention of 'purification and benefit' at the end gives the interpretation an interesting twist. It suggests that the results of Ulysses' actions are twofold. The violence with which he 'blinds the eye of sense' is not to be condoned, yet it is ultimately a source of benefit to him. The eye of sense is not, in this context, the sensibility of the physical organism, but the 'inward eye' which must replace it (according to the neoplatonic philosophers), if liberation is to be achieved. For a full account of this, we may turn to a translation of Plotinus' fourth Ennead, which Thomas Taylor published with the title 'Plotinus on the Beautiful' in 1787. The account occurs in the course of another attempt to explain the wanderings of Ulysses in neoplatonic terms[56]:

> But our true country, like that of Ulysses, is from whence we came, and where our father lives. But where is the ship to be found, by which we can accomplish our flight? . . . it is in vain that we prepare horses to draw, or ships to transport us to our native land. On the contrary, neglecting all these, as unequal to the task, and excluding them entirely from our view, having now closed the corporeal eye, we must stir up, and assume a purer eye within, which all men possess, but which is alone used by a few.

> [*Taylor's note to the above.*] This inward eye is no other than intellect, which contains in its most inward recesses, a certain ray of light, participated from the sun of Beauty and Good, by which the soul is enabled to behold and become united with her divinely solitary original. This divine ray, or, as Proclus calls it, σύνθημα, a mark or impression, is thus beautifully described by that philosopher, (Theol. Plat. p. 105). 'The Author of the universe, (says he) has planted in all beings impressions of his own perfect excellence, and through these, he has placed all beings about himself, and is present with them in an ineffable manner, exempt from the universality of things. Hence, every being entering into the ineffable sanctuary of its own nature, finds there a symbol of the Father of all. And by this mystical impression, which corresponds to his nature, they become united with their original, divesting themselves of their own essence, and hastening to become his impression alone; and, through a desire of his unknown nature, and of the fountain of good, to participate him alone. And when they have ascended as far as to this cause, they enjoy perfect tranquillity, and are conversant in the perception of his divine progeny, and of the love which all things naturally possess of goodness, unknown, ineffable, without participation, and transcendently full.

This insistence upon Ulysses' 'inward eye' as the faculty to which he must submit if he is to regain his native country, inevitably reminds one of the Mariner's 'glittering eye'. Is it fanciful to suppose a direct connection?

Lane Cooper's article, 'The Power of the Eye in Coleridge', with its emphasis upon the cult of animal magnetism and Coleridge's interest in it, has already been noticed.[57] In the course of his article, Cooper points out that there is a clear reference to magnetism in a stanza of *The Ancient Mariner* which was later excised:

> Listen, O listen, thou Wedding-guest!
> 'Marinere! thou hast thy will:
> 'For that, which comes out of thine eye, doth make
> 'My body and soul to be still.'

The doctrine of magnetic emanation, he suggests, is expressed explicitly there and implicitly in other descriptions of the Mariner's 'glittering eye'.[58]

The explanation may be accepted, but it is questionable whether it tells us the full story. There are other glittering eyes in Coleridge's poetry, as Cooper points out—the glittering eyes of Hartley, taken out to the orchard plot in the moonlight for instance[59]—where there is little suggestion of 'magnetic emanation'. In dealing with a mind as intricate as Coleridge's it is never too safe to assume that any single explanation is a sufficient account of a given phenomenon: one has to consider the possibility that as an influence it was taken up and subsumed into a growing body of thought. And in this case it is quite clear that Coleridge had long been occupied with imagery of the flashing eye. In the *Greek Ode on Astronomy*, Wisdom, the Creatrix, 'unlocked the depths of Nature' to the 'piercing eye' of Urania.[60] In the temple of his *Allegoric Vision*, there were a few 'whose eyes were bright, and either piercing or steady, and whose ample foreheads . . . bespoke observation followed by meditative thought. . . .'[61] These were presumably equivalent to those[62]

> Who in this fleshly World, the elect of Heaven,
> Their strong eye darting through the deeds of men,
> Adore with steadfast unpresuming gaze
> Him Nature's essence, mind, and energy!

in *Religious Musings*.

In all these cases, the eye is not primarily the eye of magnetism, but the eye of intellect. As such, it has a long ancestry in eighteenth-century poetry, one obvious example being the well-known lines from Akenside's *Pleasures of the Imagination*[63]:

> Say, why was man so eminently rais'd
> Amid the vast Creation; why ordain'd
> Through life and death to dart his piercing eye,
> With thoughts beyond the limits of his frame . . .?

It seems clear that Coleridge had taken this concept from his predecessors, and had endowed it with both the 'scientific' background of animal magnetism and the mystical significance of the 'inward eye' in neoplatonism. As often happened, he also carried the idea a stage further. When he uses the term 'piercing eye', his sense is usually Akenside's —it is the eye of the investigator or creator. He speaks of God's 'chaos-piercing eye', and of 'times too remote to be pierced by the eye of investigation'.[64] When he speaks of the 'glittering eye', on the other hand, the emphasis is on passiveness—as in the case of Hartley, soothed by being held in the moonlight, or the Mariner in this poem. The influence is outside human control; its magnetic force is more compelling.

With this preliminary chain of evidence before us, we may turn to an examination of the events of the poem in their due order. The opening presents few difficulties under the interpretation so far offered. The ship sets sail cheerfully enough, and if we pause to consider the first impression, it is of a company of men living according to custom and tradition. Observing the taboos of their lore, they proceed happily on their way, and, even when they sail into thick snow and ice, a combination of the helmsman's skill with fortunate circumstances keeps them from harm.

The mariners have been happily described as 'hommes moyens sensuels', in fact: they are this and more. They live in what appears to them to be a pleasant, well-ordered universe, unaware that the apparent calm is no more than the precarious equilibrium between mighty forces.

The mention of snow and mist is the first point at which

an observant reader might be aware of deeper elements in the poem than at first appear, for these are symbols which have appeared elsewhere in Coleridge's writings. In *Religious Musings*, for example, he describes how the 'dayspring of Love' rises glorious in his soul,[65]

> As the great Sun, when he his influence
> Sheds on the frost-bound waters . . .

In *Biographia Literaria*, likewise, he describes the 'alleviation that results from "*opening out* our griefs:" which are thus presented in distinguishable forms instead of the mist, through which whatever is shapeless becomes magnified and (literally) *enormous*'.[66] Mist is used again and again by Coleridge to symbolize a state where ignorance and slavery to the passions results in a distorted picture of the world, or (where the mist is veiling the sun) of God.[67]

Ice and snow, on the other hand, seem to have an ambivalent position in Coleridge's symbolism. They can stand for the coldness of the unawakened heart—but they are also attractive, by reason of their brightness and purity. This ambivalence may well be intended to represent the state of the mariners, who, if they lack insight and awareness of any world beyond that of their immediate senses, display an elementary goodness in their fellowship and their active kindness to the albatross.

The shooting of the albatross brings this state of affairs to an end; and I have already suggested that the Mariner's action combines detachment from his fellows with moral ignorance. In connection with the latter characteristic, it is interesting to discover that, some years after writing the poem, Coleridge saw a hawk being shot at from the ship on which he was travelling and wrote in his notebook a reduced but recognizable version of the idea: 'Poor Hawk! O Strange Lust of Murder in Man!—It is not cruelty/it is mere non-feeling from non-thinking.'[68]

As the ice and snow disappear, it becomes clear that in spite of causing danger and discomfort, they have been acting as a protection for the ship and its crew. The Mariner's companions hail their departure, but soon find themselves in far worse plight, exposed to the merciless, untempered heat of the sun's rays. There is a parallel to this image in a snippet of verse by Coleridge entitled, significantly, *Napoleon*[69]:

> The Sun with gentle beams his rage disguises,
> And like aspiring Tyrants, temporises—
> Never to be endured but when he falls or rises.

The heat of the sun is, as we have seen, an essential element in the speculations of Jacob Boehme. Boehme's insistence on the benevolence of God led him to the doctrine that if God at times seemed angry, this was no more than an appearance, engendered by the diseased imagination of fallen man. Cut off from the light of God, he could experience only the heat of his presence: and any exposure to his full glory would therefore be felt as nothing less than exposure to unendurable fire.

Heat and thirst are one element in the mariners' torment; solitude and endless monotony are the other. And just as the one torture is due to the fact that the sun is untempered, so the other is due to the fact that time is unmodified. A passage in *Biographia Literaria* helps to bring out the full significance of this.[70]

> It sometimes happens that we are punished for our faults by incidents, in the causation of which these faults had no share: and this I have always felt the severest punishment. . . . For there is always a consolatory feeling that accompanies the sense of a proportion between antecedents and consequents. The sense of Before and After becomes both intelligible and intellectual when, and *only* when, we contemplate the succession in the relations of Cause and Effect, which, like the two poles of the magnet manifest the being and unity of the one power by relative opposites, and give, as it were, a substratum of permanence, of identity, and therefore of reality, to the shadowy flux of Time. . . . Hence . . . the Mystics have joined in representing the state of the reprobate spirits as a dreadful dream in which there is no sense of reality, not even of the pangs they are enduring—an eternity without time, and as it were below it—God present without manifestation of his presence.

According to some vague reminiscences by De Quincey, Coleridge had, before writing *The Ancient Mariner*, meditated a poem 'on delirium, confounding its own dream-scenery with external things, and connected with the imagery of high latitudes'.[71] It seems likely that some such plan was forming in his mind when he wrote, on a page of the Gutch notebook,[72]

in that eternal & delirious misery—
wrathfires—
inward desolations—
an horror of great darkness
great things that on the ocean
counterfeit infinity—

Fallen humanity cannot bear the revelation of infinity: and the Ancient Mariner, by breaking through the veils of convention and custom with which mankind normally defends itself from the unbearable supernatural, has brought upon himself the curse of Cain. According to Boehme, Cain was regarded by his parents, Adam and Eve, as the son who would fulfil the prophecy, and vanquish the serpent, but he, in his pride as a man and a hunter, and knowing only the use of violence, destroyed not the serpent but his brother Abel.[73] Thus the serpent came to 'bruise the heel' of mankind.

This legend seems to have its place in the poem, along with a good deal more of the serpent lore and daemonology that has been examined above. We have already suggested that Coleridge was familiar with the Egyptian symbol of the Sun, the Serpent and the Wings, especially in its use as an emblem of the Trinity and the divine creativity. The sun proceeds into eternal generation in the serpent, which is in its turn exalted and winged, to soar back to the sun. We know from Coleridge's many references elsewhere that he was fond of using the image of God as the sun, already a cliché of the emblem-writers and other symbolists. In a note from the *Aids to Reflection*, cited earlier, he puts forward the theory that the serpent, in Egyptian temple-language, represented the wisdom of the flesh. And it is reasonable to suppose that he was conversant, also, with the ambivalence of the serpent in Egyptian lore, where the daemonic could represent either the serpent alone (the cacodaemon Typhon), or Cneph the winged, good daemon.[74]

We can learn more about Cneph from Maurice's *History of Hindostan*, which Coleridge read with some attention. Maurice, in discussing the rise of mythology, follows tradition in making Japhet founder and guardian of the Greek nation, and also sees him as prototype of Neptune. The connecting figure between these two is, for him, Canopus, the Egyptian god of mariners, whom he describes as follows[75]:

> Canopus is a bright star of the first magnitude in the stern of the ship Argo, which we shall presently see was no other than the ark of Noah, turned into a constellation; and Cneph, or Canupha, (for that is the Coptic and Arabian primitive) by which the Egyptians meant the guardian genius, who with his expanded wings hovered over the waters, was therefore the proper pilot of that vessel.

If we accept this final link in the chain of evidence, the albatross can be identified with the guardian daemon even more closely than before. In terms of the Egyptian hierogram, the Mariner, in killing the albatross, destroys the connection between the sun and the serpent. In consequence, the two become separate, and equally alien to man. The serpent, representative of flesh, becomes loathsome and corrupt, while the sun, now that the true inward vision is lost, is apprehended only as heat or wrath. Or, in psychological terms, the Mariner is trapped between the fearful wrath of his conscience, which is all that remains of his Reason, and his consequent loathing of the flesh. Caught in this vicious circle, he is truly in Hell.[76]

> For the sky and the sea, and the sea and the sky
> Lay like a load on my weary eye,
> And the dead were at my feet.

Further evidence that the 'slimy things' of the poem are intentional symbols of corruption may be found in *The*

Destiny of Nations, where they are used in this sense, while
Love is imaged as a winged spirit, or a breeze[77]:

> . . . Love rose glittering, and his gorgeous wings
> Over the abyss fluttered with such glad noise,
> As what time after long and pestful calms,
> With slimy shapes and miscreated life
> Poisoning the vast Pacific, the fresh breeze
> Wakens the merchant-sail uprising.

If this explanation of the symbolism of the early poem is
accepted, it becomes clear that in the killing of the albatross
and its result, Coleridge has given us an image of the fall of
mankind. This image differs in one important respect,
artistically speaking, from normal representations. The Fall,
as conventionally described, is from a static state of bliss to a
dynamic state of evil. In Coleridge's developed thinking,
however, it is a separation from 'the suspending Magnet, the
Golden Chain from the Staple Ring fastened to the Footstool
of the Throne'.[78] In other words, he evidently accepts the
idea of the Great Chain of Being, which, logically pursued,
makes the state of virtue dynamic and reduces man after the
fall to a static condition of monotony and privation. Any
redemptive force in such a condition must therefore have a
dynamic quality, if it is to help re-establish the cycle of
divine creativity.

· · · · ·

If Coleridge found the materials for his imagery of the
Fall in Egyptian mythology, he could also find the materials
for a complementary theory of redemption there. The myth
of Isis and Osiris offered him precisely the dynamic paradigm
which he was seeking. We may be encouraging in following
this line of investigation, moreover, by the fact that in the
attempts of previous critics to interpret the symbolism of
the poem, the sun and moon have usually had an important
place. It has been suggested, for example, that the work of
retribution is carried out under the light of the sun, while
the work of the redemption is carried out under the light of
the moon[79]; and while this theory is rather too broad to fit

the poem as it stands, the fact that it should be brought forward at all is significant.

There are two chief objections to the theory just described. The first is that to have the sun identified only with retribution would run counter to Coleridge's normal use of it as a symbol for benevolence. The other has been cogently put forward by Humphry House[80]:

> If the moon is to be associated always with the good and the redemption, why is it that the crew die by the star-dogged moon at the end of Part III? It is difficult to explain this and yet support the idea of a consistently developing imagery in terms of the penance and redemption and reconciliation theme alone.

This is an important difficulty, and at one time I thought that it could perhaps be met with the aid of an abstruse point made by Lowes. Dealing with the assertion by Hale White and others that the poem contained 'the mistake of a rising, horned moon at sunset', he pointed out that the objection was only valid if the crescent moon was being referred to. The waning moon rises, horned, in the early morning at certain periods, and it could be argued that it was early morning when the moon rises in the poem.[81] I had supposed from this that the Mariner's shipmates died under the waning moon, while the work of redemption took place beneath the crescent. Moreover, it was possible to back this interpretation by means of a passage in Coleridge's drama, *Zapolya*[82]:

> *Emerick (alone, looks at a Calendar).* The changeful
>   planet, now in her decay,
> Dips down at midnight, to be seen no more.
> With her shall sink the enemies of Emerick,
> Cursed by the last look of the waning moon:
> And my bright destiny, with sharpened horns,
> Shall greet me fearless in the new-born crescent.

Unfortunately for the simplicity of this theory, however, there is, as I discovered, a passage in one of Coleridge's notebooks where he discusses the superstitions of seamen: and in the course of which he remarks, 'Here Vexation, which in a Sailor's mind is always linked on to Reproach and Anger, makes the Superstitious seek out an Object of his superstition that can feel his anger. Else the Star, that dogged the Crescent or my "Cursed by the last Look of the waning moon" were the better.'[83]

This remark complicates, but also helps to solve, the problem before us. The moon remains constant as a beneficent power, and has no part in the dying and cursing. It is the star between its horns that represents the daemonic vengeance upon the Mariner.[84] When the moon ascends the sky, later on, 'with a star or two beside', she has become the symbol of reconciliation.

The theme of reconciliation has other interesting features. If the slimy creatures crawling on the sea signified corruption earlier on, it is equally fitting that the water-snakes should be the creatures which, as they move and rear, evoke the Mariner's blessing. For in this vision of the snakes interweaving harmoniously beneath the light of the moon can be discerned the wished-for harmony between *natura naturata* and *natura naturans*. The snakes and the moon are for the Mariner a revelation of the inner, ideal harmony of the universe (not unrelated to the sun and serpent of the Egyptian ideal), which is shortly to be revealed to him in more vivid form. This scene, and some of those which follow it are related in mood to that described in a note-book[85] :

Quiet stream, with all its eddies, & the moon light playing in them, quiet as if they were Ideas in the divine Mind anterior to the Creation.

There is another image of some importance in this incident. The liberating act of the Mariner in blessing the snakes seems involuntary. He is, by his own confession, unable to help himself, and when the spell breaks he can only say,[86]

A spring of love gusht from my heart,
And I bless'd them unaware!

The use of the spring as an image here is hardly fortuitous. In the Isis and Osiris mythology, the moon and the fountains are closely related, and it may be argued that the fountain-image, like that of the serpent, is an image of divine creative energy. The point may be left for fuller discussion to a later chapter, and it will be sufficient here to recall two uses of the image elsewhere in Coleridge's works. In the *Philosophical Lectures*, he invites those who rely on the heart alone in religion to soar like the lark and enjoy the light as well: their being will then 'be made fit for its appointed happiness and the extension of power which will come when the spring has been given'.[87] In *Dejection: an Ode*, likewise, he speaks of the impossibility of hoping[88]

> from outward forms to win
> The passion and the life, whose fountains are within.

It is significant of the manner in which internal and external images blend in this poem that the 'spring' in the Mariner's heart is followed by the longed-for rain.

Identification of the moon with Isis in this poem may be reinforced by the mention of 'Mary Queen' and 'Heaven's Mother'. The Heavenly Mother of Egyptian mythology is thus related to the Roman Catholic Queen of Heaven.

The 'hundred fire-flags sheen' have already been commented on in connection with Berkeley's *Siris*, and this appearance of darting lights in the elements heralds, significantly, the third phase of the poem: the phase in which the Mariner is granted a vision of the ideal universe. In this vision, the bodies of his shipmates are invested by a troop of spirits, who stop their work at dawn in order to hymn the sun. The core of the vision lies here[89]:

> Around, around, flew each sweet sound,
> Then darted to the sun:
> Slowly the sounds came back again
> Now mix'd, now one by one.

The mention of the sun here is the first since the vanishing of the spectre-ship; and it helps us to solve the problem raised earlier. For we can now suggest that the sun, in the poem as a whole, is a symbol not of wrath and retribution, but of God and the image of God in human reason—as is normal in Coleridge's writings. The sun which is unveiled by the shooting of the albatross is the angry 'Typhonian' sun, unendurable because improperly apprehended. 'Only in the Mediator', wrote Coleridge in a later notebook, 'can the Holy One, of eyes too pure to behold iniquity, cease to become a consuming fire to all Corruption.'[90] The sun of the vision, on the other hand, is the true divine, centre of light and source of harmony. It is the 'true sun' of the mystics, described by Apuleius, Plato, Boehme, and many other writers.[91]

During the vision, therefore, the Mariner sees in essence and reality the harmony which was only prefigured to him in the sight of the moon and the water-snakes. In this Platonic ideal, all human beings are in communion with God and therefore in harmony with one another.

This conception, which seems to haunt *Siris* and the neoplatonic philosophers, had probably been a favourite with Coleridge since boyhood. In the *Greek Ode on Astronomy*, for instance, he had described the paradisal condition where[92]

> round the fields of Truth
> The fiery Essences for ever feed.

The vision remained with him long after the writing of *The Ancient Mariner*, moreover. In *The Statesman's Manual*, nearly twenty years later, he was to describe how a biblical text might dawn upon a man[93]

> . . . in the pure untroubled brightness of an Idea, that most glorious birth of the God-like within us, which even as the Light, its material symbol, reflects itself from a thousand surfaces, and flies homeward to its Parent Mind enriched with a thousand forms, itself above form and still remaining in its own simplicity and identity!

The central importance of the 'vision' for the poem as allegory, is further borne out by two stanzas which appear at the end of it in the original version[94]:

> I turn'd my head in fear and dread,
> And by the holy rood,
> The bodies had advanc'd, and now
> Before the mast they stood.

They lifted up their stiff right arms,
They held them strait and tight;
And each right-arm burnt like a torch,
A torch that's borne upright.
Their stony eye-balls glitter'd on
In the red and smoky light.

This, as we may learn from Lowes, is a reference to the phenomenon known as the 'Hand of Glory'.[95] But it is also relevant that in Thomas Taylor's writings, the torch-bearer is identified as the interpreter of the mysteries.[96] The Mariner has been initiated into the meaning of the central mystery of the universe.

There is one further characteristic of the Mariner's vision which merits discussion. Writing to Tieck many years later, Coleridge recalled one of the speculations which had possessed him in boyhood and youth[97]:

Before my visit to Germany in September, 1798, I had adopted (probably from Behmen's Aurora which I had *conjured over* at school) the idea, that Sound was = Light under the praepotence of Gravitation, and Color = Gravitation under the praepotence of Light: and I have never seen reason to change my faith in this respect.

The importance of this passage lies in the portrayal of light and sound as inter-related phenomena. As soon as one looks at Coleridge's poems with this in mind, one is struck by the number of passages where this inter-relation seems to be presupposed. It seems as though the scenes and sounds which delighted him most were those where the harmony of sight and the harmony of sound seemed in some way to fuse. *The Eolian Harp*, for example, has a striking description of[98]

. . . the one Life within us and abroad,
Which meets all motion and becomes its soul,
A light in sound, a sound-like power in light,
Rhythm in all thought, and joyance every where . . .

In *Dejection*, he tells how from Joy

flows all that charms or ear or sight,
All melodies the Echoes of that Voice,
All Colors a Suffusion of that Light.

At the end of *Religious Musings* the idea recurs in a form even closer to the present poem.[99]

> Soaring aloft I breathe the empyreal air
> Of Love, omnific, omnipresent Love,
> Whose day-spring rises glorious in my soul
> As the great Sun, when he his influence
> Sheds on the frost-bound waters—The glad stream
> Flows to the ray and warbles as it flows.

This not only unites the flow of light and sound, but establishes the sun as source of both harmonies. This is precisely the concept which Coleridge is using in *The Ancient Mariner*.[100]

> Around, around, flew each sweet sound,
> Then darted to the Sun:
> Slowly the sounds came back again
> Now mix'd, now one by one.

It would be difficult to find a better example of Coleridge's lifelong quest for harmonious unity in the universe than his attempt, both in poetry and speculation, to see light and sound as varying manifestations of a single identity.

And if we return to Coleridge's hint that Boehme's *Aurora* first led him to this speculation, we find that investigation of Coleridge's source once again proves enlightening, for the passage in *Aurora* most likely to have given rise to such a speculation comes in Boehme's description of the delights of the angelic congress with God.[101]

> An angel sendeth forth Nothing but the *Divine* Power, which he takes in his Mouth, wherewith he kindles his Heart, and the Heart kindles all the *Members*, and *that* he sends forth from himself again at the Mouth, when he speaks and praises God.

The close link between Boehme's angels and Coleridge's seraph-men is typical of his visionary mind. Indeed, the emotional concentration within these stanzas is remarkable: they include many of Coleridge's most personal and essential feelings, from the days when he conjured over Boehme at school to the time of actually writing the poem: a time when his appreciation of natural beauty was at its height, and when he would often lie[102]

> On sea-ward Quantock's heathy hills
> Where quiet sounds from hidden rills
> Float here and there like things astray,
> And high o'er head the sky-lark shrills.

The vision, during which 'the Man is determined (i.e. impelled and directed) to act in harmony of inter-communion',[103] lasts only for a short time: but while it lasts the Mariner is able to apprehend the ideal communion of human spirits with each other and with God. That the vision is still present in the next brief part, is suggested by the lines:

> Still as a Slave before his Lord,
> The Ocean hath no blast:
> His great bright eye most silently
> Up to the moon is cast

It has been noted by several critics that these lines derive from Sir John Davies's poem, *Orchestra*:[104]

> For his great chrystal eye is always cast
> Up to the moon, and on her fixed fast . . .

It may now be pointed out, however, that the lines occur in Davies's description of the 'dance', or harmony of nature. The verbal borrowing thus reflects a community of symbolism between the two poems.

Soon it becomes evident that the Mariner is not to remain within the vision permanently, for it is essentially a vision granted in the course of penance. Nevertheless, the vision is an important part of his penance. He may now return to his own country—'but no longer at ease in the old dispensation': his consciousness of the full heights and depths of human experience, as revealed in his vision and his torments, means that he will from now on possess a dual consciousness, drawing him away from everyday experience. He will even be invested with strange powers—able to pass like night from land to land and forced to seek out those who will hear and perhaps profit from his story. We are reminded again of the Wandering Jew. Like the Jew, also, the Mariner has the brand of Cain—but according to Coleridge's interpretation of the Cain-story. He is daemonically possessed.

Of the dénouement of the poem, little more need be said. It should be pointed out, however, that the 'native country' has a particular significance in neoplatonic thought. It is the world which the soul leaves when it descends into generation, and which it is constantly trying to regain in this life. This doctrine is also used to account for the sense of recognition which accompanies certain mystic experiences. That Coleridge knew and accepted it is clear from the last stanza of the *Greek Ode on Astronomy* [105]:

> I may not call thee mortal then, my soul!
> Immortal longings lift thee to the skies:
> Love of thy native home inflames thee now,
> With pious madness wise.

The importance of the doctrine in the poem also springs from its central place in the neoplatonic interpretation of the *Odyssey*. Lowes mentioned the parallel between the trance of the Mariner as his ship is moved on by supernatural forces, and the corresponding incident in Homer. He also discussed a series of further parallels to which his attention had been drawn, including the abandonment of Ulysses by heaven after he killed the Cyclops; the dying, one by one, of his crew for killing creatures beloved of the sun-god; the falling asunder beneath him of his craft when he is almost safe ashore; and his subsequent wanderlust and spell-binding powers of speech. He accepted them but would not think of them as more than a background influence[106]: he did not know, presumably, the passages cited above where precisely these incidents are made central to a neoplatonic interpretation of the *Odyssey*. Once seen in this light, however, the parallels with *The Ancient Mariner* become very much more compelling.

One other parallel may be drawn—a minor and tentative one. The cock is a common symbol for the sun; and it may well be that in the lines

> The moonlight steep'd in silentness
> The steady weathercock,

Coleridge intended to combine a piece of fine atmospheric description with a resolution of symbolism. The Mariner, it might be said, is not granted a permanent vision of the Sun, but he is afforded the calm which results from having it established now in his imagination as an abiding, if latent, truth.

The home-coming of Ulysses was also commented on by the neoplatonists, and Porphyry's emphasis on the fact that he at once went to consult with a priestess reminds us of the Mariner's desire for absolution from the Hermit. The whole sequence of events at the end of the poem may be compared with Plotinus's description of the 'race of divine men'.[107]

> *In the third class is the race of divine men*, who through a more excellent power, and with piercing eyes, acutely perceive supernal light, to the vision of which they raise themselves above the clouds and darkness as it were of this lower world, and there abiding despise every thing in these regions of sense; being no otherwise delighted with the place which is truly and properly their own, than he who after many wanderings is at length restored to his lawful country.

In the light of the foregoing argument, we may accept Robert Penn Warren's description of the poem as a 'sacramental vision', but it is also clear that the sacrament is more closely religious than his article suggests. The basic theme of the poem, he declares,[108] is the 'one Life' to which Coleridge often referred throughout his writings. This is so: but it would be wrong to imagine that the 'Life' signifies simply a biological phenomenon. Even in the years following his return from Germany, when he was deeply engrossed in Spinozism, there was always a metaphysical bias in Coleridge's study of physiology. If there is one common thread in Coleridge's spiritual quest, it is his conviction that by meditating on the material universe, men will come to understand the realm of the spiritual, and, correspondingly, that the scientist who bears in mind metaphysical truths will find in them the solution to his problems and the true interpretation of physical phenomena. In *The Ancient*

Mariner, therefore, the albatross is not simply a physical organism: for Coleridge's 'reverence for life' is not to be confused with that of, say, Albert Schweitzer. The bird has to be seen as a symbol both of physical and transcendental life, both sides receiving their appropriate weight.

Similarly, Penn Warren's interpretation of the poem in terms of Understanding and Imagination, which presents several difficulties as it stands, can, with the aid of certain modifications, be made to bring out the 'psychological' implications of our interpretation. It is wrong to identify Understanding and Imagination with the sun and moon respectively, but the existence of some such relationship may be accepted. Warren, pursuing his theory that the sun is the 'understanding', has to interpret the 'vision' by saying that at that point in the poem the sun no longer exists in abstraction, no longer partakes of death, but has its proper rôle in the texture of things and partakes of the general blessedness.[109] This interpretation, however, forces the phenomena into a pattern which they do not quite fit: and indeed his theory as a whole involves a devaluation of the sun which is markedly foreign to all traditional symbolisms, including Coleridge's.

> Whene'er the mist, that stands 'twixt God and thee
> Defecates to a pure transparency,
> That intercepts no light and adds no stain—
> There Reason is, and then begins her reign!

If we apply the interpretation suggested by this verse of Coleridge's,[110] we have the counterpart of our earlier exposition. The Sun remains unchanging as a symbol of the divine Glory. Psychologically, it is the divine Reason in mankind, which the unenlightened understanding of the guilty experiences only in the heat and wrath of conscience. When, in the 'vision', therefore, the Mariner sees it in its true glory, it is because in that brief period, his understanding is transfigured. In the act of seeing the true sun, it partakes of its qualities, and becomes Reason.

Likewise, the psychological significance of the moon in the poem is subtler than Warren suggests. His argument is summarized as follows by House[111]:

Mr Warren maintains that the association is so recurrent and persistent in Coleridge's writing, between creation or the activity of the secondary imagination and the moonlight, half-lights, dim lights, gloom, luminescent clouds and so on, that the association between them can justifiably be regarded as habitual. . . .

In discussing the moon's function in the poem, I have brought forward evidence to suggest that there is a noticeable ambivalence involved, corresponding both to its phases, and at times to the positioning of certain stars. The significance of moonlight seems to vary in this way throughout Coleridge's poetry. At its best it is the quiet moonlight which

> steep'd in silentness
> The steady weathercock.

and this may well be the light of the full moon, in view of the sea's 'great bright eye' at the beginning of the section[112]:
There are two other significances beside this, however. The moonlight in which the water-snakes move and rear, coil and swim, is paralleled by the Pantisocracy sonnet, in which Coleridge looks forward to an ideal state where,[113]

> . . . dancing to the moonlight roundelay,
> The wizard Passions weave an holy spell.

Here the moon is shining upon the energy of a *natura naturata* which is coming into dynamic harmony with *natura naturans*, but has not reached the stillness and fullness of the consummated communion.
The third significance is a darker one. As early as 1788, Coleridge addressed the autumnal moon, in a sonnet, as 'Mother of wildly-working visions!' and likened her to Hope, sometimes 'hid behind the dragon-wing'd Despair', even if later, she emerges 'in her radiant might'.[114] In *France: An Ode*, ten years later, he recalled[115]

> How oft, pursuing fancies holy,
> My moonlight way o'er flowering weeds I wound,
> Inspir'd, beyond the guess of folly . . .

Here the undertone of wildness is again subdued, this

time to a suggestion of 'pious madness', but it emerges full and unchecked in a line of *Religious Musings*[116]:

Moon-blasted Madness when he yells at midnight!

If the moon is mother of visions, the blessing is a mixed one: for the power which may be the heavenly Imagination can also in unhappier minds, be wild-working fancy—even to the point of lunacy.

This paradigm of three separate functions is, it may be argued, fundamental to Coleridge, and repeated in his account of the Imagination in *Biographia Literaria*, where he distinguishes between the workings of the primary and secondary Imagination and of the Fancy.[117]

The primary Imagination is at one with the Reason, just as the full moon is at one with the Sun, figuring the orb of the lost Osiris. The primary Imagination is 'the living Power and prime Agent of all human Perception, and . . . a repetition in the finite mind of the eternal act of creation in the infinite I AM'.

The secondary Imagination, on the other hand, is the Isis which seeks to re-create the lost Osiris, to harmonize *natura naturata* with *natura naturans*. It is seen by Coleridge as

an echo of the former, co-existing with the conscious will, yet still as identical with the primary in the *kind* of its agency, and differing only in *degree*, and in the *mode* of its operation. It dissolves, diffuses, dissipates, in order to recreate; or where this process is rendered impossible, yet still . . . it struggles to idealize and to unify. It is essentially *vital*, even as all objects (*as* objects) are essentially fixed and dead.

If, on the other hand, the Isis function of the moon is overshadowed, redeeming moonlight becomes merely static moonshine. In the same way, Coleridge's Fancy

has no other counters to play with, but fixities and definites. The Fancy is indeed no other than a mode of Memory emancipated from the order of time and space; while it is blended with, and modified by that empirical phenomenon of the will, which we express by the word

CHOICE. But equally with the ordinary memory the Fancy must receive all its materials ready made from the law of association.

The Imagination, like the moon, is ambivalent in function: it can either draw the mind to the full light of Reason, or pander to the Understanding. In the latter case, it becomes the Eve in man,[118]

tempted by the same serpentine and perverted Understanding which, framed originally to be the Interpreter of the Reason and the ministering Angel of the Spirit, is henceforth sentenced and bound over to the service of the Animal Nature, its needs and its cravings, dependent on the Senses for all its Materials, with the World of Sense for its appointed Sphere: 'Upon thy belly shalt thou go, and dust shalt thou eat all the days of thy life.'

Even the Fancy has its uses in the scheme of things, however, and there is a passage in *The Destiny of Nations*, written in 1796, which not only makes this plain, but also serves as a summary of the intellectual structure of *The Ancient Mariner* (and evidently as some justification for its composition, in Coleridge's eyes)[119]:

> For Fancy is the power
> That first unsensualises the dark mind,
> Giving it new delights; and bids it swell
> With wild activity; and peopling air,
> By obscure fears of Beings invisible,
> Emancipates it from the grosser thrall
> Of the present impulse, teaching Self-control,
> Till Superstition with unconscious hand
> Seat Reason on her throne.

This 'psychological' element in the interpretation of the poem is in accord with the original intentions of its composer, as described in *Biographia Literaria*[120]:

> ... it was agreed, that my endeavours should be directed to persons and characters supernatural, or at least romantic; yet so as to transfer from our inward nature a human interest and a semblance of truth sufficient to procure for

these shadows of imagination that willing suspension of disbelief for the moment, which constitutes poetic faith.

Read quickly, this passage might seem to refer only to that process which does in fact occur triumphantly in the poem—description of supernatural incidents in such everyday language as renders them immediately plausible to the reader; and the impression is likely to be confirmed if the passage is read as complementary to the next, where Wordsworth's aim 'to give the charm of novelty to things of every day' is described (an aim which is equally often misunderstood). Coleridge does not say that his aim is to transfer the 'semblance of truth' from our everyday experience, however, but from our 'inward nature'. The meaning, surely, is that we will accept the story not just because it is narrated plausibly (which of course it is), but because the events correspond to truths which we inwardly recognize as valid. The process is further illuminated by a passage in the later fragment 'On Poesy or Art'[121]:

> In the objects of nature are presented, as in a mirror, all the possible elements, steps, and processes of intellect antecedent to consciousness, and therefore to the full development of the intelligential act; and man's mind is the very focus of all the rays of intellect which are scattered throughout the images of nature. Now so to place these images, totalized, and fitted to the limits of the human mind, as to elicit from, and to superinduce upon, the forms themselves the moral reflexions to which they approximate, to make the external internal, the internal external, to make nature thought, and thought nature,— this is the mystery of genius in the Fine Arts. . . .

Something like this aim seems to have been in Coleridge's mind when he wrote *The Ancient Mariner*; and our discussion has shown the extent to which he tried to make 'thought nature' in his poem. It also throws light on his well-known reply to Mrs Barbauld's objection that the poem had no moral. In his own judgment, he said, the poem had too much[122]; and he was apparently referring to something more than the Mariner's final words to the Wedding-guest. And these words, in their turn, gain from the weight of symbolism behind them in the poem. They must inevitably pay the price of having influenced the writer of the hymn, 'All things bright and beautiful', but we need not follow Irving Babbitt in supposing the poem's meaning to be a mere elaboration of that hymn and its sentiments.

I do not wish to suggest, of course, that the poem contains a rigid symbolic structure into which every detail can be fitted like a jigsaw puzzle. Stoll, criticizing the symbolist interpreters of the poem, has reminded us that 'in fine literature there is something of an old wives' tale',[123] and there can be no doubt that many of the supernatural touches in the poem are there simply from delight in their vividness. If the 'Spirit that bideth by himself in the land of mist and snow' reminds us of that purity which is, in Coleridge's eyes, the necessary condition of joy, it is doubtful whether the figures of Death and Life-in-Death (who were not given these names in the first version) are intended to do more than dramatize a judgment which has already been set in motion by other forces in the poem.

This delight in vividness reminds us of the other great organizing principle in the poem's composition: the apparent determination on Coleridge's part to make his poem consist of images rather than stated thoughts wherever possible. It is this quality which has delighted many generations who may never have given a thought to the meaning of the poem; and it is this quality which Imagist poets and critics have found so exciting. As a result, Coleridge was taken to be an Imagist poet *manqué*, a process which culminated in the writing of *The Road to Xanadu*. That *The Ancient Mariner* can be read in this way is not for one moment to be doubted: but it is evidently wrong to suppose that Coleridge intended that, and only that; and it is therefore also wrong to use the poem as a proof of the theory (which we will dispute again in connection with *Kubla Khan*) that true poetry is written only when the poet allows free play to his imagination, unfettered by intellectual preoccupations. Whatever the merits of this theory, it is evident that in *The Ancient Mariner* at least, the images were intended to be a secondary blossoming, and that the core of the poem was to be a body of organized symbolism, which should bind the action of the ballad into a logical, as well as narrative, sequence. This symbolic structure finds one of its poles in the concept of the ideal Sun and seraphs, where pure intelligences are in communion with a Deity who is source of light and harmony; the other pole being the Mariner himself, with a set of subtle and dynamic symbols relating him to, and alienating him from, the ideal state. Robert Penn Warren has likened him to the *poète maudit* of romanticism,[124] and there is much to be said for this identification. It has to be recognized however that his accursedness is no simple phenomenon. It is the daemonic curse of one who has experienced the angelic state: it is a curse which involves in its very nature the memory of blessedness. And thus the Mariner becomes a true romantic 'pilgrim of eternity'.

In spite of his achievement, Coleridge seems to have been dissatisfied with his poem. I suspect that one reason for his dissatisfaction was the failure of his readers to pick up any of the threads which he had so skilfully interwoven. It is likely that the remarks which he later made about Tasso's allegorizing were meant to apply to his own poem, also: the music of the poem, he felt, distracted the reader from symbolic meanings. He may also have felt that his own purpose had not properly been carried out, and that the metaphysical, so far from being brought home to his readers, had been distanced by the very unreality of the events in the poem.

At all events, he was not immediately discouraged from writing supernatural poetry as such: on the contrary, he tells us that he began preparing *Christabel*—'in which I should have more nearly realized my ideal, than I had done in my first attempt'.[125] And, if his later accounts are to be believed, *Christabel* also was written with allegorical intent—though, once again, not with a moral to be openly obtruded on the reader as a principle or cause of action.

Chapter VI

'BY ALL THE EAGLE IN THEE,
ALL THE DOVE . . .'

IT is possible that *Christabel* and *The Ancient Mariner* were planned at one and the same time. The main evidence for such a theory, however, is Wordsworth's inconclusive statement in *The Prelude*.[1] From Coleridge's account in *Biographia Literaria*, it is possibly to deduce only that there was a direct relationship between the purposes of the two poems, not that they were in the first place intended to be complementary pieces.[2] Accordingly, that is how *Christabel* will be treated in this chapter.

The existence of this apparent relationship between the two poems led Nethercot to believe that an investigation of *Christabel* conducted on the lines of *The Road to Xanadu* might prove as fruitful. The reader of *The Road to Tryermaine* is, however, forced to confess to some disappointment. The greatness of Lowes's achievement lay not so much in his ability to trace elements in the poem to remote sources, as in his demonstration of the manner in which, from sources so widely separated in space and time, Coleridge had often elicited an image or a phrase which was infinitely richer than the sum of its sources. Nethercot, on the other hand, rarely did more than discover factual sources for elements in *Christabel*, without adding very much to our appreciation of the work either as poetry or as an intellectual structure. He spends a great deal of time, for example, in identifying sources of names in the poem from Hutchinson's *History of Cumberland* without ever, apparently, considering the possibility that Coleridge acquired these names, not by remembering them from his reading of the book, but by going to the book and deliberately searching for authentic lakeland names—as any modern writer of historical fiction might do.[3]

Another reason for Nethercot's apparent failure is to be found in the nature of the poem itself. *The Ancient Mariner* is remarkable for a certain unique quality which might be described as 'isolation of vividnesses'. There is a brittleness throughout the poem, a separation between stanza and stanza, which is caused by the constant welling up of some new and brilliant image, requiring a moment of darkness before the reader is ready to assimilate the next. These images are often, as has been said, the fruits of earlier reading, and the result is that the texture of the poem is more closely bound up with Coleridge's sources and what he did with them. *Christabel*, on the other hand, relies more on present imagination for its shaping and colouring.

The meaning of the poem is a topic which Nethercot treats more briefly; his discussion is interesting, however, and less open to the objections urged above. And indeed, since Coleridge spoke of the intricacy and subtlety of the poem's organization, there would appear to be every reason for pursuing the investigation in this direction.

One is hampered, of course, by the fact that Coleridge did not bring his poem to a conclusion. It is no easy matter to discuss the pattern of a poem, when only two parts out of the intended five were actually written. On the other hand, we are fortunate in possessing several versions of the poem's projected conclusion, as given by Coleridge himself in later life. Gillman's biography, for example, contains two such accounts. The first consists of a brief outline of purpose[4]:

The story of the Christabel is partly founded on the notion, that the virtuous of this world save the wicked. The pious and good Christabel suffers and prays for

'The weal of her lover that is far away,'

exposed to various temptations in a foreign land; and she thus defeats the power of evil represented in the person of Geraldine. This is one main object of the tale.

Derwent Coleridge gives a similar account of the symbolic intentions of the poem[5]:

The sufferings of Christabel were to have been represented as vicarious, endured for her 'lover far away'; and Geraldine, no witch or goblin, or malignant being of any kind, but a spirit, executing her appointed task with the best good-will,—as she says herself:—

> All they who live in the upper sky
> Do love you, holy Christabel;
> And you love them, and for their sake,
> And for the good which me befell,
> Even I in my degree will try,
> Fair maiden, to requite you well.

In form this is of course accommodated to a 'fond superstition', in keeping with the general tenor of the piece; but that the holy and the innocent do often suffer for the faults of those they love, and are thus made the instruments to bring them back to the ways of peace, is a matter of fact, and in Coleridge's hands might have been worked up into a tale of deep and delicate pathos.

James Dykes Campbell said that he suspected and hoped that Coleridge was merely quizzing his friends with the shorter account of the ending[6]: but this theory is weakened by the appearance of the same plan in the account given to Derwent. Moreover, it is difficult to imagine Coleridge joking about this particular religious doctrine, which, as we have seen, raised crucial problems in his religious thinking.

The idea has, indeed, sometimes been put forward that by the time Coleridge wrote this poem, his religious preoccupations had disappeared altogether,[7] but this is difficult to accept. On the contrary, the accounts given above, and the pattern traced in previous chapters, suggest that *Christabel* might represent one of his most concentrated and powerful efforts to deal with the problem of evil. *The Ancient Mariner*, as we have seen, includes a redeeming principle, but only as one element in the poem. In *Christabel*, on the other hand, Coleridge makes a focal point of the redeeming principle, by personifying it in the heroine of his poem.

This view of the poem is supported by some further comments on its genesis, recorded in the *Table Talk*[8]:

Where (Crashaw) does combine richness of thought and diction nothing can excel, as in the lines you so much admire—

'Since 'tis not to be had at home,
She'l travel to a martyrdome.
No home for her confesses she,
But where she may a martyr be.
She'l to the Moores, and trade with them
For this invalued diadem,
She offers them her dearest breath
With Christ's name in't, in change for death.
She'l bargain with them, and will give
Them God, and teach them how to live
In Him, or if they this deny,
For Him she'l teach them how to die.
So shall she leave amongst them sown
The Lord's blood, or at least, her own.
Farewell then, all the world—adieu,
Teresa is no more for you:
Farewell all pleasures, sports, and joys,
Never till now esteemed toys—
Farewell whatever dear'st may be,
Mother's arms or father's knee;
Farewell house, and farewell home,
She's for the Moores and martyrdome."

These verses were ever present to my mind whilst writing the second part of *Christabel*; if, indeed, by some subtle process of the mind they did not suggest the first thought of the whole poem.

The last part of Coleridge's sentence suggests that Coleridge had in mind a link between the Teresa of Crashaw's poem and the Christabel of his own: if so, other passages in Crashaw probably played a part in forging it. When Coleridge came to discuss Saint Teresa in his philosophical lectures, it was from a different poem that he quoted—'The Flaming Heart'[9]—and the many paradoxes in this poem as a whole suggest that it too helped to mould his conception of Christabel.[10]

O sweet incendiary! shew here thy art,
Upon this carcasse of a hard, cold, hart,
Let all thy scatter'd shafts of light, that play
Among the leaues of thy larg Books of day,

Combin'd against this BREST at once break in
And take away from me my self & sin,
This gratious Robbery shall thy bounty be;
And my best fortunes such fair spoiles of me.
O thou undaunted daughter of desires!
By all thy dowr of LIGHTS & FIRES;
By all the eagle in thee, all the doue;
By all thy lives & deaths of loue;
By thy larg draughts of intellectuall day,
And by thy thirsts of love more large than they;
By all thy brim-fill'd Bowles of feirce desire
By thy last Morning's draught of liquid fire;
By the full kingdome of that finall kisse
That seiz'd thy parting Soul, and seal'd thee his;
By all the heav'ns thou hast in him
(Fair sister of the SERAPHIM!)
By all of HIM we have in THEE;
Leave nothing of my SELF in me.
Let me so read thy life, that I
Vnto all life of mine may dy.

As usual, however, it would be wrong to make a sharp, rigid identification at this point. Coleridge did not altogether approve of St. Teresa.[11] If Christabel has a strain of Teresa's whole-hearted, innocent love, moreover, she has other qualities in addition. Her temperament is altogether quieter than that of the Spanish saint; and this makes one suspect that she has her place in a series of characters which Coleridge had for some time been drawing, and which all represent, in some form or other, the 'child of nature'. Earlier figures in the series had been the foundling in *The Foster-Mother's Tale*, the 'gentle Maid' in *The Nightingale*, and the child, Enos, in *The Wanderings of Cain*; and they shared two particular qualities with Christabel: a love of nature by night, and an association with the moon. The foundling is described as having been[12]

A pretty boy, but most unteachable—
And never learnt a prayer, nor told a bead,
But knew the names of birds, and mock'd their notes,
And whistled, as he were a bird himself:

And all the autumn 'twas his only play
To get the seeds of wild flowers, and to plant them
With earth and water, on the stumps of trees.

Readers of Wordsworth will recognize touches of the 'child
of nature' described in book five of *The Prelude*, here[13]; the
last thing related of Coleridge's boy, however, is that he[14]

seiz'd a boat,
And all alone, set sail by silent moonlight
Up a great river, great as any sea,
And ne'er was heard of more: but 'tis suppos'd
He liv'd and died among the savage men.

Enos, in *The Wanderings of Cain*, is another child of
nature and lover of the moonlight. He is first shown[15]

plucking fruits
By moonlight, in a wilderness.

He loves the animals that he sees about him, and cannot
understand why they run away from him. In one respect,
also, he is an advance on the foster-child. The foster-child
suffers at the hands of Lord Velez, and subsequently the
latter feels the pangs of conscience, but there is no other
impact on him. Enos, on the other hand, is actively helping
and guiding Cain. 'A little further, O my father, yet a little
further, and we shall come into the open moonlight.'[16]

The Nightingale does not continue this line of development
for it contains no theme of guilt. The setting of the poem,
on the other hand, brings us close to the opening of *Christabel*
and the innocent maiden has clear affinities with the 'lovely
lady'.[17]

A most gentle Maid,
Who dwelleth in her hospitable home
Hard by the castle, and at latest eve
(Even like a Lady vowed and dedicate
To something more than Nature in the grove)
Glides through the pathways: she knows all their notes,
That gentle Maid! and oft, a moment's space,
What time the moon was lost behind a cloud,

Hath heard a pause of silence; till the moon
Emerging, hath awakened earth and sky
With one sensation, and those wakeful birds
Have all burst forth in choral minstrelsy,
As if some sudden gale had swept at once
A hundred airy harps! And she hath watched
Many a nightingale perch giddily
On blossomy twig still swinging from the breeze
And to that motion tune his wanton song
Like tipsy Joy that reels with tossing head.

A still more significant feature of this description is the
bringing together of the 'night-birds' and the 'Aeolian harp'
image. Coleridge, as we have already seen, was fond of using
the latter image to describe a state of harmony between the
human mind and *natura naturans*[18]: and it is therefore
reasonable to suppose that the 'tipsy Joy' of the night-birds
in *The Nightingale*, like the weaving water-snakes of *The
Ancient Mariner*, represents a vision of Nature in one of its
occasional moments of perfect harmony.[19]

The importance of this image is plain when we notice that
'night-birds' also appear in *Christabel*—but with a difference.
Instead of the melodious nightingales of the earlier poem,
Christabel has sombre owls; and whereas, in *The Ancient
Mariner* and *The Nightingale*, Aeolian imagery indicates the
central harmony of the poem, the owls of Tryermaine represent forces which are less easily defined. During the hour of
the night which was Geraldine's,[20]

By tairn and rill
The night-birds all that hour were still.
But now they are jubilant anew,
From cliff and tower, tu—whoo! tu—whoo! . . .

This suggests that the owls still represent good forces, but
differ from the nightingales in the way that the veiled moon
of the poem differs from the full moon: they are minimal
agents of good. The emergence of 'Aeolian' imagery in this
new form obviously has an importance for the poem as a
whole: among other things, it gives a binding force to our
view of Christabel as 'child of nature', and helps to suggest

how this aspect of her came to be linked with Teresa in Coleridge's mind. In his *Philosophical Lectures* of 1818, he related that at the time of his first interest in Teresa, he read of the importance which she attached to the sacraments and was led to think,[21]

. . . what if a mind like hers had attached anything like a religious meaning to the Aeolian harp, as she did to the crucifix and the holy water? What endless religious applications and accommodations all its irregular tones would produce!

Under this light, Christabel begins to emerge as a Teresa of Nature,[22]

> a lady vowed and dedicate
> To something more than Nature in the grove.

And, as usual, there is a direct relationship with Coleridge's immediate experience. At the time when he began *Christabel*, he was trying to educate Hartley, his son, as a 'child of nature'. It was in *The Nightingale*, significantly, that he wrote of his intention to make Hartley 'Nature's playmate', and told how he had once stopped his crying by taking him out into the moonlight. At the same time there is a hint that he saw Hartley's simple intuitive innocence as a guide for his own intellectual gropings, just as Enos guided Cain towards the light. In this way, his speculations mingled with the direct experience of his own relationship with Hartley in helping to mould the character and function of Christabel in the poem. The latter influence, which is in the background throughout, emerges into explicit statement at the end of part two, where a description of his occasional anger with Hartley, and possible reasons for it, is thrust in as a commentary on Sir Leoline's anger with Christabel.[23]

Although Christabel may have the innocence of a child, however, she is in all other respects a fully grown woman— even a priestess of the supernatural; and we must therefore consider whether the mythological lore which we have discussed in previous chapters is not relevant to her. From the Teresa of Nature, suffering for her lover far away, it is, after all, a single step to Isis, seeking her lost Osiris.

If this identification is to be made, however, the imagery
of the poem suggests that Coleridge is producing the myth
in a strangely inverted form. The moon of this poem is not a
crescent, but a full moon veiled and distorted; and this is
significant. The image of sun or moon veiled by cloud is one
which Coleridge uses with great frequency to express his
view that apparent evils are really good seen in distortion.
For example[24]:

> Life is a vision shadowy of Truth;
> And vice, and anguish, and the wormy grave,
> Shapes of a dream! The veiling clouds retire,
> And lo! The Throne of the redeeming God
> Forth flashing unimaginable day
> Wraps in one blaze earth, heaven, and deepest hell.
>
> *(Religious Musings)*

or

> But chiefly this, him First, him Last to view
> Through meaner powers and secondary things
> Effulgent, as through clouds that veil his blaze,
> For all that meets the bodily sense I deem
> Symbolical, one mighty alphabet
> For infant minds . . .
>
> *(The Destiny of Nations)*

The image appears frequently in his prose works. In an
appendix to *The Statesman's Manual*, he says,[25] '. . . if the
light be received by faith, to such understandings it delegates
the privilege to become sons of God, . . . expanding while it
elevates, even as the beams of the sun incorporate with the
mist, and make its natural darkness and earthly nature the
bearer and interpreter of their own glory.' And in a manuscript note he writes,[26] 'O! if Love sanctioned Desire (or
rather, as the rising Sun shoots thro' and saturates with rich
light the Cloud that veils it, took up and transfigured Desire
into its own Being) then, then I should appear such as I
should always be. . . .' From this it is clear that clouds and
mist have for him the ambivalence of the daemonic. They
may be robes of transfiguration, through which the sun
reveals itself in glory, or they may be misty exhalations,
apparitions of evil,[27] 'the shaping Mist, which the Light had

drawn upward from *the Ground* (i.e. from the mere Animal nature and instinct), and which that Light alone had made visible. . ."

In *Christabel*, it is the element of distortion, not of revelation, which dominates the moon-imagery. The change is emphasized by a slight alteration in the description of the moon from its initial formulation in the Gutch notebook. There Coleridge had written,[28]

> Behind the thin
> Grey cloud that cover'd but not hid the sky
> The round full moon look'd small.

In *Christabel*, this becomes,[29]

> The thin gray cloud is spread on high,
> It covers but not hides the sky.
> The moon is behind, and at the full;
> And yet she looks both small and dull . . .

The introduction of the word 'dull' links the passage with the later description of Geraldine 'looking askance' at Christabel[30]:

> A snake's small eye blinks dull and shy;
> And the lady's eyes they shrunk in her head,
> Each shrunk up to a serpent's eye . . .

A conscious parallel is evidently intended between the sinister veiling of the moon and the veiling of Geraldine's 'large bright eyes divine'. Both Geraldine and Christabel are related to the moon of the poem, in fact, but in different ways: Geraldine is the daemonic spirit, veiling herself until she assumes the appearance of evil, while Christabel, unconsciously imitating her gestures, is the human Isis who suffers these daemonic ravages, takes them into her own nature, and eventually transfigures them into good. And in a mysterious way, this acts for 'the weal of her lover that's far away'—probably by transfiguring his desire into true love, and reviving the lost Osiris within him.

The owls, as we have seen, help to underline this element of masked good, and it is possible that they also have a more specific significance in the poem. Coleridge twice used the idea of the owl as bird of wisdom in light poems written at this time,[31] and the fact of its sacredness to Athena would bring it into line with the general symbolism of *Christabel*. When the owls awaken the cock (bird of Osiris) it only crows drowsily. Such an interpretation gives point to the atmosphere of mystery and moral ambiguity which is already potent in the image.

I am inclined to think that further mythological signifficances were also present in Coleridge's mind. His view of the myth of Cupid and Psyche as a neoplatonic attempt to account for the fall of man, for example,[32] seems relevant to this poem, for Christabel is the observe of Psyche. Psyche, by her lack of trust, drove away her lover. Christabel, by receiving Geraldine (who actually possesses the serpentine nature which Psyche wrongly suspected in Cupid), shows an innocent trust which helps to restore her absent lover.

A further, more tentative parallel between the two myths may be drawn. Psyche, in the course of her wanderings, descended to the dark regions of Hades. There Proserpine gave her a dark box, which she opened on her return, expecting to receive a portion of the divine beauty; instead, however, she fell into an infernal Stygian sleep. Taylor comments,[33]

> This obscurely signifies, that the soul, by considering a corporeal life as truly beautiful, passes into a profoundly dormant state.

Christabel, likewise, is given a substance of magical qualities: the cordial made by her mother. Instead of using it for herself, however, she gives it to the stranger Geraldine, and achieves vicariously the result which Psyche had sought for herself—for Geraldine receives the 'divine beauty'.[34]

> Her fair large eyes 'gan glitter bright,
> And from the floor whereon she sank,
> The lofty lady stood upright:
> She was most beautiful to see,
> Like a lady of a far countrée.

The glittering eye is by now familiar to us as a Coleridgean symbol of the supernatural—and here the hint is reinforced. On both occasions when Geraldine drinks the cordial, she is betrayed temporarily into a sympathy with Christabel's mother and the forces of good, which passes with the effects of the wine.

The possible link here with Psyche and Proserpine is perhaps tenuous, but is mentioned because there is another reason for associating Christabel with Proserpine. The mastiff bitch which guards Sir Leoline's castle reminds us that Pluto's stronghold, also, was guarded by a mastiff. He had figured, indeed, in a translation of Bürger's poem, 'The *Menagerie* of the Gods', which Coleridge would have read in the *Monthly Magazine* for May, 1796.[35]

> At Pluto's black gate, in a kennel at rest,
>   A mastiff so grim has his station,
> That fearful of reaching the fields of the blest,
>   Some ghosts have made choice of damnation.

The grim castle of Tryermaine has certain resemblances to Hades, which are strengthened by Sir Leoline's obsession with death.[36]

> Each matin bell, the Baron saith,
> Knells us back to a world of death.

The 'one last leaf, the last of its clan' also is part of a favourite Coleridgean image for that mockery of life which is really death. It reminds us of the 'products of the mere *reflective* faculty', which 'partook of DEATH, and were as the rattling twigs and sprays in winter'.[37] And in a later notebook, describing the 'dedication of all ranks . . . to the fiend Mammon, and the fiend-hag, Anxiety', he says: 'The Men are corpses: while the Charnel-house, the Dry Bones, are dancing and eddying like the fallen leaves, with which the Gust of November strikes up a mockery of Life.'[38]

It seems clear that the world of Tryermaine is a world of death, therefore, and one cannot help wondering whether Coleridge did not intend a connection with Greek mythology. Pluto, it will be remembered, carried off Proserpine while she was gathering wild flowers—an action of the 'Fancy' which reminds one both of the Mariner shooting the albatross and of the theory discussed earlier whereby the Fall was

from Love to Lust.[39] There is the possibility of a detailed
connection, as this interpretation would make Christabel's
mother identifiable with Proserpine, and the 'wild-flower
wine' bequeathed by her would fall neatly into the pattern,
as a symbol of lost innocence. Since first formulating this
theory, moreover, I have come across a passage in a late
notebook which shows that Coleridge sometimes thought of
this myth in allegorical terms[40]:

> The Manichæan Error consists in ante-dating Nature
> —i.e. characterizing the Base or Ground-stuff (?) under
> the name of that which began to exist only by the super-
> induction and combination of an Antagonist Element—
> in denouncing Nature as if she had remained Hades. The
> Desiderium of Proserpine charmed up the dark King into
> the sunny flower-field of Enna: that he carried her down
> with him, sunk down again to the Region of Hollowness
> and endless Burning—the fiery Esurience, was the Fall.

This line of interpretation is inviting, but is of course
slightly peripheral to the poem as we have it. A further
identification on these lines may be made between Sir
Leoline and Cain, for Christabel, like Enos in *The Wanderings of Cain*, is both the innocent 'child of nature' and a
redeeming force in presence of her father's hopelessness and
grief. But it is time for us to develop a full interpretation of
the evil, negative forces in the poem, which will find a place
for these various tributary symbolisms.

Such an interpretation may be introduced by considering
Coleridge's detailed plans for the poem's development, as
they have come down to us. Here there are two main
sources. The first is a brief entry in a notebook of 1823[41]:

> Were I free to do so, I feel as if I could compose the third
> part of Christabel, or the song of her desolation.

The second is the lengthy plan of the poem's future
course, which Coleridge gave to Gillman[42]:

> Over the mountains, the Bard, as directed by Sir
> Leoline, 'hastes' with his disciple; but in consequence of
> one of those inundations supposed to be common to this

country, the spot only where the castle once stood is discovered,—the edifice itself being washed away. He determines to return. Geraldine being acquainted with all that is passing, like the Weird Sisters in Macbeth, vanishes. Re-appearing, however, she waits the return of the Bard, exciting in the mean time, by her wily arts, all the anger she could rouse in the Baron's breast, as well as that jealousy of which he is described to have been susceptible. The old Bard and the youth at length arrive, and therefore she can no longer personate the character of Geraldine, the daughter of Lord Roland de Vaux, but changes her appearance to that of the accepted though absent lover of Christabel. Next ensues a courtship most distressing to Christabel, who feels—she knows not why —great disgust for her once favoured knight. This coldness is very painful to the Baron, who has no more conception than herself of the supernatural transformation. She at last yields to her father's entreaties, and consents to approach the altar with this hated suitor. The real lover returning, enters at this moment, and produces the ring which she had once given him in sign of her betrothment. Thus defeated, the supernatural being Geraldine disappears. As predicted, the castle bell tolls, the mother's voice is heard, and to the exceeding great joy of the parties, the rightful marriage takes place, after which follows a reconciliation and explanation between the father and daughter.

This may well represent Coleridge's sincere plan for the poem's development, but being a bare narrative, it leaves some important questions unanswered. It establishes the relationship between Geraldine and the absent lover more firmly, by making Geraldine actually assume his form; but it does not explain how or why the lover was to be benefited or restored by Christabel. In other words, it represents the plot of the poem, without telling us how the symbolic structure of the poem would have been developed and finally resolved. How is it, for example, that Geraldine is 'a spirit, executing her task with right good will'?

The question remains unanswered, and we can only

return to the completed parts of the poem for hints as to how Geraldine's nature was meant to be understood. Nethercot has quoted some variant lines from *The Destiny of Nations* which are relevant to the subject—the lines where Coleridge describes those 'Beings of higher class than Man', who make[43]

> Of transient Evil ever-during Good
> Themselves probationary, and denied
> Confess'd to view by preternatural deed
> To o'erwhelm the will, save on some fated day . . .

There is, indeed, every reason to think of Geraldine as a daemonic being: particularly as she possesses that ambivalence which we have already noticed as characteristic of the daemonic nature. The wild-flower wine raises her to her full heavenly stature, and if she relapses from it immediately afterwards, it is not without a struggle[44]:

> Deep from within she seems half-way
> To lift some weight with sick assay,
> And eyes the maid and seeks delay;

It is only by summoning up 'scorn and pride', (primary characteristics of the fallen angel) that she is able to resume her purpose, and lie down with Christabel.

Nethercot also argues at some length that Geraldine was intended to be a vampire—probably the first in English literature. There is strong supporting evidence for this in the well-known incident where Shelley, hearing the poem read aloud, rushed from the room, declaring afterwards that he had seen eyes in the breasts of Mary Godwin. To have eyes in the breasts is a characteristic of the vampire, and Shelley had evidently interpreted Geraldine in this light.[45]

To stress this element too strongly, however, is probably to mistake Coleridge's main intention. It was well understood at the time that the art of the supernatural writer lay in keeping his reader 'on the very edge and confines of the world of spirits'. 'The secret,' said a contemporary reviewer,[46] 'which the reader thinks himself every instant on the point of penetrating, flies like a phantom before him, and eludes his eagerness till the very last moment of protracted expectation.' In the case of Christabel, moreover, one is not sure whether Coleridge would have revealed Geraldine's secret even then. It seems likely, on the contrary, that he wished to make the evil side of her nature deliberately ambiguous. If the tree where she is found helps to suggest the serpentine, the general location of the poem's action suggests a different form of daemon. One does not normally find serpents in northern climates, but one does find wolves: and I suspect that there is an element of the werewolf,[47] as well as the serpent, in Geraldine's depravity.

In Tooke's *Pantheon*, which Coleridge pored over at school, there is mention of a figure which fits this idea and relates it to Coleridge's theme. Scylla, the figure in question, is described as having the upper parts resembling a woman, and lower parts resembling a serpent and a wolf: she is identified by Tooke with lust.[48] Alongside this, we may place a passage which E. H. Coleridge quotes from *Mizaldus Redivivus*[49]:

When Alexander the Great was in the East the King of Inde presented him with a damsel of singular beauty and comeliness. Fair though she was she had been reared and nourished on the poisonous wolf's bane, and mischief and treachery lurked in the gift. Now it chanced that Aristotle when he looked at the maiden perceived that one moment her eyes blazed and sparked, and then blinked and closed like the eyes of a snake.

The parallel with Geraldine is close. It is related just after this, moreover, that 'as many as wooed the damsel were smitten of her poison and died'. This, it will be remembered, was also the case with Sarah in the *Book of Tobit*, which we earlier suggested Coleridge to have read as an allegory of love and lust.[50]

There is, of course, one difficulty raised by the discussion so far. How is it possible to combine the characteristics of serpent and wolf *visibly*? Are we to suppose that Coleridge was thinking so abstractly that the point did not occur to him?

It would be tempting to do so, but if we did, we should be wrong. The point had been nagging at the back of my mind when, just before going to press, my attention was drawn to a collection of Coleridge's poems which contained his own manuscript corrections. And there I found his description of Geraldine altered to read as follows[51]:

> ... and full in view,
> Behold! her bosom and half her side—
> It was dark & rough as the Sea-Wolf's hide
> A sight to dream of, not to tell!

The combination of vulpine and reptilian characteristics is completed neatly in this image. Coleridge, as always in his great poetry, is thinking as vividly as he is thinking subtly.

Apart from this image, however, it is the snake-imagery of the poem which dominates the portrayal of Geraldine; and the evil element in her personality is thus related to a concept of evil which, in previous chapters, we saw Coleridge eliciting from his study of Boehme and the mythologists. The evil of Geraldine is 'daemonic' evil: it is the unrestrained riot of that which, properly tempered, is a necessary and indispensable element in the good.

And it is in precisely these terms that Christabel is intended to redeem the daemonic evil—she is to accept it, subsume it, and finally transfigure it. The daemonic must nevertheless enter her so deeply that she takes on, temporarily, its actual appearance to unenlightened eyes. Her involuntary imitation of Geraldine's snake-like behaviour deceives even her own father.

In the first of these silent struggles between Christabel and Geraldine, neither principle is victorious. The position is stated accurately in Bracy's dream, a central statement of the poem's imagery[52]:

> ... in my sleep I saw that dove,
> That gentle bird, whom thou dost love,
> And call'st by thy own daughter's name—
> Sir Leoline! I saw the same,
> Fluttering and uttering fearful moan,
> Among the green herbs in the forest alone ...
> I stooped, methought, the dove to take,
> When lo! I saw a bright green snake

Coiled around its wings and neck.
Green as the herbs on which it couched,
Close by the dove's its head it crouched;
And with the dove it heaves and stirs,
Swelling its neck as she swelled hers!

This dream, describing Christabel's sufferings, only adds
to Sir Leoline's misunderstanding of the position, for he
identifies the dove not with her, but Geraldine. He is
distressed and angered when Christabel again behaves like a
snake and confirms him in his misapprehension.

The image of the snake struggling with the bird occurs
elsewhere in Coleridge's writings. A notebook entry describes his opium-taking and its causes, as follows[53]:

I have never loved Evil for it's own sake; no! nor ever
sought pleasure for it's own sake, but only as the means of
escaping from pains that coiled round my mental powers,
as a serpent around the body & wings of an Eagle! My
sole sensuality was *not* to be in pain!—

The same metaphor is used, tightly compressed, in
Dejection: an Ode[54]:

Hence, viper thoughts, that coil around my mind,
Reality's dark dream!

Earlier, it had appeared in the description of the desolation
through which Cain passed, in *The Wanderings of Cain*[55]:

Never morning lark had poised himself over this desert;
but the huge serpent often hissed there beneath the talons
of the vulture, and the vulture screamed, his wings
imprisoned within the coils of the serpent.

Nethercot has shown several places where this image
occurred in Coleridge's reading, and it is only necessary to
add to his list Plutarch's description of a 'River-Horse', with
a hawk on its back fighting a serpent, which he interpreted
as a symbol of Typhon's misuse of power.[56]

In *Christabel*, of course, there is one important difference.
The struggle is not violent, but gentle, insidious: Christabel
is not hawk or vulture, but dove.

The figure of Bracy seems subordinate when one reads
Christabel for the first time, but the importance of his dream
suggests that Coleridge was planning to give him a more
important rôle as the poem progressed. When Derwent
Coleridge was born in September, 1800, his father called
him 'Bracy' in various notebook entries[57]: and we know from
elsewhere of the peculiar veneration which he attached to the
figure of the 'bard'.

Bracy's poetic insight, as displayed in his dream, is
followed immediately by his bardic plan for exorcising any
evil spirit that may linger in the woods. The plan, however,
is brusquely rejected by the Baron[58]:

> 'Sweet maid, Lord Roland's beauteous dove,
> With arms more strong than harp or song,
> Thy sire and I will crush the snake!'

Sir Leoline thus stands revealed as the Typhonian male.
His reliance on force to win his ends recalls Boehme's Cain,
who also set out to crush the serpent—but succeeded only
in killing his innocent brother Abel.[59] Sir Leoline is in equal
danger of crushing Christabel. He is like the Cain of Gessner's *Death of Abel*, who inquires contemptuously, 'Does the
towering eagle coo like the timorous dove?'[60]

In contrast to this, Bracy's plan for overcoming the evil
forces reminds us[61] significantly of Coleridge's early speculations[62]:

> '. . . I vowed this self-same day
> With music strong and saintly song
> To wander through the forest bare,
> Lest aught unholy loiter there.'

The serpent is not to be crushed, but charmed by the
power of music. This is Coleridge the harmonist speaking.
He is advocating that the method of Typhon be replaced by
the way of Osiris, who, according to Plutarch,[63]

> . . . travelled over the rest of the world, inducing the
> people every where to submit to his discipline, not indeed
> compelling them by force of arms, but persuading them
> to yield to the strength of his reasons, which were con-

veyed to them in the most agreeable manner, in hymns and songs accompanied with instruments of music: from which last circumstance, the Greeks conclude him to have been the same person with their *Dionysius* or *Bacchus*. . . .

. . . . . .

At this point, the poem reaches its abrupt cessation, and it is not easy to decide how the patterns of imagery so far raised in the poem would have been eventually resolved. Nevertheless, one or two suggestions can be offered with some confidence.

The serpent imagery of the poem would clearly have appeared again, but with some development to illustrate the subjugation of evil. One of Boehme's memorial emblems, we may recall, was that of the eagle, with the serpent in its talons, gazing at the sun[64]: and this image, suggesting the conquest of evil by a combination of power and insight, might well have had its place.

Another favourite image of Coleridge's, which he might have used in some way, was that of the divine man or god wrestling with and overcoming the serpent. He used it several times in later years to describe Humphry Davy, whom he felt to be in danger of becoming a 'Theo-Mammonist', and allowing the age to strangle him. 'I see two Serpents at the cradle of his genius,' he wrote, '. . . but the Hercules will strangle both the reptile monsters.'[65] And again,[66]

> Davy . . . seems more and more determined to mould himself upon the Age in order to make the Age mould itself upon him. . . . And as I once before said, may that Serpent, the World, climb around the Club, which supports him, & be the symbol of Healing—even as if in Tooke's Pantheon you may see the thing *done* to your eyes in the Picture of Esculapius.

A simple resolution of the imagery of *Christabel* in such terms is, however, hardly possible if, as seems likely, Coleridge wished not only to bring out the active virtue of his heroine, but also to lay particular stress upon her passive virtue as innocent child of nature. It seems possible that not she but her lover was intended to be the protagonist of active virtue: or it may be that Coleridge intended Christabel to display both active and passive power until the actual return of her lover—the point when[67]

> ... Love rose glittering, and his gorgeous wings
> Over the abyss fluttered ...

Her work thus accomplished, Christabel would then be enabled to assume her normal feminine rôle of passive innocence.

Such speculations, however, lead one to wonder whether the imagery of the poem could have been worked out convincingly in the manner suggested. Just how could Christabel's sufferings have been made to serve 'the weal of her lover'?

The question is a pressing one, and I am inclined to think that Coleridge had set himself an insoluble problem in the poem as we have it. He had, in fact, raised the problem which is involved as soon as we ask how innocence can ever redeem experience. The problem is not peculiar to Coleridge: it runs through the whole of Victorian literature, and remains unsolved. It is the central problem involved in creating a doctrine of redemption when good and evil are identified with innocence and experience respectively.

For most Victorian writers, however, the problem was not so complicated as for Coleridge. They mostly followed the pattern which he had used in writing *Osorio*, whereby innocence, by virtue of its own innate appeal, must necessarily awaken remorse in the evil-doer. The result is that they created complete works, but works which often carry little conviction for the modern reader. Very often the whole weight of a Victorian novel, for example, will fall upon a small incident which is not strong enough to carry it—some incident which relies on the assumption that evil must needs respond to virtue—and that the highest form of virtue is, necessarily, innocent virtue.

For Coleridge, writing *Christabel*, however, there were further complications. He had evolved a system of good and evil by which evil was the basis of good, which had become separated from its true functioning and now existed autonomously. It is Christabel's task to bring back this evil 'ground' into its proper place, to raise it to its true angelic stature. But at the same time, Coleridge was sufficiently tied to the morality of his age to feel that this process could not be carried out in her consciousness. In consequence, he was reduced to the task of making it take place, by some means, in her unconscious. And it is difficult to see how he could have solved the problem posed by this demand.

It is interesting to notice that a romantic writer without this particular inhibition finds no difficulty in working out an appropriate redemptive pattern. D. H. Lawrence used very much the same pattern of imagery as Coleridge: for him, also, the snake was a symbol of moral ambivalence— of apparent evil, representing the necessary potency of good. But he is quite content that the mind should take up experience of this 'evil ground' into its consciousness.[68]

> If there is a serpent of secret and shameful desire in my soul, let me not beat it out of my consciousness with sticks. It will lie beyond, in the marsh of the so-called subconsciousness, where I cannot follow it with my sticks. Let me bring it to the fire to see what it is. For a serpent is a thing created. It has its own *raison d'être*. In its own being it has beauty and reality. Even my horror is a tribute to its reality. And I must admit the genuineness of my horror, accept it, and not exclude it from my understanding.

The result of this attitude, expressed also in his poem *Snake*, is that this particular problem and imagery involve no difficulties for Lawrence. He can in fact use it at length in a novel such as *The Plumed Serpent*. Coleridge, on the other hand, can accept the potential beauty of the serpent as a concept, but shrinks from drawing the logical conclusion of such acceptance. In consequence, the 'evil' remains in Christabel's unconscious and the poem remains incomplete.

This theory is supported by the fact that Coleridge did not stop writing poetry of the type of *Christabel*. On the contrary, one is surprised to find him, nearly twenty years later, composing *Zapolya*, a full-length verse play which incorporates many of the themes and images of the earlier poem.[69] The soldier who wishes to crush the 'venomous snake', his enemy, fails: the victory is won by Sarolya, who is described as having a dove-like capacity to detect evil, despite her own innocent nature, and Glycine, child of nature, who succeeds in killing the real traitor and is eulogized at the end of the play as

Thou sword that leapd'st forth from a bed of roses:
Thou falcon-hearted dove.

There is an important difference in this play, however. Although the images are often the same as in *Christabel*, they are used rhetorically: they are not a necessary part of the working out of the poem's meaning. The attempt to achieve such an integration of imagery in the intellectual structure of a poem had failed, for reasons which we have examined. 'The reason of my not finishing *Christabel*', said Coleridge, a year before his death, 'is not, that I don't know how to do it —for I have, as I always had, the whole plan entire from beginning to end in my mind; but I fear I could not carry on with equal success the execution of the idea, an extremely subtle and difficult one.'[70]

Nevertheless, if the attempt to represent redemption of evil by innocence was the rock on which the poem foundered, parts of Coleridge's intention shine clear through the achieved poetry and the projected conclusion. Like *The Ancient Mariner*, it was to have represented evil as something which was not completely separate from good, but a distortion of it, a lapse of daemonic energies. The way to deal with such evil was not to crush it, but to temper it, harmonize it, and raise it to its proper heavenly stature.

Coleridge's theory of good and evil, like all his theories, was thus dominated by the necessity for all-inclusiveness. It is the same spirit which made him unable to produce poetry of the imaginative order of *The Ancient Mariner*, *Christabel* and *Kubla Khan* unless his reasoning and inquiring powers were also at full stretch. But between the vision and the achievement there often lay an impassable barrier. In the case of *Christabel*, as we have seen, it was the working through that was difficult—the idea, on the other hand, was

197

straightforward, and had in fact been expressed succinctly in some lines from *Religious Musings*[71]:

> Thus from the Elect, regenerate through faith,
> Pass the dark Passions and what thirsty cares
> Drink up the spirit, and the dim regards
> Self-centre. Lo they vanish! or acquire
> New names, new features—by supernal grace
> Enrobed with Light, and naturalised in Heaven.

Chapter VII

THE RIVER AND THE CAVERNS

'I had been thinking all the time, while I was asleep, of what I had just been reading, but my thoughts had run into a channel of their own, until I myself seemed actually to have become the subject of my book . . .'

Proust: *A la Recherche du Temps Perdu*: Overture

KUBLA KHAN is a poem surrounded by mystery, and an important element in the mystery is Coleridge's own reticence on the subject. He never referred to it in any of his letters or published works, except on the occasion when he wrote a preface for it on its first publication in 1816. The account which he then gave of its origins is well known[1]:

In the summer of the year 1797, the Author, then in ill health, had retired to a lonely farm-house between Porlock and Linton, on the Exmoor confines of Somerset and Devonshire. In consequence of a slight indisposition, an anodyne had been prescribed, from the effects of which he fell asleep in his chair at the moment that he was reading the following sentence, or words of the same substance, in 'Purchas's Pilgrimage': 'Here the Khan Kubla commanded a palace to be built, and a stately garden thereunto. And thus ten miles of fertile ground were inclosed with a wall.' The Author continued for about three hours in a profound sleep, at least of the external senses, during which time he has the most vivid confidence, that he could not have composed less than from two to three hundred lines; if that indeed can be called composition in which all the images rose up before him as *things*, with a parallel production of the correspondent expressions, without any sensation or consciousness of effort. On awaking he appeared to himself to have a distinct recollection of the whole, and taking his pen, ink, and paper, instantly and eagerly wrote down the lines that are here preserved. At this moment he was unfortunately called out by a person on business from Porlock, and detained by him above an hour, and on his return to his room, found, to his no small surprise and mortification, that though he still retained some vague and dim recollection of the general purport of the vision, yet, with the exception of some eight or ten scattered lines and images, all the rest had passed away like the images on the surface of a stream into which a stone has been cast, but, alas! without the after restoration of the latter! . . .

Yet from the still surviving recollections in his mind, the Author has frequently purposed to finish for himself what had been originally, as it were, given to him . . . but the tomorrow is yet to come.

The account has sometimes been criticized, in substance or in detail, but the accumulation of various pieces of evidence has tended to confirm many features of it. In a notebook of 1810 he wrote of a quarrel with Charles Lloyd, and the effort involved in his forbearance,[2] '. . . it prevented my finishing the Christabel—& at the retirement between Linton & Porlock was the first occasion of my having recourse to Opium'. A year or two later, Collier records that he recited[3] 'some lines he had written many years ago upon the building of a Dream-palace by Kubla-Khan: He had founded it on a passage he had met with in an old book of travels'. In a recently recovered fragment of his table talk, in 1830, he said,[4] 'I wrote *Kubla Khan* in Brimstone Farm between Porlock and Ilfracombe—near Culbone'. Further evidence is provided by his desire to live near Porlock after his return from Germany,[5] and by the coming to light of the Crewe holograph manuscript, with its independent account of the writing of the poem, as follows[6]:

This fragment with a good deal more, not recoverable, composed, in a sort of Reverie brought on by two grains of Opium taken to check a dysentery, at a Farm House between Porlock & Linton, a quarter of a mile from Culbone Church, in the fall of the year, 1797.

Various attempts have been made to assign other dates to the poem, but without carrying complete conviction: E. K.

Chambers, who examined the question more thoroughly and over a longer period than anyone else, finally came to favour a date early in October, 1797.[7] On the 14th of that month, Coleridge wrote to Thelwall, mentioning that he had 'been absent a day or two', and that he was sending off the completed *Osorio*; he also made some remarks about the state of mind which was necessary in him before rocks, waterfalls, mountains or caverns could give him the sense of sublimity or majesty.[8]

H. M. Margoliouth has suggested that the retirement might have taken place in the course of a walking expedition with the Wordsworths, pointing out that Culbone seems a long way for a retirement from Stowey, whereas it would be on the route of a trip to, say, the Valley of Rocks.[9] There are certain objections to this theory, however. The main one is the presence of the copy of Purchas. No one would be likely to carry such a great folio volume on a walking expedition pure and simple, though Coleridge did sometimes carry books with him when it was strictly necessary.[10] I am inclined to think it more likely that the retirement was deliberate, Coleridge's intention being to get away from domestic anxieties for a while and complete *Osorio* in peace. In this case, he might well have taken Purchas with him as a potential source of local colour and Oriental imagery.

But can we accept the statement that the poem was composed in a 'Reverie'? The point is a difficult one, but the various name-fabrications, and a certain inconsequence, superficially, in the poem's action, suggest that the poem was in fact composed in something less than a state of full consciousness, whatever the reason may have been. With the example of George Dyer's artificially stimulated induced states of poetic creativity before us, of course,[11] we may well wonder whether the laudanum might not have been taken for help in writing poetry: but this is an issue which is unlikely ever to be clarified.

Although the circumstances in which the poem was written are a matter of great interest, however, it is not necessary to prove, for the purposes of the present study, that the poem was written at any particular time or place, or even that it was written in a dream. The interpretation which follows does, however, rest on the theory that however it was composed, *Kubla Khan* the poem is not a meaningless reverie, but a poem so packed with meaning as to render detailed elucidation extremely difficult. It will be suggested that many of the images in the poem can be related to several patterns of meaning which run parallel and are held together not by the 'story', but by a separate argument which runs through the poem, at times explicitly stated, at times implicit in the imagery.

The idea that very intricate mental processes can take place in states of imperfect consciousness may be surprising at first sight, but there is substantial evidence to support it. Dalbiez, in the course of a long discussion on the subject, gives two good examples of such phenomena[12]:

. . . the dreamer passes by association from one image to another; he uses relations, but he does not isolate them; he does not understand them. On the other hand the scientist, after the action of the unconscious relation has caused the rise of a new idea, perceives the relation as a thing apart; he understands. Discovery, in fact, is made in two stages. The first stage is comparable to the evocation with unconsciousness of the relation in the case of the animal or the dreamer, but with this difference that concepts of a high order of abstraction are involved. The second stage is strictly rational, the intellection of relation considered simply in itself as a thing apart. Sometimes discovery consists in the rising-up process and the intellectual appreciation of a relation between two ideas already possessed; the unconscious action of the relation is then confined to the appropriate evocation. The accounts given by Poincaré of the origin of several of his discoveries seem to show that their origins can be traced to a process of this kind. The discovery of several structural schemata by Kékulé seems to have been brought about by a process whereby relational unconsciousness has developed into the creation of a new schema. He was dozing on the top of an omnibus, and atoms were dancing before his eyes, first two and two and then in groups of three or four. He spent most of the night working out on paper the hypnagogic or oneiric images which had thus appeared to him, and in the morning he had the result. Another time the process was even more definitive. Atoms were again dancing before his eyes; they executed a snake-like movement, then the snake bit its own tail. Kékulé suddenly awoke with the impression of illumination, and spent the rest of the night in perfecting his idea. 'Let us learn to dream, gentlemen,' the great chemist concluded, 'and perhaps the truth will come to us while we sleep; but do not let us publish our dreams before having passed them through the sieve of the waking reason.'

Both the dreamers cited by Dalbiez were scientists, which strengthens the theory that there is a kinship between creative intellectual processes in different fields. In view of Coleridge's observations on the ideal form of epic poetry, Kékulé's vision, where the snake actually bit its own tail, is particularly interesting.

For further comment on the place of reason in certain forms of dream, we may go to a poet singularly close to Coleridge in nature. Yeats's views on this subject have been recorded as follows by L. A. G. Strong[13]:

[Yeats's] insistence on the function of intellect in the writing of poetry is of particular interest to us today, when poetry has tended to divide itself into two camps, with purely cerebral work at one extreme and dithyrambic excitement at the other. Yeats would never allow this division. I remember telling him one evening about a phase in the work of that fine lyric poet, Wilfred Rowland Childe, who died less than two years ago. Childe was devoutly religious, and a medievalist. He had been favoured with a number of visionary poems during a period of strong inspiration, in which he seemed to have little to do but record what presented itself so splendidly before him. The period passed and, hoping to regain it, Childe formed the habit of inducing in himself a kind of trance, a suspension of the faculties almost like that of a medium.

Yeats strongly condemned this passive approach to the problem of poetic composition. 'The only legitimate passivity is that which follows exhaustion of the intellect. Then guidance comes.' He saw the whole thing as a struggle in which all the poet's faculties were united in order to grasp, receive, and wrestle with the visiting angel of inspiration. Intellect could never be left out, at any stage of the process, and it always had the final task of editing and polishing the poem so that it could stand the world's inspection. One had to remember the world, and do all that integrity allowed and courtesy enjoined in order to meet it. The thought of the poem might be difficult, but the syntax should be clear.

Coleridge was aware that the solution of a problem in the mind sometimes comes as an image: and there is a passage elsewhere in his writings which is in close parallel with Yeats's views—particularly his comments on the 'exhaustion of the intellect'. It is his attempt, in *The Friend*, to offer a psychological explanation of Luther's celebrated vision of the Devil.

The interest of the passage for our purposes is twofold. Firstly, the circumstances in which Coleridge places Luther correspond in two ways with those of his own 'retirement' at Culbone: he is poring over an old book, and is conscious of past quarrels and disputes. Secondly, there is a correspondence in the language used by Coleridge to interpret both events. In composing *Kubla Khan*, he says, all the images rose up before him 'as *things*, with a parallel production of the correspondent expressions, without any sensation or consciousness of effort'. In the account of Luther's vision, it is supposed that 'he sinks, without perceiving it, into a Trance of Slumber: during which his brain retains its waking energies, except that what would have been mere *Thoughts* before, now (the action and counterweight of his outward senses . . . being withdrawn) shape and condense themselves into *Things*, into Realities!' Images in the one case, thoughts in the other, 'rise up as things'; and in Luther's case, the process is supposed to follow exhaustion of the intellect[14]:

Methinks I see him sitting, the heroic Student, in his Chamber in the Warteburg, with his midnight Lamp before him, seen by the late Traveller in the distant Plain of *Bischofsrode*, as a Star on the Mountain! Below it lies the Hebrew Bible open, on which he gazes, his brow pressing on his palm, brooding over some obscure Text, which he desires to make plain to the simple Boor and to the humble Artizan, and to transfer its whole force into their own natural and living Tongue. And he himself does not understand it! Thick Darkness lies on the original Text: he counts the Letters, he calls up the Roots of each separate Word, and questions them as the familiar Spirits of an Oracle. In vain! thick Darkness continues to cover it! . . . With sullen and angry Hope he reaches for the VULGATE, his old and sworn enemy, the treacherous confederate of the Roman Antichrist. . . .

(The Vulgate, he discovers, has an interpretation which favours Romish doctrines: the Septuagint offers no help.)

Disappointed, despondent, enraged, ceasing to *think*, yet continuing his brain on the stretch, in solicitation of a thought; and gradually giving himself up to angry Fancies, to recollections of past persecutions, to uneasy Fears, and inward Defiances, and floating Images of the evil Being, their supposed personal Author; he sinks, without perceiving it, into a Trance of Slumber: during which his brain retains its waking energies, except that what would have been mere *Thoughts* before, now (the action and counterweight of his outward senses and their impressions being withdrawn) shape and condense themselves into *Things*, into Realities! Repeatedly half-wakening, and his eyelids as often re-closing, the objects which really surround him form the place and scenery of his Dream. All at once he sees the Arch-fiend coming forth on the Wall of the Room, from the very spot perhaps, on which his Eyes had been fixed vacantly during the perplexed moments of his former Meditation: the Ink-stand, which he had at the same time been using, becomes associated with it: and in that struggle of Rage, which in these distempered Dreams almost constantly precedes the helpless Terror by the pain of which we are finally awakened, he *imagines* that he hurls it at the Intruder, or not improbably in the first instant of awakening, while yet both his imagination and his eyes are possessed by the Dream, he *actually* hurls it!

This account does not correspond in all details, of course, but it is close enough to make one ask whether *Kubla Khan* may not have been, like Kékulé's dream, the resolution of a series of images which had been up till then the subject of intense thought on Coleridge's part. If so, it might be possible to trace a coherent and logical shape there, instead of merely the 'unchecked subliminal flow of blending images' which Lowes found.[15] And in that case, the poem, coming as it does at the heart of Coleridge's intensest creative period, might turn out to be something in the nature of a paradigm in which some of his major problems were stated, and a tentative resolution essayed.

To examine the validity of such sweeping claims, it is clear that a very detailed analysis of the poem must be undertaken; but before it is begun, there are one or two other points to be made. The first is of bibliographical interest. After studying the poem for some time, I became convinced that the last six lines of the second stanza, as normally printed in the standard editions, marked a departure in sense from the preceding lines. On examining the first edition of the poem, as published in 1816, I found that they in fact appeared there as a separate stanza.[16] In the discussion that follows, therefore, I shall refer to them as the 'third' stanza, and the last stanza, where necessary, as the fourth.

A brief word may also be said about previous studies of the poem. Professor Wilson Knight and Maud Bodkin, in works mentioned earlier,[17] have treated the poem as a piece of symbolism, made up of unconscious and archetypal images. Dorothy Mercer's article, 'The Symbolism of "Kubla Khan"',[18] is concerned mainly with the influence of Jacob Boehme's images within the poem. She does not succeed in revealing any convincing and logical pattern in the poem, however, and the main reason for this seems to be that Boehme's images only arrived in the poem after being taken up and conjured over in Coleridge's own mind. A logical but brief interpretation of the poem appears in the Clark Lectures of Humphry House[19] and my own discussion, although taking a broader line and disagreeing at some points, does not, I think, conflict fundamentally with his.

.   .   .   .   .

If the poem *Kubla Khan* has a unity, it is clearly not a unity of either space or time.[20] The hero of the poem is a Tartar king in China, yet his pleasure-dome is to be built beside a river which seems to be the Alpheus, sacred river of Greece. In the last stanza, an Abyssinian maid is introduced, 'singing of Mount Abora'—which sounds like the Abyssinian Mount Amara. And as soon as we begin examining the associations of the imagery, we find ourselves carried further afield: according to Lowes, Alph is related to another sacred river—the Nile, and the 'caves of ice' were located in Kashmir when Coleridge first read of them.[21]

In such a confused landscape, the best plan is to begin at the beginning of the poem—but not with Kubla Khan himself. The most significant point of departure in the poem, after all, is not in the lines based on Purchas, but the third, fourth and fifth lines, where he suddenly breaks away from Purchas, to return again immediately afterwards:

> Where Alph, the sacred river, ran
> Through caverns measureless to man
> Down to a sunless sea.

Symbolist critics tend to interpret the river here as the river of life, and the sunless sea as death: they would probably paraphrase simply, 'where human life runs its course, through sublime splendours, until it merges in the sea of death'. The interpretation may be accepted as a first step: but to make it, as it stands, the core of the poem is as un-Coleridgean as to interpret *The Ancient Mariner* purely in terms of the 'one Life'. To find the pattern within which this conception of the poem has its place, we need to look more closely at some of the other statements in it, and consider whether they are not related to the complicated lore which we considered earlier.

To begin with, the name of the sacred river is not Alpheus but 'Alph', and I do not think that the shortening is accidental. We have already discussed the widespread preoccupation with primeval lore in Coleridge's day, and this included great interest in the origins of language. The history of the alphabet was much studied, and treatises concerning the relationship between various languages were not uncommon. Even as late as 1854 it was possible for a treatise entitled *The One Primeval Language* to be published and receive serious attention.[22] In general, most writers on the subject shared the belief that all languages could be traced to a single original, and this was not surprising, since, like Coleridge himself, they had somewhere in their minds the picture of God acting as a parent to Adam, teaching him language and the divine social state, and revealing the alphabet to him.[23] To discover this original, therefore, might lead to discovery of the cradle of civilization—that traditional point of dispute among scholars—and even of the nature of that antediluvian civilization. And this in its turn might lead them to the secrets of the Creation itself.

Many theories were offered as to the site of the original civilization in Coleridge's day: even the claims of Tartary were canvassed[24], together with more traditional candidates such as Mesopotamia or Egypt. In the case of language, however, there seemed to be a strong case for regarding the Ethiopic language as one of the oldest—particularly as the first letter of the alphabet in the Amharic dialect, 'Alph', could be regarded as prototype of the Hebrew Aleph on one hand, and the Greek Alpha on the other. Eusebius, indeed, in his *Praeparatio Evangelica*, called the first letter of the Hebrew alphabet Alph.[25]

Now the Hebrews have in all twenty-two letters: of which the first is 'Alph', which translated into the Greek language could mean 'learning': and the second 'Beth', which is interpreted 'of a house'. . . .

Bruce, in his *Travels to Discover the Source of the Nile*, went further. He claimed that the first three letters of the human alphabet had been invented by the troglodytes of Ethiopia; he also maintained that the second letter, 'Beth', did not signify the door of a house, but the door of the troglodytes' caves—because of the resemblance to a rounded door in the shape of the letter.[26]

The interest of these theories lies not only in their claim of priority for the Ethiopic alphabet, but also in their assumption that some of the letters, at least, have a symbolic meaning. Coleridge apparently had his own theories on these lines, for we find him, many years later, mentioning a theory of his that words in original languages were really sentences, each syllable being a distinct symbol, and very often each letter being the relict of a syllable—perhaps of several. Another note is even more revealing[27]:

A hint.
Whether the Absence of Vowels in the Hebrew is not a clue to the Alphabet, as according to my old old theory consisting of symbols of whole words/ & whether the Aleph does not add to the proof.

Many of Coleridge's friends and acquaintances shared his interest in language. When Edmund Fry published his *Pantographia* in 1796, for instance, the subscribers included J. P. Estlin, Benjamin Flower and John Disney; and Gilbert Wakefield had written a paper on 'The Origin of Alphabetical Characters' in 1784.[28]

The Cabbalists, also, were deeply interested in language. Robert Fludd, in his *Mosaicall Philosophy*, dwelt upon the fact that Ayin meant both 'nothing' and 'a fountain', and explained this by suggesting that the fountain was nothing in the darkness, but became infinite when it flowed from dark Aleph to light Aleph.[29] In the Zohars, the birth of language was expounded in terms of the sexual dialectic which we have already examined[30]:

... When the Supreme Thought experienced a mysterious joy, a luminous ray escaped from the Thought and drew the forty-two letters together, and it was this union which resulted in the birth of the world above and of the one below. This is the mystery which God makes known to those who fear him. The letter Beth with which the Scriptures begin is the female Element; the letter Aleph is the male Element. . . .

From this wealth of tradition and speculation, a possible pattern emerges. If Alph the sacred river is associated with

Beth, the cavern, we do not need to go to the cabbalistic writings to remind ourselves that the river and the cavern are themselves male and female symbols, and were used with this significance in such neoplatonic writings as Porphyry's exposition of the Cave of the Nymphs in Homer. Moreover, when the two letters are put together, they make up the word AB, which appears on the first page of Holwell's *Mythological Dictionary* as a name of Apollo.

There is a curious passage in Carlyon's account of Coleridge's punning talk in Germany which may be relevant here[31]:

> In order to illustrate, as was supposed, the inscrutable nature of the Deity, His name 'Abba' was bandied through all its changes, as, for instance, AB—BA——AB—BA— backwards and forwards—forwards and backwards AB— BA.

As it stands, the anecdote is singularly pointless, since it requires very little ingenuity to see that the word Abba is a palindrome. If on the other hand, we suppose that Coleridge was treating his companions to a disquisition on the letters A and B, with their combination as a representation of the Apollo, the lost Shechinah, it will be seen that he could indulge in a very pretty piece of speculation, while Carlyon would be left completely bewildered.

The chief importance of this excursion into alphabetic lore, however, lies in the symbolic possibilities which it raises, and which can exist quite independently of it. In particular, we may recall that caverns appeared frequently in ancient lore. The chief mysteries were celebrated in them. It was a cave in Dodona, according to one tradition, where the infant Dionysus, the re-created sun, was nursed and cherished by the nymphs, until he could emerge in his full glory. Caverns were also associated with the moon, both being sacred to Isis.[32] Thomas Taylor has an interesting passage on the symbolism of the cave[33]:

> A cave, as we learn from Porphyry, . . . is an apt symbol of the material world; since it is agreeable at its first entrance on account of its participation of form, but is involved in the deepest obscurity to the intellectual eye,

which endeavours to discern its dark foundation. So that, like a cave, its exterior and superficial parts are pleasant; but its interiour parts are obscure, and its very bottom, darkness itself.

The cavern is a symbol not only of the hope of restoring the true sun, the Dionysus, but, in its own nature, of the material world. In this it resembles the Isis of Plutarch's treatise.

The river and the caverns, therefore, may be taken together as symbolizing the elements of dialectic creativity, but in a fallen world. Alph is not the river that watered Milton's Paradise, for as he himself tells us, that river had returned in part to Eden, to well up in an everlasting fountain. Milton's fountain symbolized immortality, and exists no longer—'Though Sin, not Time, first wraught the change.'[34] Alph is the sacred river, as it flows after the Fall. It no longer returns to the fountain, but flows down to be lost in the sterility of the sunless sea.

Equivalent legends surrounded the sacred rivers of antiquity. The Nile of fact flowed to the Mediterranean, where its life-giving waters were lost in the sterile sea; the Nile of legend, on the other hand, was Osiris, the immortal one, the snake with the tail in its mouth. Similarly, Lowes has pointed out that when Coleridge spoke of Alph running to a sunless sea, he was being true to Pausanias, who said that the Alpheus rose from a vast sea in the depths of the earth, and returned to it.[35] The Alpheus of legend behaved differently, however, flowing under the sea to Syracuse, and there springing forth in the fountain Arethusa. Lowes draws attention to Seneca's account of 'the belief that the Alpheus makes its way right from Achaia to Sicily, stealing under sea by secret sluice, and reappearing only when it reaches the coast of Syracuse'. A source which echoed Seneca and lay even closer to Coleridge's hand, was the description of the Arcadians in Milton's *Arcades*.[36]

> Of famous *Arcady* ye are, and sprung
> Of that renowned flood, so often sung,
> Divine *Alpheus*, who by secret sluse,
> Stole under Seas to meet his *Arethuse*.

Another of Milton's references to the legend ('Return Alpheus, the dread voice is past/ That shrunk thy streams!') was actually quoted by Coleridge in a lecture.[37] The fact is that it had long been a part of the classical imagery at the disposal of English poets, who had used it both decoratively and symbolically.[38] A good example of such usage by a minor poet may be found in Fenton's poem, *To Caelia on her Birthday*, published in 1773[39]:

> O, may thy life in even current flow,
> Not fiercely rapid, nor too dully slow:
> And, when the hand of death shall change its course,
> Like Alpheus to his Arethusa's source,
> Pass subterraneous through the realms of night,
> To join the fountain of eternal light.

The eternal pursuit of Arethusa by Alpheus is another tradition which fits the pattern of the 'lost Shechinah'. After the Fall, the male principle, separated from the female, seeks eternally to unite with her again, in order that they may mingle in the creative fountain, and recover the lost glory. But the fountain of Eden is lost, and the river runs away fruitlessly. Instead of the river, the 'secret sluice' and the Arethusa fountain, there exist only the river, the caverns measureless to man, and the sunless sea.

Having thus established the context of the poem in the fallen world of the cabbalistic writers, we may proceed to an interpretation of the first stanza as a whole. First of all, we may remind ourselves of the fact, already dwelt upon in these pages, that Coleridge's world-picture was a picture still dominated by the cosmogony of Genesis. Evolutionary theories were beginning to be voiced abroad, but were not yet taken seriously. When the general reader thought of ancient history before the major empires of Egypt, Persia, Greece, Rome and so on, his mind went back to the Flood and then to the Fall. Racial theories were therefore related to the supposed dispersal of races after the Flood, and the origins of civilization either to that dispersal or, earlier still, to the civilization revealed to Adam in Eden. In consequence it was not uncommon for pagan traditions and myths to be regarded simply as corruptions and distortions of a single pure source, which had also been preserved in the Bible. When striking parallels were discovered between cultures separated from each other by many thousands of miles, this seemed to confirm the theory that they must have originally sprung from a common source.

A glance at eighteenth-century literature reveals the great interest in the subject, and I have already mentioned the weight of evidence that Coleridge shared this interest, particularly in the period which he spent at Bristol and Stowey. Another work which reflects this interest is the translation of the *Edda Saemundar* by Amos Cottle, brother of Coleridge's Bristol publisher, which Coleridge read on its appearance in 1797.[40] The work is prefaced by a long essay, which examines in detail the relationship between the Scandinavian and Greek mythologies.

Apart from his general interest in mythology, Coleridge had a particular interest in those studies of the subject which were hostile to the Christian faith. His interest in Dupuis's book, which set out to prove that Christ was the sun, and the early Christians sun-worshippers, was no doubt partly due to the immediacy of the problem involved, and it is noticeable that J. P. Estlin, the Bristol Unitarian minister, introduced a long attack on Dupuis and his theories into a pamphlet which he published in 1797.[41] He had presumably been introduced to Dupuis by Coleridge himself. With such theories in the air, Coleridge would feel that there was an immediate relevance in the study of mythology.

The sun-worship which, for all these reasons, fascinated Coleridge, was interpreted in various ways. We have already mentioned the eighteenth century theory that it had been introduced by Cain and his descendants, who found themselves deprived of the heavenly Shechinah and therefore worshipped that object in the universe which most reminded them of it. If Coleridge accepted this theory, it seems likely that he connected it with another which dominated a good deal of contemporary mythological study. Bryant's *Analysis of Ancient Mythology*, which we have already discussed, was also concerned primarily with sun-worship, associating it not with Cain but Ham. After describing how the Cuthites were the family which at an early time colonized the whole world, being the first mariners, and a highly enterprising people, Bryant continues,[42]

> They stood their ground at the general migration of families: but were at last scattered over the face of the earth. They were the first apostates from the truth; yet great in worldly wisdom. They introduced, wherever they came, many useful arts; and were looked up to, as a superiour order of beings: hence they were stiled Heroes, Dæmons, Heliadæ, Macarians. They were joined in their expeditions by other nations; especially by the collateral branches of their family, the Mizraim, Caphtorim, and the sons of Canaan. These were all of the line of Ham, who was held by his posterity in the highest veneration. They called him Amon: and having in the process of time raised him to a divinity, they worshiped him as the Sun: and from this worship they were stiled Amonians, . . .

It is impossible, in the absence of evidence, to know the precise position which Coleridge adopted, confronted with these varying theories: and the situation is further complicated by the fact that one is uncertain to what extent he would have regarded these traditions as factual, or simply as symbolic explanations of certain elements in human experience. An entry in the Gutch notebook reads[43]:

> Ham—lustful rogue—Vide Bayle under the Article Ham. Nimrod, the first king, taught Idolatry, & persecuted for Religion's sake. He was the first who wore a crown— (according to the Persian writers) having seen one in the Heavens—made war for conquest—

Both notes point to a reading of the Bible which is influenced by the search for good symbols—particularly of the origins of lust and violence. I am inclined to think that Coleridge went further, and identified Cain and Cham as varying personifications of the fallen man who has lost the light of the Shechinah, and therefore lives by heat—whether the heat of violence, like Cain, or the heat of lust, like Ham.

The relevance to *Kubla Khan* of this digression into sun-mythology begins to emerge when we recall that according to one tradition, the sons of Ham, having rebelled against the other tribes, were driven into the wastes of Tartary: this being made to explain both the violence of the Tartars, and the fact that Tartarus became a name for Hell.[44] Coleridge seems to have been interested in Tartary, which he often uses as a source of imagery. One of the projects listed in the Gutch notebook was to 'Describe a Tartarean Forest all of Upas Trees'.[45] Writing a letter at sea, he describes how detachments of foam 'scour out of sight, like a Tartar Troop over a Wilderness'.[46] Poole's works are 'Tartarean tan-pits'.[47] A pain in his cheek concentrates 'all the Rays of a Tartarean Sun'.[48] Jeremy Taylor's unusually violent Advent sermon is a 'Tartarean drench'.[49]

It seems clear from this that in Coleridge's eyes, Tartary and violence were so closely linked as to provide him with a stock image which he could develop both literally and symbolically. In a later notebook he accounted for the Tartar race as having sprung from a predominance of the Ham strain over the Shem strain, both being in degeneracy.[50] He was fully aware of the common antithesis between the uncivilised Tartars and the civilized Chinese.[51] And the Tartars apparently had their place in Coleridge's conception of the Satanic. In a lecture on Milton, he declares that Satan's prime character of pride and sensual indulgence is 'often seen *in little* on the political stage'—'It exhibits all the restlessness, temerity, and cunning which have marked the mighty hunters of mankind from Nimrod to Napoleon.'[52] In *The Friend*, he spoke of Napoleon's attempts to 'transform Europe into a Tartar Empire'[53] and elsewhere of Timur Khan as being, like Napoleon, an agent of God's wrath.[54]

The Tartars also had something of Satan's 'singularity of daring, grandeur of sufferance and ruined splendour'.[55] The harsh splendour of the Tartar Empire and the mysterious grandeur of the Khans had haunted English literature since the sixteenth and seventeenth centuries. Apart from Purchas's two great works, Coleridge would have come across them in Mandeville and lesser travel-writers, and in English literature from Marlowe to Milton. In view of the Abyssinian element in the poem before us, it is also interesting to notice that the grand and mysterious Prester John was identified by Ludolphus as Prester-Chan, an Asian king who had been driven out of his kingdom by the king of the Tartars and was later wrongly regarded as an African king.[56] Elsewhere, Prester John is again discussed in close conjunction with the Tartars. According to Herbert's *Travels*, he lived in Abyssinia, his chief fort being at Amara, and was descended from '*Maqueda* the *Sabæan* Queen that gave *Solomon* an affectionate visit, which made her People Jewish Proselytes'. Herbert then describes Tartary as an equally remote and unknown civilization, describing Cambalu (Kubla Khan's summer palace) and discussing the title 'Chan'—called by Venetus 'Shadow of Spirits, Monarch of the whole World, and Son of the immortal God'.[57] Coleridge also, in one place, relates the two areas.[58]

From all this, Kubla Khan, the Tartar ruler in China, begins to assume a much wider significance than at first sight: and the investigation may still be pursued with some profit, for there is evidence to connect him directly with a theme which we have already discovered in the first lines of the poem: that of the lost glory and the lost paradise. To make the connection plainer, it should be pointed out that in the volume of Purchas from which Coleridge drew the immediate inspiration of his poem, the name of the Tartar emperor was spelt 'Cublai Can'.[59] The spelling is important, for it was that used by Milton. In a later lecture, Coleridge was to deplore that some parts of *Paradise Lost* were hardly read by most readers, and to single out for special mention Adam's vision of future events in the eleventh and twelfth books.[60] And when, in reading Purchas, his eye lighted on the words 'In *Xamdu* did *Cublai Can* build a stately Palace', it was, no doubt, the beginning of this vision, where Adam is led into the highest part of Paradise, which leapt to his mind:[61]

> His Eye might there command wherever stood
> City of old or modern Fame, the Seat
> Of mightiest Empire, from the destind Walls
> Of *Cambalu*, seat of *Cathaian Can* . . .

These lines of Milton, which refer to Kubla's summer palace, serve to set Xanadu literally in the context of a fallen world; but they do more than that, for they had been quoted by Bryant in a passage where he was trying to demonstrate that the Chinese were sun-worshippers and descendants of Ham.[62]

> In China the Deity upon the Lotos in the midst of waters has long been a favourite emblem, and was imported from the west. . . . The Cuthites worshiped Cham, the Sun; whose name they variously compounded. In China most things, which have any reference to splendour, and magnificence, seem to be denominated from the same object. Cham is said in the language of that country to signify anything *supreme*. . . . Cambalu, the name of the ancient metropolis, is the city of Cham-Bal: and Milton styles it very properly, *Cambalu, seat of Cathaian Chan*. By this is meant the chief city of the Cuthean Monarch; for Chan is a derivative of Cahen, a prince.

If we suppose that Coleridge read the Purchas account with Milton's lines in mind, we have a clear reason for the transmutation of Xamdu into the trisyllabic Xanadu, and for the Miltonic strain which runs through the rest of the poem. If we go further, and suppose that he remembered Milton's lines in the context of Bryant's theories, a further prospect opens. In that case, Kubla Khan is directly connected with the sons of Ham, the violent ones who worship the sun as a substitute for the lost Shechinah.

There are other reasons why Kubla Khan should be associated with sun-worship. His very name established the connection, according to Bryant[63]:

> Chan signified a Priest; also a Lord or Prince: these two offices being formerly united.
>
> Rex Anius, Rex idem hominum, Phœbique Sacerdos.
>
> The term was sometimes used with a greater latitude, and denoted any thing noble and divine. Hence we find it prefixed to the names both of deities and men; and of places denominated from them.

Warburton, in his *Divine Legation of Moses*, quoted a tradition that Genghis Khan was divine, and said by his mother to be a son of the Sun.[64] And Coleridge's contemporary, Condorcet, dwelt upon the versatile genius of the Eastern priesthood in general[65]:

Such was, in remote periods, the art of the Eastern priests, who were at once, kings, pontiffs, judges, astronomers, surveyors, artists and physicians.

The Alpheus, also, had its due place in sun-worship, according to Bryant[66]:

There was an Omphalis in Elis; and here too was an oracle mentioned by Pindar and Strabo. . . . In this province was an ancient city Alphira; and a grove of Artemis Alpheionia, and the whole was watered by the sacred river Alpheus. All these are derived from El, the prophetic Deity, the Sun; and more immediately from his oracle, Alphi. The Greeks deduced every place from some personage: and Plutarch accordingly makes Alpheus— Εἰς τῶν τὸ γένος ἀφ' ἡλίου καταγόντων, one of those who derived their race from the Sun.

Alpheus, sacred river of Greece, was sacred to the sun, and ran through a region containing a sun-city and sun-groves. Moreover, there was a walled enclosure on its banks, According to the ancient geographers, this was Altis, sacred grove of Olympia, in the centre of which stood a temple to Zeus.[67] In Dupuis's book on sun-worship, it is stated that the temple of Jupiter Olympus there contained a consecrated place, which was shown as the point from which the waters of the flood drained away, under Deucalion.[68]

After Cain had killed Abel, he built a walled city, east of Eden,[69] and it was noticeable that sun-worshippers in general built cities or enclosures sacred to the sun. According to Bishop Huet, in his book on the site of the original Paradise, the 'curious gardens' which the princes of East enjoyed making, were intended to represent the garden of Eden.[70] It might be suggested, in fact, that the sun-worshippers, who feared and reverenced the sun because it reminded them of the lost Shechinah, also built cities and enclosures sacred to the sun in memory of the lost Paradise.

There were sun-cities in many parts of the world, of course. On the banks of the Nile, sacred river of Egypt, there was an enclosure sacred to the sun. Bryant described it as follows[71]:

> Here was the city On (of the Scriptures, the same with Heliopolis) so famous for its temple and religious rites; whose inhabitants are reported to have been the wisest of the Egyptians. The temple is said to have been very magnificent: and its original name was Ains Shems, or Shemesh, *the fountain of the Sun.*

Elsewhere, Bryant has more to say about the etymology of the name On.[72]

> Plato therefore with great justice rendered the term in his own language by το 'Ον, when he treated of the first cause, the *Lord of Life*: for the name among the Egyptians was perfectly analogous to ὀν, ὀντα, ἐοντα, εἰναι among the Greeks. It was the name of the true God; of whom the Egyptians at first made the sun only a type. But when the substitute was taken for the original, it was then adapted to the luminary: at least so far, as that the city of On was called the city of the Sun: and the orb of day was worshipped as the *living God.*

Having made this further link between the sun which the sons of Ham worshipped and the God, τὸ "Ον, of Platonic speculation (Coleridge frequently used τὸ "Ον or ὁ "Ων for God the father when describing the Platonic trinity, it may be noted),[73] Bryant goes on to point out that Heliopolis had another claim to fame: it had produced the man who had seen beyond the sun of the material universe to the one true God[74]:

> . . . this people 'chose themselves a leader; one who was a priest of *Heliopolis*, and whose name was *Osarsiph*. He enjoined them to pay no regard to the gods of the country nor to the animals which were held sacred by the *Egyptians*; but to sacrifice and feed indifferently: and not to have any connections out of their own community.—In short, this priest of *Heliopolis* was the founder of their republic, and their lawgiver: and after he had listed himself with this body of men, he changed his name to *Moses.*'

There was another sun-city in the ancient world, with which the Heliopolis of Egypt had connections. This was Heliopolis in Syria, better known to the eighteenth century as Balbec. Robert Wood's *Ruins of Balbec* and *Ruins of Palmyra*,[75] were two of the great archaeological books of the century and were well known to the Coleridge circle. Robert Lovell wrote of[76]

> The spot once dear to fame,
> Where Balbec flourish'd, or Palmyra stood.

and Coleridge of the commanding genius which could at its best, 'give a Palmyra to the desert'.[77]

Maundrell, the traveller, whose account of Syria ran into many editions, visited Balbec, describing its Walls and Towers and mentioning the Sun-city tradition.[78] He also visited the valley between the mountains of Libanon and Antilibanon, popularly supposed to be the Eden mentioned by the prophet Amos,[79] and elsewhere found a structure which was said to be the tomb of Abel near the fountain of the river Barrady.[80] His description of Barrady and the vale of Damascus is particularly striking[81]:

> It is situate in an even Plain of so great extent, that you can but just discern the Mountains that compass it, on the farther side. It stands on the West side of the Plain, at not above two miles distance from the place where the River *Barrady* breaks out from between the Mountains: it's Gardens extending almost to the very place.
>
> The City it self . . . is thick set with Mosques, and Steeples, the usual ornaments of the Turkish Cities, and is encompass'd with Gardens, extending no less, according to common estimation, than thirty miles round; which makes it look like a noble City in a vast Wood. The Gardens are thick set with Fruit Trees of all kinds, kept fresh, and verdant by the Waters of *Barrady*. You discover in them many Turrets, and Steeples, and Summer-Houses, frequently peeping out from amongst the green Boughs, which may be conceiv'd to add no small advantage and beauty to the Prospect. On the North side of this vast Wood, is a place called *Solhees*, where are the most beautiful Summer-Houses and Gardens.

The greatest part of this pleasantness, and fertility proceeds . . . from the Waters of *Barrady*, which supply both the Gardens, and City in great abundance. This River, as soon as it issues out from between the cleft of the Mountain . . . into the Plain, is immediately divided into three Streams, of which the middlemost, and biggest runs directly to *Damascus* . . . and is distributed to all the Cisterns and Fountains of the City. . . .

Barrady being thus describ'd, is almost wholly drunk up by the City and Gardens. What small part of it escapes, is united . . . in one Channel again, on the South East side of the City; and after about three or four hours course, finally loses it self in a Bog there, without ever arriving at the Sea.

I have quoted this passage at length because it is both representative of many descriptions of earthly paradises which Coleridge must have known, and nearer to Xanadu, in detail and in general atmosphere, than any other that I have read.

In looking at such descriptions, one sees recurring patterns. Just as the Heliopolis of Egypt is mirrored by the Heliopolis of Syria, there are resemblances between the cults in both cities, including the wailing of the women for their dead god.[82] Again, there was a Heliopolis in Arabia. A memorable passage in *Paradise Lost* describes the mariners lingering enchanted while[83]

> . . . off at Sea North-East windes blow
> *Sabean* Odours from the spicie shoare
> Of *Arabie* the blest . . .

Milton's source was no doubt Diodorus Siculus, whose description of the Holy Islands forms one of the finest paradise-gardens of ancient literature. Diodorus describes the fruitfulness of 'Arabia the happy' and especially the Sacred Isle, which 'chiefly produces Frankincense, and in that abundance, as suffices for the Service and Worship of the Gods all the World over. . . . The Tree is very small, like to the white *Egyptian* Thorn, and bears a Leaf like to the Willow: It puts forth a Flower of a Golden Colour; from the

Bark of this Tree by incision made, distils the Frankincense in Drops like Tears.' In the nearby island of Panchæa was the town of Panara, notable for being governed by a democracy and for the temple of Jupiter Triphylius, greatly venerated 'because of it's Antiquity and the Stateliness of the Structure, and the Fertility of the Soyl'. The fields round the Temple were 'Planted with all sorts of Trees, not only for Fruit, but for Pleasure and Delight', and a fountain near the temple threw up a river 'from whence flows most clear and sweet Water, the drinking of which, conduces much to the Health of the Body. This River is called the Water of the Sun'.[84]

Incense was associated with sun-worship in many parts of the ancient world. According to Plutarch, the Egyptians burnt different kinds of incense at sunrise, mid-heaven and sunset.[85] And the Tartars, who were not the least of sun-worshippers (for a tradition had it that the Mexicans and Peruvians were descended from the nations whom Kubla Khan sent to conquer Japan)[86] were no exception. On the page which Coleridge was reading when he began the poem, Purchas relates that they believed in immortality and in a heavenly God, to whom they daily burned incense, asking of him health and understanding.[87]

The more one reads such accounts, the clearer it becomes that the images of the first stanza form a tightly-knit pattern and are bound together by two concepts: those of sun-worship and the earthly paradise. The two ideas are mutually interdependent. Because fallen man fears and propitiates all things which remind him of the inward Shechinah which he has lost, his cult focuses itself on the sun; similarly the memory which persists through his fallen nature leads him to strive to re-create a paradise-garden for himself. The sun-temple in the enclosed garden expresses both his fears and his aspirations.

Kubla Khan is the Tartar king of tradition: fierce and cruel, he bears the brand of Cain. But like Cain in *The Wanderings of Cain*, he yearns to break the shackles which enslave him, and to regain the happiness of paradise before the Fall. In consequence, he turns from violence to the arts of civilization. He encloses a garden and constructs a dome.

The dome itself is a further link with sun-worship and pantheism. According to Maurice's theory, the earliest temples of mankind were in the shape of pyramids, and later quadrangular. Finally, 'the piety of theologians and the fancy of philosophers' united to build the dome: 'an epitome of the universe itself in which all the phenomena of nature should be exhibited at one glance to the astonished spectator'. They thus made their temples resemble the cavern of Mithra, in the lofty roof of which the zodiac was painted and the sun and planets represented, moving in their orbits. The greatest example of such a dome was the Pantheon with its central cavity, 'to admit the fountain of light'.[88]

During the period when *Kubla Khan* was written, Coleridge's feeling for nature, and for the significance of nature in religion, was at its height. In *This Limetree Bower my Prison*, *Frost at Midnight* and *The Nightingale* he stressed again and again the importance of Nature as teacher and guide. Correspondingly, he reproved those who cut themselves off from such beneficent influences and expressed pity for the[89]

> youths and maidens most poetical,
> Who lose the deepening twilights of the spring
> In ball-rooms and hot theatres . . .

This feeling found a natural complement in antipathy towards buildings dedicated to religion. Lovell, one of the pantisocrats, had written,[90]

> In vain may priests their mystic rites repeat,
> The dome still moulders with th'unhallow'd dust;
> For virtue only consecrates her seat,
> Her sacred temple is the heart that's just.

Coleridge echoed the contempt, but broadened his idea of the true temple of God to include natural piety. In 1795, he wrote of the view from a hill overlooking the Bristol Channel,[91]

> It seem'd like Omnipresence! God, methought,
> Had built him there a Temple: the whole World
> Seem'd *imag'd* in its vast circumference . . .

The theme was to recur. At the end of *France: An Ode*, he

was standing on the cliffs, shooting his being through earth, sea and air, 'possessing all things with intensest love'.[92] In *Fears in Solitude*, he wrote[93]

> O divine
> And beauteous island! thou hast been my sole
> And most magnificent temple, in the which
> I walk with awe, and sing my stately songs,
> Loving the God that made me!

'The blue sky bends over all': and this 'dome' is the only temple in which God should be worshipped (as Christabel and the hermit in *The Ancient Mariner* recognize). The man-made dome is a mistaken ideal, an attempt to escape from the true temple and create a private world. The theme is stated more explicitly in a much later poem, *To Nature*[94]:

> So will I build my altar in the fields,
> And the blue sky my fretted dome shall be.
> And the sweet fragrance that the wild flower yields
> Shall be the incense I will yield to Thee,
> Thee only God! and thou shalt not despise
> Even me, the priest of this poor sacrifice.

It is the flaw in Kubla Khan's personality that he cannot possess this innocent attitude towards nature. Instead, he must enclose his paradise with walls and towers and build a private pleasure-dome in the middle of it.

The dome, then, emphasizes the theme of enclosure and separation from the world which was introduced by the building of the walls and towers. As Kubla is priest and king, so his dome is both temple and palace.

I suspect that Coleridge may also have had another significance in mind for the pleasure-dome. E. H. Coleridge was the first to draw attention to the apparent influence of a passage from Maurice's *Hindostan* upon the poem.[95] This passage, which describes an image of ice in the mountains of Kashmir, was transcribed by Coleridge into his notebook under the heading '*Hymns Moon*', and was followed by another quotation from Maurice, which was evidently intended to find a place in another of the projected *Hymns*—the one to the air and other elements.[96]

Air &c—Five Mathem. spend every night in the lofty tower—one directs his eye to the Zenith—2nd to the E. 3rd to the W. 4. S. 5th. N. They take notice of the Wind & rain & stars—Grand Observatory in Pekin—

There is a work of the Italian Renaissance which bears an interesting resemblance to this passage at one point. Campanella's *City of the Sun* is an early utopian fantasy about an ideal city where a form of communism, not unlike Coleridge's own Pantisocracy, was established. In the middle of this city, there stood a large temple with a dome, on the inside of which were painted the sun, moon and other heavenly bodies. Philosophers of the city stood in the dome, making observations of the heavenly bodies. The heavenly bodies were not worshipped, however: they were highly honoured, but worship was offered only to God.[97]

This work is so like a Coleridgean speculation, that if he did not know of it, one can only say that he ought to have done. In any case, however, it seems that there is a strand of meaning in the poem which corresponds to this. It was traditionally believed that the secrets of the universe had been revealed to Adam in the paradise-garden, and that the garden itself had been laid out in a form which provided a picture of the workings of the universe.[98] This knowledge was for the most part lost at the Fall; but man was constantly striving to rediscover it: and Kubla's dome is an apt symbol of that striving.

The final significance of the dome brings us back more firmly to the central imagery of the poem. I have already dwelt upon the Miltonic note which seems to be present throughout, and it is therefore interesting to turn to a note written many years later, on the subject of the Church as a material institution—turned into a Palace, in fact[99]:

The Gospel Truths in worldly Health, Wealth, and Lustihood = Lightning flashed across Sunshine. Even the Outward Church, or the Ecclesia in Domino petrified by the Mammon of Apostacy into Ædes Kyriacas, 'from whose arched roof Pendent by subtle Magic many a Row of starry lamps and blazing Cressets, fed With Naphtha and Asphaltus, yielded Light As from a Sky,' may need the Thunderbolt to reduce it to ruins & a wilderness of dark Caverns & Dungeons avenging the bedimmed Flashes from Heaven/ that now glare on the amazed Consciences of the prisoners inclosed & underwhelmed.

The passage from *Paradise Lost*, so casually introduced here, had evidently long been impressed on his mind as a symbol. And it comes, of course, from the description of the building of Pandaemonium[100]:

> Anon out of the earth a Fabrick huge
> Rose like an Exhalation, with the sound
> Of Dulcet Symphonies and voices sweet:
> Built like a Temple, where *Pilasters* round
> Were set, and Doric pillars overlaid
> With Gold'n Architrave; nor did there want
> Cornice or Freeze, with bossy Sculptures grav'n;
> The Roof was fretted Gold.

The palace which the daemons built for themselves is a characteristic fruit of daemonic energies, and it helps us to see Kubla Khan's true nature. He has been seen, by Humphry House and others, as the poet in action, but it seems clear that he is much more than that. He is nearer to the ancient Eastern priests who were at one and the same time 'kings, pontiffs, judges, astronomers, surveyors, artists and physicians'.[101] He personifies genius in all its forms: and his genius is the manifestation of daemonic powers.

Nevertheless, it would be wrong to see Kubla as representing the highest type of genius. Coleridge thought that Napoleon was a genius, but he did not approve of him. When he spoke of Napoleon as building a Tartar empire, or of Timur Khan as being, like Napoleon, an agent of God, he did not intend the comparison to be flattering to either party.[102] He thought of Napoleon with respect, but not with admiration. According to Hazlitt, he put him in the class of active rather than of intellectual characters,[103] and this distinction is clarified by a passage in *The Statesman's Manual* where Napoleon is mentioned by name. In this, Coleridge describes how the will, when linked with reason and religion, manifests itself as wisdom or as love (that is, as the third person of the Platonic trinity). But when it is abstracted from such qualities, the will becomes Satanic pride and rebellious self-idolatry, coupled with despotism over other men. Obdurate, it can subdue sensual impulses, and is superior to toil, pain and pleasure. After holding up Milton's Satan as the apotheosis of this spirit, he enumerates its characteristic qualities, concluding,[104]

> . . . these are the qualities that have constituted the COMMANDING GENIUS! these are the Marks, that have characterized the Masters of Mischief, the Liberticides, and mighty Hunters of Mankind, from NIMROD to NAPOLEON.

The character of the genius is further elaborated elsewhere. In the *Philosophical Lectures*, Coleridge says that to have a genius is to live in the universal, and thus to know no self except that which is reflected from around one.[105] Here, as elsewhere, Coleridge's view of divinity and genius seem to coincide. The genius, like God, can only truly realize himself in the act of creation, in seeing by his own light. It is as if the sun were to wish to see, and to discover that it can only see the objects which reflect its light.

This is not the genius of Napoleon, however: on the contrary, he is 'the evil genius of our planet'.[106] The distinction is made clear in *Biographia Literaria*, where Coleridge draws a further distinction between men of absolute genius, and men of commanding genius, such as Napoleon. Men of absolute genius are on the whole contented, because they exist between thought and reality: they live in an inter-mundium of which their own living spirit supplies the substance, and their imagination the ever-varying form, and are therefore self-sufficing. In one of his lectures, however, he declares that even this type of genius has certain longings[107]:

> . . . Yet,—and here is the point, where genius even of the most perfect kind, allotted but to few in the course of many ages, does not preclude the necessity in part, and in part counterbalance the craving by sanity of judgment, without which genius either cannot be, or cannot at least

manifest itself,—the dependency of our nature asks for some confirmation from without, though it be only from the shadows of other men's fictions.

In the men of commanding genius, these longings become daemonic urges. They have to force their preconceptions upon the world without, in order to present them back to their own view with a satisfying degree of clearness, distinctness and individuality[108]:

> ... These in tranquil times are formed to exhibit a perfect poem in palace, or temple, or landscape-garden; or a tale of romance in canals that join sea with sea, or in walls of rock, which, shouldering back the billows, imitate the power, and supply the benevolence of nature to sheltered navies; or in aqueducts that, arching the wide vale from mountain to mountain, give a Palmyra to the desert. But alas! in times of tumult they are the men destined to come forth as the shaping spirit of Ruin, to destroy the wisdom of ages in order to substitute the fancies of a day, and to change kings and kingdoms, as the wind shifts and shapes the clouds.

In other words, the man of commanding genius has an ambivalent nature, which moulds itself to the demands of the age. When Coleridge spoke of Timur Khan as being, like Napoleon, an agent of God, he was ascribing to him, not divine virtue, but the function of God's scourge—that of 'the shaping Spirit of Ruin', or the thunderbolt that will destroy the Palace of Mammon.

In the poem before us, the scene is tranquil, for Kubla Khan is the man of commanding genius in time of peace. He must still impress himself upon the world, but can do it peacefully, by building his pleasure-dome and garden-paradise. Nevertheless, the ambivalent nature of the daemonic and of genius has already initiated a dialectic in the poem. Kubla Khan may seem a peaceful and prosperous ruler, but his garden is not and cannot be the garden of Eden, just as the sacred river is not and cannot be the river of paradise. The dome which he builds is therefore as precarious as the 'Russian palace of ice, glittering, cold and transitory' (an image of Cowper's which Coleridge used to describe Darwin's poetry),[109] or the 'Wealth's glittering fairy-dome of ice' of his poem *Separation*.[110] Kubla's position as a man of commanding genius is equally precarious. His river flows down to a sunless sea, and his garden is enclosed by walls and towers. The ominous is only a hint in such images, but is to become explicit in the next stanza.

Chapter VIII

FOUNTAIN OF THE SUN

'Government, like dress, is the badge of lost innocence; the palaces of Kings are built on the ruins of the bowers of paradise.'

THOMAS PAINE.[1]

PAINE'S image states the theme of the second stanza of *Kubla Khan* neatly—though naturally his application of it is very different from Coleridge's. Paine's eye was on government, as on a necessary evil, a substitute for the paradise that was irrevocably lost. Coleridge, on the other hand, saw civilization in a different light, regarding it partly as an attempt to regain the lost paradise. The eighteenth-century bid to impose rational order on the universe had been an attempt of this nature, which had failed because it had not taken sufficiently into account the extent of the ruin. Similarly, the medieval mind had included not only the rational order of scholasticism, but also primitive emotion—an emotion largely made up of fear and fascination[2]:

This was the other part of the Gothic mind—the inward, the striking, the romantic character, in short the genius, but genius marked according to its birthplace; for it grew in rude forests amid the inclemencies of outward nature where man saw nothing around him but what must owe its charms mainly to the imaginary powers with which it was surveyed. There nothing outward marked the hands of man. Woods, rocks and streams, huge morasses, nothing wore externally the face of human intellect; and yet man cannot look but intellect must be either found or placed. There arose therefore, among the Gothic nations, a superstition or a worship of fire.

This is the spirit which haunts the second stanza, and the note of fear which attends it should make us hesitate before saying that the stanza is simply a vivid presentation of Gothic splendours. It is often read in this sense, of course. Humphry House speaks of the 'sense of inexhaustible energy, now falling now rising, but persisting through its own pulse',

230

which is conveyed by the description of the 'mighty fountain'.[3] These lines he takes to be symbolic of the poet's creative energy at its most sublime; and it is only when he comes to deal with the 'ancestral voices' that he says,

> This is essential to the full unity of the conception: the Paradise contains knowledge of the threat of its own possible destruction.

That there is an image of energy in the fountain may be accepted: but I cannot agree that it is creative energy of the highest type. On the contrary, it participates in the threat to the ordered security of the Paradise—a threat which I take to be a feature of the whole stanza, and not simply the last line.

One reason for saying this is that many of the images in the stanza appear elsewhere in Coleridge's poetry, in contexts of disaster and ruin. In *Religious Musings*, for example, the Scarlet Woman of Babylon, identified by a footnote with 'the union of Religion with Power and Wealth, wherever it is found', is 'she that worked whoredom with the Daemon Power'.[4] One of her children is[5]

> pale Fear
> Haunted by ghastlier shapings than surround
> Moon-blasted Madness when he yells at midnight!

In the same poem the terrors of the French Revolution are described as letting loose the Giant Frenzy, who[6]

> Uprooting empires with his whirlwind arm
> Mocketh high Heaven; burst hideous from the cell
> Where the old Hag, unconquerable, huge,
> Creation's eyeless drudge, black Ruin, sits
> Nursing the impatient earthquake.

Passages like this recur throughout Coleridge's poetry. In the fragment *Mahomet*, for example, probably written in 1799, a frenzied crowd of enthusiasts is described[7]:

> Loud the tumult in Mecca surrounding the fane of the idol;—
> Naked and prostrate the priesthood were laid—the people with mad shouts

Thundering now, and now with saddest ululation
Flew, as over the channel of rock-stone the ruinous
river
Shatters its waters abreast, and in mazy uproar
bewilder'd,
Rushes dividuous all—all rushing impetuous onward.

In *The Night-Scene*, written in 1813, an absent character is
addressed as follows[8]:

. . . . always striv'st thou to be great
By thine own act—yet art thou never great
But by the inspiration of great passion.
The whirl-blast comes, the desert-sands rise up
And shape themselves; from Earth to Heaven they
stand,
As though they were the pillars of a temple,
Built by Omnipotence in its own honour!
But the blast pauses, and their shaping spirit
Is fled: the mighty columns were but sand,
And lazy snakes trail o'er the level ruins!

The importance of these instances is heightened by the
specific resemblances in imagery and even wording to *Kubla
Khan*. I take such imagery to represent the 'Typhonic'
element in the poem. In the second stanza there may not be
actual disaster, but there is strong threat of it, finally
reinforced by the 'ancestral voices prophesying war'. This
contrast between the tremendous powers of Nature and
man's puny efforts to control and shape them to his purposes
is a constant theme with Coleridge. It is well expressed in a
note[9]

Of the sentimental *Cantilena* respecting the benignity
and loveliness of *Nature*—how does it not sink before the
contemplation of a pravity of nature, on whose reluctance
and inaptness a form is forced (the mere reflex of that form
which is itself absolute Substance!) and which it struggles
against, bears but for a while and then sinks with alacrity
of self-seeking into dust or sanies, which falls abroad into
endless nothings or creeps and cowers in poison or
explodes in havock—What is the beginning? What the

end? And how evident an alien is the supernatant in the brief interval?

The same sense of foreboding haunts his speculations more and more as the years go by, until in 1830 he is declaring that the Earth is not a goddess in petticoats, but the Devil in a strait waistcoat.[10] In a passage of his political writing which echoes Paine's metaphor he writes, of good government,[11]

But whence did this happy organization first come?—Was it a tree transplanted from Paradise, with all its branches in full fruitage? Or was it sowed in sun-shine? Was it in vernal breezes and gentle rains that it fixed its roots, and grew and strengthened?—Let History answer these questions!—With blood was it planted—it was rocked in tempests—the goat, the ass, and the stag gnawed it—the wild boar has whetted his tusks on its bark. The deep scars are still extant on its trunk, and the path of the lightning may be traced among its higher branches. And even after its full growth, in the season of its strength, 'when its height reached to the heaven, and the sight thereof to all the earth,' the whirlwind has more than once forced its stately top to touch the ground: it has been bent like a bow, and sprang back like a shaft. Mightier powers were at work than Expediency ever yet called up! yea, mightier than the mere Understanding can comprehend!

All this has its place in the second stanza and its imagery. Kubla Khan, the man of commanding genius, has temporarily imposed his will upon nature, but untamed forces still exist which can in a moment destroy the fragile pattern of order, security and pleasure which he has set up. In consequence, the imagery here brings out and develops the theme which was foreshadowed in the sacred river and the sunless sea: the theme of a *natura naturata* out of harmony with *natura naturans*. The 'waning moon', for example, fits the pattern which we have traced elsewhere: the redemptive forces of nature are not in the ascendant.

The presence of echoes from Milton's description of Eden

might seem at first to weigh against such an interpretation of the second stanza, until one examines them more closely. The point is missed if this scene is regarded merely as another reminiscence from Milton's first, idyllic description of Paradise. The echoes in the second stanza come not from this but from the ninth book where, in contrast with the clear innocence of the earlier description, a sense of foreboding invests the scene. Eve and the scenery through which she walks are beautiful as before, but a new presence has entered the garden. Satan lurks there, seeking an opportunity to achieve the downfall of the human race.[12]

> Neerer he drew, and many a walk travers'd
> Of stateliest Covert, Cedar, Pine, or Palme . . .

It is no accident that these lines give Coleridge's poem its 'cedarn cover', for the same trees recur, with more tragic significance, in Adam's lament at the end of the same book[13]:

> How shall I behold the face
> Henceforth of God or angel, earst with joy
> And rapture so oft beheld? Those heav'nly shapes
> Will dazle now this earthly, with thir blaze
> Insufferably bright. O might I here
> In solitude live savage, in some glade
> Obscur'd, where highest Woods impenetrable
> To Starr or Sun-light, spread their umbrage broad,
> And brown as Eevning: Cover me, ye Pines,
> Ye Cedars, with innumerable boughs,
> Hide me, where I may never see them more.

Just as the sun and the daemonic are ambivalent, inducing both terror and fascination, so with the 'sublime' scenery of this stanza. Because it recalls the lost paradise, it awakens opposing emotions in the human mind. It is at once attractive and terrifying, holy and haunted.

The wailing woman is closely linked with the scene, and her emotions, too, are ambivalent. She is woman after the Fall. She fears her demon-lover and yet is attracted by him—she is 'wailing' and yet 'wailing for' him. The duality of her feelings corresponds, evidently, to the duality of the daemon, his twin nature of 'seraph' and 'saraph', his heavenly nature which is still glorious, though in ruin. The woman longs for her daemon lover, for only in him can she hope to find the lost Shechinah: yet in reality he is always the demon-lover, an angel of heat rather than light, of lust rather than love. At first sight, wailing beneath the waning moon, she is a personification of crazy terror—even of the Queen Aso whose whoredom with Typhon releases the shaping spirit of ruin. Yet in her very yearning she expresses something of the Isis who longs for her lost Osiris.

The woman herself should probably be associated also with the cults of 'wailing women' which often had a place in sun-worship. In Greece, the women wailed for Adonis, in Egypt for Osiris, in Phoenicia for Thammuz. Ostensibly, the cult represented the tears of Isis, but its celebration was commonly accompanied by sexual orgies, as the prophet Ezekiel saw.[14] Once again, *Paradise Lost* is relevant[15]:

> *Thammuz* came next behind,
> Whose annual wound in *Lebanon* allur'd
> The *Syrian* Damsels to lament his fate
> In amorous ditties all a Summers day,
> While smooth *Adonis* from his native Rock
> Ran purple to the Sea, suppos'd with blood
> Of *Thammuz* yearly wounded: the Love-tale
> Infected *Sions* daughters with like heat,
> Whose wanton Passions in the sacred Porch
> *Ezekiel* saw, when by the *Vision* led
> His eye survayd the dark Idolatries
> Of alienated *Judah*.

In his *Death of Moses*, published in 1795, Southey refers to 'Thammuz' annual dirge',[16] and there is evidence, as we have seen, that Coleridge and Southey, as they worked together, were interested by biblical accounts of 'daemon-lovers' in the Book of Tobit and the sixth chapter of Genesis, and that Coleridge intended to use this imagery to symbolize the difference between lust and love.[17]

The image of the fountain, which comes next in the stanza, maintains the association with *Paradise Lost*. Indeed, some critics have tended to identify it directly with the fountain in the paradise-garden[18]:

> Southward through *Eden* went a River large,
> Nor chang'd his course, but through the shaggie hill
> Pass'd underneath ingulft, for God had thrown
> That Mountain as his Garden mould high rais'd
> Upon the rapid current, which through veins
> Of porous Earth with kindly thirst up drawn,
> Rose a fresh Fountain, and with many a rill
> Waterd the Garden; thence united fell
> Down the steep glade, and met the nether Flood,
> Which from his darksom passage now appeers,
> And now divided into four main Streams,
> Runs divers, wandring many a famous Realme
> And Country . . .

A closer comparison, however, reveals that the resemblances in Coleridge's poem occur mainly in the first stanza: the fountain and glade of the second differ in important respects. Milton's fountain is actually in the paradise garden, on top of the 'steep savage hill'; Coleridge's fountain would appear to be away from the garden and the river-plain, whether or not it is within the walls and towers. And there is nothing in Milton to suggest that his fountain is anything but a gentle outpouring, drawn up by 'kindly thirst' and flowing out into a myriad of rills. The violent, cataclysmic upheaval of Coleridge's 'mighty fountain' has no place in it.

The relation between the two fountains, like the relation between the two savage scenes, is in fact an oblique one, and has to be approached by way of the ninth book of Milton's poem.[19]

> There was a place,
> Now not, though Sin, not Time, first wraught the
>   change,
> Where *Tigris* at the foot of Paradise
> Into a Gulf shot under ground, till part
> Rose up a Fountain by the Tree of Life;
> In with the River sunk, and with it rose
> *Satan* involv'd in rising Mist . . .

In view of the fountain's proximity to the Tree of Life, and the statement that it disappeared at the Fall, it is clear that Milton intended to make it a symbol of immortality; and in doing this he was echoing an age-old image. One need go no further than the New Testament to find references to the 'well of water springing up into everlasting life', or 'the fountain of the water of life'.[20] Coleridge's fountain, on the other hand, is an image of that which replaces eternal life—the distortion of angelic energies into daemonic, so that that which should be a quiet steady welling up becomes an untamable force, a spirit of ruin, rising up in destruction, proceeding in tumult, and finally sinking to the lifeless ocean of death.

This train of imagery was evidently present in Coleridge's mind when, in discussing *King Lear*, he spoke of Shakespeare's knowledge, from his reading of nature, that 'to power in itself, without reference to any moral end, an inevitable admiration and complacency appertains, whether it be displayed in the conquests of a Napoleon or Tamerlaine, or in the foam and thunder of a cataract'.[21] But imagery of this sort was in any case basic with him: one can discover throughout his writings fountain-images which are sufficiently subtle to suggest an organized body of thinking on the subject.

I am inclined to think that this thinking first originated with his interest in Egyptian theology. We have already examined his opinion that Egyptian religion was founded upon the cyclical, and that wherever the Egyptian philosophers discovered a cycle, they postulated a manifestation of the divinity.[22] Examples of such cycles (symbolized by the snake with its tail in its mouth) would be the movements of the heavenly bodies and the apparent perpetual replenishment of the waters of the Nile.

We have seen how such speculations were given contemporary significance in Coleridge's day by the interest in sun-worship and in the Nile fountains. Coleridge shows his interest in the latter not only by his enthusiasm for Bruce, but also by use of Nile images. One of the plans in his notebooks was 'to make a detailed comparison, in the manner of Jerome Taylor, between the searching for the first Cause of a Thing & the seeking the fountains of the Nile'[23]; he spoke of the 'many headed Nile of Credulity'[24]; and said of Napoleon's office, the 'Chief Consulate', 'It pretends to no sacredness; it is no Nile, made mysterious by the undiscover-ableness of its fountain-head'.[25] He would also have been familiar with the neoplatonist use of the image of the fountain for God, as it is displayed in Taylor's translations[26]:

But with the ancient philosopher, the deity is an immense and perpetually exuberant fountain; whose streams originally filled and continually replenish the world with life . . .

Where streams ambrosial in immortal course
Irriguous flow, from Deity their source.

Of course, Coleridge often uses this common image in a straightforward and traditional way. As in many other cases, however, there is evidence that he had also worked up a detailed body of imagery around it. In particular, he used it frequently to express his sense of a link between divinity and genius.

A good example of this process at work may be found in his well-known description of a spring[27]:

The spring with the little tiny cone of loose sand ever rising & sinking at the bottom, but it's surface without a wrinkle.—W.W. M.H. D.W. S.H.

Humphry House has commented on the evocative accuracy of this image, and on its use in one of Coleridge's poems.[28] It is also clear, however, that Coleridge intended it to have symbolical significance. Commenting on Mrs Gillman's health many years later, he said, 'But still her Flow of Strength, the tiny Spring at the bottom of the natural Fountain, requires careful *husbanding*—too much (and but a little is often too much) must not be drawn at once from the Basin. Wait for it's own gentle overflowing.'[29] He also used the image to describe the ideal of sexual love[30]:

O best reward of Virtue! to feel pleasure made more pleasurable, in legs, knees, chests, arms, cheeks—all in deep quiet, a fountain with unwrinkled surface yet still the living *motion* at the bottom that 'with soft and even pulse' keeps it full . . .

It is used yet again to describe joy[31]:

> . . . but oh Sara! I am never happy, never deeply glad-dened—I know not, I have forgotten, what the *Joy* is of which the Heart is full as of a deep & quiet fountain overflowing insensibly, or the gladness of Joy, when the fountain overflows ebullient.

One has only to turn to *Dejection: an Ode* to see how this relates to genius. Of Sara, he can there hope,[32]

> Joy lift her spirit, joy attune her voice:
> To her may all things live, from pole to pole
> Their life the eddying of her living soul!

Of himself, on the other hand, he has to say[33]

> I may not hope from outward forms to win
> The passion & the life whose fountains are within.

This fountain represents the ideal state within which happiness and creative power are together evident. It is the crown of his dialectic. For example the 'copula' which often appears in his philosophical diagrams is directly linked with it: he speaks in a note of the Sabbath as 'the Copula . . . the renewing Fountain' of the Hebrew religion.[34] And the 'sabbath' in its turn becomes endowed with the same properties, as when he speaks of the 'eddying of the mind' in some sabbath of the soul.[35]

This concept of 'eddying' has its own importance, which may again be traced to one of his naturalistic notes[36]:

> The *white rose* of Eddy-foam, where the stream ran into a scooped or scolloped hollow of the Rock in it's channel —this Shape, an exact white rose, was for ever over-powered by the Stream rushing down in upon it, and still obstinate in resurrection it spread up into the Scollop, by fits & starts, *blossoming* in a moment into a full Flower.

This note is not only a piece of highly accurate observation[37]: it also provides the most perfect expression of a thought which Coleridge used many times: namely that the true test of genius is not whether it flows, but whether it progresses—or revolves and merely spins upon itself.[38] He noted as a defect in Wordsworth that there was an occasional eddying, instead of progression, in his thought.[39] Some preachers had this defect of 'eddying' permanently, and as a result, sterility of mind followed their ministry.[40] Don Quixote's madness was 'the circling in a stream which should be progressive and adaptive . . .'[41] Similarly, it was the 'eddy without progression', the 'brooding of the one anguish' which distinguished Lear's true madness from Edgar's feigned insanity.[42] In the ideal, on the other hand, there was a progression through the eddying which, at its best, resembled the perpetually re-created rose of eddy-foam.

Even within the ideal, however, the fountain could flow in different modes. Love, for example, could manifest itself 'now as the sparkling and ebullient spring of well-doing in gifts and in labours; and now as a silent fountain of patience and long-suffering . . .'[43] Likewise, he could picture truth as a gentle fountain in the snow[44] or as a natural and gentle spring.[45] The ideal fountain, moreover, had a still nobler form. At its best, the fountain reflected the sun and thus gave forth a light of its own—the light of the sun imaged in the fountain.[46] Thus Ideas to him were fountains, by the light of which all other knowledges needed to be frequently revised.[47] The Church at its best could be described as 'shooting aloft in a stately column, that reflects the light of heaven from its shaft, and bears the "Iris, Coeli decus, promissumque Iovis lucidum" on its spray'.[48] And the true scholar, 'his mental Eye-sight purged and potenziated by this celestial Euphrasy, as he beholds the Sun in a Fountain, so will he in the miracles of Religion behold the abbreviations of the Miracle of the Universe'.[49]

This being the ideal, however, it is more relevant to the last stanza of *Kubla Khan* than the second. Here we are still dealing with the dialectic of a fallen world, and the fountain shoots aloft not in a stately column but in destruction. Nevertheless, the ideal is not entirely lost to view. The river Alph may be Lethe, river of oblivion, but all is not lost: As Coleridge wrote in the Gutch notebook,[50]

There is not a new or strange opinion—Truth returned from banishment—a river run under ground——fire beneath embers—

So-called 'originalities', he wrote in his 'Commemoration Sermon' of 1799, are[51]

indeed but transmigrated Absurdities—! Exploded out of the world, they were plunged, like Plato's Souls, into the waters of oblivion, after a lapse of ages once again to repass it.

In this connection, the various traditions of the 'two fountains' become relevant. In the Niflheim of the *Eddas*, there was a river from which flowed both sweet and bitter streams.[52] The fountain of lost paradise in Dante's *Purgatorio* had twin streams of Lethe and Eunoe.[53] Dupuis described the two fountains in Abyssinia—one, the source of the Nile, and another among the troglodytes, called the 'fountain of the sun'.[54] Coleridge himself had described the 'twy-streaming fount' of Property in *Religious Musings*.[55]

The 'two fountains' are an important organizing concept in the poem: on the one hand the fountain of the lost paradise, fountain of the sun, cyclical and immortal; on the other the river of oblivion, its cycle broken and its fountain a whirling intermittent pillar of destruction. This latter is the fountain of the second stanza, and it brings us back to the Isis-Osiris theme in the poem. In Coleridge's day, the moving whirling pillar of water which we call a typhoon was known as a Typhon[56]: and the Typhonic, destructive fountain of *Kubla Khan* stands in the same relation to the stately fountain of immortality as the burning Typhonic sun of *The Ancient Mariner* to the harmonious ideal sun of the Mariner's vision.

Elisabeth Schneider has stated that the 'ancestral voices prophesying war' have no proper place in *Kubla Khan*, and gives this as one of her reasons for not thinking it a great poem.[57] Under the interpretation offered here, however, it will be seen that their position in the poem is both logical and integral. The prophecies of war simply make explicit the 'other side of the daemonic' which is equally implicit in the fountain of destruction.

As in *The Ancient Mariner*, the Typhonic may be regarded as the scourge of God—the apparent 'wrath of God' which is really a distorted version of his goodness, educed by the imperfect vision and consequently distorted actions of fallen man. This element is reinforced by the image of chaff and thresher's flail which is used to describe the fountain. In September, 1796, Coleridge had read the following passage on the sublime, in Lowth's *De Sacra Poesi Hebraeorum*[58]:

> It would be a tedious task to instance particularly with what embellishments of diction, derived from one low and trivial object, (as it may appear to some) the barn, or the threshing-floor, the sacred writers have contrived to add a lustre to the most sublime, and a force to the most important subjects: Thus 'JEHOVAH threshes out the heathen as corn, tramples them under his feet, and disperses them. He delivers the nations to Israel to be beaten in pieces by an indented flail, or to be crushed by their brazen hoofs. He scatters his enemies like chaff upon the mountains, and disperses them with the whirlwind of his indignation.'

But whether the sublime is viewed as the Typhonic or as the wrath of God is immaterial; the main point is that the dominating images of the second stanza, the savage scenery, the cedarn cover, the demon-lover and the destructive fountain, are all anti-types of features of the true paradise, and thus induce those feelings which we have associated with the ambivalent sublime: namely fascination and dread.

The traditional associations of wild scenery with the daemonic could be demonstrated from several sources: but I propose simply to quote at length from a work which Coleridge admired very much: Burnet's *Theory of the Earth*. 'Burnet's book', he wrote many years later, 'is a grand Miltonic romance; but the contrast between the Tartarean fury and turbulence of the Burnetian and the almost supernatural tranquillity of the Mosaic Deluge is little less than comic.'[59] In earlier years, nevertheless, he had been so impressed by the passage on mountains in it that he had wished to turn it into English blank verse.[60] Burnet's description of the earth after the Flood, one of the high spots of the book, had no doubt appealed to him strongly[61]:

That the inside of the Earth is hollow and broken in many places, and is not one firm and united mass, we have both the Testimony of Sence and of easie Observations to prove: How many Caves and Dens and hollow passages into the ground do we see in many Countries, especially amongst Mountains and Rocks; and some of them endless and bottomless so far as can be discover'd. We have many of these in our own Island, in *Derbyshire, Somersetshire, Wales,* and other Counties, and in every Continent or Island they abound more or less. These hollownesses of the Earth the Ancients made prisons, or storehouses for the winds, and set a God over them to confine them, or let them loose at his pleasure. For some Ages after the Flood, as all Antiquity tells us, These were the first houses men had, at least in some parts of the Earth; here rude mortals shelter'd themselves, as well as they could, from the injuries of the Air, till they were beaten out by wild beasts that took possession of them. The Ancient oracles also us'd to be given out of these Vaults and recesses under ground, the *Sibyls* had their Caves, and the *Delphick* Oracle, and their Temples sometimes were built upon an hollow Rock. Places that are strange and solemn strike an awe into us, and incline us to a kind of superstitious timidity and veneration, and therefore they thought them fit for the seats and residences of their Deities. They fansied also that steams rise sometimes, or a sort of Vapour in those hollow places, that gave a kind of Divine fury or inspiration. But all these uses and imployments are now in a great measure worn out, we know no use of them but to make the places talkt on where they are, to be the wonders of the Country, to please our curiosity to gaze upon and admire; but we know not how they came, nor to what purpose they were made at first.

It would be very pleasant to read good descriptions of these Subterraneous Places, and of all the strange works of Nature there; how she furnisheth these dark neglected Grottoes; they have often a little Brook runs murmuring through them, and the roof is commonly a kind of petrifi'd Earth, or Icy fret-work; proper enough for such rooms. But I should be pleas'd especially to view the Sea-caves, where the waves roll in a great way under ground, and wear the hard Rock into as many odd shapes and figures as we see in the Clouds. 'Tis pleasant also to see a River in the middle of its course throw itself into the mouth of a Cave, or an opening of the Earth, and run under ground sometimes many Miles; still pursuing its Way thorough the dark pipes of the Earth, till at last it find an out-let. There are many of these Rivers taken notice of in History in the several parts of the Earth, as the *Rhone* in *France*, *Guadiana* in *Spain*, and several in *Greece*, *Alpheus*, *Lycus*, and *Eracinus*; then *Niger* in *Africa*, *Tigris* in *Asia*, &c.

Of all the sublime places which Burnet mentions, the most interesting is Delphi, for this is the landscape in Greece which most corresponds to the savage landscape of the second stanza. It was wild, it had a hideous fountain and mighty chasm, and it was here that the priestess of the Oracle prophesied, wearing the skin of the python.[62] It was, in fact, the place where[63]

> stood the healing God,
> When from his bow the arrow sped that slew
> Huge Python.

—to quote Coleridge's own lines in *The Destiny of Nations*. The healing God was Apollo Belvedere, the sun-god, and the Python, as Maurice pointed out at some length in the *History of Hindostan*, could be identified with Typhon.[64]

. . . the waters of the Nile were gradually subsiding, and the unwholsome damps and pestilential vapours that arose after so vast a body of waters was withdrawn, were denominated Typhon, and symbolically represented by Scorpio. These could alone be dissipated and rendered innoxious by the beams of the sun, the mighty archer, whose rays, like burning arrows, pierced through and annihilated the mud-generated monster. The Greeks, during their frequent migrations into Egypt, learned this ingenious allegory, and as ingeniously built upon it the story of Apollo and the serpent Python. By the mere transposition of a letter, Typhon was converted into Python. . . .

There is one other daemonic landscape which seems to contribute to the poem. I have already dwelt upon the 'Typhonian' element in the allegory of Cupid and Psyche, the fatal doubt in the mind of Psyche that her unknown lover might really be a serpent. When Cupid flies away from her, and she 'falls in love with love', she is in the position of the wailing woman of the poem—dangerously attached to physical love, yet yearning for her lost lover, and ready to undertake many labours to regain him. One of the labours which Venus prescribes is as follows[65]:

Do you see the summit of yonder lofty mountain, from which the dusky waters of a black fountain fall, and which, confined in the channel of the neighbouring valley, irrigate the Stygian marshes and supply the hoarse streams of Cocytus? Bring me immediately in this little urn liquid dew drawn from the inmost influx of the lofty fountain' . . .

But Psyche with the utmost celerity ascended to the very summit of the mountain, presuming that there at least she should find the period of her most miserable life. However, when she arrived at the confines of the vertex she saw the deadly difficulty of the vast undertaking: for a rock enormously lofty, and inaccessibly rugged, vomited from its middle the horrid waters of the fountain, which immediately falling headlong in winding streams, rushed suddenly through a narrow channel into the neighbouring valley.

This labour of Psyche serves to introduce a further and final significance of the savage landscape. It is the holy and haunted place of the lost paradise; but it is also the wilderness through which man must pass if paradise is to be regained. For the making explicit of this idea, we may turn to the remaining stanzas of the poem.

I have already pointed out that the six lines which are often joined to the end of the second stanza appear as a stanza in their own right in the first edition of the poem: and examination shows that they mark a new departure in the poem's argument.

> The shadow of the dome of pleasure
>   Floated midway on the waves;
> Where was heard the mingled measure
>   From the fountain and the caves.
> It was a miracle of rare device,
>   A sunny pleasure-dome with caves of ice!

The 'caves of ice' are the new, transforming element in the poem. The dome of pleasure is not the pleasure-dome which Kubla decreed, a 'temple built by Omnipotence in its own honour'[66]—and thus liable to perish. It is the 'miracle' in which two seemingly irreconcilable principles are held together: heat and ice.

But how is the 'miracle' related to the symbolism of the rest of the poem? In searching for an answer to this question, we may avail ourselves of the work of E. H. Coleridge and J. L. Lowes, who pointed out and discussed the relevance of two passages from Maurice which Coleridge had mentioned in the Gutch notebook.[67] The first, noted under the heading 'Hymns—Sun', reads as follows in Maurice[68]:

> (Quintus Curtius) declares it to have been an immemorial custom among the Persians for the army never to march before the rising of the sun; that a trumpet, sounding from the king's pavilion, proclaimed the first appearance of its beam, and that a golden image of its orb, inclosed in a circle of crystal, was then displayed in the front of that pavilion, which diffused so wide a splendour that it was seen through the whole camp. . . .

Coleridge actually transcribed the second passage, under the heading, 'Hymns Moon'.[69]

> In a cave in the mountains of Cashmere an Image of Ice, which makes it's appearance thus—two days before the new *moon* there appears a bubble of Ice: which increases in size every day till the 15th day, at which it is an ell or more in height: then, as the moon decreases, the Image does also till it vanishes.

Did Coleridge transcribe these passages merely because they struck him as vivid and picturesque? I think that they lie too close to his favourite trains of symbolism for that. The Persians, for example, in the extract quoted, are behaving like true sons of Cain. They have to propitiate the sun, which they see only as a symbol of power: and the glory of the rising sun thus becomes to them merely a favourable signal for battle.

Similarly, Maurice's description of the cave in Kashmir follows a long account of the work of the goddess Isis in swelling the waters of the Nile,[70] and there would seem to be a connection between the two. The image of ice, waxing and waning in unison with the phases of the moon would be, in Coleridge's eyes, a unique symbol of *natura naturata* in harmony with *natura naturans*. One thinks of his[71]

> silent icicles,
> Quietly shining to the quiet Moon.

The present image takes that harmony and perfects it.

Many years later, Coleridge jotted down in a notebook a series of brief notes on the connection between the architecture and general ideals of a number of civilizations. Among them, he noted, 'Moorish—Palace and Paradise—Self-centering Pride, Splendor and Voluptuousness, with lust of exclusive Possession . . .' and 'Indian Cavern/a multiform Idol of Nature/levelling Man & Beast, as Avatars of the ἐν καὶ παν/ Their Worship sought for the foundations of Nature or Hades—hence the Caverns. . . .'[72]

The opposition between these two ideals, which in the notebook is partly hidden by their inclusion in a longer list, was more present to Coleridge's mind at the time of which we are thinking. In 1799, he was planning to write with Southey a poem entitled 'The Flight and Return of Mohammed' in which he would have introduced a disputation between Mahomet, as representative of unipersonal Theism, and a 'Fetisch-Worshipper who adored the sensible only', who would have been an 'Okenist+Zoo-magnetist with the Night-side of Nature'.[73]

It seems clear, then, that the dome and caves respectively represent a synthesizing of the ideals of monotheism and pantheism, which, separated, lead only to self-centred rationalism on the one hand or idolatry of nature on the other. I think it possible that Coleridge in coming to formulate the latter symbolism may also have been influenced by a passage in Churchill's *Voyages*, which described a hollow mountain, in which could be visited a series of caves. The most spectacular of these, the 'room of heaven', was described as follows[74]:

> . . . in the Roof of it are the Sun, Moon, and Stars, so beautiful and bright, that our Father told me, he stood long in doubt thinking what it might be, for he was satisfy'd the sun could not pierce into that place, nor the Stars shine with him . . . He says, the Water that dropt from the Walls and run about the ground was as could as Ice, tho it was in the Month of *July* that he went in.

This image would bind together still more tightly and narrowly the symbolism of the dome and the cavern, for it would once again juxtapose the ideals of reason and of nature: the painted heavenly bodies in the man-made dome,[75] and the impression of the true heavens in the vast roof of the cave.

It seems clear, then, that Coleridge, as early as this, would have regarded caves as symbols of the ἕν καί πᾶν—and therefore of Isis.[76] The link between moon and caves in symbolism is a common one, of course—and there is even, in *Samson Agonistes*, the well-known description of the moon as dark and silent, 'hid in her vacant interlunar cave'.[77] Both images were used as symbols of passive love by Coleridge: in the case of the moon, he took Milton's image a stage further[78]:

> Infinite Love,
> Whose latence is the plenitude of All,
> Thou with retracted beams, and self-eclipse
> Veiling, revealest thine eternal Sun.

Here the moon is the Isis of passive love, and her veil of self-eclipse acts as a revelation of the sun.

The position of the dome as symbol of the active principle in human creation is fortified by its use in this stanza. In the previous part of the poem, it stood for the genius who was trying to imitate *natura naturans*, to achieve that work of the Primary Imagination which would be a repetition in the finite mind of the eternal act of creation in the infinite I AM[79]: against it were ranged the forces of a *natura naturata* which was, in a fallen world, out of harmony with *natura naturans*. In the third stanza, on the other hand, the miracle is achieved. The dome has caves of ice: it is no longer the precarious dome of self-sufficiency or Cowper's 'Russian palace of ice, glittering, cold and transitory'.[80]

The miraculous harmony thus achieved exists in more than one dimension, moreover, for the caves provide a harmony which is appreciated by several senses at once. If the ice in the caves represents visually and tangibly a perfect response to the moon, there is also a perfect response of *natura naturata* to *natura naturans* in terms of sound. The

> mingled measure
> From the fountain and the caves

is not to be identified with the tumult in the midst of which Kubla heard ancestral voices prophesying war: that tumult is now transmuted into a measured harmony. And this, like the ice in the caves, represents the perfection of art, love and divine creativity. It corresponds to the relationship ('the circulation and choral eddying of the Divine *Life*, the eternal Act of Communion')[81] between God the Father and God the Son—between the great I AM and 'the filial WORD that re-affirmeth it from Eternity to Eternity, whose choral Echo is the universe'.[82] Coleridge used this imagery several times elsewhere in his poetry. In one poem, he used it to describe the ideal relationship between man and woman[83]:

> The Almighty, having first composed a Man,
> Set him to music, framing Woman for him,
> And fitted each to each, and made them one!
> And 'tis my faith, that there's a natural bond
> Between the female mind and measured sounds . . .

In the poem *Ad Vilmum Axiologum* he extended this image to art. Wordsworth could continue to create because he was surrounded by those who responded to his song[84]:

COLERIDGE THE VISIONARY

Ad Vilmum Axiologum

This be the meed, that thy song creates a thousand-fold
echo!
Sweet as the warble of woods, that awakes at the gale of
the morning!
List! the Hearts of the Pure, like caves in the ancient
mountains
Deep, deep *in* the Bosom, and *from* the Bosom resound
it,
Each with a different tone, complete or in musical
fragments—
All have welcomed thy Voice, and receive and retain
and prolong it!
This is the word of the Lord! it is spoken, and Beings
Eternal
Live and are borne as an Infant; the Eternal begets the
Immortal:
Love is the Spirit of Life, and Music the Life of the
Spirit!

One may detect a slight note of envy here—a reference to
the fact that Wordsworth, unlike Coleridge, has the good
fortune to be surrounded by women who are devoted to his
genius.[85] The full pathos of the poem emerges if it is read in
conjunction with *Dejection: an Ode*, which again refers to
the harmony of the Wordsworth household, and, in the first
version addressed to Sara Hutchinson, promises her the
qualities which he evidently feels would produce the
'mingled measure' of full creative harmony, could they only
be united with his own.

If this interpretation is accepted, it is plain that an extraordinary condensation of imagery is achieved within these
six lines. As with *The Ancient Mariner*, there is a moment of
vision at the heart of this poem. The ideal is revealed for a
moment; visual and auditory harmonies fuse into a single,
intricate pattern. The moon and ice are in harmony together,
and so are the fountain and cave. There is a cross-harmony
between the two pairs, moreover; the ice and the echo are
linked together by the fact that both are associated with
caves, while the moon and fountain are equally linked—for

between them they figure that lost sun which, according to the mystics, is fountain both of light and sound. In addition, a more comprehensive harmony is evident in the first two lines of the stanza, for the shadow of the dome of pleasure, floating midway on the water in the centre of the scene, figures the age-old ideal of a harmony between permanence and flux, between time and eternity. The contents of the Bible, said Coleridge many years later, 'present to us the stream of time continuous as Life and a symbol of Eternity, inasmuch as the Past and the Future are virtually contained in the Present'.[86]

If the ideal harmony has been stated in the third stanza, the images which compose it stand only in a formal pattern: their fusion is achieved statically, not organically. This state mirrors accurately the place of the 'vision' in the poem. The poet is still left with the problem of achieving the harmony which he has for a moment envisaged: and the figure of Kubla appropriately merges at this point into the figure of Coleridge himself.

A relationship between poet and hero is evident throughout the poem, but I do not think that Coleridge would have identified himself with the Kubla of the first stanza. He, as we have seen, is the man of steadfast, commanding genius, whereas Coleridge seems to have seen himself as a man whose genius was intermittent and unpredictable, but when it did appear, absolute. Kubla Khan can create within his own self-imposed limitations, but his achievements will be correspondingly limited, and liable to perish. Coleridge's genius, on the other hand, takes the whole of human experience for its field, and would, if successful, achieve the miracle of finding the pattern—of reconciling *natura naturata* with *natura naturans*. He is left with the problem of achieving this vision and this creative ecstasy, and it is around this problem that the final stanza of the poem is constructed.

In examining this stanza, it is clear that the figure of the 'Abyssinian maid' is the most difficult and puzzling of the images to be dealt with. Lowes himself found her baffling, and confessed on one occasion that he was not satisfied with the comments which he had made on the subject.[87]

In one of Coleridge's earliest surviving letters, the one

which he sent to his brother George with the poem *A Mathematical Problem*, there is an image which seems relevant to our discussion here. He says,[88]

> I may justly plume myself, that I *first* have drawn the Nymph Mathesis from the visionary caves of Abstracted Idea, and caused her to unite with Harmony.

Even before going to Cambridge, then, he had this image in his mind, and associated the nymph with learning. He may well have derived it from Porphyry's allegorical interpretation of the Cave of the Nymphs in Homer, which had been included (appropriately enough) in Thomas Taylor's translation of Proclus' *Philosophical and Mathematical Commentaries* a few years before.[89]

In this case, the nymph would emerge as a guardian of knowledge. This is interesting, for I have already mentioned that there was a whole race of cave-dwellers who were associated with the guardianship of hidden knowledge—namely, the troglodytes of Abyssinia. They were reputed to have been androgynous, to have invented the first three letters of the alphabet, and to have within their territory the 'fountain of the sun'. Burnet relates that after the Flood, mankind lived for some time in caves: and the impression was often conveyed that the troglodytes were an antediluvian people, surviving from the very beginning of civilization.

Coleridge would have read of the troglodytes in Bruce's *Travels*: and he was also familiar with the account of them in Herodotus. The evidence for this lies in a stray remark in a letter to Southey where, describing his conversation with an American land-agent, he says, 'He never saw a *Byson* in his Life—but has heard of them—They are quite backwards.'[90] The remark is puzzling at first sight, but can in fact be explained by reference to Herodotus' description of the oxen of the Garamantes 'which walk backwards whilst they are feeding; their horns are so formed that they cannot do otherwise, they are before so long, and curved in such a manner, that if they did not recede as they fed, they would stick in the ground'. Coleridge's pleasantry needs no further explanation: the importance for our present purpose is that this observation by Herodotus occurs just after his description of the 'Fountain of the Sun' that was cold at noon and boiled at midnight, and in a passage which is, outside Diodorus Siculus, the *locus classicus* on the subject of troglodytes.[91]

Troglodyte lore is also relevant to the 'dulcimer' which the Abyssinian maid was playing. There was some interest in the dulcimer at Bristol in Coleridge's time,[92] but that does not explain how it should have found its way into a poem where every other image seems to refer to ancient history and mythology. If we look at Eusebius' *Praeparatio Evangelica* or Calmet's *Antiquities Sacred and Profane*, however, we find it asserted that the troglodytes invented one of the oldest musical instruments known to man, namely the sambuca.[93] And the English word used to translate this in Coleridge's day was always 'dulcimer'.[94] It seems reasonable to suppose, therefore, that this is another link between the Abyssinian maiden and the troglodyte guardians of ancient truth.

A further clue to the symbolism of the dulcimer may be found by examining Burney's *History of Music*—a work which Coleridge knew.[95] Towards the end of the first volume, in a quotation from Montfaucon, there is this account of the relationship between the sambuca and the lyre[96]:

'Among the stringed instruments, you will find the Lyre of a character analogous to *masculine*, from the great depth or gravity, and roughness of its tones; the *Sambuca* of a *feminine* character, *weak* and *delicate*, and from its great *acuteness*, and the *smallness* of its *strings*, tending to *dissolve* and *enervate*. Of the intermediate instruments, the *Polyphthongum partakes* most of the *feminine*; but the *Cithara differs not much* from the *masculine character* of the *Lyre*.' Here is a scale of stringed instruments; the *Lyre* and *Sambuca* at the extremes; the *Polyphthongum* and *Cithara* between; the one next to the *Sambuca*, the other next to the *Lyre*.

The lyre is the traditional instrument of Apollo and the bards: and I do not think it fanciful to suppose that Coleridge had seen in the sambuca a symbol of the feminine complement for which he was seeking—of the passive, delicate music which would sustain his own, stronger music and turn it into the mingled measure of his ideal vision.

So far in our interpretation, the Abyssinian maid has emerged as a symbol of the lost tradition of knowledge for which mankind is seeking, and a symbol of Coleridge's own feminine ideal, the passive complement to his active rôle as creative artist. She has another significance, however, and one which knits her still more closely to the central symbolism of the poem as we have interpreted it. The key to this further significance is to be found in a work well known in English up till Coleridge's time, and used by Sidney as a source of his *Arcadia*[97]—Heliodorus' *Aethiopian History*. At the beginning of this history, a band of Egyptian robbers have come upon the scene of a mutiny and are preparing to board the ship and rob the bodies when they see an even more astonishing sight[98]:

> It was a young Lady, sitting upon a Rock, of so rare and perfect a Beauty, as one would have taken her for a Goddess, and though her present misery opprest her with extreamest grief, yet in the greatness of her affliction, they might easily perceive the greatness of her Courage: A Laurel crown'd her Head, and a Quiver in a Scarf hanged at her back; she rested her left Arm upon her Bow, and let her Hand carelessly hang down upon her right Thigh; she leaned on her other Arm, laying her Cheek upon her hand, and fixing her eyes upon a young Gentleman that lay not far distant from her. . . .

Shortly afterwards,

> she leaped from the Rock, and the Thieves upon the Mountains suprized with fear and astonishment ran to hide themselves behind the Bushes: for she appeared more Divine when she was upon her Feet; her Arrows in her Quiver clashing as she stepped, her Robe (that was Cloth of Gold) glittering in the Sun, and her Hair that flowed under her Coronet (like the Priestesses of *Bacchus*) reaching almost to the ground. One said she was a Goddess, and sure the Goddess *Diana*, or *Isis* the Patroness of their Country. . . .

There can be little doubt that Coleridge was familiar with Heliodorus, for in 1795, when he and Southey were working in close collaboration, the latter used the Aethiopian history in a poem which he published, referring to it specifically in a footnote to the following stanza[99]:

> The holy prelate owns her power;
> In soft'ning tale relates
> The snowy Ethiop's matchless charms,
> The outlaws den, the clang of arms
> And love's too-varying fates.

This helps us to identify Coleridge's 'Abyssinian maid'— and incidentally suggests that he pictured her as white. The likelihood that he also followed Heliodorus in regarding her as an Isis-figure is strengthened when we remember that he borrowed a Latin volume of Apuleius containing the *Metamorphoses* in November, 1796.[100] Towards the end of the story, Aristomenes prays for help to the goddess Isis, and at last a radiant figure appears, carrying a timbrel of brass in her right hand, which gives forth a shrill and clear sound, and a boat-shaped cup of gold in her left hand; and breathing out 'the pleasant spice of fertile Arabia'. After a time she reveals her identity[101]:

> Some know me as Juno, some as Bellona of the Battles; others as Hecate, others again as Rhamnubia, but both races of Aethiopians, whose lands the morning sun first shines upon, and the Egyptians who excel in ancient learning and worship me with ceremonies proper to my godhead, call me by my true name, namely, Queen Isis.

It seems then that Coleridge's damsel has the place of Queen Isis within the visionary structure of the poem. She is its redemptive figure, the complement to the woman wailing for her demon-lover beneath the waning moon in the second stanza. Like the Indian maid of Keats's *Endymion*, she stands at last revealed as the radiant white moon goddess.

One now begins to see why she is singing of Mount Abora. A source was long ago pointed out in Milton's lines comparing Eden with the place[102]

> ... where *Abassin* Kings thir issue Guard,
> Mount *Amara*, though this by som suppos'd
> True Paradise under the *Ethiop* Line
> By *Nilus* head, enclos'd with shining Rock,
> A whole dayes journey high ...

This Abyssinian paradise recurred several times in eighteenth-century literature: there is a particularly good description of it in Thomson's *Seasons*.[103] Moreover, it is easy to see why Coleridge should have used it here. His maid is singing of the lost paradise, which lies by the fountain of the sacred river. But why has Amara been changed to Abora?

Two reasons may be suggested. The first is that the word 'Abor' appears on the second page of Holwell's mythological dictionary with the comment that 'the Sun was called Abor, the parent of light'.[104] The second is that Beth-Abara was the place where Christ was baptized in Jordan by John the Baptist, and where the spirit descended upon him 'like a dove'.[105] Milton used it in *Paradise Regained*,[106] and Coleridge used it as a symbol for the place where Truth is revealed to man. After his discussion of Arctic superstitions in *The Destiny of Nations*, he continued[107]:

> Wild phantasies! yet wise,
> On the victorious goodness of high God
> Teaching reliance, and medicinal hope,
> Till from Bethabra northward, heavenly Truth
> With gradual steps, winning her difficult way,
> Transfer their rude Faith perfected and pure.

The change from Amara to Abora thus adds to the Abyssinian paradise the further symbolism of the sun, the descending dove, and the revelation of divine Truth.

The mountain-top is, of course, a powerful Romantic and pre-Romantic symbol in its own right, and one that is often used to express the sublime. The young Hazlitt was to remember for the rest of his life Coleridge, as a Unitarian preacher, giving out his text at Shrewsbury: 'And he went up into the mountain to pray, HIMSELF, ALONE.'[108]

> ... and when he came to the two last words, which he
> pronounced loud, deep, and distinct, it seemed to me,

who was then young, as if the sounds had echoed from the bottom of the human heart, and as if that prayer might have floated in solemn silence through the universe.

Later in life, this image was still present with Coleridge as an example of the true sublime, as distinguished from the majestic, or the grand[109]:

I would say that the Saviour praying on the Mountain, the Desert on one hand, the Sea on the other, the city at an immense distance below, was sublime. . . .

In *The Prelude*, Wordsworth pictured Coleridge[110]

On Etna's summit, above earth and sea,
Triumphant, winning from the invaded heavens
Thoughts without bound, magnificent designs,
Worthy of poets who attuned their harps
In wood or echoing cave, for discipline
Of heroes . . .

And there is some reason to believe that Lamb associated with Coleridge the well-known lines of Matthew Roydon on Sir Philip Sidney[111]:

When he descended down the mount,
His personage seemed most divine:
A thousand graces one might count
Upon his lovely chearful eyne.
To hear him speak, and sweetly smile,
You were in Paradise the while.

The mountain-top has long been associated with inspiration, and the twin-peaked Parnassus is a familiar image. But there is one passage which particularly aroused Coleridge's enthusiasm. It occurs in a poem which he once praised in terms as extravagant as he ever used of any work of literature[112]:

Now Collins' Ode on the poetical character—that part of it, I should say, beginning with—'The Band (as faery Legends say) Was wove on that creating Day', has inspired & whirled *me* along with greater agitations of enthusiasm than any the most *impassioned* Scene in Schiller or Shakspere. . . .

The passage in question may be quoted in full[113]:

The band, as fairy legends say,
Was wove on that creating day,
When he, who call'd with thought to birth
Yon tented sky, this laughing earth,
And drest with springs, and forests tall,
And pour'd the main engirting all,
Long by the lov'd Enthusiast woo'd,
Himself in some diviner mood,
Retiring, sate with her alone,
And plac'd her on his saphire throne,
The whiles, the vaulted shrine around,
Seraphic wires were heard to sound,
Now sublimest triumph swelling,
Now on love and mercy dwelling;
And she, from out the veiling cloud,
Breath'd her magic notes aloud:
And thou, thou rich-hair'd youth of morn,
And all thy subject life was born!
The dangerous passions kept aloof,
Far from the sainted growing woof:
But near it sate ecstatic Wonder,
Listening the deep applauding thunder:
And Truth, in sunny vest array'd
By whose the Tarsol's eyes were made;
All the shadowy tribes of Mind,
In braided dance their murmurs join'd,
And all the bright uncounted Powers,
Who feed on heaven's ambrosial flowers.
Where is the Bard, whose soul can now
Its high presuming hopes avow?
Where he who thinks, with rapture blind,
This hallow'd work for him design'd?

High on some cliff, to heaven up-pil'd,
Of rude access, of prospect wild,
Where, tangled round the jealous steep,
Strange shades o'erbrow the vallies deep,
And holy Genii guard the rock,
Its glooms embrown, its springs unlock,

While on its rich ambitious head,
An Eden, like his own, lies spread,
I view that oak, the fancied glades among,
By which as Milton lay, his evening ear,
From many a cloud that drop'd ethereal dew,
Nigh spher'd in heaven its native strains could hear:
On which that ancient trump he reach'd was hung:
   Thither oft his glory greeting,
   From Waller's myrtle shades retreating,
With many a vow from Hope's aspiring tongue,
My trembling feet his guiding steps pursue;
   In vain—Such bliss to one alone,
   Of all the sons of soul was known,
   And Heaven, and Fancy, kindred powers,
   Have now o'erturn'd th'inspiring bowers,
Or curtain'd close such scene from every future view.

This poem probably gave Coleridge the 'ideal tribes' of the brain which Hartley charted in *Religious Musings*[114]: certainly it haunted his imagination, and contributed richly to *Kubla Khan*. The movement of the verse in Collins's poem has a strange resemblance to that of Coleridge's last stanza: and by enshrining Milton in his own mountain-paradise, Collins gives a twist to tradition which is typical of the eighteenth century and relevant to 'Mount Abora'. Coleridge, of course, would not have followed Collins strictly, to make Milton sole possessor of the peak. He himself followed the classical tradition of the twin-peaked Parnassus, and placed Shakespeare 'on one of the two glory-smitten summits of the poetic mountain, with Milton as his compeer, not rival'.[115] Yet there is an important sense in which he would follow Collins. Mount Abora is not simply the lost paradise of the past, where the secrets of the universe lay hid: it is also the mountain of inspiration, where the bard attains his creative ecstasy. For Coleridge, as for Collins, ecstasy and the vision of truth are the same, and constitute the true sublime.[116]

Inspiration, with poetic inspiration as its centre, is thus the keynote in the remaining lines of the poem. Elisabeth Schneider has quoted a relevant passage from Plato's *Ion*[117]:

For as the Priests of Cybele perform not their Dances, while they have the free Use of their Understandings; so these Melody-Poets pen those beautiful Songs of theirs, only when they are out of their sober Minds. But as soon as they proceed to give Voice and Motion to those Songs, adding to their Words the Harmony of Musick and the Measure of Dance, they are immediately transported; and possessed by some Divine Power, are like the Priestesses of Bacchus, who, full of the God, no longer draw Water, but Honey and Milk out of the Springs and Fountains; tho unable to do any Thing like it, when they are sober. And in Fact there passes in the Souls of these Poets that very Thing, which they pretend to do. For they assure us, that out of certain Gardens and flowery Vales belonging to the Muses, from Fountains flowing there with Honey, gathering the Sweetness of their Songs, they bring it to us, like the Bees; and in the same Manner withal, flying.

The inspiration of the 'Awennydion, or people inspired', as described in Giraldus Cambrensis, is equally apposite[118]:

These gifts are usually conferred upon them in dreams: some seem to have sweet milk or honey poured on their lips. . . . They invoke, during their prophecies, the true and living God, and the Holy Trinity, and pray that they may not by their sins be prevented from finding the truth.

The Bard was also a Druid: and in Coleridge's eyes the poet's function extended far beyond the creation of melodious verses. The bardic ecstasy was one with all creative ecstasy, secular or sacred. The poet on Parnassus was not far removed from Moses on Mount Sinai or Christ on Mount Tabor—and to see how readily these conceptions blended in the romantic mind, we need only glance at Lamb's description of George Dyer[119]:

At the very time when, personally encountering thee, he passes with no recognition—or, being stopped, starts like a thing surprised—at that moment, reader, he is on Mount Tabor—or Parnassus—or co-sphered with Plato —or with Harrington, framing 'immortal commonwealths'. . . . The Cam and the Isis are to him 'better than all the waters of Damascus'. On the Muses' hill he is happy, and good, as one of the Shepherds on the Delectable Mountains. . . .

The creative ecstasy is thought of in the same terms as religious transfiguration. 'For genius, all over the world, stands hand in hand, and one shock of recognition runs the whole circle round.'[120] The scientist or the philosopher, the poet, prophet or king share the same needs and the same nature[121]:

> There, Priest of Nature! dost thou shine,
> NEWTON! a King among the Kings divine,
>   Whether with harmony's mild force,
>   He guides along its course
> The axle of some beauteous star on high,
>   Or gazing, in the spring
>   Ebullient with creative energy,
> Feels his pure breast with rapturous joy possest,
>   Inebriate in the holy ecstasy.

The inspired figure of the last stanza is the apotheosis of all the 'divine men' who had haunted Coleridge's youthful imagination. And the fact of his 'glory', of his transfiguration, brings this figure into the full symbolic pattern of the poem. Just before Milton described Mount Amara in *Paradise Lost*, he spoke of another earthly paradise, also in Ethiopia—[122]

>   . . . that *Nyseian* Ile
> Girt with the River *Triton*, where old *Cham*,
> Whom Gentiles *Ammon* call, and *Libyan Jove*,
> Hid *Amalthea* and her Florid Son
> Young *Bacchus* from his stepdame *Rhea's* eye . . .

The lost paradise is regained in the song of the Abyssinian maid, and with it the lost Dionysus. Her song corresponds to the inscription in the Egyptian temples of Minerva, which was recorded in the *Pantheon* that Coleridge pored over at school[123]:

I am what is, what shall be what hath been: My Veil hath been unveil'd by none: The Fruit which I have brought forth is this, the Sun is born.

If Coleridge could revive within him her symphony and song, the work of Isis would be complete: he would be the restored Osiris, and his 'music loud and long' would be as potent as the 'music strong and saintly song' of Bard Bracy.[124] He would be the Apollo, the prince of bards.

According to the Homeric hymn dedicated to him, the Pythian Apollo came to earth to build a temple for himself. After some time he came to Crisa, below the glades of Parnassus; before building his temple there, however, he was obliged to slay the ravaging she-dragon Python (guardian of the monster Typhaon). Then he looked for ministers to serve him, and diverted a ship manned by Cretans to Crisa. He appeared to the crew 'bearing the form of a man, brisk and sturdy, in the prime of his youth, while his broad shoulders were covered with his hair'[125] and explained that they had been brought to be the keepers of his temple.[126]

And when they had put away craving for drink and food, they started out with the lord Apollo, the son of Zeus, to lead them, holding a lyre in his hands, and playing sweetly as he stepped high and featly. So the Cretans followed him to Pytho, marching in time as they chanted the Ie Paean after the manner of the Cretan paean-singers and of those in whose hearts the heavenly Muse has put sweet-voiced song. With tireless feet they approached the ridge and straightway came to Parnassus and the lovely place where they were to dwell honoured by many men. There Apollo brought them and showed them his most holy sanctuary and rich temple.

The weaving of the circle also had a place in sun-worship. In Coleridge's day, it was probably best known as a dance of the Druids, as in Mason's *Caractacus*[127]:

> Circle, sons, this holy ground;
> Circle close, in triple row.

According to an article in Ouseley's *Oriental Collections*, the three circular spirals beloved of the Druids might represent the three attributes of their God: fire, light and spirit.[128] Another article in the same volume described the ritual dances of the Indians round their fires, quoting classical parallels to suggest that they were dances in honour of the sun, or Dionysus. [129] Such dances might take place round any object which had solar significance, but were especially reserved for personages or gods representing the sun.[130]

Coleridge apparently knew all about such dances: he referred to the Pyrrhic dance in a notebook,[131] and was even aware that dancing around the maypole on May Day was a survival of the worship of Priapus.[132] He would have associated all this lore with the idea of the 'magic circle',[133] which fascinated him, and with the cyclical lore of the Egyptians.[134] And there is one example of the circular dance which evidently impressed him particularly. In the Gutch notebook, he wrote, 'Read the whole 107th page of Maurice's Indostan.'[135] 'Why Coleridge meant to re-read the page *in toto*,' says Lowes, 'we can only guess.'[136] With the present discussion in mind, however, our guesses have a more secure foundation: for at the foot of the page the following passage begins[137]:

The RAAS JATTRA, or circular dance, which is the nineteenth festival, must by no means be passed over, as I have the strongest reasons for thinking it allusive to that of the planetary train, and the very dance mentioned by Lucian. Some slight glance at the character of CREESHNA, the Indian Apollo, has already been taken, and a more ample account of this important personage will be given hereafter. This feast, Mr Holwell informs us, falls on the full moon in October, and is universally observed through Hindostan; but in a most extraordinary manner at Bindoobund, in commemoration of a miraculous event, which is fabled to have happened in the neighbourhood of that place. A number of virgins having assembled to celebrate in mirth and sport the descent of Kissen (Creeshna) in the height of their joy the god himself appeared among them, and proposed *a dance* to the jocund fair. They objected the want of partners with whom to form that dance: but Creeshna obviated the objection by dividing himself (his rays) into as many portions as there were virgins, and thus every nymph had a Creeshna to

attend her in the circular dance. The author of this
account has illustrated his narration by an engraving, and
whether by accident or design I cannot say, but the
number of the virgins thus engaged is exactly *seven*, while
the radiant god himself stands in an easy, disengaged
attitude in the *centre* of the engraved table.

The bard stands revealed in these images as the divine
priest of nature. Just as the Son of God transubstantiates the
materials of the earthly Temple into the 'pattern in the
mount', the eternal Temple in Heaven,[138] so the bard
displays man as 'the sole magnificent temple of the world of
visible existence',[139] as 'an edifice not built with human
hands, which needs only to be purged of its idols and idola-
trous services to become the temple of the true and living
light'.[140] He is the Shakespeare whose 'whole harmonious
creation of light and shade with all its subtle interchange of
deepening and dissolving colors rises in silence to the silent
fiat of the uprising Apollo'.[141]

Since this is the climax of the poem, moreover, it is fitting
that there should be another echo from that poem which had
its place in the 'vision' of *The Ancient Mariner*: Davies's
Orchestra. Just before the passage already quoted, Davies
describes how Love, who created the world, is able sometimes to step in and resolve the discords which he sees[142]:

'Then with such words as cannot be exprest,
He cuts the troops, that all asunder fling,
And ere they wist, he casts them in a ring.

Then did he rarefy the element,
    And in the centre of the ring appear,
The beams that from his forehead spreading went,
    Begot an horror, and religious fear
    In all the souls that round about him were;
        Which in their ears attentiveness procures,
        While he, with such like sounds their minds
        allures.

As the poem draws to its close, dominated by this central
image, one is conscious of an inevitability in the final
imagery, matched by an increasing weight of significance.

It is like hearing a number of themes resolved in the conclusion of an intricate piece of music. Almost every strand which we have traced in the poem is reflected in the honey-dew and the milk of paradise.

I have already quoted two passages which speak of the honey on the lips of the bard in ecstasy, and there can be little doubt that this was a favourite theme with Coleridge. When Wordsworth thought of him absent in Sicily, it was precisely this image from the Sicilian poet which came to his mind[143]:

> . . . yea, not unmoved,
> When thinking on my own beloved friend,
> I hear thee tell how bees with honey fed
> Divine Comates, by his impious lord
> Within a chest imprisoned; how they came
> Laden from blooming grove or flowery field,
> And fed him there, alive, month after month,
> Because the goatherd, blessed man! had lips
> Wet with the Muses' nectar.

The fact that Coleridge speaks not of 'honey' but of 'honey-dew', however, reminds us that there are other associations involved: for in the Eddas, where this term is mainly used, it has a wider connotation. The true 'hydromel' flows from one of the two celestial fountains.[144]

> . . . under this root is the fountain *Vergelmer*, whence flow the infernal rivers: this root is gnawed upon below by the monstrous serpent *Nidhoger*. Under that root, which stretches out towards the land of the Giants, is also a celebrated spring, in which are concealed Wisdom and Prudence. He who has possession of it is named *Mimis*; he is full of wisdom, because he drinks thereof every morning.

The mead which flows from this fountain is described again later[145]:

> 'The great and sacred Ash is besprinkled with a white water, whence comes the dew which falls into the valleys, and which springs from the fountain of PAST-TIME.' Men call this the Honey-dew, and it is the food of bees.

Honey-dew is thus related to the true fountain of the lost Paradise—the Arethusa for which Alpheus seeks. And this gives a special point to all the other associations of milk and honey with Paradise which come to mind.

In the eighteenth century, this association was almost commonplace, for the image had occurred in connection with many paradises, both past and future, from the ancient Brahman Paradise[146] to Moses' Promised Land. It was particularly welcome to an age which was interested in 'natural religion'. Maurice, for example, praised the Golden Age, when 'rivers of milk and nectar flowed through nature's universal garden'.[147] The contemporary student of mythology, however, could hardly fail to notice that the image also had esoteric significance. In the mysteries, honey purged the initiate from evil[148]; and in Abyssinia, which was described as a land of honey and butter, Christian initiates were given milk and honey.[149] In many widely scattered civilizations, moreover, they were food for the young god. Krishna was fed on milk by his maidens: and the infant Zeus was fed with honey and the milk of the goat Amaltheia, while the Curetes danced about him clashing their arms to prevent his cries from reaching the ears of Kronos.[150] The same element entered into Isaiah's prophecies concerning the Messiah[151]:

. . . Behold, a virgin shall conceive, and bear a son, and shall call his name Immanuel. Butter and honey shall he eat, that he may know to refuse the evil, and choose the good.

Once again, therefore, the same pattern emerges. As the god of Love, descending to earth, shines forth with the rays of the sun, so the bard in ecstasy, the inspired genius, partakes of the divine.

.   .   .   .   .   .

Kubla Khan, to sum up, is a poem with two major themes: genius and the lost paradise. In the first stanza the man of commanding genius, the fallen but daemonic man, strives to rebuild the lost paradise in a world which is, like himself, fallen. In the second stanza, the other side of the daemonic re-asserts itself: the mighty fountain in the savage place, the wailing woman beneath the waning moon, the daemon-lover.

The third stanza is a moment of miraculous harmony between the contending forces: the sunny dome and the caves of ice, the fountain and the caves, the dome and the waves all being counterpoised in one harmony. Finally, in the last stanza, there is a vision of paradise regained: of man re-visited by that absolute genius which corresponds to his original, unfallen state, of the honey-dew fountain of immortality re-established in the garden, of complete harmony between Apollo with his lyre and the damsel with the dulcimer, of the established dome, and of the multitude, reconciled by the terrible fascination of the genius into complete harmony.

In spite of the over-riding pattern of the poem, however, the imagery is so complicated and interwoven that a complete interpretation cannot be presented in one straightforward exposition. Instead, one is forced to establish the dialectic of thesis, antithesis, static harmony and desired consummation in the four stanzas, and then suggest how various images and ideas pass through it. Alph, as the sacred river, runs through measureless caverns to a sterile sea and is thus separated from the fountain, which becomes in its turn destructive; but even in this state, a harmony between fountain and caves is possible, and one may also envisage a re-establishment of the original honey-dew fountain of immortality in a regained paradise. Again, Alph is also Alpheus, the male principle for ever seeking Arethusa the female principle: in this rôle he becomes assimilated with the Kubla of the first stanza and re-emerges in the last stanza in the harmony of the inspired bard with the Abyssinian maid. Or again we may trace in the Cain-like figure of Kubla the Typhonian sun of heat and violence, with the wailing woman beneath the waning moon as his confederate, the usurping Aso of Ethiopia: the harmony of ice and moon figures the redeeming work of Isis, who becomes explicit in the Abyssinian maid, and finally restores Osiris, the sun-god of divine love. As in *The Ancient Mariner*, all these symbols may be translated psychologically. Kubla is the eighteenth-century man of understanding, trying to impose a rational order on the universe, while the second stanza represents that other side of the eighteenth-century mind—the Gothic love of horrible sublimity and powerful destruction—for which the unregenerate Reason can find no place. A powerful genius may impose a harmony even upon these warring elements: but the only true solution lies with the true genius, who in his moment of inspiration is restored temporarily to the state of unfallen man, and so enabled to overcome the sterile conflict between the impotent understanding and the unrestrained energies of destruction by subsuming these elements into the Sun-fountain of the sublime Reason—at once powerful and compellingly attractive.

That this intricate pattern of imagery represents the fruit of long speculation on Coleridge's part is supported by the fact that one can consider some of his other 'divine men' in connection with it and find so many detailed parallels as to render coincidence impossible. This is true of minor parallels such as that of Phaeton, who tried to drive the sun-chariot of his father, but crashed to the earth, with the result that the River Alpheus boiled, the Nile hid its head-waters, and the Ethiopians were turned black.[152] It is easy to see how this could be read as a distortion of the Fall-myth. The same is true of more important parallels. In an earlier chapter, we considered Coleridge's enthusiasm for Moses, visionary and 'Veil of the Light',[153] and this enthusiasm is reflected throughout the poem. Moses ('beyond doubt a man of great intellectual powers naturally, a Man of Commanding Genius . . . learned in all the learning of Egypt')[154] is 'an alumnus of the Temple of Isis or On'[155] who deplores the decline of the true religion into an idolatry of nature with male and female animal gods and dreams of a better and purer community for his people. This cannot, however, be achieved in Heliopolis by the Nile. He must first lead his people through the wilderness, where it is recorded that he struck out a fountain of water from the rock. He married an Abyssinian woman, according to tradition,[156] and went up into Mount Sinai, where it is recorded that 'the Mountain was in smoke because the Lord descended on it in Fire'. Coleridge later commented on this statement as follows[157]:

The Light commences it's action as a stimulant, & raises the dark and dank Stagnum into Mist, where it thins, and is pierceable, there is a Gleam, and the Light becomes a pale Stain; then it is densest, it is a darkness that ferments, till by its light-enkindled internal action it breaks forth in rending flashes, & the darkness explodes into *Light*, the Dionysus from *Semele*, of *Jove*/—the *Ground*-Lightning.

Thus transfigured into the 'Dionysus from Semele of Jove' Moses receives 'the credentials of a law-giver'.[158] On coming down from the mountain, radiant as the sun-god, his people, who have relapsed into Egyptian animal-worship, are fear-struck by his awesome appearance. Having given them the divine Laws, however, he is not allowed to enter the promised land, but only to see, from Mount Abarim, 'the far prospect beyond, thro' the breaches and sudden thinnings of the intervening Mists, close at hand sad and savage wastes, ruggedness, and desolation while from the far distance a fair landscape, indistinct but green & sunny and bathed in Light of Freshness, gleams thro' in snatches!—[159] Thus he has a glimpse, at least, of the 'land flowing with milk and honey'.

Another Old Testament figure who is relevant to the paradigm is King Solomon. The *Song of Solomon* had a considerable vogue in the eighteenth century (nine separate translations, several of them in verse, are recorded in the British Museum Catalogue for that period), and it is difficult to believe that there is no connection between its imagery and that of *Kubla Khan*. Coleridge refers to it several times in his later notebooks,[160] and it is clear from these references that he originally regarded the poem as an epithalamium on the marriage between Solomon and an Egyptian princess. In his longest discussion, in 1830,[161] he says that he had once held the book to be a simple love-poem, but had eventually, following the analogy of the Cupid and Psyche myth and Oriental poetry in general, come to see it as an allegory of the Messiah, and his communion with the soul.

Solomon was the king of Israel who came nearest to realizing the splendours of a typical Eastern potentate. He built a pleasure-house for himself, and a paradise-garden—[162]

   . . . that, not Mystic, where the Sapient King
Held dalliance with his faire *Egyptian* Spouse.

Tradition held that the Queen of Sheba was queen of both Egypt and Ethiopia: and when the Canticle was associated with Solomon's Wisdom writings, the 'woman' of the poem was identified with the feminine Wisdom of the Apocryphal writings.

In the cabbalistic writings, King Solomon is the great archetype of the King. In the *Song of Solomon* and the Wisdom writings, two of the most important sources of cabbalistic imagery, the King remains constant: but his Beloved, the Matrona, is imaged in three different ways. She is herself, the ideal woman; she is the earthly paradise for which the king is seeking; and she is the heavenly Wisdom.

Here we reach the heart of Coleridge's visionary speculations. His vision of his own potentialities remained constant during these years—he could, he felt, be the man of absolute genius: but there was a constant and threefold problem concerning the means of achieving that state. At times, he hoped to create a community of spirits like that depicted in the central vision of *The Ancient Mariner*, on the banks of the Susquehannah or elsewhere, and thus literally re-create the earthly paradise; at times, he hoped to discover the ideal woman, who should be his inspiration; and at times the 'ideal woman' became, like Solomon's Beloved, or the celestial bride of Jacob Boehme,[163] the image of a psychological state—the recovery of Wisdom and the lost Shechinah.

The Abyssinian maid carries all these significances within the poem, and examination of the *Song of Solomon* helps to establish this. When the bridegroom describes his bride as a Paradise-garden, his imagery corresponds with that of Coleridge's poem[164]:

A garden inclosed is my sister, my spouse; A spring shut up, a fountain sealed.

Thy plants are an orchard of pomegranates, with pleasant fruits; camphire, with spikenard,

Spikenard and saffron; calamus and cinnamon, with all trees of frankincense; myrrh and aloes, with all the chief spices:

A fountain of gardens, a well of living waters, and streams from Lebanon.

(the bride replies)

Awake, O north wind; and come, thou south; blow upon my garden that the spices thereof may flow out.

Let my beloved come into his garden, and eat his pleasant fruits.

(and much later)

I am a wall, and my breasts like towers: then was I in his eyes as one that found favour.

Other, more specifically sexual images[165] throw light upon the final lines of the poem. Coming to the bride, the King says,[166]

Thy lips, O my spouse, drop as the honey-comb: honey and milk are under thy tongue; and the smell of thy garments is like the smell of Lebanon.

and later,

I am come into my garden my sister, my spouse. I have gathered my myrrh with my spice; I have eaten my honeycomb with my honey; I have drunk my wine with my milk: eat, O friends; drink, yea drink abundantly, O beloved.

Similarly, in one eighteenth-century verse translation, the bride says of her beloved,[167]

The floating ringlets wanton in the wind
Salute his cheek, or, graceful, fall behind . . .
His lips are lilies dropping honey-dew . . .

It is important to notice in connection with our identification of the maid with Wisdom that several of these images recur in the book of Ecclesiasticus. There Wisdom compares herself with the trees of the paradise-garden; she declares that the memorial of herself is sweeter than honey; and finally, she compares herself with the stream that waters a garden and then becomes a river, and finally a sea.[168]

It is interesting to turn directly from this Old Testament imagery to the work of a modern poet exploring the same theme. Rainer Maria Rilke is perhaps the writer who has come closest to expressing the significance of the 'maiden' in terms of the poet's vision, though he concentrates on the inward psychological experience more specifically than Coleridge does. His second Sonnet to Orpheus has been translated by J. B. Leishman as follows[169]:

> And almost maiden-like was what drew near
> from that twin-happiness of song and lyre,
> and shone so clearly through her spring attire,
> and made herself a bed within my ear.

> And slept in me sleep that was everything:
> the trees I'd always loved, the unrevealed,
> treadable distances, the trodden field,
> and all my strangest self-discovering.

> She slept the world. O singing god, and stayed,
> while you were shaping her, with no desire
> to wake, and only rose to fall asleep?

> Where is her death? Oh, shall you find this deep
> unsounded theme before your song expire?
> Sinking to where from me? . . . Almost a maid . . .

In the *Notebook of Malte Laurids Brigge*, moreover, there is a passage concerning artistic consummation which bears a startling and detailed resemblance to the imagery of *Kubla Khan*: though Rilke's final conclusion is as pessimistic as Coleridge's is optimistic. It may fittingly be quoted in full, to conclude our discussion of the poem's meaning[170]:

> The moulder of plaster casts, before whose shop I pass every day, has hung two masks outside his door. The face of the young drowned woman, which was cast in the Morgue, because it was beautiful, because it smiled, smiled so deceptively, as though it knew. And beneath it, the face that did know. That hard knot of senses drawn tense; that unrelenting concentration of a music continually seeking to escape; the countenance of one whose ear a god had closed that he might hear no tones but his own,

so that he might not be led astray by what is transient and confused in sounds, but in whom dwelt their clarity and enduringness; so that only soundless senses might bring in the world to him silently, a waiting world, expectant, unfinished, before the creation of sound.

Consummator of the world! As that which comes down in rain on the earth and the waters, falling down carelessly, falling by chance, inevitably rises again, joyous and less visible, out of all things, and ascends and floats and forms the heavens: so through you came the ascent of our down-cast spirits and domed the world about with music.

Your music! it should have encircled the universe, not us alone. An organ should have been built for you in the Thebais, and an angel should have led you to that solitary instrument, through the desert mountain ranges, where kings repose and hetairæ and anchorites. And he should have flung himself up and away, fearful lest you begin.

Then you, O welling fountain, would have poured forth, unheard, giving back to the All that which only the All can endure. Bedouins would have swept past in the distance, superstitiously, but merchants would have flung themselves to the ground on the skirts of your music, as if you were the tempest. Only a few solitary lions would have prowled around you by night, far off, afraid of themselves, menaced by the stirring of their own blood.

For who will now withhold you from lustful ears? Who will drive them from the concert halls, the venal company with sterile ears that prostitute themselves but never conceive? The seed streams forth, and they stand under it like sluts and play with it, or it falls, while they lie there in their abortive satisfaction, like the seed of Onan amongst them.

But, master, if ever a virginal spirit were to lie with unsleeping ear beside your music, he would die of blessedness, or he would conceive the infinite and his impregnated brain would burst with so great a birth.

If the interpretation offered here is correct, there is a clear reason for Coleridge's reticence on the subject of the poem's meaning. Normally, he was modest in public to a fault: but he was conscious of latent powers within himself, and there were times when he could not help speaking of them. Writing to Humphry Davy in February, 1801, he said of the work that he hoped to write, on poetry and the pleasures derived from it, 'I have faith, that I do understand this subject/and I am sure, that if I write what I ought to do on it, the Work would supersede all the Books of Metaphysics hitherto written/and all the Books of Morals too.—To whom shall a young man utter *his Pride*, if not to a young man whom he loves?—'[171]

This 'pride' also emerges in the *Greek Ode on Astronomy*, where he hoped to join Newton in Heaven,[172]

> gazing, in the spring
> Ebullient with creative energy,

and in *Religious Musings*, where he hoped to become one of the 'Contemplant Spirits',[173]

> that hover o'er
> With untired gaze the immeasurable fount
> Ebullient with creative Deity!

In a poem addressed to his brother in 1797, he spoke of[174]

> that divine and nightly-whispering Voice
> Which from my childhood to maturer years
> Spake to me of predestinated wreaths,
> Bright with no fading colours!

When he spoke of such hopes to his friends, however, his modesty forbade such forthright expression. He would either play down his powers, or, in certain circumstances, speak of them with a light-hearted, ironic mock-arrogance. At Nether Stowey, he was fond of striking this second attitude: he was known to his friends there as 'the Bard',[175] and on one occasion wrote a humorous letter to Thomas Ward, appointing him 'Penmaker to my immortal Bardship', which concluded as follows[176]:

> Given from Apollo's|Temple in the|odoriferous Lime-grove—alias|Street—in what|olympiad our Inspiration| knows not, but of the|usurping Christian Æra|1799— Oct. 8.

Four years later, he received a letter from Mr Welles, offering him some medicine for the gout. 'I have in my possession,' the letter ran, 'a kind of Nectar/for it removes pain, & of course promotes pleasure—& may in the end immortalize—me/which I freely offer to you.'[177] This sentence seems to have stirred and awakened the imagery of *Kubla Khan* in Coleridge's mind, for in his reply he promised, if the medicine cured him, to raise a new sect in honour of Welles . . .[178]

> . . . then, joining party with Thomas Taylor, the Pagan (for whom I have already a sneaking affection on account of his devout Love of Greek) to re-introduce the Heathen Mythology, to detect in your person another descent & metamorphosis of the God of the Sun, to erect a Temple to you, as Phoebo Sanatori; & if you have a Wife, to have her deified, by act of Parliament, under the name of the Nymph, Panacea. But probably it would not be agreeable to you to be taken up, like the Tibetan Delha Llama, and to be imprisoned during life for a God.

Even in a playful letter like this, it may be noted, the reference was introduced with hesitation and followed by an apology. It was evidently a similar instinct of modesty which led him to describe *Kubla Khan*, when he published it, as a 'psychological curiosity'. This it is, of course, but by reason of its wealth of meaning rather than any lack of it. Coleridge's own assertion that the poem was unfinished was probably sincere, for his notebooks contain various notes on Kubla Khan and the Tartars which were no doubt collected with a continuation in mind.[179] One can continue a poem in the middle, however, as well as at the end: and it is likely that this was his plan. Certainly it is difficult to see how the poem could be carried on after the last stanza: the argument is there brought to an end with overwhelming finality.[180]

The argument of the poem as a whole might conceivably provide the basis of expansion at other points in the poem: its general drift is not very far removed from that of *Religious Musings*, for example, a much longer poem. Nevertheless, it is clear that such an attempt on Coleridge's part would have been mistaken and probably impossible. The images of the

poem are so tightly drawn together and so closely interlocked that any addition would upset its balance.

The chief characteristic of the poem, indeed, is its extraordinary compression: and if one is to make any objection to
the poem it must be on these lines. As with the 'moral' of
The Ancient Mariner,[181] the trouble is not that the poem has
no meaning, but that it has too much. The reader can hardly
be expected to bring to mind all the complicated involutions
of sense which it contains in the time that it takes him to
read fifty lines of poetry. On the contrary, his attention is far
more likely to be caught throughout by the fascination of
the sensuous imagery in its own right.

Nevertheless, if *Kubla Khan* is a petrified forest, it is also
an enchanted forest. At every point it glows directly, and at
every point, also, it reflects the intense subterranean energy
of a mind which could not rest in its endeavour to apprehend
all experience and reduce it to one harmony. It will always
remain possible to enjoy it as a simple stream of images, and
to ignore the opportunity which it affords of exploring the
intricacies of Coleridge's visionary world. To be fascinated
by these intricacies, one has first to share something of
Coleridge's excitement at the potentialities of the basic
images involved. Once we begin to sense this excitement,
however, and its climax in the writing of a poem where, for a
moment, his visionary world modelled itself into a single
pattern, a paradigm that was also a focus of his major
speculations in art and life, we may see that in this context
more than any other the poem is what Coleridge himself was
the first to call it: 'a vision in a dream'.

Chapter IX

THE VISIONARY GLEAM

NO man is an island, entire of himself, and it is hard for a poet to stand apart for long from either his peers or his audience. Coleridge at various times shared each of the twin romantic dreams: there were times when he wished that he could become either a rock in the ocean, completely self-sufficient, or be dispersed upon the winds in ideal sympathy.[1] Nevertheless he, as much as his contemporaries, worked within a tradition: the tradition helped to shape him and he in his turn was able to influence its future course. When he thought of his own output, it was the visionary poems which he prized: he named *The Ancient Mariner*, *Christabel* and *The Destiny of Nations*. But these, as we have seen, were not appreciated by the age for what they were; his drawing-room poems, on the other hand, were valued too highly by the age. Between these extremes, he wrote a number of poems, notably his conversational nature-poems, which were appreciated by his contemporaries in a way which corresponds roughly to their permanent value in English poetry.

Since it has long been customary to take these last, 'agreed' poems as the yardstick for judging the rest, and to find in the poems of the *annus mirabilis* a more exotic flowering of the spirit which breathes in them, it might be objected that the investigation which we have been carrying out is irrelevant to the main purposes of literary criticism. It might be said that the value of Coleridge's poems lies in what they communicate to a sensitive modern reader, and to a lesser extent what they communicated to Coleridge's contemporaries: the speculation and associations in the poet's mind being of no account except insofar as he succeeds in making them readily communicable upon the printed page.

To say this is to say that poetry must ultimately be judged by life: and it is a statement that needs to be made. But it is equally necessary to say, with Matthew Arnold, that poetry is a criticism of life: and the two viewpoints are not irreconcilable. For the common reader always reads in a tradition of some sort, and his responses are never governed solely by reference to direct experience. The Victorians used to read Coleridge as a predecessor of Tennyson, and therefore they enjoyed him above all for his sensibility—his sensitivity to nature, his feeling for love and friendship, and the gentle music of his verses. The Imagist critics read him as an Imagist poet, and valued his ability to produce images of unsurpassable vividness. 'After more than a hundred years,' wrote Sir Arthur Quiller-Couch, ' "The Ancient Mariner" is the wild thing of wonder, the captured star, which Coleridge brought in his hands to Alfoxden and showed to Dorothy and William Wordsworth,'[2] and his words have been the text for a hundred essays on the poem, including *The Road to Xanadu*. To the symbolist critics, again, Coleridge was chiefly interesting as a poet who could organize symbols into patterns which are as exciting for the psycho-analyst as for the literary critic.

In all these ways, Coleridge has been criticized by life, and we have seen how all these excellencies are to be found in his poetry by the sympathetic critic. Nevertheless, when we try to find Coleridge himself, we do not see, first and foremost, any of the figures which have been projected for our attention. We see instead a man who tried to take as his sphere all human experience, whether in the world of measurable sense-perception or in the universe of the imagination, and to harmonize it into a single pattern. In this man, the shaping spirit and the inquiring spirit were equally strong, and he was never happier than when exercising both to the limit of their powers. If the life by which we are to judge poetry is the life of external sense-experience, he was at fault to do so: but if that life is to include all the shapings of the human imagination as well, then his poetry not only criticized life, but is criticized by life to its advantage.

Kubla Khan is the test case. As a poem, it was born out of Coleridge's visionary speculations: it was also projected forward as a myth within which much of his later thinking took place. How relevant is either of these facts to poetry, or to human experience?

Their relevance to poetry has already been discussed. Whether or not we are interested in them depends on whether we prefer our own personal reaction to the poem, or to read it vicariously through the mind of Coleridge, for whom each of the images had associations which bound them together in an intricate logical and sensuous pattern.

Their relevance to human experience is a more complicated issue, and our attitude to it is likely to be associated with our attitude towards Coleridge's thought in general, with its over-riding emphasis upon the importance of the human imagination. For many critics and readers, the human imagination is in the last analysis a peripheral mental function: it has an important biological function, in enabling human beings to deal with situations which cannot for one reason or another be dealt with by direct physical action, but it must be disciplined by the body, and constantly checked against sense experience.

If this view is adopted, *Kubla Khan* is, for all its merits, a tragic poem, and a focusing point of all that was unsatisfactory in its author. It has its basis in a visionary world which even in Coleridge's day was under heavy fire. Evolutionary theories were already abroad, but he refused to listen to them.[3] In the same way, he dismissed as ridiculous the claims of Sanskrit for priority to other languages,[4] because he could hardly believe that Hebrew, or some language immediately prior to it, was not the language taught by God to Adam in Paradise. He spent a good deal of time, all his life, in trying to interpret basic scientific phenomena in terms of theories which he elicited from the Bible. And if he was conservative about the past, he was an impossible idealist concerning the future. His 'Abyssinian maid' was an ideal being who did not and could not exist in this life, and his attempts to find her brought nothing but unhappiness to his wife, his children, his intimate friends and himself. The political scheme of Pantisocracy was a prime example of his inability to see man as he is, weak and potentially vicious, and the best that can be said is that he did at least come to value traditional human institutions more highly in his later thinking. His philosophy as a whole, nevertheless, consisted of a long series of attempts to impose theories on an experience which refused to fit them, and his vision of himself as an inspired genius was a pitiful delusion.

This is the Benthamite indictment of Coleridge: and ultimately, it is the Wordsworthian indictment, also. There is at the heart of Wordsworth's attitude to the world a distrust of the human imagination, a fear of it even, which binds him as decisively to the eighteenth century as Coleridge's faith in the imagination points him forward into the nineteenth. And it is precisely this difference between the two poets which makes their relationship so important and fascinating, for it is nothing less than an encounter between the two attitudes of mind which were to dominate Victorian literature. That relationship cannot be examined in detail here, but some of the salient points of agreement and disagreement may be briefly indicated, for the sake of the light which they throw on the Coleridgean attitude.

Keats's characterization of Wordsworth as the 'egotistical sublime'[5] is still the necessary starting-point for any study of his personality, whether expressed in art or life; in the same way, the ideal communion of spirits is the most important single element in Coleridge's universe. The divergeness to which these respective attitudes lead may be illustrated concisely by their use of cabbalistic imagery. When Wordsworth speaks of 'marriage' in connection with his philosophy, the marriage which he envisages has little to do with male and female love as Coleridge thought of it: it is a dignified marriage between the human mind and the world around it[6]:

> . . . the discerning intellect of Man,
> When wedded to this goodly universe
> In love and holy passion, shall find these
> A simple produce of the common day.
> —I, long before the blissful hour arrives,
> Would chant, in lonely peace, the spousal verse
> Of this great consummation . . .

On the rare occasions when Coleridge took over this image, he immediately transformed it by subordinating it to a cabbalism of real life. Thus he speaks of the marriage

between the mind and nature as something which is actually
made by Joy[7]:

> Joy, Sara! is the Spirit & the Power,
> That wedding Nature to us gives in Dower
>   A new Earth & new Heaven
> Undreamt of by the Sensual and the Proud!
> Joy is that strong Voice, Joy that luminous Cloud—
>   We, we ourselves rejoice!
> And thence flows all that charms or ear or sight,
> All melodies the Echoes of that Voice,
> All Colors a Suffusion of that Light.

And he at once makes it clear that this joy which 'weds
nature to us' is itself the result of purity of heart combined
with happiness in personal relationships.

> Thou being innocent & full of love,
> And nested with the Darlings of thy Love,
> And feeling in thy Soul, Heart, Lips, & Arms
> Even what the conjugal & mother Dove
> Feels in her thrill'd wings, blessedly outspread—
> Thou free'd awhile from Cares & human Dread
> By the Immenseness of the Good & Fair
>   Which thou see'st every where—
> Thus, thus should'st thou rejoice!

The difference of attitude between the two poets which is
implicit in these passages can thus be clarified and to some
extent explained by examining their respective attitudes
towards love and marriage in the ordinary sense. Coleridge
expressed their disagreement succinctly in a letter of 1811[8]:

> . . . no man who has not been in love, (can) understand
> what Love is, tho' he will be sure to imagine and believe,
> that he does. Thus, Wordsworth is by nature incapable of
> being in Love, tho' no man more tenderly attached—
> hence he ridicules the existence of any other passion, than
> a compound of Lust with Esteem and Friendship, con-
> fined to one Object, first by accidents of association, and
> permanently, by the force of Habit and a sense of Duty.

It is interesting, in passing, to notice that precisely the same
argument is carried on in the mind of one of the characters

in Forster's *A Passage to India*. As she walks up the hill towards the Marabar caves, Adela Quested thinks about her relationship with her betrothed, and suddenly realizes that she is not in love with him. 'Vexed rather than appalled, she stood still, her eyes on the sparkling rock. There was esteem and animal contact at dusk, but the emotion that links them was absent.'[9]

'The emotion that links them' in Coleridge's case took the form of an outgoing of spirit that was foreign to Wordsworth's nature. It was a difference between them that extended to other fields than human relationships. At one point in his *Hymn before Sunrise, in the Vale of Chamouni*, Coleridge expresses, as elsewhere,[10] a sense of identity with the mountain before him[11]:

> . . . the dilating Soul, enrapt, transfused,
> Into the mighty vision passing—there
> As in her natural form, swelled vast to Heaven!

According to Coleridge, Wordsworth censured these lines as 'strained and unnatural'—a judgment which he could not accept[12]:

> For from my very childhood I have been accustomed to *abstract* and as it were unrealize whatever of more than common interest my eyes dwelt on; and then by a sort of transference and transmission of my consciousness to identify myself with the Object.

The difference can be traced even in their attitudes to one another. Coleridge, in a note written at Malta, expressed a longing to share Wordsworth's very identity which Wordsworth would not have reciprocated[13]:

> To W[ordsworth] in the progression of Spirit/once Simonides, or Empedocles—or both in one?—'O that my Spirit, purged by Death of its weaknesses, which are, alas! my *identity*, might flow into *thine*, & live and act in thee & be Thou.'

The statement, of course, does not necessary imply uncritical admiration of Wordsworth: it may suggest rather that a combination of Coleridge's Aeolian genius with

Wordsworth's strength of purpose would form a perfect identity. Nevertheless, the 'outgoing' is there. Coleridge seems eventually to have grasped that there was a deep-rooted difference between their respective outlooks, however, and to have recognized that in spite of their apparent agreement on many points the agreement was often only verbal, and masked a fundamental divergence of views. '. . . We begin to suspect', wrote Coleridge in 1802, 'that there is, somewhere or other, a *radical* Difference in our opinions'[14]; and he repeated the doubts a fortnight later, sowing seeds which were to bear fruit in his *Biographia Literaria*.[15] Some time before this he had expressed a more bitter opinion: 'Wordsworth', he wrote, 'appears to me to have hurtfully segregated & isolated his Being.'[16] The doubts grew as the years passed. Later on, when he was fond of characterizing Wordsworth as 'spectator ab extra',[17] he apparently came to regard his inflexibility of attitude as a direct limitation of his genius. This at least is the conclusion to be drawn from putting together several isolated pieces of evidence.

The first is a comment on Wordsworth in the *Table Talk*[18]:

> Of all the men I ever knew, Wordsworth has the least femineity in his mind. He is *all* man. He is a man of whom it might have been said,—'It is good for him to be alone.'

This may be taken in conjunction with a semi-humorous comment on Wordsworth's untidiness and the 'dusty Paper-wilderness' of his room, as opposed to the combination of 'Lady-like *Wholeness* with creative delight in *particular* forms' which he felt to characterize himself and Southey.[19] And these two passages may in their turn be read in the light of a passage on greatness[20]:

> I have known *strong* minds, with imposing, undoubting, Cobbett-like manners, but I have never met a *great* mind of this sort. And of the former, they are at least as often wrong as right. The truth is, a great mind must be androgynous. Great minds—Swedenborg's for instance—are never wrong but in consequence of being in the right, but imperfectly.

If this conflation of separate statements represents a fair statement of Coleridge's views, it would seem that he denied to Wordsworth the ultimate heights of greatness in later years. And in any case, his comment on Wordsworth's lack of femineity points back to comments on Wordsworth's self-sufficiency which he had ventured as early as 1798, along with other shrewd criticisms. Hazlitt recorded them as follows[21]:

He lamented that Wordsworth was not prone enough to believe in the traditional superstitions of the place, and that there was a something corporeal, a *matter-of-fact-ness*, a clinging to the palpable, or often to the petty, in his poetry, in consequence. His genius was not a spirit that descended to him through the air; it sprung out of the ground like a flower, or unfolded itself from a green spray, on which the gold-finch sang. He said, however (if I remember right), that this objection must be confined to his descriptive pieces, that his philosophic poetry had a grand and comprehensive spirit in it, so that his soul seemed to inhabit the universe like a palace, and to discover truth by intuition, rather than by deduction.

The same spirit which prevented Wordsworth from believing in the traditional superstitions of Devonshire prevented his giving to mythological studies anything like the importance which Coleridge assigned to them. Nevertheless, he seems to have tried faithfully to incorporate myths and travellers' tales in his poetry from time to time. One is startled, for example, to find a Tartarean paradise in the middle of *The Prelude*—[22]

... Gehol's matchless gardens, for delight
Of the Tartarian dynasty composed ...
A sumptuous dream of flowery lawns, with domes
Of pleasure sprinkled over, shady dells
For eastern monasteries, sunny mounts
With temples crested, bridges, gondolas,
Rocks, dens, and groves of foliage taught to melt
Into each other their obsequious hues ...

But Coleridge's peculiar magic was not for Wordsworth. We have already seen how their respective attitudes to the imagination are revealed in their attitudes to nature. Coleridge does not normally speak of climbing mountains: his concern is with the emotions felt when gazing at a mountain from a distance or when standing on its summit. One feels with Wordsworth, on the other hand, that the climbing of a mountain symbolizes his relationship with nature and indeed with life. He has a feeling of exhilaration in struggle, coupled with a touch of hostility or, at times, fear. His emotions as he climbs Snowdon are a good example[23]:

> With forehead bent
> Earthward, as if in opposition set
> Against an enemy, I panted up
> With eager pace, and no less eager thoughts . . .

Similarly, his emotions at the top are not of transfiguration, of harmony at the heart of nature, but of splendid isolation from nature. The moon which for Coleridge is a harmonizing power is for Wordsworth a symbol of this isolation,[24]

> the emblem of a mind
> That feeds upon infinity, that broods
> Over the dark abyss, intent to hear
> Its voices issuing forth to silent light
> In one continuous stream.

As with the moon, so with the imagination. Both poets found the visionary power slipping from them as life passed by. For Wordsworth, the transience of the imagination meant automatically that it could have no place in his permanent philosophy. If he did not renounce it, he bade it farewell, content to accept the remaining glimmerings as welcome visitations, but careful to regard them merely as windfalls, not to be budgeted for in the life of common day.[25] For his permanent philosophy, he looked to those figures who had achieved self-sufficient isolation: the leech-gatherer on the moor, the lonely shepherd, the old Cumberland beggar.

Coleridge could not accept this sort of loneliness. 'I *love* but few,' he once said, 'but those I love as my own Soul; for I feel that without them I should—not indeed cease to be kind and effluent, but by little and little become a soulless fixed Star, receiving no rays of influence into my Being, *a*

Solitude which I so tremble at, that I cannot attribute it even to the Divine Nature.'[26]

Thus, and in countless ways, the myth which we have examined in these pages projected itself into the later years of his existence. His inability to conceive of true happiness in isolation is apparent in *Dejection*. Prohibited from finding with Sara Hutchinson the fulfilment of his happiness, he sought instead to make the Wordsworth household as a whole a substitute for his lost community by the Susquehannah, and to find happiness in their happiness[27]:

> When thou, & with thee those, whom thou lov'st best,
> Shall dwell together in one happy Home,
> One House, the dear *abiding* Home of All,
> I too will crown me with a Coronal . . .

Sara Hutchinson and the Wordsworth household are but two of the forms under which he sought his Abyssinian maid. He could not follow Wordsworth in making the imagination a marginal factor in creativity—it was for him the *sine qua non*. He therefore set out to find the Isis who would release the Osiris-power locked in his imagination, seeking her by turns in an ideal woman, a community of true spirits or discovery of truth.

The relationship with Sara Hutchinson was a failure, but in the circumstances, it is not clear that it was a necessary failure. The situation in which they found themselves, affectionate to each other but unable to express their affection in physical terms, was almost certain to lead to the nervous strain which eventually brought the relationship to an end.[28] And if his attempt to find community of spirits in the Wordsworth household was a failure, it is only fair to point out that another household, that of the Gillmans, later gave him a community in which, if he did not find his ideal, he at least found the emotional security that enabled him to produce a succession of completed works.

The attempt to find Truth, and thus create a complete poetic universe, is a more complicated issue, for here Coleridge was limited, far more than in the other cases, by the biblical-visionary world in which he had grown up. Again and again, he was haunted by the hope that that world would be vindicated. At its purest, this hope is voiced in the imagery of the 'vision' in *Kubla Khan*. Referring to the inspired writings of Scripture, he says, 'The unsubstantial, insulated Self passes away as a stream; but these are the shadows and reflections of the Rock of Ages, and of the Tree of Life that starts forth from its side.'[29] And this vision, being cast over the whole of human knowledge, could emerge in the most unlikely places. '. . . All the vast & stately edifice of the present Geometry', we find him saying, 'well worthy to be the pride of the human soul awaits only the descent of the glory to become at once the temple & the Shekinah of the divine humanity.'[30]

Coleridge's intellectual quest was much more than an attempt to impose a pattern upon facts, however. The pattern was held ready all the time—any phenomenon which could be described in terms of the first chapter of St John's gospel was seized upon[31]—but Coleridge was also a disinterested inquirer. We have seen in earlier chapters how he was for a time held by the moral challenge presented to him by Southey, and by the intellectual challenge presented by the Necessitarians. It is characteristic of his range of sympathies that he was also held by the Wordsworthian challenge. Side by side with his visionary world of speculation, there is in his mind a positivist world of rationalist investigation, which he no doubt hoped would eventually be harmonized with it, but which none the less seems at times to contradict it flatly. It was part of the spirit which had caused him, after writing a passage concerning the progress of the soul towards God, in *Religious Musings*, to write in a foot-note[32]:

See this *demonstrated* by Hartley, vol. 1, p. 114, and vol 2, p. 329. See it likewise proved, and freed from the charge of Mysticism, by Pistorius. . . .

From 1798 onwards, powerful influences were at work to reinforce this desire within him. Wordsworth, with his deep respect for the imagination, yet 'matter-of-fact-ness' and insistence on devotion to the actual, was one. Tom Wedgwood, also, had interested him in psychological speculations and investigations. As early as June, 1798, he reported that he had been metaphysicizing so long and so closely with Tom Wedgwood, that he had become a caput mortuum, mere lees & residuum'.[33] And while Wedgwood was encouraging him to analyze his own faculties, Humphry Davy was holding out even greater hopes for the scientific approach to metaphysical problems. He seems to have impressed Coleridge deeply with the prospect of discovering truth by understanding physical nature, so that he even considered setting up a small chemistry laboratory of his own.[34] Some years later he became disillusioned with Davy, when it became clear that his work was coming to have less and less reference to the metaphysical speculations which they had shared. Nevertheless, during the first years of their friendship, from 1799 onwards, he held him in high regard, as he showed by his remark that if Davy had not been in the first rank of England's philosophers and scientific benefactors he would have been in the first rank of her poets.[35] The remark is an illuminating one, for the poems of Davy which have survived bear a marked resemblance to Coleridge's visionary poetry and speculations, one of them actually being called 'The Sons of Genius'.[36] It is important to recognize the visionary strain in Davy if one is to understand Coleridge's growing interest in scientific analysis and investigation in the years following his return from Germany. His interest reflected a desire to reach empirically an understanding of the hidden harmony between *natura naturata* and *natura naturans*.

Unfortunately, the development of nineteenth-century science, with its ever-expanding horizons, turned out to be uncongenial to such ideals, and Coleridge soon discovered that, so far from fulfilling his vision, his researches were in danger of destroying his own visionary powers[37]:

> And haply by abstruse Research to steal
> From my own Nature all the Natural Man—
> This was my sole Resource, my wisest plan!
> And that, which suits a part, infects the whole,
> And now is almost grown the Temper of my Soul.

The process had begun in Germany, however, where in his physiological and New Testament studies he had been

brought up against a form of scientific analysis more penetrating and destructive than anything which existed in
England. There he must have learnt how little basis existed
in history for his visionary world. This experience was
accompanied by a more ominous one. In March, 1799, he
wrote to his wife of the state of mind brought on by his
separation from those he loved: 'I have, at times, experienced
such an extinction of *Light* in my mind, I have been so
forsaken by all the *forms* and *colourings* of Existence, as if the
organs of Life had been dried up; as if only simple BEING
remained, blind and stagnant!'[38]

During the years that followed, this twofold process
continued. The scientific assault on his visionary world was
accompanied by a steady waning of his imaginative powers.
The process of attrition was extremely slow; and it has been
pointed out that many of the finest touches in *The Ancient
Mariner* occur not in the edition of 1798, but in the revised
editions of later years, demonstrating his continued poetic
strength. One also remembers that strange revival which
enabled him to produce the second part of *Christabel* in 1800.
Nevertheless, by 1825, he could write the following commentary on his loss of visionary powers in a letter to Gillman[39]:

. . . the more we have seen, the less we have to say. In
youth and early manhood the mind and nature are, as it
were, two rival artists both potent magicians, and
engaged, like the King's daughter and the rebel genii in
the Arabian Nights' Entertainments, in sharp conflict of
conjuration, each having for its object to turn the other
into canvas to paint on, clay to mould, or cabinet to
contain. For a while the mind seems to have the better in
the contest, and makes of Nature what it likes, takes her
lichens and weather-stains for types and printer's ink,
and prints maps and facsimiles of Arabic and Sanscrit
MSS, on her rocks; composes country dances on her
moonshiny ripples, fandangos on her waves, and waltzes
on her eddy-pools, transforms her summer gales into
harps and harpers, lovers' sighs and sighing lovers, and
her winter blasts into Pindaric Odes, Christabels, and

Ancient Mariners set to music by Beethoven, and in the insolence of triumph conjures her clouds into whales and walruses with palanquins on their backs, and chases the dodging stars in a sky-hunt! But alas! alas! that Nature is a wary wily long-breathed old witch, tough-lived as a turtle and divisible as the polyp, repullulative in a thousand snips and cuttings, *integra et in toto*. She is sure to get the better of Lady *Mind* in the long run and to take her revenge too; transforms our to-day into a canvas dead-coloured to receive the dull, featureless portrait of yesterday: not alone turns the mimic mind, the ci-devant sculptress with all her kaleidoscopic freaks and symmetries! into clay, but *leaves* it such a *clay* to cast dumps or bullets in; and lastly (to end with that which suggested the beginning) she mocks the mind with its own metaphor, metamorphosing the memory into a *lignum vitæ* escritoire to keep unpaid bills and dun's letters in, with outlines that had never been filled up, MSS. that never went further than the title-pages, and proof-sheets, and foul copies of Watchmen, Friends, Aids to Reflection, and other *stationary* wares that have kissed the publishers' shelf with all the tender intimacy of inosculation!

It might seem from this stream of pessimism that all was lost—until one notices how imaginatively the case is presented. Something at the centre had gone, some essential shaping and organizing power, but apart from that his mind ranged as vividly as before.

That the decline in creative power was by no means absolute is evident from the persistence of his conversational powers, and the influence which he was able to exercise over a section of his contemporaries and the next generation. It is hard to find an imaginative writer or thinker who did not come under the spell. If Coleridge's stimulation had been paramount in making Wordsworth a poet of stature, the younger poets were now affected equally strongly. Coleridge met Keats in a lane near Highgate one day in April, 1819, and discoursed to him about nightingales, poetry and many other topics.[40] (Perhaps he even spoke of his wish that he could die amidst the prospect of Caen Wood and the sound of the birds there.—'Death without pain at such a time, in such a place as this, would be a reward for life.")[41] A few months later Keats wrote his *Ode to a Nightingale*. Shelley bought Coleridge's works as fast as they came out, with an urgency which bears witness to his enthusiasm[42]: and his use of visionary landscapes closely resembling that of *Kubla Khan* has been noticed by more than one critic.[43] When Shelley missed seeing Coleridge in the Lake District and found only Southey to talk to, Coleridge commented, 'I *might* have been of use to him, and Southey could not; for I should have sympathized with his poetics, metaphysical reveries, and the very word metaphysics is an abomination to Southey, and Shelley would have felt that I understood him.'[44]

And so the list may be continued. 'I think with all his faults,' wrote Thomas Arnold, 'old Sam was more of a great man than any one who has lived within the four seas in my memory'.[45] 'The only person I ever knew who answered to the idea of a man of genius,' said Hazlitt.[46] 'The largest and most spacious intellect, the subtlest and most comprehensive . . . that has yet existed among men,' said De Quincey.[47] Carlyle wrote a bitingly satirical account of Coleridge at Highgate[48]: yet his writings show the influence everywhere.[49] Sterling, Hare, Maurice and many others each acknowledged their debt, so that a whole generation of Cambridge men, including the original 'Apostles', grew up with a reverence for his name,[50] and Mill could designate him as the most influential teacher of English youth in the years between 1820 and 1840.[51]

Coleridge's influence on the nineteenth century is matter for another book, however, and it will be enough to draw attention to one particular writer of the next generation upon whom the 'visionary' influence of Coleridge fell more strongly than on most, namely Coventry Patmore. His father, D. G. Patmore, was closely associated with Lamb, Hazlitt and other friends of Coleridge,[52] and it seems that a certain amount of their talk was handed down to him. Thus some records of this intercourse eventually found its way into Hall Caine's life of Rossetti,[53] while other notes can be found scattered through Patmore's writings and correspondence. Writing to a friend, he declared,[54]

Tennyson's best work, though in its way a miracle of grace and finish, is never of quite the highest kind. It is not finished *within*. Compare the finish of 'Kubla Khan' with that of the 'Palace of Art'.

That this was not merely a passing gesture, but a fully worked-out view of the poem is evident from Patmore's own poem 'The Contract'. In this he uses an imagery which can only have sprung from his own interpretation, or one that had come down to him[55]:

> Twice thirty centuries and more ago,
> All in a heavenly Abyssinian vale,
> Man first met woman; and the ruddy snow
> On many ridgëd Abora turn'd pale,
> And the song choked within the nightingale.
> A mild white furnace in the thorough blast
> Of purest spirit seem'd She as she pass'd;
> And of the Man enough that this be said,
> He look'd her Head.

It was probably from Coleridge, also, that he first derived his idea of genius as 'that divine third, quickening, and creative sex, which contains and is the two others'.[56] In a letter of April, 1847, in which he was giving advice to Sutton about his son, he wrote, 'If he *really* studies Coleridge it will do him immense good,' and added, a few lines later, 'Tell him that enthusiasm without knowledge is fanaticism; that knowledge without enthusiasm or love is demoniacal, but that knowledge wedded to enthusiasm is Angelic.'[57]

In this and countless other ways Coleridge's visionary speculations lived on after his death. Nevertheless, one is always forced to return to the whole man in his situation, and to evaluate his achievement in those terms.

Here, it seems to me, there was an ultimate failure of purpose. The 'visionary' period, culminating in the poetry of 1797-8, was a period of undeniable achievements; and the period between 1799 and 1804, when he devoted himself to Nature in more empirical fashion, contained much that was seminal. His attempt to weave together the two worlds of thought was, on the other hand, a failure.

It was a failure, as we have seen, for two reasons. On the

one hand, his failure in the field of personal relationships meant that his mythologizing could not evolve into the personal myth which some romantic artists were to make the basis of their art. On the other, that failure interacted in many ways with the relentless logic of his intellectual development, which left him faced with his quest for creative stimulation from a woman, or community, or line of investigation, each eluding him by turns.

This remorseless dialectic was set in motion in September, 1798, when Coleridge departed for Germany. The encounter there with an intellectual world far less accommodating than that in which he had hitherto lived, coupled with the subsequent emotional crisis which followed his meeting with Sara Hutchinson set in motion forces which were ultimately to destroy the emotional poise and intellectual innocence on which he had for a brief period been able to build his visionary world. And since he was half aware of this, there may have been a wistfulness for him, even at this early date, in the passage from Jeremy Taylor which he copied into one of his notebooks[58]:

> He to whom all things are one, who draweth all things to one, and seeth all things in one, may enjoy true peace & rest of spirit.

When we look at the later work of Coleridge, it is just this unity which is missing. The elements of what we have looked at in the preceding pages are still there, but in fragmentary form. Every now and then, for example, a piece of the pure visionary will emerge into the light of day[59]:

> Idly talk they who speak of Poets as mere Indulgers of Fancy, Imagination, Superstition, &c.—/ They are the Bridlers by Delight, the Purifiers, they that combine these with *reason* & order—the true Protoplasts, Gods of Love who tame the Chaos.

or this, from a notebook of 1833[60]:

> The Pure of Heart are not therefore Poets; but no man can be a great Poet, that Apotheosis of a Philosopher, the transfigured Philosopher with seraph wings on his shoulders, who has not a pure Heart.

In moments such as these, Coleridge is his own Ancient Mariner, haunted by his vision of the inner harmony of the universe, or the poet of *Kubla Khan*, seeking to recover the 'symphony and song' which are the necessary conditions of his genius. Equally, when he looks at Wordsworth in the prime of his creative powers, possessed of his lonely self-sufficient strength, he can adapt the same imagery to meet the occasion[61]:

[Wordsworth] is devoting himself to his great work— grandly imprisoning while it deifies his Attention & Feelings within the sacred Circle & Temple Walls of great Objects & elevated Conceptions . . . now he is at the Helm of a noble Bark; now he sails right onward—it is all open Ocean, & a steady Breeze; and he drives before it . . .

For himself, he was mostly content to pursue truth disinterestedly, in the hope that this pursuit would, in its own time, lead him back to the over-riding intellectual and poetic vision which he sought. There were darker times, also, when he could hardly do more than work mechanically at any routine task that lay to hand. Even then, however, a memory of the Stowey days would sometimes break through to sustain him. Thus he wrote, in Malta,[62]

I work hard, I do the duties of common Life from morn to night/but verily 'I raise my limbs, like lifeless *Tools*.' The organs of motion & outward action perform their functions at the stimulus of a galvanic fluid applied by the *Will*, not by the Spirit of Life that makes Soul and Body one. Thought and Reality two distinct corresponding Sounds, of which no man can say positively which is the Voice and which the Echo. O the beautiful Fountain or natural Well at Upper Stowey! The images of the weeds which hung down from it's sides, appeared as plants growing up, straight and upright, among the water weeds that really grew from the Bottom/& so vivid was the Image, that for some moments & not till after I had disturbed the water, did I perceive that their roots were not neighbours, & they side-by-side companions. So— even then I said—so are the happy man's *Thoughts* and

Things—(in the language of the modern Philosophers, Ideas and Impressions.)—

After reading a passage like this, it is hard to think of Coleridge as a man born to unhappiness. If he did not reach the comprehensive harmony for which he sought there were many occasions, 'sabbaths of the soul' as he would call them, when Thoughts rose up as Things and left, if not another *Kubla Khan*, some permanent record of insight, whether in a poem, or a sympathetic appreciation, or a critical aperçu, or an acute description of nature. His *Biographia Literaria* is an array of such moments.

It is these moments which represent the challenging element in Coleridge's nature. His constant insistence upon the rôle of the imagination in human life and happiness is an insistence upon the one human faculty which has been patronized by a scientific age, but which still gives us constant reminders of its importance and of the deadly consequences which follow its neglect. All artistic experience poses this problem, of course: but Coleridge posed it the more convincingly because he was also willing to accept the scientific universe of discourse, as far as that was possible. Since his time, scientific thinkers have become more imaginative and imaginative writers have become more scientific: but that simply means that each group has fortified its own position—not that the gap has been bridged.

Coleridge has his place among the potential bridge-builders, and in that capacity also he is still a figure to be reckoned with. It is perhaps idle to look for an 'essential' Coleridge. 'Essentially', he was the lifelong pilgrim towards truth; 'essentially', also, he was the inspired poet of the brief *annus mirabilis*. But if one is looking for an enduring *persona*, one may perhaps find it somewhere between the two—in those moments of insight which characterized him all his life. In this character, fallen angel and questing pilgrim merge into a new figure—a figure which, though excluded from the Penetralia of the universe, is sufficiently aware of harmony to have a sense of being near the inner shrine. At such moments, when inquiring reason and shaping imagination momentarily fuse, angel and pilgrim meet in the figure which he himself apparently chose as a symbol with which to conclude one volume of his great projected philosophical work[63]—'even that most religious philosophy, which listening in child-like silence in the outer courts of the temple, blended fragmentary voices from the shrine with the inward words of her own meditation'.

Appendix I

TRANSLATION OF COLERIDGE'S GREEK ODE ON ASTRONOMY

Written by S. T. Coleridge, for the prize at Cambridge, 1793

I

HAIL, venerable NIGHT!
O first-created, hail!
Thou who art doom'd in thy dark breast to veil
The dying beam of light,
The eldest and the latest thou,
Hail, venerable NIGHT!
Around thine ebon brow,
Glittering plays with lightning rays
A wreath of flowers of fire.
The varying clouds with many a hue attire
Thy many-tinted veil.
Holy are the blue graces of thy zone!
But who is he whose tongue can tell
The dewy lustres which thine eyes adorn?
Lovely to some the blushes of the morn;
To some the glories of the Day,
When, blazing with meridian ray,
The gorgeous Sun ascends his highest throne;
But I with solemn and severe delight
Still watch thy constant car, immortal NIGHT!

2

For then to the celestial Palaces
Urania leads, Urania, she
The Goddess who alone
Stands by the blazing throne,
Effulgent with the light of Deity.
Whom Wisdom, the Creatrix, by her side
Placed on the heights of yonder sky,
And smiling with ambrosial love, unlock'd
The depths of Nature to her piercing eye.
Angelic myriads struck their harps around,

And with triumphant song
The host of Stars, a beauteous throng,
Around the ever-living Mind
In jubilee their mystic dance begun;
When at thy leaping forth, O Sun!
The Morning started in affright,
Astonish'd at thy birth, her Child of Light!

3

Hail, O Urania, hail!
Queen of the Muses! Mistress of the Song!
For thou didst deign to leave the heavenly throng.
As earthward thou thy steps wert bending,
A ray went forth and harbinger'd thy way:
All Ether laugh'd with thy descending.
Thou hadst wreath'd thy hair with roses,
The flower that in the immortal bower
Its deathless bloom discloses.
Before thine awful mien, compelled to shrink,
Fled Ignorance abash'd with all her brood
Dragons, and Hags of baleful breath,
Fierce Dreams that wont to drink
The Sepulchre's black blood;
Or on the wings of storms
Riding in fury forms,
Shriek to the mariner the shriek of Death.

4

I boast, O Goddess to thy name
That I have raised the pile of fame;
Therefore to me be given
To roam the starry path of Heaven,
To charioteer with wings on high,
And to rein-in the Tempests of the sky.

5

Chariots of happy Gods! Fountains of Light!
Ye Angel-Temples bright!
May I unblamed your flamy thresholds tread?
I leave Earth's lowly scene;
I leave the Moon serene,
The lovely Queen of Night;
I leave the wide domains,
Beyond where Mars his fiercer light can fling,

And Jupiter's vast plains,
(The many belted king;)
Even to the solitude where Saturn reigns,
Like some stern tyrant to just exile driven;
Dim-seen the sullen power appears
In that cold solitude of Heaven,
And slow he drags along
The mighty circle of long-lingering years.

6

Nor shalt thou escape my sight,
Who at the threshold of the sun-trod domes
Art trembling, . . . youngest Daughter of the Night!
And you, ye fiery-tressed strangers! you,
Comets who wander wide,
Will I along your pathless way pursue,
Whence bending I may view
The worlds whom elder Suns have vivified.

7

For Hope with loveliest visions soothes my mind,
That even in Man, Life's winged power,
When comes again the natal hour,
Shall on heaven-wandering feet
In undecaying youth,
Spring to the blessed seat;
Where round the fields of Truth
The fiery Essences for ever feed;
And o'er the ambrosial mead,
The breezes of serenity
Silent and soothing glide for ever by.

8

There, Priest of Nature! dost thou shine,
NEWTON! a King among the Kings divine.
Whether with harmony's mild force,
He guides along its course
The axle of some beauteous star on high,
Or gazing, in the spring
Ebullient with creative energy,
Feels his pure breast with rapturous joy possest,
Inebriate in the holy ecstasy.

299

9

I may not call thee mortal then, my soul!
Immortal longings lift thee to the skies:
Love of thy native home inflames thee now,
With pious madness wise.
Know then thyself! expand thy wings divine!
Soon mingled with thy fathers thou shalt shine
A star amid the starry throng,
A God the Gods among.

(Translated by Robert Southey, London,
1802. SP, II, 170-4.)

THE IMAGERY OF *ZAPOLYA*

Zapolya, a 'dramatic poem . . . in humble imitation of the *Winter's Tale* of Shakespeare', was offered to the Committee of Management of Drury Lane Theatre, and rejected in March, 1816. It was subsequently published in 1817. The imagery of this play, while marking no new departure, repeats many of the trends which have been noticed in Coleridge's earlier poetry. The imagery is here much more incidental —it is not, as in *Christabel*, absorbed into the action of the plot—but this makes its overt significance all the more apparent, and reinforces a good deal that we have said about Coleridge's intentions.

At the beginning of the play, Count Emerick usurps the throne, which has been left to the baby prince, under guardians, after the death of the king. The play is constructed round the theme that where all efforts to overthrow the tyrant by force fail, a combination of innocence and courage is successful.

The first part of the play is dominated by the figure of Raab Kiuprili, who as a strong soldier typifies physical force. Infuriated by news of the usurpation, he declares,

> The venomous snake! My heel was on its head,
> And (fool!) I did not crush it.   (60-1)

and, just afterwards,

>   And now
> Must I, hag-ridden, pant as in a dream?
> Or, like an eagle, whose strong wings press up
> Against a coiling serpent's folds, can I
> Strike but for mockery, and with restless beak
> Gore my own breast?   (87-92)

He then taxes Emerick with his crime and, detecting a lie in his words of self-justification cries,

>   Mark how the scorpion, falsehood,
> Coils round in its own perplexity, and fixes
> Its sting in its own head!   (348-50)

Emerick claims that he has popular support. Kiuprili replies that this is merely mob fanaticism, and declares,

> Better, O far better
> Shout forth thy titles to yon circling Mountains,
> And with a thousand-fold reverberation
> Make the rocks flatter thee, and the unvolleying air
> Unbribed, shout back to thee, King Emerick!   (358-62)

Emerick endeavours to have him made away with, but Kiuprili's friend, Chef Ragozzi, allows him to escape, deploring Emerick's tyranny:

> O rare tune of a tyrant's promises
> That can enchant the serpent treachery
> From forth its lurking hole in the heart.   (452-4)

Between Part One and Part Two of the play, a civil war takes place, in which Emerick is triumphant. The second part opens twenty years later with a complete change of atmosphere. Glycine, orphan daughter of Ragozzi, is living in the mountains with Sarolta, wife of Kipriuli's son Casimir. Sarolta has little desire to see members of the court.

> A spring morning
> With its wild gladsome minstrelsy of birds
> And its bright jewelry of flowers and dewdrops
> (Each orbéd drop an orb of glory in it)
> Would put them all in eclipse.   (II, I, i, 32-6)

Laska, steward of Casimir and betrothed to Glycine, becomes jealous of her liking for young Bethlen (true heir to the throne). She asks him if a serpent has stung him. He replies,

> No, serpent! no; 'tis you that sting me; you!
> What! you would cling to him again?   (182-3),

Glycine replies by bantering him, calling him 'Calm as a tiger, valiant as a dove', and says that she is grieving for Bethlen because she has dreamt that the war-wolf gored him as he hunted in the haunted forest. Bethlen himself enters, and she tells him that he is sought on account of his rash words and treason to the king. He mutters to himself, and she says, aside,

> So looks the statue, in our hall, o' the god,
> The shaft just flown that killed the serpent!   (258-9)

Throughout it is she who is conscious of evil and danger in the wood:

> Madam, that wood is haunted by the war-wolves,
> Vampires, and monstrous . . .   (339-40)

302

Bethlen is told that he was found in an oak, while the lady who had brought him lay dying nearby. He replies with a longing to discover his mother, whom he feels cannot be dead.

> O that I were diffused among the waters
> That pierce into the secret depths of earth,
> And find their way in darkness! Would that I
> Could spread myself upon the homeless winds!   (379-82)

Sarolta, who is slowly revealed as the spirit of wisdom and innocence in the play, reassures him:

> . . . may the light that streams from thine own honour
> Guide thee to that thou seekest!   (418-9)

When Glycine speaks again of the evils in the wood, Sarolta replies that beasts in the shape of men are worse than war-wolves.

As the second act of Part Two opens, Raab Kiuprili, in his cavern in the forest, is telling Zapolya that he has just been dreaming that he was entwined by a huge serpent (the image which he used earlier). Just afterwards, he hears Glycine singing of a bird caught in a shaft of sunlight, 'His eyes of fire, his beak of gold/All else of amethyst!'

Bethlen enters, thinking at first that he has come to a monster's den. Kiuprili tells him to stop. Bethlen asks,

> Voice of command! and thou, O hidden Light!
> I have obeyed! Declare ye by what name
> I dare invoke you! Tell what sacrifice
> Will make you gracious,   (196-9)

Kiuprili replies,
> Patience! Truth! Obedience!
> Be thy soul transparent! so the Light,
> Thou seekest, may enshrine itself within thee!
>   (199-201)

Bethlen then discovers his mother, Zapolya, in the cave. He returns to old Bathory, his foster-father, and reports to him the message which she has given him:

> 'The shadow of the eclipse is passing off
> The full orb of thy destiny! Already
> The victor Crescent glitters forth and sheds
> O'er the yet lingering haze a phantom light.
> Thou canst not hasten it! Leave then to Heaven
> The work of Heaven: and with a silent spirit
> Sympathize with the powers that work in silence!'
>   (96-102)

At this point, Sarolta, personification of wisdom and innocence, has revealed herself also as representative of the 'passive' side of Coleridge's philosophy, voicing that philosophy in terms which are reminiscent of *Frost at Midnight* and *The Ancient Mariner*.

At the beginning of Act Four, there is a speech by Casimir, in which he comments on Sarolta's ability to detect evil in spite of her own innocence, and compares her to the dove which knows the prowlers of the air, and the young steed that recoils on its haunches at the first hiss of an adder which it has never yet seen. Meanwhile the royal hunt comes on the scene, and Glycine, seeing Laska, her betrothed, about to shoot Bethlen treacherously from behind, shoots and kills him. Zapolya exclaims joyfully,

> In vain we trenched the altar round with waters,
> A flash from Heaven hath touched the hidden incense—
> (179-80)

The hunt approaches again, accompanied by the noises of a storm. Old Bathory comments,

> The demon-hunters of the middle air
> Are in full cry, and scare with arrowy fire
> The guilty! (201-2)

At the end of this act, which concludes the play, Bethlen is restored triumphantly to the throne, and Sarolta makes a final speech praising the domestic virtues, which flourish,

> While mad ambition ever doth caress
> Its own sure fate, in its own restlessness! (397-8)

Just before this, Bethlen, now Andreas, makes his final speech in which he praises those who have restored him to his throne, mentioning particularly Raab Kiuprili (around whom he hopes that his youth may climb as a vine round an elm) and Glycine, whom he addresses as

> Thou sword that leap'dst forth from a bed of roses:
> Thou falcon-hearted dove. (375-6)

NOTES

CHAPTER I

1. PMLA, 1924, XXXIX, 229-53; reprinted in his *Essays in the History of Ideas*, N.Y., 1955, pp. 228-53.
2. 'The Concept of "Romanticism" in Literary History', *Comp. Lit.* 1949, I, 1-23; 147-172.
3. CPL, 289-92.
4. CPL, 47. Miss Coburn stresses that her own conviction remains open on the point.
5. He himself suggests in his lecture that the form of medieval poetry is comparable with the couplet verse of Dryden and Ben Jonson.
6. Review of *The Monk* by M. G. Lewis in the *Critical Review* for February, 1797. (CMC, 370); Letter to Bowles, March, 1797. CLG, I, 318.
7. CMC, 386.
8. E. Heller, *The Disinherited Mind*, Cambridge, 1952, p. 165.
9. T. E. Hulme, *Speculations*, 1936, p. 118.
10. This theme recurs several times in the long journal-letter of February-May, 1819. KL, 295-341.
11. F. Scott Fitzgerald, *The Great Gatsby*, 1926, p. 118.
12. WPR, xii, 246-61. See Basil Willey, *The Eighteenth Century Background*, 1940, 274-93, for a discussion of this and related passages.
13. WPR, xiv, 111-129.
14. C. Connolly, *The Condemned Playground*, 1945, pp. 71-2.
15. R. M. Rilke, *Briefe aus Muzot*, 1921-6, Leipzig, 1936, p. 337. I have partly used a translation by J. B. Leishman (in his edition of Rilke's *Duino Elegies*, 1948, p. 101). For a use of similar imagery by Coleridge, see the account of his dreams in CNB 36. 4ᵛ.
16. R. M. Rilke, *Briefe aus den Jahren 1914-21*. Leipzig, 1937, p. 80. (tr. J. B. Leishman, *op. cit.*, p. 18). It is interesting to compare this with Shelley's account of Coleridge (p. 36 below).
17. Letter to George and Thomas Keats, December, 1817. KL, 71.
18. W. B. Yeats, *Collected Poems*, 1950, pp. 391-2.
19. T. E. Hulme, *Speculations*, 1936, p. 117.
20. See above, note 17. I suspect that Keats's image here was prompted by a review of *Biographia Literaria* in *Blackwood's Magazine* (1817, II, 6) which described Coleridge as a man who 'presumptuously came forward to officiate as High-Priest at mysteries beyond his ken—and who carried himself as if he had been

familiarly admitted into the Penetralia of Nature, when in truth he kept perpetually stumbling at the very Threshold.'

21. Edith Coleridge, *Memoir and Letters of Sara Coleridge*, 1873, I, 193. Quoted by Virginia Woolf in *The Death of the Moth* (1942, p. 76).

22. CNB 21.121ᵛ-2 (CAP, 104).

23. CBLC, II, 13 and n. See also HH, 30-3; 167; and CNC, 1070n.

24. See below, p. 92.

25. S. Potter, *Coleridge and S.T.C.*, 1935, *passim*.

26. *Ibid.*, p. 267.

27. T. S. Eliot speaks of 'the disastrous effects of long dissipation and stupefaction of his powers in transcendental metaphysics.' (*The Use of Poetry and the Use of Criticism*, 1933, p. 67.) E. H. Coleridge refers to fragments, 'the *disjecta membra* not, alas! of the poet, but of the metaphysician and the divine.' (Ath., 1894, (i), 114.) Such comments are not without justice, of course, but without some qualification they encourage the tendency referred to in the text.

28. V. Woolf, *The Death of the Moth*, 1942, p. 70.

29. 'On Consistency of Opinion.' H, XVII, 27.

30. London, 1948. See, in particular, chapter xii.

31. CPW, I, 100-2.

32. See, e.g., his letter to George Coleridge of March, 1794. CLG, I, 77-8.

33. See, e.g., his letter to Sotheby, 1802: 'If there be any two subjects which have in the very depth of my Nature interested me, it has been the Hebrew & Christian Theology, & the Theology of Plato.' CLG, II, 866. Cf. CTT, 42; 130.

34. *London University Magazine*, 1830, II, 318.

35. A. Gilchrist, *Life of William Blake*, 1880, I, 380.

36. For a note on Coleridge's three-year anxiety concerning a letter attacking Newton, see CLG, II, 1014, note 1. Coleridge retained a distaste for the 'cold System of Newtonian Theology' over a considerable period however. (CLG, II, 866).

37. See below, p. 74. Cf. 'from the naked savage up to Newton'. (CPL, 275).

38. Newton was eventually to have a place in the firmament—presumably when he awakened from his 'sleep'. See *Jerusalem* 93 (K, III, 318).

39. CLC, II, 686-8; G. Keynes, *Blake Studies*, 1949, pp. 95-8.

40. Op. cit., II, 323n: 'Blake and Coleridge, when in company, seemed like congenial beings of another sphere. . . .' The phrase 'in company' is ambiguous, but seems to refer to the meetings

between the two men. These probably took place at the house of Mr Aders in Euston Square. (Gilchrist, *Life of Blake*, 1880, I, 379-80.) Coleridge's poem, *The Two Founts* was addressed to Mrs Aders.

41. G. Keynes, *Blake Studies*, 1949, pp. 99-100.
42. Letter to Poole, Oct., 1797. CLG, I, 354.
43. Letter to Thelwall, Oct., 1797. CLG, I, 349.
44. Letter to Cottle, March, 1815. CLU, II, 128-9.
45. CBLC, I, 202.
46. 'On the Living Poets', H, V, 165-8. (Cf. Cowper's description of Milton in *The Task*, iii: *Poems*, 1785, II, 104.)
47. *Dejection: An Ode*. CPW, I, 365; cf. CLG, II, 797.
48. Arnold on Shelley (*Essays in Criticism*, 2nd Ser., 1888, pp. 203-4).
49. Letter to Thelwall, Dec., 1796. CLG, I, 280-1. Coleridge later projected a verse translation of the Apocalypse. See CLS, 14n.
50. Letter of May, 1798. LCL, I, 123-4.
51. H, XIX, 210.
52. H, XVIII, 369. (Cf. MPL, i, 20-2.)
53. H, XVII, 108; 107. (Cf. *Coriolanus*, V, vi, 115-16.)
54. H, VII, 117; 118.
55. Letter of April, 1816. LCL, II, 190.
56. *Dedication to Don Juan*. BP, VI, 3-4.
57. SW, IV, 8 (ll. 202-8).
58. Variant to ll. 23-6. CPW, I, 132.
59. CPW, II, 1001.
60. Letter to Cottle, April 1797. CLG, I, 320.
61. Letter to Flower, Dec. 1796. CLG, I, 267. See also CGNB, f. 26ᵛ. (CNC, 182 and note, tracing part of the phrase to a sermon by Jeremy Taylor.)
62. CPW, I, 102; 491-2.
63. CBLC, I, 272, note to p. 202, l. 8.
64. *i.e.*, the poem later given the title of *Self-Knowledge*. CPW, I, 487. For the earlier belief, see CBLC, II, 212n.
65. CBLC, I, 115.
66. CBLC, I, 136-7.
67. CNB 21½, 10-10ᵛ (CAP, 195-7).
68. CNB 21. 2ᵛ, and CAP, 79. Oct. 5, 1804.
69. CNB 21. 104ᵛ (CAP, 80). Oct. 11, 1804.
70. *Morning Light*, 1883, VI, 518.
71. The full tide of misfortune descended on him in the summer of 1798. (CLG, I, 403-414.) But as early as April 1797, he had written 'I am not the man I have been—and I think never shall.' (CLG, I, 320.)

72. See WL, II, 67-9, for Dorothy Wordsworth's shocked reaction.
73. See Note 55.
74. *The Leisure Hour*, 1864, XIII, 831.
75. T. S. Eliot, *The Use of Poetry and the Use of Criticism*. 1933, p. 69.

CHAPTER II

1. See, e.g., the timetable of Warrington Academy. H. McLachlan, *Warrington Academy*, Manchester, 1943, p. 63.
2. Thomas Amory, *The Life of John Buncle, Esq.*, 1756, pp. 418-9.
3. CBLC, I, 12. It is clear from a reference in Christopher Wordsworth's diary that this 'literary society in Devonshire' was the Society of Gentlemen at Exeter. See below, p. 325, n. 42.
4. See his letter to George Dyer of Feb., 1795. CLG, I, 151-3.
5. CNB 36. 47. See below, p. 78.
6. EKC, 49-51. In 1800, he visited the 'Liverpool literati'. (Letter of July 24, 1800. CLG, I, 607-8.)
7. See X, Index entry 'Manchester Memoirs', for examples of one such influence.
8. LW, II, 21. The spelling 'Mirandula' suggests that Lamb's immediate reference is to John Donne's first appearance in Oxford at the age of ten, when, according to Walton, his remarkable abilities 'made one give this censure of him, *That this age had brought forth another Picus Mirandula*'. Izaak Walton, *Lives of Dr. John Donne, Etc.*, 1670, pp. 12-13.
9. J. M. Murry, *Between Two Worlds*, 1935, pp. 50-1.
10. Leapidge Smith, 'Reminiscences of an Octogenarian', *Leisure Hour*, 1860, IX, 633-4. See my note, NQ, 1958, CCIII, 114-16.
11. X, 233.
12. Charles Jenner, *Town Eclogues*, 1722, p. 38.
13. Annotation to Berkeley's *Siris*, K, III, 354; 'A Vision of the Last Judgment', K, III, 146.
14. 'The Everlasting Gospel', sect. h, K, III, 333.
15. My account here is taken from R. J. Z. Werblowsky's article, 'Milton and the *Conjectura Cabbalistica*', *Journ. Warb. & Court. Instit.*, 1955, XVIII, 90-113.
16. Shelley, 'Alastor', ll. 116-28. SW, I, 180.
17. Letter to Thelwall, Nov. 1796. CLG, I, 260.
18. Lane Cooper, 'The Power of the Eye in Coleridge', in *Studies Presented to J. M. Hart*, N.Y., 1901, pp. 78-121. Reprinted in his *Late Harvest*. Ithaca, N.Y., 1952.
19. CNBG, f. 2. (CNC, 13 and n.). See below, p. 103.
20. CPW, I, 99-100 and n. See below, p. 62.

21. CPW, I, 242.
22. CLG, II, 791-2. Cf. Wordsworth, WPR, vi, 264-70.

> Of rivers, fields,
> And groves I speak to thee, my Friend! To thee,
> Who, yet a liveried schoolboy, in the depths
> Of the huge city, on the leaded roof
> Of that wide edifice, thy school and home,
> Wert used to lie and gaze upon the clouds
> Moving in heaven.

23. GWS, 17-18.
24. CBLC, I, 170n. (The original reading is 'eight hymn', usually amended (e.g. X, 230) to 'eight hymns'. The reading 'eighth hymn' seems more likely to have given rise to the misprint, however—and Synesius wrote ten hymns in all.) CLG, I, 76.
25. CLG, I, 93.
26. Francis Okely, *Memoirs of Jacob Behmen*. Northampton, 1780, p. 26. It is also in one edition of Coleridge's favourite *Aurora* (JB, I, xxiii). Coleridge had a liking for such personal emblems. See his design for one for himself: E. Betham (ed.) *A House of Letters*. 1905, p. 108; and his motto" EΣTHΣE". (CLG, II, 867 and n.)
27. Letter to Lamb, May, 1798. CLG, I, 404-5.
28. CPW, II, 964.
29. C. Lloyd, *Edmund Oliver*. Bristol, 1798, I, x-xi.
30. Letter of Dec. 1796. CLG, I, 286-7; CPW, I, 157-8.
31. C. Lloyd, op. cit., I, 66-7; 14-15.
32. Quoted in letter to Poole, Dec. 1796. CLG, I, 271.
33. Isa. xxx, 26. Quoted in J. Clowes, *Dialogues on ... Swedenborg*, 1788, p. 140. CCS, 213-14 seems to refer to this text.
34. Clowes, op. cit., pp. 57, 60.
35. In 1782 and 1783, the first Theosophical Societies were formed, in London and Manchester respectively; in London, the society normally worshipped at the Female Orphan Asylum, under the Rev. J. Duché. At first it was hoped that the movement would flourish within existing sects, as Swedenborg himself wished; and the dialogues of John Clowes (see n. 31) were designed to welcome the new doctrines, and show that they could be held without difficulty by a member of the Church of England. As the missions prospered, however, several Methodist ministers were converted to the new teaching and subsequently disowned by their own denomination. As a result, a separate religious body was formed, and a church established in Great Eastcheap. In 1789, a General

Conference was called in London, and in the following year the *New Jerusalem Magazine* began publication.

(see art., 'New Jerusalem Church', Enc. Brit. (11th ed.)
Coleridge's first reference to the sect takes the form of a laconic note in the Gutch notebook: 'Mem. To reduce to a regular form the Swedenborgian's Reveries—' CNBG, f. 22.^{v} (CNC, 165 and n.).

36. See above, p. 46 and n. 8.

37. ' 'Twas observ'd, at his first appearance in the Schools, that his Fancy was Gay and Bright, his Wit strong and ready, and he had a Richness of Memory that had hardly been enjoy'd before him; For it was observ'd, that, what he had but once heard, he would Repeat forward and backward without mistaking the least Sylable; and it was peculiar to him, never to lose, what he had obtain'd, tho' but once Reading, or hearing a thing made it his own.'

(E. Jesup, *Life of John Picus, Prince of Mirandula*, London, 1723, pp. 6-7.)

'Ever and anon, a pamphlet issued from the pen of Burke. There was no need of having the book before us. Coleridge had read it in the morning, and in the evening he would repeat whole pages verbatim.'

(C. V. Le Grice, 'College Reminiscences of Mr Coleridge'.
Gentleman's Magazine, Dec. 1834, p. 606.)

38. Art. 'Kabbalah', *Enc. Brit.* (11th ed.); Lowes, X, 230.

39. See article by Werblowsky (note 15 above).

40. See D. Saurat, *Literature and Occult Traditioon*, 1930, for a full account.

41. CNB 18. 91^v; 50. 24^v; 11. 29-29^v. Cf. also his reference to love as the Light which 'glorifies the darkness into a Shechinah of it's own Beauty.' (CNB 48. 22.)

42. CNB 26. 58. Cf. his dismissal of some 'Cabalistic Fancies' of Irving's. (Marginal note, E. Irving, *Sermons* (BM, C. 126. i. 8) 1828, I (140) xxxiv-v.)

43. CPL, 299-300 and n. 21, p. 444.

44. CNB 36. 35-6. (Cf. 34. 14^v; 41. 41.)

45. CNB 36. 35^v.

46. Letter of Jan. 1810. CC, II, 105.

47. H. Crabb Robinson, *Diary*, (ed. T. Sadler) 1869, I, 388. (May 29, 1812.)

48. CLU, II, 201-2.

49. CBLC, I, 98.

50. JB, I, 47.

51. CFB, III, 259; CSC, I, 133; CLG, I, 103. Cf. CLG, I, 110:

'[the Mayor of Cambridge] would certainly be a Pantisocrat, were his head & heart as highly illuminated as his Face.'

52. CLG, I, 279. In the *Biographia*, however, he describes Bowles and Cowper as 'the first who combined natural thoughts with natural diction; the first who reconciled the heart with the head.' (CBLC, I, 16.)

53. CLC, II, 501.

54. CNBG, f. 77ᵛ (CNC, 272).

55. CPW, I, 99-100 and n.

56. Lowes (X, 464-5) first pointed out that Coleridge found the passage from Haggern in Erasmus Darwin's *Loves of the Plants* (1789, pp. 183-4, = *Botanic Garden*, 1791, II, 183-4). See also G. Grigson, *The Romantics*, 1942, pp. 343-4 (note 156).

57. CLU, II, 46, corrected from the original MS in Dr. Williams's Library. The idea that Coleridge associated Boehme's image with the magnetic lore which was being discussed in his day may be supported by reference to an entry in an early notebook: "It is not true that men always go gradually from good to evil or evil to good. Sometimes a flash of lightning will turn the magnetic poles." CNB 3½, f. 53 (CNC, 432.) Elsewhere he indulges in a long meditation on this general theme, as it affects not only love, but religion and moral conduct (CIS, p. 60 from CMSB Egerton 2801, f. 106.)

58. CNB 14. 41ᵛ-41. Tentatively dated 1808-10.

59. I am hoping to elaborate this point elsewhere.

60. CNB 46. 5ᵛ.

61. LW, II, 211.

62. Shelley, 'Alastor'. See above, p. 50.

63. For a full discussion of this point, see SH, 80-5.

64. The *rationale* of this is considered by A. O. Lovejoy in an article, 'The Parallel of Deism and Classicism'. *Mod. Phil.*, 1932; re-printed in his *Essays in the History of Ideas*, N.Y., 1955, pp. 78-98.

65. '... among the Ancients, the Bard and the Prophet were one and the same character,' Letter to Poole, Dec. 1796. CLG, I, 289. For Coleridge's praise of a passage in Southey's *Madoc*, 'respecting the Harp of the Welch Bard & it's imagined Divinity with the two Savages', see CLG, II, 1071.

66. Burns, *Tam o' Shanter*,. (*Poems* ..., Edinburgh, 1794, II, 199.) Coleridge often quoted the previous two lines,

> Or like the snow falls in the river,
> A moment white—then melts for ever;

in various forms. See, e.g., CIS, pp. 43, 185.

67. *The Historical Library of Diodorus the Sicilian*. Made English by G. Booth. 1700, pp. 77-8. A side-note at 'Island' reads, 'This seems to be *Brittain*'.

68. Letter to Poole, Oct. 1799. CLG, I, 538. For Coleridge's intoxication by the 'bardic' passages in Gray and Collins, see CNC, 383 and below, pp. 72, 258-9.

69. ll. 193-7. CPW, I, 262-3.

70. This account of the Druids is taken mainly from HEL, 588-9. Sampson also gives a list of contemporary works on the subject.

71. HA, 78.

72. BG, 59.

73. See below, p. 194. Coleridge also mentions this work in his notebooks (CNB 14. 20^v) and puts forward a plan for a 'true Pantheon of Heathen mythology, to include the Brahman, Tartar, Otaheitan, Northern, etc.' (CNB, 15. 87).

74. HA, 76.

75. HM.

76. BA, III, 601; Ruthven Todd, *Tracks in the Snow*, 1946, pp. 37-8 and plate 12.

77. CNB 36. 79-80.

78. CNB 53. 6. Elsewhere he declares that he would like to believe an 'interior and spiritual' sense of the Bible—and 'risk being called Swedenborgian, or Cabalistic.' (CNB 35. 47^v.)

79. CSC, II, 154.

80. CTT, 130.

81. CPL, 85.

82. CTT, 56.

83. CPL, 88. (Coleridge refers in his notes to Herodotus, vi, 52: Sections 53-4 are also relevant.)

84. CPL, 89n.

85. CTT, 80.

86. CEP, 2-3.

87. CNB 43. 69.

88. CEP, 4. Cf. CNB 43. 68^v-9.

89. CNB 18. 164.

90. CNB 43. 68^v-9.

91. CAR, 277.

92. CPL, 221.

93. CNB 36. 55-6.

94. Letter to Roger Gale, 1726-7. This letter, the original of which was later printed in *Family Memoirs of the Rev. William Stukeley*, Surtees Society, 1882, III, 266, is here quoted, with one correction, from W. Hutchinson, *History of Cumberland*, Carlisle, 1794,

I, 241-2. Coleridge apparently knew the latter work: see below, p. 175. Stukeley's theories may also be examined in his *Abury* (1743). Ruthven Todd (*Tracks in the Snow*, 1946, pp. 47-50 and Plate 14) has noticed Blake's evident interest in Stukeley, and his use of the serpent-temple as an image in *Jerusalem*.

95. BA, I, 488, plate VIII; BT, I, 415. See M. Oldfield Howey, *The Encircled Serpent*, 1926, ch. i, for further illustrations and a discussion of the hierogram.

96. CBLC, II, 11.

97. CSC, II, 323.

98. CNB 4. 7-8 (CNC, 609 and n.) quoting MPL ix, 498-503; 516-7.

99. H, XVIII, 371.

100. Letter to Cottle, 1815. CLU, II, 128. (See above, p. 33.)

101. CCS, 219.

102. CNB 16. 118^v (cf. CAP, 162). Elsewhere in the notebooks he speaks of and draws the serpentine orbit of the moon. (CNB 33. 6^v.)

103. Cf. the terms of Hazlitt's tribute to Coleridge, 'to whom I owe it that I have not crept on my belly all the days of my life like the serpent, but sometimes lift my forked crest or tread the empyrean . . .', H, VIII, 251.

104. Gen. iii, 15.

105. See below, p. 156.

106. G. Grigson, *The Romantics*, 1942, p. 335, n. 44.

107. Gray 'Progress of Poesy', ll. 96-102. Collins, 'Ode on the Poetical Character'. (See below, pp. 258-9.) Cf. Byron:

> Time the Avenger, execrates his wrongs,
> And makes the word 'Miltonic' mean 'Sublime' . . .
> (Preface to *Don Juan*, BP, VI, 6.)

108. Note to 'The Nightingale', CPW, I, 264, n. 2.

109. CNB 10. 50. (CNC, 658). The entry is dated about February, 1800.

110. LCL, I, 126. (as sent to Southey).

111. CBLC, I, 195. Cf. MPL, v, 482-90.

112. Note in Anderson's *British Poets*. CMC, 189.

113. Letter of May, 1794. CLG, I, 80.

114. SP, II, 170-4. Apart from influence from Gray, Collins, Akenside, etc., there are touches reminiscent of Synesius. (See *Essays and Hymns of Synesius of Cyrene*, tr. A. Fitzgerald, Oxford, 1930, II, 372-92.) It is perhaps a feature of his disappointment that shortly afterwards he was calling Synesius 'the hyper-Platonic

Jargonist' (CGNB, f. 28ᵛ). For later, more favourable references to Synesius, see CNB 17. 123ᵛ-4; CBLC, I, 169n-170n.
115. MPL, vii, 1-12.
116. Letter of Mary Evans to Coleridge, quoted in his letter to Southey of Oct. 1794. CLG, I, 112.

CHAPTER III

1. Christopher Wordsworth's diary for November, 1793. C. Wordsworth, *Social Life at the English Universities in the Eighteenth Century*, Cambridge, 1894, p. 589.
2. Maximus Tyrius, *Dissertations*, tr. T. Taylor, 1804, I, 33.
3. See JCE, I, 177-83 and below, note 8.
4. See R. V. Holt, *The Unitarian Contribution to Social Progress in England*, 1938, pp. 14-15 and ch. i *passim*.
5. Coleridge signs a letter of February, 1792, 'Reverend in the future tense, and Scholar of Jesus College in the present tense'. (CLG, I, 33.) The only evidence I have discovered of Unitarian leanings lies in his friendship with Frend, and with John Hammond of Fenstanton. (See *Athenaeum* 1893, i, 757, and Venn, *Alumni Cantabrigienses*, entry 'Hammond'.) One of his biographers says, of this period, 'Coleridge announced—though not to George—that he was a Socinian'. (HC, 31 and note 7, p. 427). The grouped references which he cites for this part of his book do not support this statement, however.
6. CNB 36. 32ᵛ.
7. '. . . he told us a humorous story of his enthusiastic fondness for Quakerism, when he was at Cambridge, and his attending one of their meetings, which had entirely cured him.' ('Recollections of Mr Coleridge', CTT, 319.) In the *Omniana*, however, Coleridge states that Quakerism, 'with all its bogs and hollows is still the prime sunshine spot of Christendom in the eye of the true philosopher'. (CTT, 363.)
8. Cottle gives the date as 1796 (JCE, I, 180) but this can hardly be correct. By February, 1796, Coleridge had preached several times on his *Watchman* tour, and mentioned that he had not worn the blue coat which had been a feature of his first sermons. (CLG, I, 180-2.) Cottle's reference to Coleridge's recent lectures in Bristol suggests a date in the latter part of 1795. In a letter of November, Coleridge reminded Southey of an occasion when they had been standing in the house of Mr Jardine, the Unitarian minister at Bath, apparently during the late summer of that year: this may well have been the same occasion. (CLG, I, 165.) If so,

however, Cottle's mention of the failure of the harvest (which took place in 1795) makes a date in the very late summer necessary. September-October, 1795, seems the likeliest date, therefore.

9. Letter to Southey, CLG, I, 87-8. (Cf. pp. 91-2).
10. Unitarian chapels were not then licensed for marriages however. Mr Morchard Bishop tells me that Estlin, the Unitarian minister at Bristol, gave the Coleridges a set of spoons (which are still in the family) as a wedding present. This is further evidence of Coleridge's intimacy with the Bristol Unitarians by this date.
11. CNB 36. 47. (See above, p. 46.)
12. CNB 26. 17ᵛ. Quoted, GWT (I, *Notes*, pp. 9-10).
13. See above, p. 38.
14. From CNBN (29). Quoted GWT, II, 4.
15. See Section lxii (Contra Sabellianos) of his *Adversus Haereses*. Epiphanii Constantiae . . . *Opera Omnia*. Paris, 1622, I, 513. Coleridge discusses Sabellianism, with Epiphanius as one of his authorities, in CNB 18. 131ᵛ and refers to Epiphanius on the Ebionites in his Table Talk (CTT, 290). His theology was later to be accused, independently, of being 'Neoplatonized Sabellianism'. See J. H. Rigg, *Modern Anglican Theology*. 1857, pp. 7; 12n.
16. CBLC, I, 114.
17. See H. N. Fairchild, *Religious Trends in English Poetry*, N.Y., 1949, III, 273. Fairchild bases his assumption mainly upon an undated poetic fragment by Coleridge:

> Where'er I find the Good, the True, the Fair,
> I ask no names—God's spirit dwelleth there!
> The unconfounded, undivided Three,
> Each for itself, and all in each, to see
> In man and Nature, is Philosophy.   (CPW, II, 1011.)

I feel, however, that Coleridge's own description of his Trinitarian beliefs, given below, outweighs this evidence.
18. CBLC, I, 136-7. (See above, p. 38.)
19. CPL, 175-6. See also CFB, III, 157-8.
20. CNB 17.21.
21. CPW, I, 110-11, ll. 29-33; 35-6; 41-5.
22. Ibid., ll. 105-113.
23. CLG, I, 239 (Sept. 28, 1796).
24. LCL, I, 49 (Oct. 24, 1796).
25. CLU, II, 104-6, 109, 113, 122-3.
26. CLU, II, 109. Coleridge cites MPR, iv, 196 onwards and 500 onwards. I have quoted ll. 196-7, 514-20.
27. CLG, I, 612.
28. C. Carlyon, *Early Years and Late Reflections*, 1836-58, I, 193.

29. CNB 16.32 (CNC, 1710 and n), commenting on Kant's *Grundlegung zur Metaphysik der Sitten*.

30. CPL, 295.

31. A brief résumé and harmony of the conflicting accounts can conveniently be found in EKC, 20-1.

32. Which was carried out by a future Lord Chancellor. JG, 49-50.

33. *The Friend*, Oct. 26, 1809. CFA, 161. (Cf. CFB, II, 38-9.) It is interesting, in view of the discussion of his visionary imagery which takes place in later chapters, that he speaks of his Reason having drawn a 'circle of Power' around him at this time.

34. CBLC, I, 49n.

35. CPJ, 476-7, and note, pp. 653-4.

36. CBLC, I, 49n. Cf. his earlier, more bitter memory of this mood, in November, 1795. CLG, I, 173.

37. Letter of October, 1795. SS, I, 247. Southey's part in Pantisocracy is fully discussed by W. Haller, (SH, ch. iii).

38. Letter of Sept. 18, 1794. CLG, I, 103.

39. CLG, I, 103.

40. CPW, I, 68-9.

41. CLG, I, 119.

42. CLG, I, 122; 119-120.

43. See note by J. P. Collier. CSC, II, 50n.

44. CLG, I, 115. The final two sentences were incorporated into a lecture of 1795. (*Conciones ad Populum*, Bristol, 1795, p. 34; CET I, 28-9.)

45. London, 1793.

46. G. Dyer, *Poems*, 1802, II, 123-6.

47. CLG, I, 147.

48. CPW, I, 79. (Cf. CLG, I, 147-8.) For Coleridge's recantation, see his note of 1797 to this passage (CPW, I, 79).

49. J. Priestley, *Doctrine of Philosophical Necessity Illustrated*, 1777, p. 108.

50. CPW, I, 102. Professor John Danby has pointed out to me a probable source for the ideas in this passage in Akenside's *Pleasures of Imagination* (1st vn.), I, 73-4; 109-32.

51. CPW, I, 84.

52. CFA, 114; CFB, I, 215-16.

53. Text as first published in the *Cambridge Intelligencer*, Dec. 31, 1796. Cf. CPW, I, 160. Coleridge later criticized the idea of the 'pre-established harmony' in its *common* interpretation. (CBLC, I, 89; cf. CPL, 350.) Nevertheless, he retained some such idea at the back of his mind—see, e.g., his speculation that the Creation of the Universe must have been achieved during a grand prevailing

harmony of spheral music. (C. & M. C. Clarke, *Recollections of Writers*, 1878, p. 64.)

54. CLG, I, 168; 334.

55. CPW, I, 84, n. 2.

56. See CPW, I, 81; 147.

57. CLG, I, 155. The Memnon image, also, probably comes from the Akenside passage. (*Pleasures of Imagination*, I, 109-24, where it is used for the harmonizing power upon the imagination of Nature's most beautiful forms.)

58. Letter of Dec., 1794. CLG, I, 137.

59. Letter to Sara Hutchinson. CLG, II, 790.

60. Note of 1818 in Boehme's *Aurora*, describing his state of mind when he first read Boehme. (JB, I, 127; BM copy C. 126. k. 1.)

61. CLG, II, 798.

62. CPL, 313-14.

63. CNB 54.13ᵛ. Transcribed CIS, 185.

64. CBLC, I, 80 and n.

65. In CNB 21½.51ᵛ, he opposes the 'Sol intelligibilis, Lux lucifica', to the 'Cosmos (Sol) sensibilis, Lux elucens', which are 'the *passive* existence, the outmost *Body*, of the Agent'.

66. See, e.g., CAR, 5, and CMC, 99.

67. WPR, xiv, 63-77.

68. 'Ode: Intimations of Immortality', ll. 197-9. WP, IV, 285.

69. CBLC, II, 5-6. Cf. Hazlitt's account of Wordsworth and the sunset. 'My first Acquaintance', H, XVII, 118.

70. Letter to Poole, Oct., 1803. CLG, II, 1014.

71. 'To H. C. Six years old', ll. 5-8 (WP, I, 247). Cf. 'Peter Bell' (prologue), WP, II, 331-2, and Coleridge's reference to it in the first version of *Dejection* (CLG, II, 791). Wordsworth acknowledged his debt to a passage in Jonathan Carver's *Travels* (*Athenaeum*, 1894, (i), 246).

72. CLG, I, 530; 553. Cf. Derwent Coleridge's memoir, Hartley Coleridge, *Poems*, 1851, I, xlviii.

73. CNB 6.25ᵛ. (CNC, 1159, *variatim*.)

74. See CNB 36.26ᵛ-7. He also calls him 'the Veil of Christ' and 'Christ under the Veil' (CNB 41.40ᵛ; 45.27ᵛ). The source of this image seems to be II Cor. iii, 13-16. Boehme often refers to it, and More states that 'Christ is nothing but Moses unveiled' (*Conjectura Cabbalistica*, Ep. Ded., in *A Collection of several philosophical writings of Dr. Henry More*, 1662).

75. CAR, 96 (from Leighton).

76. J. Davy, *Memoirs of the Life of Sir Humphry Davy*, 1836, I, 125.

The plan was apparently drawn up after Davy's arrival in Bristol (Ibid., pp. 124, 129).

77. AT, 71-2.
78. CBLC, II, 92-3.
79. See CSC, I, 184-5; II, 7-8 (probably the same lecture). Cf. CSC, II, 263. Nietzsche exploits the same idea in *The Birth of Tragedy*.
80. CSM, 52. (Coleridge's italics.)
81. CNB 53.10^v. See below, p. 269.
82. CBLC, I, 176. For some contemporary references to Moses, see CNC, 50n.
83. See above, pp. 46-7.
84. CBLC, I, 98.
85. e.g. CNB 17.83 (CAP, 213).
86. CLG, I, 249 (cf. CLG, I, 73).
87. CNB 5.2 (CNC, 467). See below, p. 117, and cf. CFB, I, 175; CSM, 60.
88. CPL, 226.
89. In the *Aids to Reflection* it is used for life without immortality. CAR, 303n.

CHAPTER IV

1. CFA, 161. (Cf. CFB, II, 38-9 and n.) Coleridge also used the metaphor of the Mexican temple in his Bristol Lectures of 1795.
2. ll. 85-8. CPW, I, 247.
3. CLG, I, 338.
4. Letter of March, 1798. CLG, I, 397.
5. See, e.g., HH 114-15, G. Whalley, 'A Library Cormorant', *The Listener*, Sept. 9, 1954, p. 396, and CNC, 177n.
6. X, 75.
7. X, 76.
8. X, 229.
9. X, 33.
10. X, 33-7. (Lowes's italics.)
11. Notably in *The Road to Tryermaine* (N).
12. CBLC, I, 77. Cf. his MS. note in J. G. E. Maass: *Versuch über die Einbildungskraft*, Halle and Leipzig, 1797, p. 29 (BM copy C. 126. d. 15).
13. CNBG, f. 2. Coleridge found the observation in Priestley (CNC, 13 and n.).
14. X, 39.
15. X, 233-5.

16. Library of Congress Notebook, quoted, N. Rogers, *Shelley at Work*, Oxford, 1956, p. 67.
17. Rogers, op. cit., p. 70 and ch. v *passim*.
18. CPL, 138-9 and n., p. 408; 296; CFB, I, 9; CNB 30.34-37^v (see also CLG, I, 532).
19. CIS, 252; CNB 49.31^v.
20. CFB, II, 61-2.
21. CCS, 41 (quoting from Sir Philip Sidney).
22. A. Cobban, *Edmund Burke and the Revolt against the Eighteenth Century*, 1929, p. 165.
23. CTT, 96.
24. CMSV, Envelope V (Notebook 60), plate 3.
25. CNB 44.70.
26. CNB 50.13.
27. ll. 332-4. Coleridge specifically mentions the 'great Whore' of *Revelation* xvii in a note to this passage. CPW, I, 121.
28. CNB 36.72.
29. CNB 36.77.
30. Letter to Thelwall, CLG, I, 215. Cf. his letter in *The Watchman* of April 1, 1796 (CLG, I, 198-200). Hazlitt refers to his low estimate of Godwin in their conversation of January, 1798 ('My First Acquaintance . . .', H, XVII, 112 and n.). In 1796, Coleridge was planning to write a 'six-shilling Octavo' against him (CLG, I, 253; 267; 293). The plan did not materialize, but he achieved the more remarkable feat of converting Godwin himself to a theistic position. See C. Kegan Paul, *William Godwin: his Friends and Contemporaries*, 1876, I, 357-8.
31. (1784 ed.) BB, 122, no. 75.
32. See CLG, I, 245; 278; 335 and n.; LCL, I, 86; H, XVII, 113. In May, 1798, Coleridge named his second son Berkeley.
33. M, 46.
34. W. B. Yeats, *Pages from a Diary Written in Nineteen Hundred and Thirty*, Dublin, 1944, p. 18.
35. CNBG, f. 25^v (CNC, 174 and n.) has a reference to the *Maxims*, the page number corresponding to that in the edition which Coleridge borrowed. See above, n. 31.
36. CBLC, I, 201. Coleridge refers to *Siris* in slighting terms in CNB 4.21 (CNC, 893), but this belongs to a period just after that in which his visionary enthusiasms were dominant, and probably represents a reaction against them following the impact of German thought.
37. CLG, I, 262. Coleridge also requested Proclus, Porphyrius, Sidonius Apollinaris and Plotinus.

38. Sections 206; 269. BW, II, 556, 585.
39. CLG, I, 350-1.
40. Coleridge devoted a long note to Newton and aether in *Joan of Arc* (II, 34. 1796 ed., pp. 41-2; CPW, II, 1112-3.) For other discussions see CAR, 394n.; CMSV, I, plate 39, and CMSV, Envelope II, plate 29, where he describes aether as the hush, the brooding, before the 'fiat of the heavenly Lucina'.
41. These schemes of study recur both as a projected course of instruction for young men and preparation for writing an epic poem. (CLG, I, 256; 320-1; 209.) It is probable that he wished to combine the two schemes. His plan to write the *Evidences of Religion* may also have been relevant. (LCL, I, 1.)
42. CAR, 252n. See below, pp. 112-13.
43. LCL, I, 33.
44. BB, 123, no. 81.
45. CNBG, f. 45^v (CNC, 240). See below, p. 263.
46. BB, 124, no. 89.
47. BB, 124, nos. 93-4; and 115 note 4.
48. CLG, I, 260.
49. Omniana, 1812 (CTT, 334). Kathleen Coburn points out the importance of South's *Sermons* (quoted here) for the image of the rising sun in *The Ancient Mariner*. CNC, 327 and n.
50. Section 299 (BW, II, 599).
51. CPL, 371.
52. He refers elsewhere to the use of this concept by Aristotle and Bacon: CAR, 244-5n.; CCS, 5. He would also have come across it in Spinoza.
53. MW, I, 429.
54. 'Essay on Fasts', CTW, March 9, 1796, p. 33.
55. CPW, I, 110, n. 1. The full title of the work would appear to be 'De Mysteriis Aegyptorum' (as in Iamblichus). I have not traced a work of this title in the writings of Damascius, Nicolaus Damascenus or Joannes Damascenus. Is this one of Coleridge's jokes? (Cf. 'Groscollius': CPW, II, 1142.)
56. A good picture of the knowledge generally available may be gained from Charles Rollin's *Concise History of the Antiquities of Egypt* (1753).
57. CPL, 90-1.
58. CPW, I, 132.
59. AT, 107.
60. CAR, note to pp. 251-2. Coleridge also refers to Origen's discussion of myths in CNB 23.82^v-3.
61. LCL, I, 95.

62. For a discussion of this preoccupation, see C. J. Smith, 'Wordsworth and Coleridge: the Growth of a Theme', *Stud. Phil.*, 1957, LIV, 53-64.
63. Letter of May 30, 1815. CLC, II, 648.
64. CLG, I, 396.
65. CBLC, I, 114-15.
66. Plutarch, *De Iside et Osiride Liber: Graece et Anglice*, ed. Samuel Squire, Cambridge, 1744 (II), 2-3.
67. Ibid., 41; 43.
68. Ibid., 52.
69. Ibid., 56-7.
70. Ibid., 59; 71-2.
71. See above, p. 67.
72. CNB 21.48 (CNC, 1233). For the earlier, more optimistic version 'that shall unite', see above, p. 97.
73. E. Swedenborg, *True Christian Religion*, 1795, p. 46. The centrality of this concept is indicated by the fact that twenty pages of the *Swedenborg Concordance* (1893) are devoted to 'heat' and 'light'.
74. CNB 13.34-33^v (CAP, 190).
75. 'What honest Bunyan terms heart-work' (Lamb, letter to Coleridge of Jan., 1797: LCL, I, 78) was also a favourite term with early Methodists. See Wesley's Journal for Jan 16, 1751 (1909-1916 ed., III, 511), and R. A. Knox, *Enthusiasm*, Oxford, 1950, pp. 588-9. For the 'moonshine heartless Head-work' of Unitarian sermons, according to Coleridge, see CNB 11.48^v (CAP, 167-8).
76. CLG, I, 103. See above, p. 85.
77. *The Piccolomini*, IV, i, 24-7. CPW, II, 686.
78. CNB 44.70^v-72. Cf. ff. 15-16.
79. MS. note in N. Grew, *Cosmologia Sacra*, 1701 (BM copy C. 44. g. 1), p. 6. Printed, CIS, 120. See also CNC, 209.
80. CAR, 382-6.
81. CPW, I, 285-92. In the first published version, however (*Athenaeum*, Jan. 27, 1894, p. 114), the two drafts are separated and entitled respectively 'The Wanderings of Cain' and 'Cain'. Coleridge always retained a doubt as to whether Cain and Abel should be regarded as historical beings or mythical and symbolical figures. See CNB 44.79.
82. CNB 26.152. Plutarch also identifies Typhon with Seth (op. cit. pp. 56-7).
83. CPW, I, 287.
84. Section 187 (BW, II, 547-8). It is conceivable that this was the

paragraph for which Coleridge originally went to Berkeley in March, 1796. I have mentioned above that he ordered Dupuis's work from London, and it seems likely that he would have heard about it from the review which appeared on the first page of the *Analytical Review* for March, 1796. In this case, he might have been reminded that the same view as that of Dupuis had been expressed in *Siris*, and borrowed the volume on March 10 in order to look at it again. At this time he was still busy with *The Watchman*.

85. Chs. i-ii. Quoted in S. Hobhouse, *Selected Mystical Writings of William Law*, 1938, p. 339.
86. Hobhouse, *op. cit.*, pp. 370-1.
87. CPW, I, 285n. The *Athenaeum* version has minor variations.
88. CPW, I, 286n.
89. CPW, I, 289.
90. ll. 119-21. CPW, I, 113.
91. CNBG, ff. 73ᵛ-74 (CNC, 258 and n.).
92. X, 470-1.
93. CPW, I, 456 and n.; CSC, II, 163 (here Coleridge specifically cites the Brocken and Messina). For his later use of it as an image for the human imagination see CMSV Envelope 3 (CNBV 56), page 19.
94. CAR, 220n. For a marginal note by Coleridge to this passage, describing the 'glory', see CIS, 243.
95. Coleridge visited the Brocken twice in 1799, hoping to see the 'spectre', but was disappointed on both occasions. See EKC, 107-8; 113; and refs.
96. The copy which he presented to a Paris Library was translated into French earlier, however.
97. BT, I, 499.
98. CNBG, f. 4ᵛ. (CNC, 39 and n.) This notebook has a number of references to giants and pigmies.
99. X, 14-5; 457. MW, I, 4.
100. For this and other references by Southey and Davy at this time, see OKK, 294-5 and 359 note 5.
101. CNBG, f. 23ᵛ; 24ᵛ (CNC, 172, 174 and nn.). See also his letter to Charles Lloyd, Senior, Oct., 1796 (CLG, I, 240), and X, 25; 466-7.
102. MPL, iv, 168-70.
103. Tobit, vi-viii. Cf. T. Copeland, 'A Woman Wailing for her Demon Lover'. RES, XVIII, 87-90.
104. CNB 44.13. Cf. Boehme's *Aurora*, xvii (JB, 168-71).
105. MPL, x, 504-84.

106. Gen. iii, 14.
107. MPL, ix, 494-531. See above, p. 70.
108. CAR, 253n. See above, pp. 112-13.
109. MH, I, 338; 500-1.
110. See below, pp. 325, n. 42.
111. *Essays by a Society of Gentlemen at Exeter*, 1796, pp. 220-2. DNB, entry 'Hugh Downman', identifies the author and refers to unpublished MSS. of the society. Perhaps the contribution which Coleridge helped with is still extant somewhere.
112. W. Jones, 'On the Gods of Greece, Italy and India', *Asiatic Researches*, 1788, I, 223. Sir William is referred to in *The Friend* (CFB, III, 189n) and Southey used his work as a source for *Thalaba*.
113. T. Taylor, *Cupid and Psyche*, 1795, Introd., p. viii.
114. CNB 16.76^v-7. CFB, I, 126.
115. CFB, III, 198 and n. (Cf. CPL, 335-6.)
116. CPW, I, 412; CBLC, I, 57 and n.
117. Letter to Sotheby, July, 1829. CLU, II, 427.
118. CMC, 30; 33 (probably separate reports of the same remark); and 194.
119. CAR, 277-8.
120. CLC, II, 648; CLG, I, 396. See above, p. 114.
121. 'Hope and Time'. GWS, 18.
122. Akenside, 'Pleasures of Imagination' (1st vn.), I, 99-101; 105-7; 56-9. (*Poems*, 1772, pp. 15; 13.)
123. CAR, 220n. See above, pp. 123-4.

CHAPTER V

1. Letter to Thelwall, 13 May, 1796. CLG, I, 215.
2. M, 43.
3. See e.g., WL, I, 225-7.
4. L. Stephen, *Hours in a Library*, 1892, III, 358. Quoted in part by Muirhead, M, 43n.
5. R. Graves, 'The Integrity of the Poet', *The Listener*, March 31, 1955, pp. 579-80.
6. '. . . a work of such pure imagination': Coleridge on *The Ancient Mariner*. CTT, 106.
7. Irving Babbitt, *Rousseau and Romanticism*, Boston, 1919, p. 287. Quoted, X, 301.
8. Leslie Stephen, op. cit., III, 359.
9. R. Graves, *The Meaning of Dreams*, 1924, pp. 145-58 (for a

powerful attack on it see X, 593-6); M. Bodkin, *Archetypal Patterns in Poetry*, 1934, ch. ii and pp. 90-115.

10. G. Wilson Knight, *The Starlit Dome*, 1941. Kenneth Burke, *The Philosophy of Literary Form*, Louisiana, 1941. R. P. Warren, 'A Poem of Pure Imagination', *Kenyon Review*, 1946, VIII, 391-427.

11. London, 1953.

12. E. E. Stoll, 'Symbolism in Coleridge', PMLA, 1948, LXIII, 214-33.

13. OKK, 252.

14. OKK, 254-5.

15. See, e.g., G. Garrigues, 'The Ancient Mariner', *Journal of Speculative Philosophy*, XIV, 1880, 327-38. *Sew. Rev.* VI, 200. H. B. Cotteril, *Introduction to the Study of Poetry*, 1882, p. 201. J. Sterling, *Essays and Tales*, 1848, pp. 101-10. Also below, pp. 291-2.

16. OKK, 258.

17. See above, pp. 128-30.

18. CSM, 36-7.

19. OKK, 258.

20. Letter to Sotheby, Sept., 1802. CLG, II, 864.

21. CPW, II, 1139.

22. Note of April 14, 1805. CNB 17.69-69^{v}.

23. C. Carlyon, *Early Years and Late Reflections*, 1836-58, I, 138-9.

24. Ibid., I, 140-1.

25. Crit. Rev., Feb., 1797, XIX, 194-200.

26. N, 199-200, et3 eqq.

27. CLG, II, 707.

28. JG, 334.

29. CBLC, I, 202.

30. CBLC, II, 256-7.

31. CAR, 244.

32. 'Religious Musings', ll. 45-9. CPW, I, 111.

33. See above, p. 107.

34. From sections 195, 205. BW, II, 551, 555.

35. ll. 163-8, 261-5, 305-9. I have used throughout the version of 1798. (CPW, II, 1030-48.)

36. X, 257-9.

37. CNBG, f. 5^{v}. (CNC, 45), X, 243-50.

38. X, 251.

39. X, 250.

40. 'It is an enormous blunder . . . to represent the An. M. as an old man on board ship. He was in my mind the everlasting wandering

Jew—had told this story ten thousand times since the voyage, which was in his early youth and 50 years before.' MS. fragment of table talk, now in Victoria College Library: CNC, 45n.

41. CBLC, I, 12.

42. 'Coleridge spoke of the esteem in which my brother was holden by a society at Exeter, of which Downman and Hole were members.' Christopher Wordsworth's diary, in C. Wordsworth, *Social Life at the English Universities in the Eighteenth Century*, Cambridge, 1894, p. 589.

43. CLG, I, 347. WPR, v, 460-76.

44. RH, 150-1.

45. CPW, I, 286.

46. WP, I, 360.

47. J. W. Robberds, *Memoir of William Taylor*, 1843, I, 223; *Crit. Rev.*, Oct., 1798, p. 201.

48. e.g. X, 335-6.

49. W. Scott, *The Chase* and *William and Helen*, Edinburgh, 1796.

50. RH, 142-3.

51. See below, p. 177.

52. X, 223-8.

53. See his gloss to ll. 131-4. CPW, I, 191 (cf. X, 234 et seqq.).

54. CSC, II, 147.

55. T. Taylor, *Philosophical and Mathematical Commentaries of Proclus*, 1788, II, 295n.

56. T. Taylor, *Plotinus on the Beautiful*, 1787, pp. 39-40 and 40n.

57. See above, p. 51.

58. Lane Cooper, *Late Harvest*, Ithaca, N.Y., 1952, p. 66. CPW, II, 1040.

59. CNBG, f. 32 (CNC, 219 and n.). CPW, I, 267.

60. See below, Appendix I, st. ii.

61. CPW, II, 1094.

62. See above, p. 143.

63. Bk. i, ll. 151-4.

64. CLG, I, 237; 303.

65. CPW, I, 125.

66. CBLC, II, 208-9. Cf. Wordsworth's account in *The Prelude* of how he would see a shepherd,

> distant a few steps,
> In size a giant, stalking through thick fog,
> His sheep like Greenland bears . . .
> (WPR, viii, 265-7)

67. The idea that 'fears will set the fancy at work, and haply, for a time, transform the mists of dim and imperfect knowledge into

determinate superstitions' (CAR, 22) is basic with Coleridge. In a copy of *Aids to Reflection* now in the British Museum, he wrote, 'When the Invisible is sought for by means of the Fancy in the world *without*, and the Awe is transferred to imaginary Powers (Dæmons, Genii, &c) or to sensible Objects (*Fetisches*, *Gri gris*, Saints' Images, Relics, &c) the Man becomes a Phantast in the one case and superstitious in the other.—The *Idea* of God is contained in the Reason: and the *Reality* of this Idea is a Command of the Conscience. Yet by placing even this *out of* ourselves, as if it existed in Space, we change it into an *Idol*.' (CMSB Add. 34,047, pp. 98-9.) See also CSC, II, 100, and CNB 47.44^v-45.

68. CNB 15.42^v.
69. CPW, II, 1010, Coleridge's authorship is likely but not certain.
70. CBLC, II, 207-8.
71. Q, II, 145.
72. CNBG, f. 78 (CNC, 273, *variatim*).
73. Boehme, *The Three Principles of the Divine Essence*. (JB, I (ii), 204.) Coleridge refers obliquely to this idea in a later notebook. (CNB 36.35.)
74. See above, p. 128.
75. MH, I, 241; cf. I, 67. Kathleen Coburn has noticed, independently, the relevance of this paragraph. (CNC, 240n.)
76. ll. 242-4. Coleridge was fond of speculating on the theme of Hell as a state of mind, a projection of the imagination diseased by sin. In a late notebook, also, he reflects on the Hell which would result from a human being existing in vital connection with a deranged organism (CNB 35.39^v) and elsewhere that which results from possessing human mental powers with the will withdrawn (CTT, 132) or from the survival of the soul without God or Love (CNB 46.36-36^v).
77. CPW, I, 140.
78. CNB 37.36.
79. See HH, 100.
80. HH, 103.
81. X, 181-3.
82. CPW, II, 897 (ll. 427-32).
83. CNB 15.25^v.
84. I suspect that at this point there may have been some association of ideas in Coleridge's mind between the dog-star, Siris and Osiris (there is a passage in Maurice's *Hindostan* (MH, 186) on this connection: the passage has been marked, not impossibly by Coleridge himself, in the Bristol Library copy).

85. CNB 6.37 (CNC, 1154 and n.).
86. ll. 276-7.
87. CPL, 226.
88. ll. 45-6. CPW, I, 365.
89. ll. 343-6.
90. CNB 44.35.
91. See above, p. 56. Coleridge occasionally uses snatches of the poem in later speculations, with this significance. In a passage on the 'light that lighteth every man coming into the world' he says, 'Abstracting the process of refraction which is a virtual remaining presence of the Luminary, or between the Tropics where it does not exist, or at the instant of a total eclipse of the sun, do the Rays remain—No! "at one Stride comes the Dark"' (CNB 37.67).
92. App. I, st. 7.
93. CSM, 63-4.
94. ll. 489-98.
95. X, 274n.; 555-8.
96. Thomas Taylor, *Dissertation on the Eleusinian and Bacchic Mysteries*, 'Amsterdam', 1790, p. 50.
97. Letter to Tieck, 1817, CLU, II, 201-2.
98. ll. 26-9 (CPW, I, 101); CLG, II, 798.
99. ll. 414-9. CPW, I, 124-5.
100. ll. 343-6.
101. JB, I, 53.
102. From *Recollections of Love*, CPW, I, 409.
103. CAR, 70.
104. Sir John Davies, *Poetical Works*, 1773, p. 155.
105. App. I, st. 9.
106. X, 286-7; n. 99, pp. 566-7.
107. Plotinus, *Enneads*, v, 9, 1 (tr. T. Taylor). I do not know of any place in Taylor's early translations where this appears. Unless one exists, Coleridge would probably have found it only in the original Greek.
108. R. P. Warren, 'A Poem of Pure Imagination,' *Kenyon Review*, 1946, VIII, 391-427.
109. Ibid., p. 414.
110. CCS, 227.
111. HH, 105-6.
112. ll. 419-22.
113. CPW, I, 69.
114. CPW, I, 5.
115. CPW, I, 244.
116. l. 338. CPW, I, 121.

117. CBLC, I, 202.
118. CAR, 253n.
119. CPW, I, 134.
120. CBLC, II, 6.
121. CBLC, II, 257-8.
122. CTT, 106.
123. E. E. Stoll, 'Symbolism in Coleridge', PMLA, 1948, LXIII, 228.
124. R. P. Warren, op. cit., pp. 413; 423.
125. CBLC, II, 6.

CHAPTER VI

1. WPR, xiv, 395-401.
2. CBLC, II, 6.
3. N, 167ff, 179ff, discussing W. Hutchinson, *History of the County of Cumberland*, Carlisle, 1794-7.
4. JG, 283.
5. Preface, *Poems* (ed. Derwent and Sara Coleridge), 1868, p. xlii, n.
6. CPJ, 604.
7. See S. F. Gingerich, 'From Necessity to Transcendentalism in Coleridge'. PMLA, 1920, XXXV, 1-59. Reprinted in his *Essays on the Romantic Poets* (N.Y., 1924).
8. CTT, 441.
9. CPL, 316.
10. ll. 85-108. *Poems of Richard Crashaw*, ed. L. C. Martin, Oxford, 1927, pp. 326-7.
11. He apparently associates her with fanaticism, according to a note in which he declares that 'a host of female Nuns and young Theresas in all Catholic Countries have the same stove-like Heat & devout yearning for the Virgin Mary' (CNB 41.77).
12. CPW, I, 183.
13. WPR, v, 364-425.
14. CPW, I, 184.
15. CPW, I, 287.
16. Ibid., 288.
17. Ibid., 266.
18. CPL, 371.
19. Ten years later, he used the image to describe a bird which he could hear from the *Courier* office. 'Has the Bird Hope? Or does it abandon itself to the Joy of its Frame—a living Harp of Eolus? O that I could do so!' (CNB 20.2; CAP 193.)
20. ll. 306-9. CPW, I, 226.

21. CPL, 314 (see above, p. 91). In a notebook he discusses the potential benefits from having the Aeolian harp as 'an appreciated part of religious furniture, like the crucifix—and a means, to which a promise of grace had been affixed—on a mind like Teresa's or Mad. Guyon's!' (CNB 18.57.) Elsewhere he mentions the 'incalculable advantage of chiefly dwelling on the virtues of the Heart, of Habits of Feeling & harmonious action, the music of the adjusted string at the impulse of the Breeze—and on the other hand the evils of books concerning particular actions, minute care-of-conscience, hair-splitting directions and decisions . . .' (CNB 17.10.)

22. 'The Nightingale', ll. 72-3. CPW, I, 266.

23. See Conclusion to *Christabel*, Part 2, and CNB 8.55 (CNC, 1392 and n.).

24. *Religious Musings*, ll. 396-401; *The Destiny of Nations*, ll. 15-20. CPW, I, 124; 132.

25. CSM, Appendix, xxxiii.

26. CMSB. Eg. 2800, f. 86 (CIS, 62 *variatim*).

27. CAR, 228n.

28. CNBG, f. 31 (CNC, 216 and n.).

29. ll. 16-9. CPW, I, 216.

30. ii, 583-5. Ibid., p. 233.

31. See *Drinking* versus *Thinking*, CPW, II, 979, and *Parliamentary Oscillators*, CPW, I, 211-13.

32. See above, p. 130.

33. T. Taylor, *Cupid and Psyche*, 1795, p. xiii.

34. ll. 221-5. CPW, I, 223.

35. p. 313.

36. ii, 332-3. CPW, I, 227.

37. CBLC, I, 98.

38. CNB 36.72.

39. See p. 126.

40. CNB 37.23^v. For another reference to Ceres and Proserpine see CNB 16.102-102^v (CAP 110). In a lecture of 1818, on the other hand, he describes as an 'extravagance' Boccaccio's identification, in a romance, of God the Father with Jupiter, the Saviour with Apollo, and the Evil Being with Pluto. 'But,' he says, 'for this there might be some excuse pleaded . . .' (CMC, 22-3.)

41. CNB 30.60^v. Quoted by K. Coburn, *University of Toronto Quarterly*, 1956, XXV, 127. It is interesting to notice that one of the few overt pieces of allegorizing in the Bible is concerned with the desolation of Hagar (Gal. iv, 22-v, 1), which Coleridge

mentions in a notebook (CNB 42.49^v). The parallel is not to be pressed without further evidence, however.

42. JG, 301-2.
43. N, 201-5; HH, 129. Variant ll. 126-30. CPW, I, 136. The lines read strangely, and one suspects some corruption of the text. It is however the reading adopted in all editions, and I know of no manuscript. Perhaps lines 128 and 129 ought to be interchanged.
44. ll. 257-9. CPW, I, 224.
45. The incident occurred on June 18, 1816, at a time when all the party were engaged on writing stories of the supernatural, including Byron's fragment of *The Vampyre*, Polidori's story, *The Vampyre*, and Mrs Shelley's *Frankenstein*. See the two accounts by J. W. Polidori in his *Diary* (ed. W. M. Rossetti), 1911, pp. 125-8, and in the preface to *The Vampyre* (1819, xv-xvi). See also, *Letters and Journals of Lord Byron* (ed. R. E. Prothero), 1900. IV, 296-8 and nn.
46. CMC, 356. (The review in question is not by Coleridge, however: see C. I. Patterson, 'The Authenticity of Coleridge's Reviews of Gothic Romances'. JEGP, 1951, L, 517-21.)
47. It is possible that a tradition exists whereby the werewolf longs to sleep in a human bed. The only reference I have found to such a conception, however, is that which appears in Gwen Raverat's *Period Piece* (1952, 165-6), and this is by no means conclusive. Coleridge occasionally refers to the 'war-wolf' in his writings: there are many references, for example, in *Zapolya*. For werewolves in the *Eddas*, see CNC, 170n.
48. AT, 241-4.
49. *Christabel*, ed. E. H. Coleridge, 1907, pp. 29-31.
50. See above, p. 126.
51. Coleridge, *Poems*, 1828, II, 54. (MS. amendment by Coleridge to copy now in Fitzwilliam Museum, Cambridge.)
52. ii, 531-6; 548-54. CPW, I, 232.
53. CNB 21.120^v.
54. ll. 94-5. CPW, I, 367.
55. CPW, I, 289-90.
56. *Plutarchi de Iside et Osiride Liber* (ed. S. Squire), Cambridge, 1744, (ii), 70.
57. N, 175 and refs.
58. ii, 569-71. CPW, I, 233.
59. See above, p. 156.
60. S. Gessner, *Death of Abel*, 1768, p. 20.
61. See above, pp. 88-9.

62. ii, 560-3. CPW, I, 232.
63. *Plutarchi de Iside et Osiride Liber* (ed. S. Squire), Cambridge, 1744 (ii), 16-17.
64. See above, p. 54.
65. CLG, II, 927.
66. Ibid., 1042; cf. p. 745. He did not regard the process in itself as reprehensible, however. '. . . every man of genius, who is born for his age, and capable of acting *immediately* and widely on that age, must of necessity *reflect* the age in the first instance, though as far as he is a man of genius, he will doubtless be himself reflected by it reciprocally' (Allsop's *Recollections*, 1820, CTT, 414).
67. *The Destiny of Nations*, ll. 283-4. CPW, I, 140.
68. D. H. Lawrence, 'The Reality of Peace' (ii), *English Review*, 1917, XXIV, p. 518.
69. See Appendix II for a completer account of these images.
70. CTT, 259.
71. CPW, I, 112-13. The last line is quoted in *The Friend* (CFB, II, 134), as 'Made pure by Thought, and naturalized in Heaven'.

CHAPTER VII

1. CPW, I, 295-7.
2. E. K. Chambers, 'The Date of Coleridge's *Kubla Khan*', RES, 1938, XI, 78-80.
3. CSC, II, 47. The terms of Coleridge's statement here make one wonder whether he was not aware of the tradition that Kubla Khan constructed his palace according to a dream. Lowes (X, 358) has pointed out that the Arabic account of Shang-du was not translated into any occidental language until after the composition of the poem, but the tradition might have filtered through by way of some other account. It should be noted, however, that the translation of the Arabic is itself disputed. H. Yule, *The Book of Ser Marco Polo*, 1921, I, 305-6n.
4. Morchard Bishop, 'The Farmhouse of Kubla Khan', TLS, May 10, 1957, p. 293. Mr Bishop identifies the farm as Broomstreet Farm. Comparison with the published table talk of the same date (Sept. 26, 1830) shows that the statement evidently arose in the course of a discussion of picturesque scenery, including that of north Devon. (CTT, 130-1.)
5. While in Germany, he wrote of the 'great rocky fragments which jut out from the Hills both here & at Porlock & which (alas!) we have not at dear Stowey!' (CLG, I, 498; and cf. 501, 528 for

further praise of 'Quantock, Porlock, Culbone, & Linton'.) In June, 1800, Coleridge was looking for a house at Porlock, but could find one neither there nor at Stowey. (CLG, I, 591.)

6. The best account of this manuscript, which came to light in 1934 (TLS, 2.8.34, p. 541), is given in a later letter by E. H. W. Meyerstein (TLS, 12.1.51, p. 21; and ensuing correspondence, pp. 53; 85).

7. See his three discussions in *Essays and Studies . . . of the English Association*, 1934, XIX, 102-11; RES, XI, 78-80; EKC, 100-3. More recently, H. M. Margoliouth has suggested, by detailed analysis of Coleridge's movements between May 13, 1798 and Sept. 16, 1798 (the date of his departure for Germany), that there is no place for a retirement during this period. (NQ, 1953, CXCVIII, 352-4.)

8. CLG, I, 348-52.

9. H. M. Margoliouth, *Wordsworth and Coleridge, 1795-1834*, 1953, p. 18.

10. '. . . in my 24th year I walked with Southey on a desperate hot Summer day from Bath to Bristol with a Goose, 2 vols of Baxter on the Immortality of the Soul, and the Giblets, in my hand.' (CNB 35.36.)

11. See above, pp. 87-8.

12. R. Dalbiez, *Psychoanalytic Method and the Doctrine of Freud* (tr. T. F. Lindsay), 1941, I, 91-2, citing Poincaré, *Science and Method* (tr. F. Maitland), 1914, pp. 52-5; O. Pfister, *The Psycho-analytic Method* (tr. Payne), pp. 240-1.

13. L. A. G. Strong, 'Reminiscences of W. B. Yeats', *The Listener*, Apr. 22, 1954, pp. 689-90.

14. CFA, 123-5. (Cf. CFB, I, 238-41, and CPL, 309-10.)

15. X, 401.

16. The mistake perhaps arose from the printer using a copy where stanza 2 ended at the foot of a page. Coleridge did not correct it in the 1828 edition.

17. See above, p. 135.

18. *Journal of Aesthetics and Art Criticism*, 1953, XII, 44-66.

19. HH, 114-22.

20. Humphry House is quoted as having commented on this point. (See D. Mercer, *loc. cit.* (note 18 *supra*), p. 44, n. 1A.)

21. Lowes has discussed all these points. X, 393-6; 374-6; 390-4; 379-80.

22. See Matthew Arnold, 'The Literary Influence of Academies', *Essays in Criticism*, 1865, pp. 58-9.

23. CNB 33.3; CSC, II, 232. Coleridge, however, also parodied the

extravagant use of alphabetic lore by Bryant's followers (CNB 36.79).

24. See J. S. Bailly, *Lettres sur l'Origine des Sciences, etc.*, London and Paris, 1777.

25. Eusebius, *Praeparatio Evangelica*, 474a-b (ed. and tr. E. H. Gifford, 1903, III (ii), 507).

26. BT, I, 420.

27. CNB 18.28, 17.24.

28. See *Memoirs of the Literary and Philosophical Society of Manchester*, 1785, II, 278-93. Kathleen Coburn has drawn attention to this paper by a fellow of Coleridge's college. CPL, 404, n. 55.

29. R. Fludd, *Mosaicall Philosophy*, 1659, pp. 48-50. Mentioned by Kathleen Raine: Coleridge, *Poems and Prose*, 1957, p. 15.

30. Zohar IV, as quoted by D. Saurat, *Literature and Occult Tradition*, 1930, p. 95.

31. C. Carlyon, *Early Years and Late Reflections*, 1836-58, I, 94-5.

32. T. Keightley, *Mythology of Ancient Greece and Italy*, 1838, pp. 439-40.

33. T. Taylor, *Hymns of Orpheus*, 1792, note, pp. 131-2.

34. MPL, ix, 70.

35. X, 393-6.

36. ll. 28-31. (MP, II, 159-60.)

37. CSC, I, 205.

38. Keats, of course, uses it in *Endymion*. (ii, 936-1017).

39. R. Fenton, *Poems*, 1773, pp. 150-1.

40. The original Latin version was borrowed by Southey from the Bristol Library twice in 1795, in July and October. Cottle's translation was published in November, 1797, and had passed through Coleridge's hands on its way to Wordsworth, by December 13. On December 11, Coleridge borrowed the original Latin from the Bristol Library, retaining it until February. (BB, nos. 63, 67, 99 (and n.), 102.)

41. J. P. Estlin, *The Nature and the Causes of Atheism*, Bristol, 1797, pp. 35-85.

42. BA, I, vii-viii; HM, vii-ix.

43. CNBG, f. 80ᵛ (CNC, 280 and n.); X, 30. The article referred to appears in the editions of 1710 and 1734-8 under 'Cham'; in the 1734-41 edition under 'Ham' at the end. It describes various traditions of Ham's lust.

44. T. Maurice, *Indian Antiquities*, 1793-1800, V, 874-5.

45. CGNB, f. 19 (CNC, 151).

46. CLG, I, 416 (Letter of Sept., 1798). Cf. CBLC, II, 141.

47. CLG, I, 204 (Letter of April, 1796).
48. CLG, I, 250 (Letter of Nov., 1796).
49. Preface to *Fire, Famine and Slaughter* (first published in *Sibylline Leaves*, 1817). CPW, II, 1102.
50. CNB 27.77-76^v. See also CNB 28.34^v-5.
51. CNB 3$\frac{1}{2}$.104.
52. CMC, 163.
53. CFB, I, 208.
54. CFB, II, 55n.
55. CMC, 163 (see above, n. 52).
56. J. Ludolphus, *A New History of Ethiopia* (tr. by J. P.), 1682, pp. 151-3.
57. Sir Thomas Herbert, *Some Years' Travels into Divers Parts of Africa and Asia the Great, etc.*, 1677, pp. 31-3.
58. CNB 41.88^v.
59. It is possible that Coleridge was reading the third edition of 1617, which was in Wordsworth's library at his death and might have been owned by him as early as this (*Trans. Wordsworth Society*, VI, 225, no. 285). It should be mentioned that the first and second editions read 'Xaindu', the third and fourth 'Xamdu'. The alteration evidently arose from a misreading of the second edition, where the print is poor at this point. All editions, however, read 'Cublai Can'; and it is in Purchas's other great work, the *Pilgrims*, that the other, more common, spelling appears.

In the Crewe holograph MS. the name is spelt 'Kubla Khan' in line 1, but 'Cubla' in line 29. According to E. H. W. Meyerstein (TLS, 12.1.51, p. 21) a MS. sold in 1859 and now lost to view had 'Cubla' in line 1. In Dorothy Wordsworth's journal, there is an entry which puzzled early editors, who took it to refer to a manuscript of the poem. '. . . I breakfasted and carried *Kubla* to a fountain in the neighbouring market-place, where I drank some excellent water' (WDJ, I, 34). Professor Irwin Griggs and H. M. Margoliouth have since pointed out that this was evidently a private joke of the Wordsworths, and a nickname for their drinking-can—and it seems likely that Coleridge originated the joke. But whoever *did* originate it was evidently familiar with the spelling 'Cubla Can'. See also OKK, 305.
60. CMC, 165.
61. MPL, xi, 385-8. Cf. S. Purchas, *Pilgrimage*, 1617, p. 472.
62. BA, III, 557-8; HM, 108. Cambalu is described overleaf in Purchas, on p. 475.
63. HM, 118 (from BA, I, 40-1). For another copious etymology, see Leibnitz, *Miscellanea Berolinensis*, Berlin, 1710, p. 3.

64. W. Warburton, *Divine Legation of Moses*, 1738, I, 103 and n. (On the ascription of divinity to kings and law-givers).
65. M. de Condorcet, ... *Progress of the Human Mind*, 1795, p. 148.
66. BA, I, 243-4; (HM, 18-9), with copious references.
67. See Lemprière's *Classical Dictionary*, art. 'Altis'.
68. Dupuis, *Origine de Tous les Cultes*, Paris, 1795, II, 270.
69. Coleridge's interest in this tradition is shown by the fact that he transcribed two Greek passages on the subject from Josephus into the Gutch Notebook. CNC, 277; 279 and nn.
70. P. D. Huet, *Treatise of the Situation of Paradise* (tr. T. Gale), 1694, p. 17.
71. HM, 175: quoted, with interpolations, from BO, 114.
72. BOP, 216-17.
73. For the first, see CNB 16.105; for the second, CCS, 223, and CTT, 266.
74. BO, 145 (HM, 386).
75. R. Wood, *Ruins of Balbec, otherwise Heliopolis in Coelosyria* (1757); *Ruins of Palmyra, otherwise Tedmor, in the Desert* (1753).
76. R. Lovell and R. Southey, *Poems*, Bath, 1795, p. 35.
77. See below, p. 228.
78. MJ, 135.
79. MJ, 119-20.
80. MJ, 133-4.
81. MJ, 122-3.
82. See below, p. 235.
83. MPL, iv, 161-3 (just before the mention of Asmodeus—see above, p. 126).
84. *Historical Library of Diodorus the Sicilian* (tr. G. Booth), 1700, pp. 194-5.
85. Plutarch, *De Iside et Osiride*, Cambridge, 1744 (ii), pp. 73; 108-12. For other information available to Coleridge see B. Picart, *Ceremonies and Religious Customs of ... the Known World*, 1733, III, 155-6.
86. J. R. Forster, *Observations made during a Voyage round the World*, 1778, p. 316.
87. S. Purchas, *Pilgrimage*, 1617, p. 472.
88. T. Maurice, *Indian Antiquities*, 1793-1800, III, 504-16 (see also Macrobius, *Saturnalia: Opera*, Biponti, 1788, I, 300).
89. CPW, I, 265, ll. 35-7.
90. R. Lovell and R. Southey, *Poems*, Bath, 1795, p. 43.
91. ll. 38-40. CPW, I, 107.
92. ll. 99-105. CPW, I, 247.
93. ll. 193-7. CPW, I, 262-3.

94. CPW, I, 429.
95. CPW, I, 298n. Cf. X, 379.
96. CNBG, f. 49 (CNC, 245 and n.).
97. T. Campanella, *Civitas Solis*, This work was reprinted in, e.g., Mercurius Britannicus, *Mundus Alter et Idem* (ed. W. Knight). Ultrajecti, 1643.
98. Duncan Forbes, *Letter to a Bishop*, 1732, p. 16.
99. CNB 26.74v.
100. MPL, i, 710-17. Cf. ll. 726-30.
101. See above, p. 218.
102. See above, p. 215.
103. H, VIII, 110.
104. CSM, App., ix-x.
105. CPL, 179.
106. CSC, II, 165.
107. CMC, 101.
108. CBLC, I, 20-1.
109. CBLC, I, 12. Cf. *The Task*, v. (Cowper, *Poems*, 1785, II, 187-90.)
110. CPW, I, 398.

CHAPTER VIII

1. T. Paine, *Common Sense: addressed to the Inhabitants of America*, Newport, 1776, p. 1.
2. CPL, 291.
3. HH, 118-21.
4. l. 332 and n. 1. CPW, I, 121.
5. ll. 336-8.
6. ll. 318-22.
7. CPW, I, 329-30.
8. ll. 74-83. CPW, I, 423.
9. CNB 21½.40 (CAP, 276), c. 1817-19.
10. CTT, 81.
11. CSM, 25-6.
12. MPL, ix, 434-5. Additional proof of Coleridge's familiarity with this part of the poem is afforded by his employment, more than once, of phrases closely based on line 445: 'As one who long in populous City pent...' (See, e.g., CPW, I, 93; 179; 314.)
13. Ibid., ll. 1080-90. Perhaps the word 'cover' here helped change the 'Covert' of the previous passage into Coleridge's 'cover'.
14. Ezek. viii.

15. MPL, i, 446-57.
16. R. Lovell and R. Southey, *Poems*, Bath, 1795, p. 117.
17. See above, p. 126.
18. MPL, iv, 223-35.
19. Ibid., ix, 69-75.
20. John, iv, 14; Rev. xxi, 6.
21. CSC, I, 58.
22. See above, p. 68.
23. CNB 21.37 (CNC, 1056).
24. CNB, 16.100ᵛ.
25. CIS, 279-80.
26. T. Taylor, *Hymns of Orpheus*, 1792, p. 14; and part of an oracle to Plotinus, quoted in his *Philosophical and Mathematical Commentaries of Proclus*, 1788, II, 234.
27. CNB 21.32 (CNC, 980 and n.).
28. HH, 51, citing CPW, I, 381-2, ll. 8-12.
29. CNB 30.62ᵛ. Cf. the note copied by one of the Gillmans into their copy of *Sibylline Leaves* (now at Harvard: reproduced in GWS, 123n.). (The original MS. note is in the Fitzwilliam Museum.)
30. CNB 17.41.
31. CNB 21.109ᵛ (cf. CAP, 84).
32. CPW, I, 368 (ll. 134-6).
33. Ibid., ll. 45-6.
34. CNB 36.39.
35. CFB, II, 272.
36. CNB 21.56 (CNC, 1589 *variatim*; and n. giving earlier form).
37. This note, also, has been praised by Humphry House; see HH, 55.
38. CTT, 194. (My emendation.)
39. CBLC, II, 109.
40. CTT, 204.
41. CMC, 102.
42. CSC, I, 65.
43. CSM, Appendix, p. xxix.
44. *Omniana* (CTT, 375). Cf. the poem *To Asra* (1801), CPW, I 361-2.
45. CFB, I, 101.
46. CFB, I, 171.
47. CNB 36.74ᵛ. Cf. the 'fontal light of ideas', CTT, 241.
48. CCS, 59.
49. CNB 39.19. The 'Euphrasia' refers to Adam's vision. MPL, xi, 411-22.

50. CNBG, f. 26^v (CNC, 177 and n., tracing the image to Jeremy Taylor).

51. CMSB, Eg. 2800, ff. 51-2. Transcribed, GWT, II, 107. Coleridge quotes *Aeneid* vi, 750-1 and 713-15.

52. See below, p. 265.

53. *Purgatorio*, xxviii, 121-32. Coleridge is less likely to have known this, but he knew the *Inferno* (BB, no. 80). I am indebted to Mr R. P. Wickham for this reference and for pointing out resemblances to the second stanza of *Kubla Khan* in Cooke's Hesiod. (See the description of Tartarus and the Styx in the *Theogony*: Hesiod, *Works* (tr. T. Cooke), 1728, II, 92-3 (ll. 1082-1109).)

54. Dupuis, *Origine de Tous les Cultes*, Paris, 1795, I, 101.

55. l. 204. CPW, I, 116. Thomson describes the fountains of virtue and vice in the *Seasons*.

56. The connection was not lost on Coleridge's contemporaries. His friend Hugh Downman discussed it in the essay mentioned above (op. cit., 222n; see above, p. 128).

57. OKK, 248-9.

58. BB, 123, no. 84. I am quoting the translation by G. Gregory, 1787, I, 148-9.

59. CMC, 291.

60. See two entries in the Gutch notebook: 'Burnet's Mountains translated into blank Verse, the Original at the bottom of the page'; 'Burnet's de montibus in English Blank Verse'. CNBG, ff. 7; 24^v (CNC, 61 *variatim*; 174; and 61n.). See also *Biographia Literaria*: 'The writings of PLATO, and Bishop TAYLOR, and the "Theoria Sacra" of BURNET, furnish undeniable proofs that poetry of the highest kind may exist without metre, and even without the contra-distinguishing objects of a poem.' (CBLC, II, 11.)

61. T. Burnet, *Theory of the Earth*, 1684-90, (i), 115-16. Cf. Bryant's description of the effect of fountains on inspiration and prophecy. (HM, 197; BA, I, 192, 276-80.)

62. Cf. Bryant on Delphi. HM, 152; BA, I, 79; 219-20.

63. *Destiny of Nations*, ll. 435-7. CPW, I, 146. He also refers to the Paean Apollo as '*Healer & Python-killer*' in a letter of Dec., 1796. CLG, I, 291. See also App. II, p. 302.

64. MH, I, 328.

65. T. Taylor, *Cupid and Psyche*, 1795, pp. 76-7.

66. See above, p. 232.

67. CPW, I, 298n.; X, 379-81.

68. MH, I, 105. Cf. CNBG, f. 47, and Lowes's discussion, X, 380-1. CNC, 241n. is also important.

69. CNBG, f. 45ᵛ from MH, I, 106-7 (CNC, 240).
70. See e.g. MH, I, 102. Lowes comments, but in connection with sun and moon imagery alone, X, 380-1.
71. 'Frost at Midnight', ll. 73-4. CPW, I, 242.
72. CNB 43.3; 2 (corrected).
73. CNB 25.2-1 (CAP, 290).
74. A. and J. Churchill (ed.), *Collection of Voyages and Travels*, 1704, I, 48. The volume contains more that may have been taken up by Coleridge, including notes on footless birds of paradise (p. 45) the speed of Tartar horsemen (p. 43; above, p. 215) and the course of the 'red river' (pp. 39; 28-9). The tradition of the bloody river seems to lie just beneath the surface of *Kubla Khan* (see above, p. 235). (See CNB 16.100ᵛ for a vivid use of the Nile running blood in the Egyptian plagues as a metaphor.)
75. See above, p. 223.
76. See above, pp. 109-10; 247.
77. *Samson Agonistes*, ll. 87-9. MP, II, 67.
78. *Destiny of Nations*, ll. 23-6. CPW, I, 132.
79. See above, p. 34.
80. See above, p. 228.
81. CNB 20.37ᵛ.
82. CBLC, II, 218.
83. 'To Matilda Betham . . .'. CPW, I, 375. Quoted, OKK, 234.
84. CPW, I, 391-2.
85. This envy is voiced occasionally as an 'involuntary Jealousy' in the notebooks, e.g. CNB 12.45ᵛ-47.
86. CSM, 36.
87. OKK, 352, n. 118, citing T. O. M. in the *Explicator*, Oct., 1948.
88. Letter of March, 1791. CLG, I, 7.
89. T. Taylor, *Philosophical and Mathematical Commentaries of Proclus*, 1788, II, 278-307. The whole passage is of interest as showing the sort of allegorical theories which could be found in the neoplatonic writings.
90. Letter of Sept., 1794. CLG, I, 99.
91. Herodotus, iv, 181-3. (*History*, tr. W. Beloe, 1791, II, 339-41.)
92. A visitor to Bristol heard one played in a private house: see W. D. Templeman in TLS, 2.4.31, p. 271.
93. Eusebius, *Praeparatio Evangelica*, 476b; A. Calmet, *Antiquities Sacred and Profane*, 1724 (i), 81. Eusebius' source was probably Clem. Alex., *Stromaton*, I, xvi.
94. See 'sambuca' in Ainsworth's Latin Dictionary and 'dulcimer' in the O.T.

95. BB, 124, no. 97. Coleridge borrowed the *second* volume.

96. C. Burney, *General History of Music*, 1789, I, 492. Elsewhere (pp. 205-14) a letter from Bruce describes other instruments of Abyssinia, brought from Egypt by Thot in the first ages of the world and from Palestine with Menelek, son of the Queen of Sheba.

97. C. S. Lewis, *English Literature in the Sixteenth Century*, Oxford, 1954, pp. 333-4.

98. Heliodorus, *Aethiopian History* (tr. by a Person of Quality and N. Tate), 1686, pp. 3-5.

99. R. Lovell and R. Southey, *Poems*, Bath, 1795, pp. 18-19 and n.

100. BB, 124, no. 89.

101. *Opera*, Paris, 1688, I, 364-5. Tr. R. Graves, *Golden Ass*, 1950, p. 271.

102. MPL, iv, 280-4. (See L. Cooper 'The Abyssinian Paradise...', *Mod Phil*. III, 327-32, and below, p. 261.) For variants of 'Abora', see Crewe MS., TLS, 12.1.51. I take Coleridge's alteration to be *towards* the original version.

103. Summer, 750-83. Cf. Johnson's *Rasselas*.

104. HM, 1-2 (BA, I, 12-13; 105).

105. John i, 28-34.

106. MPR, i. 184; ii, 20.

107. ll. 121-6. CPW, I, 135-6. See above, p. 171.

108. 'My First Acquaintance...'. H, XVII, 108.

109. CTT, 442.

110. WPR, xi, 454-9.

111. LW, II, 219. I hope to expand this point elsewhere.

112. CLG, I, 279.

113. Collins, *Poetical Works*, 1771, pp. 52-4.

114. ll. 368-70. CPW, I, 123, n. 1.

115. CBLC, II, 20.

116. For Collins's ode, *The Passions* and the third stanza of *Kubla Khan*, see X, 399-400.

117. Plato, *Ion*, 534 (tr. F. Sydenham, 1759, pp. 42-4). Cf. E. Schneider, 'The "Dream" of *Kubla Khan*', PMLA, 1945, LX, 800; and HH, 115.

118. Ifor Williams, *Lectures on Early Welsh Poetry*, Dublin, 1944, p. 8.

119. 'Oxford in the Vacation', LW, II, 11-12.

120. Melville, 'Hawthorne and his Mosses' (1850). Reptd., Edmund Wilson, *The Shock of Recognition*, N.Y., 1943, p. 199.

121. App. I, p. 299.

122. MPL, iv, 275-9. For siting in Ethiopia, see Herodotus, ii, 146, iii, 97.
123. See above, p. 112.
124. See above, p. 193.
125. *Homeric Hymns*, iii, 207-450 (Loeb).
126. Ibid., ll. 513-23.
127. W. Mason, *Poems*, 1764, p. 184.
128. W. Ouseley, *Oriental Collections*, 1798, II, 18.
129. Ibid., I, 348-9. Cf. Bryant, BA, I, 285-7 (HM, 356-7).
130. See J. B. Gross, *Heathen Religion*, 1856, pp. 309-11 (cf. Wordsworth's *Humanity*, WP, IV, 103), for oaks and druids. Laplanders turned their boats round three times with the course of the sun when praying for the sick (J. Pinkerton, *Voyages*, 1808, I, 484). (For Coleridge's knowledge of Leemius, see CPW, I, 134n.) The infant Dionysus was circled by the Curetes: Eusebius, *Praeparatio Evangelica*, 64d.
131. CNB 18.66.
132. CNB 21.81ᵛ-2 (CNC, 1637). Richard Payne Knight's *Discourse on the Worship of Priapus* (1786) was later withdrawn. Nevertheless a good deal of knowledge about Priapus was probably derived from surviving copies.
133. Cf. CFB, I, 337; CPL, 342; CSC, II, 69; 84.
134. See above, p. 68.
135. CNBG, f.45ᵛ (CNC, 240 and n.). The passage is marked, not impossibly by Coleridge, in the Bristol Library copy. This passage would have been relevant to his *Hymn to the Sun*.
136. X, 33.
137. MH, I, 107-8.
138. CNB 44.35.
139. CPL, 249.
140. Coleridge is endorsing a sentiment of Bacon's. CPL, 333.
141. CSC, I, 126.
142. Sir John Davies, *Poetical Works*, 1773, p. 248.
143. WPR, xi, 441-9. Wordsworth also pictures Coleridge by the Arethusa fountain (ll. 464-70).
144. P. H. Mallet, *Northern Antiquities*, tr. Bp. Percy, 1770, II, 49-50. (Cf. II, 186.) For Coleridge's knowledge of the Eddas, see CTW, 65-8.
145. Ibid., II, 53. In his *Death of Odin*, Southey writes of

the Roman skull,
With hydromel sweet-smiling full . . .

R. Lovell and R. Southey, *Poems*, Bath, 1795, p. 108.

146. J. Z. Holwell, *Ancient Brahmins*, 1779, II, 173.
147. MH, I, 376.
148. T. Taylor, *Philosophical and Mathematical Commentaries of Proclus*, 1788, II, 284-6, during a long passage on the significance of honey.
149. J. Ludolphus, *History of Ethiopia*, 1682, pp. 387-8; 289; J. Lobo, Voyage to Abyssinia (tr. S. Johnson), 1735, pp. 53-4.
150. AT, 12-13.
151. Isa. vii, 14-15. (Mentioned in an allegorical note on the Bible, CNB 35.47.)
152. Ovid, *Metamorphoses*, ii, 235-56.
153. See above, p. 95.
154. CNB 43.63^v. Moses was called Alpha (BOP, 248).
155. CNB 43.69.
156. According to Josephus (*Antiquities*, II, x-xi), Moses undertook a campaign against the Ethiopians, in the course of which he married an Ethiopian princess and visited the troglodytes.
157. CNB 53.10^v-11.
158. CSM, 52. See above, p. 96.
159. CNB 45.13^v. Cf. also his preoccupation with the education of the second generation in pantisocracy (see above, p. 86) and his interest in Moses' solution of the same problem (CNB 44.26^v-7).
160. CNB 44.16^v; 45.6^v-7.
161. CNB 47.18^v-19^v (CIS, 150).
162. MPL, ix, 442-3.
163. See above, p. 63.
164. *Song of Solomon*, iv, 12-15; 16; viii, 10.
165. It might be possible to interpret *Kubla Khan* in terms of the human body—particularly in view of a later attempt by Coleridge to explain his dream-symbolism in this way. (CNB 36.4^v.) It would be difficult to make a stringent interpretation on these lines, however.
166. Song of Solomon, iv, 11; v, 1.
167. Song of Solomon (tr. Ann Francis), 1781, pp. 65-6.
168. Ecclus. xxiv. For Coleridge's reading of this book in 1796 see CNC, 264-9 and nn.
169. R. M. Rilke, *Sonnets to Orpheus* (tr. J. B. Leishman), 1946, p. 37.
170. R. M. Rilke, *Notebook of Malte Laurids Brigge* (tr. J. Linton), 1930, pp. 72-3.
171. CLG, II, 671.
172. st. 8. App. I, p. 299.
173. ll. 403-4. CPW, I, 124.

174. CPW, I, 174. (Cf. CLG, I, 321: Letter to Cottle of 1797; for 'rightly-whispering' read 'nightly-whispering'.)
175. See, e.g., CLG, I, 527.
176. CLG, I, 538.
177. Quoted by Griggs, CLG, II, 986.
178. CLG, II, 987.
179. See, e.g., CNB $3\frac{1}{2}$.40^v; 8.40^v; 67^v-68 (CNC, 424; 1281 and n.; 1840 and n.; cf. 1131 and n.).
180. E. H. W. Meyerstein held a similar view. TLS, 30.10.37, p. 803.
181. See above, p. 172.

CHAPTER IX

1. Letter of April, 1804. CLG, II, 1116. Cf CPW, II, 913.
2. Preface to edition of Coleridge's poems (1907, p. xii).
3. See, e.g., CPL, 239; CCS, 68. In private he does not seem to have been so positive: see his discussion in CNB 51.22-3.
4. CTT, 196.
5. Letter of Oct., 1818. KL, 226.
6. *The Excursion*, Preface (1814), ll. 52-8 (WP, V, 4-5). Cf. M. H. Abrams, *The Mirror and the Lamp*, N.Y., 1953, p. 66 and note, p. 348.
7. *Dejection* (earliest version). CLG, II, 798.
8. Letter to H. C. Robinson, CLU, II, 46-7. Coleridge again referred to Wordsworth's opinion (without mentioning him by name) in 1830. CTT, 131.
9. E. M. Forster, *A Passage to India*, 1924, p. 152.
10. 'One travels along with the Lines of a mountain/ I wanted, years ago, to make Wordsworth sensible of this' (CNB 21.118^v; cf. CAP, 101). 'When Lady Beaumont was a child, she told me, that previously to her saying her Prayers she endeavoured to think of a mountain, or a great River, or something *great*, in order to raise up her Soul & kindle it.' (Feb. 1804: CNB 9.10^v; cf. CAP, 67 and CC, I, 69; also CNC, 189n.)
11. ll. 21-3. CPW, I, 378.
12. Letter of 1820. CLU, II, 261.
13. CNB 16.96^v. (Cf. CAP, 163.) From the *Aids to Reflection* it seems that Coleridge thought of Simonides as one who, like Wordsworth, had 'yielded up moral questions in despair'. CAR, 231-2.
14. CLG, II, 812.

15. CLG, II, 830-1. Cf. G. Whalley, 'The Integrity of BIOGRAPHIA LITERARIA', *Essays and Studies . . . of the English Association*, 1953.
16. Letter of May, 1799. CLG, I, 491.
17. CTT, 188-9; 210-11.
18. CTT, 470.
19. CNBN (29). Transcribed, CIS, 216-17.
20. CTT, 201.
21. 'My First Acquaintance with Poets', H, XVII, 117. Coleridge developed his opinion of Wordsworth's 'matter-of-fact-ness' in *Biographia Literaria*. (CBLC, II, 101ff.)
22. WPR, viii, 77-8; 84-9 (cf. vii, 77-86).
23. Ibid., xiv, 28-31; cf. the episode of the stolen boat: i, 377-400.
24. Ibid., xiv, 70-4.
25. See *Intimations of Immortality* (WP, II, 279-85).
26. See Allsop's Recollections, 1822. CTT, 462-3.
27. *Dejection*, earliest version, ll. 133-6. CLG, II, 793.
28. See Dorothy Wordsworth's account in 1810. WL, II, 365-7.
29. COIS, 80.
30. From a note on the 'philosophized science of Geometry'. CMSV, Envelope II, plate 43 (corrected).
31. See, e.g., CNB 43.32^v-33 for a discussion of consciousness in these terms.
32. CPW, I, 110, n. 2.
33. CLG, I, 413.
34. See his letter to Davy, Feb., 1801. CLG, II, 670-2.
35. CPW, II, 1097-8.
36. Printed in J. Davy, *Memoirs of . . . Sir Humphry Davy*, 1836, I, 34-6.
37. *Dejection*, earliest version, ll. 267-71. CLG, II, 797.
38. CLG, I, 470.
39. Letter to Gillman, Oct., 1825. CLC, II, 742-3.
40. See his journal-letter: KL, 323.
41. Allsop's Recollections, 1820. CTT, 420-1.
42. See, e.g., his urgent letter requesting *Sibylline Leaves* in July, 1817. SW, IX, 234. He had read *Biographia Literaria* by early Dec., 1817 (*Mary Shelley's Journal*, ed. F. L. Jones, Oklahoma, 1947, p. 87). For other flattering references to Coleridge see SW, IX, 43; 180; vol. X, 346; 371.
43. See R. Ackermann, *Quellen, Vorbilder, Stoffe zu Shelley's Poetischen Werken*, Erlangen and Leipzig, 1890, p. 14. Also N. Rogers, *Shelley at Work*, Oxford, 1956, 109-14.
44. T. J. Hogg, *Life of Shelley*, 1858, II, 44. The original letter is

mislaid according to N. I. White (*Shelley*, N.Y., 1940, I, 620). Coleridge is more likely to have written 'poetic, metaphysical reveries'.

45. A. P. Stanley, *Life of Arnold*, 1844, II, 56.
46. 'Lectures on the English Poets' (1818). H, V, 167.
47. 'Samuel Taylor Coleridge', *Tait's Edinburgh Magazine*, 1834, I(N.S.), p. 509.
48. Carlyle, *Life of Sterling*, 1851, ch. viii.
49. See, e.g., *Sartor Resartus, passim*.
50. C. R. Sanders, *Coleridge and the Broad Church Movement*, Durham. N.C., 1942, gives a comprehensive account.
51. A. Brandl, *Samuel Taylor Coleridge*, 1887, p. 388.
52. D. Patmore, *Life and Times of Coventry Patmore*, 1949, pp. 14-27, etc.
53. T. H. Caine, *Recollections of Dante Gabriel Rossetti*, 1882, pp. 151-66.
54. D. Patmore, op. cit., p. 98.
55. Coventry Patmore, *The Unknown Eros*, 1877, p. 21.
56. See his essay, 'Emotional Art'. Quoted, O. Burdett, *The Idea of Coventry Patmore*, 1921, p. 196.
57. Letter to Sutton, April, 1847. B. Champneys, *Memoirs and Correspondence of Coventry Patmore*, 1900, II, 153.
58. From Taylor's *Via Pacis*. CNB 21.20^v (CNC, 876 and n.).
59. CNC, 1546.
60. CNB 21.118 (cf. CAP, 96).
61. CNB 51.6.
62. CNB 17.76 (transcribed, *variatim*, CIS, 37).
63. CMSV, 'opus maximum'. This phrase concludes the volume numbered 'Vol. II' in the series of three. (For a further opinion, see M, 268-9, however.)

BIBLIOGRAPHY

The appearance of an abbreviation in brackets indicates that the work in question has not been directly referred to in the text. This bibliography is also indexed by authors in the General Index. The place of publication is London unless otherwise stated.

AT   Andrew Tooke, *The Pantheon, representing the Fabulous Histories of the Heathen Gods*. 14th edition. 1738.

Ath.   *The Athenaeum*. 1828-1921.

BA   Jacob Bryant, *A New System, or an analysis of ancient mythology*. 3 vols. 1774-6.

BB   G. Whalley, 'The Bristol Library Borrowings of Southey and Coleridge, 1793-8'. *The Library*, 5th Series, IV, 114-32. Oxford, 1950.

BG   *Coleridge: Studies by Several Hands on the Hundredth Anniversary of his Death*. Edited by Edmund Blunden and Earl Leslie Griggs. 1934.

BO   Jacob Bryant, *Observations and Inquiries Relating to various parts of Ancient History*. Cambridge, 1767.

BOP   Jacob Bryant, *Observations upon the Plagues inflicted upon the Egyptians*. 1794.

BP   *The Works of George Gordon Noel, Lord Byron. Poetry*. Edited by E. H. Coleridge. 7 vols. 1898-1901.

BT   James Bruce, *Travels to discover the Source of the Nile in the years 1768-1773*. 5 vols. Edinburgh, 1790.

BW   *The Works of George Berkeley, D.D.* 2 vols. 1784.

CAP   *Anima Poetae. From the Unpublished Notebooks of Samuel Taylor Coleridge*. Edited by Ernest Hartley Coleridge. 1895.

CAR   S. T. Coleridge, *Aids to Reflection*. 1825.

(CBE)   *Biographia Epistolaris, being the Biographical Supplement of Coleridge's Biographia Literaria, with additional letters, etc.* Edited by A. Turnbull. 2 vols. 1911.

(CBLA)   S. T. Coleridge, *Biographia Literaria*. 2 vols. 1817.

(CBLB)   S. T. Coleridge, *Biographia Literaria*. 2nd edition. Edited by Henry Nelson and Sara Coleridge. 2 vols. 1847.

CBLC   S. T. Coleridge, *Biographia Literaria*. Edited, with his aesthetical essays, by J. Shawcross. 2 vols. Oxford, 1907.

346

BIBLIOGRAPHY

CC — *Memorials of Coleorton.* Edited by William Knight. 2 vols. Edinburgh, 1887.

(CCP) — S. T. Coleridge, *Conciones ad Populum, Or Addresses to the People.* Bristol, 1795.

CCS — S. T. Coleridge, *On the Constitution of the Church and State.* 1830.

CEP — S. T. Coleridge, *On the Prometheus of Aeschylus. Transactions of the Royal Society of Literature,* II. 1834.

CET — S. T. Coleridge, *Essays on his own Times,* forming a second series of 'The Friend'. Edited by Sara Coleridge. 3 vols. 1850.

CFA — S. T. Coleridge, *The Friend; a literary, moral and political weekly paper.* Penrith, 1 June 1809—15 March 1810.

CFB — S. T. Coleridge, *The Friend: a series of Essays in Three Volumes.* New edition. 1818.

(CFC) — S. T. Coleridge, *The Friend.* 3rd edition. Edited by H. N. Coleridge. 1837.

CIS — *Inquiring Spirit. A new presentation of Coleridge from his published and unpublished prose writings.* Edited by Kathleen Coburn. 1951.

CLC — *Letters of Samuel Taylor Coleridge.* Edited by Ernest Hartley Coleridge. 2 vols. 1895.

CLG — *Collected Letters of Samuel Taylor Coleridge.* Edited by Earl Leslie Griggs. Vol. I-. 1956-.

(CLP) — *Letters from the Lake Poets . . . to Daniel Stuart.* Printed for Private Circulation. 1889.

CLS — S. T. Coleridge, *'Blessed are ye that sow beside all waters'. A lay sermon, addressed to the higher and middle classes, on the existing distresses and discontents.* 1817.

CLU — *Unpublished Letters of Samuel Taylor Coleridge.* Edited by Earl Leslie Griggs. 2 vols. 1932.

CMC — *Coleridge's Miscellaneous Criticism.* Edited by T. M. Raysor. 1936.

CNC — *The Notebooks of Samuel Taylor Coleridge.* Edited by Kathleen Coburn. Vol. I (two parts). 1957.

COIS — S. T. Coleridge, *Confessions of an Inquiring Spirit.* Edited by H. St J. Hart. 1956.

Comp. Lit. — *Comparative Literature,* Eugene, 1949-.

CPJ — *The Poetical Works of Samuel Taylor Coleridge.* Edited, with biographical introduction, by J. D. Campbell, 1893.

CPL — *The Philosophical Lectures, hitherto unpublished, of Samuel Taylor Coleridge.* Edited by Kathleen Coburn. 1949.

CPW   *The Complete Poetical Works of Samuel Taylor Coleridge.* Edited with textual and bibliographical notes by E. H. Coleridge. 2 vols. Oxford, 1912.

(CR)   *The Literary Remains of Samuel Taylor Coleridge.* Edited by H. N. Coleridge. 4 vols. 1836-9.

Crit. Rev.   *The Critical Review.* 1756-1811.

CSC   *Coleridge's Shakespearean Criticism.* Edited by T. M. Raysor. 1936.

CSL   *Coleridge on Logic and Learning, with selections from the unpublished manuscripts.* Edited by A. D. Snyder. New Haven, 1929.

CSM   S. T. Coleridge, *The Statesman's Manual; or, the Bible the best guide to political skill and foresight. A lay-sermon, etc.* 1816.

CTT   *The Table Talk and Omniana of Samuel Taylor Coleridge.* With additional Table Talk from Allsop's 'Recollections', etc. Oxford ed., 1917.

CTW   S. T. Coleridge, *The Watchman.* Bristol, 1 March-13 May 1796.

(CW)   *The Complete Works of Samuel Taylor Coleridge.* Edited by W. G. T. Shedd. 7 vols. New York, 1853-4.

DNB   *Dictionary of National Biography.* 1885-1900.

EKC   E. K. Chambers, *Samuel Taylor Coleridge.* Oxford, 1938.

Enc. Brit.   *Encyclopaedia Britannica*, 11th edition.

GWS   G. Whalley, *Coleridge and Sara Hutchinson and the Asra Poems.* 1955.

GWT   G. Whalley, *Library Cormorant.* Unpublished and confidential Ph.D. thesis in the University of London Library. 2 vols. 1950.

H   *The Complete Works of William Hazlitt.* Edited by P. P. Howe. 21 vols. 1930-4.

HA   *The Autobiography of Leigh Hunt.* Edited by J. E. Morpurgo. 1949.

HC   Lawrence Hanson, *The Life of S. T. Coleridge. The Early Years.* 1938.

HEL   George Sampson. *The Concise Cambridge History of English Literature.* Cambridge, 1941.

HH   Humphry House, *Coleridge. The Clark Lectures*, 1951-2. 1953.

HM   William Holwell, *A Mythological, Etymological and Historical Dictionary.* 1793.

JB   Jacob Boehme, *Works, . . . with figures, illustrating his Principles, left by the Rev. W. Law.* 4 vols. 1764-81.

BIBLIOGRAPHY

JCE   Joseph Cottle, *Early Recollections, etc.* 2 vols. 1837.

J.E.G.P.   *Journal of English and Germanic Philology.* Urbana, 1903-.

JG   James Gillman, *The Life of Samuel Taylor Coleridge.* Vol. I. 1838.

K   *The Writings of William Blake.* Edited by G. Keynes. 3 vols. 1925.

KL   *The Letters of John Keats.* Edited by H. B. Forman. 4th edition. 1952.

LCL   *The Letters of Charles Lamb.* Edited, with those of Mary Lamb, by E. V. Lucas. 3 vols. 1935.

LW   *The Works of Charles and Mary Lamb.* Edited by E. V. Lucas. 7 vols. 1903-5.

M   J. H. Muirhead, *Coleridge as Philosopher.* New issue. 1939.

MH   Thomas Maurice, *The History of Hindostan.* 2 vols. 1795-8.

MJ   H. Maundrell, *A Journey from Aleppo to Jerusalem at Easter, A.D. 1697.* Oxford, 1707.

MLN   *Modern Language Notes.* Baltimore, 1886-.

Mod. Phil.   *Modern Philology.* Chicago, 1903-.

MP   Milton, *Poetical Works.* Edited by H. Darbishire. 2 vols. Oxford, 1952-5.

MPL   Milton, *Paradise Lost.* (Text from MP.)

MPR   Milton, *Paradise Regained.* (Text from MP.)

MW   Milton, *Prose Works.* Edited by J. Toland. 2 vols. Amsterdam, 1698.

N   A. H. Nethercot, *The Road to Tryermaine.* Chicago, 1939

NQ   *Notes and Queries.* 1849-.

OED   *Oxford English Dictionary.*

OKK   E. Schneider, *Coleridge, Opium and Kubla Khan.* Chicago 1953.

PMLA   *Publications of the Modern Language Association of America.* Baltimore, 1889-.

Q   *The Collected Writings of Thomas De Quincey.* Edited by D. Masson. 14 vols. Edinburgh, 1889.

RES   *Review of English Studies.* 1925-.

RH   Richard Hole, *Remarks on the Arabian Nights' Entertainments.* 1797.

SH   W. Haller, *The Early Life of Robert Southey,* 1774-1803. New York, 1917.

SP   *The Complete Poetical Works of Robert Southey. Collected by himself.* 10 vols. London, 1837-8.

SS   *Life and Correspondence of Robert Southey*. Edited by C. C. Southey, 6 vols. 1849.

Stud. Phil.   *Studies in Philology*. Chapel Hill, 1906-.

SW   *The Complete Works of Percy Bysshe Shelley*. Edited by R. Ingpen and W. E. Peck. 10 vols. London, 1926-30.

TLS   *Times Literary Supplement*. 1902-.

WDJ   *Journals of Dorothy Wordsworth*. Edited by Ernest de Selincourt. 1941.

WL   *The Letters of William and Dorothy Wordsworth*. Edited by E. de Selincourt. 6 vols. Oxford, 1935-9.

WP   *Poetical Works of William Wordsworth*. Edited by E. de Selincourt. 5 vols. Oxford, 1940-9.

WPR   Wordsworth, *The Prelude*. Edited by E. de Selincourt. Oxford, 1926. (All quotations from the 1850 version.)

X   J. L. Lowes, *The Road to Xanadu*. 1951 edition.

LIST OF MANUSCRIPTS USED

CMSB   Coleridge manuscripts in the British Museum.

CMSV   Microfilm copies (at Reading University) of Coleridge manuscripts now at Victoria College, Toronto.

CNB   Coleridge notebooks in the British Museum (Add. 47496-550).

CNBG   Coleridge's 'Gutch' notebook in the British Museum (Add. 27901).

CNBN   Coleridge notebook '29' in New York Public Library.

CNBV   Coleridge notebooks, no. 56 onwards, among CMSV above.

INDEX

(*Note.*—Abbreviations refer to the Bibliography. Entries in heavy type refer to central discussions of the topic, or important references to it by Coleridge.)

I. SAMUEL TAYLOR COLERIDGE

INDEX

IV. PROJECTED WORKS

II. GENERAL INDEX

INDEX

Arcadians, 211
' Archangel a little damaged ', 35, 43
Archetypes, 135
Arctic, 256
Arethusa, fountain and goddess, 211f, 266f, 341
Argo, 157
Arianism, 78
Aristotle, 190, 320
Ark, 66f
Arnold, Matthew, 34, 277, 332
Arnold, Thomas, 291
Asmodeus, 126, 221n
Aso, queen of Ethiopia, 115, 235, 267
Association theory, 103
Astrology, 113, 218
Astronomy, 113. *See* Coleridge, S. T., *Works :* Poems
Atheism, 101, 105
Athena, 185
Atonement, 57, 176-7
Aurora, 65-6. *See also* Boehme, Jacob
' Automatism of man ', 88
Avebury, 69
Awenyddion, 260
Ayin, 209, 219

Babbitt, Irving, 134, 173
Babel, Tower of, 45
Bacchus, 58, 67, 194, 260, 261 ; as Moses, 95f. *See also* Dionysus
Bacon, Francis, 49, 320, 341
Bailly, J. S., 208n
Balbec, 220. *See also* Wood, R.
Ballad, 147, 174
Barbauld, Mrs, 172
Bard, 46, 64-5 and n, 187-8, 193-4, 253, 258-62, 264ff, **274**, **311**
Barrady, River, 220-1
Basilidians, 119
Bath, 314, 332
Baxter, Andrew, 332
Bayle, P., 214 and n
Beaumont, Sir George, 40
Beaumont, Lady, 60, 343
Beauty, 56, 100, 131, 151, 165, 185, etc.
Beckford, William, 44
Beerbohm, Max, 27
Beethoven, 290
Behmen. *See* Boehme
Belief, 32
Benevolence, 86, 90, 155, 159

Bentham, Jeremy, 280
Berkeley, George (BW), 101, **106-10**, 118 and n ; *Siris*, 49n, **106-10**, 119, **143-5**, 161f, 319
Beth, 208-10
Beth-Abara, 256
Betham, E., 309
Betham, Matilda, 249
Bible, 67, 71f, 205, 213, 235, 237, 256, 279, 288, **312**, 317, 329, 342. *See also* Genesis, Isaiah, Ezekiel, St John, St Paul, Revelation, Apocrypha
Biblical cosmology, 50, 286-7, etc.
Bishop, Morchard, 315, 331
Bison, 122, 252
Blackwood's Magazine, 305
Blake, W. (K), 29-30 and nn, 49, 66 ; *Jerusalem*, 306, 313
Bloody river, 235, 339
Blunden, Edmund, BG
Boccaccio, Giovanni, 329
Bodkin, Maud, 135, 206
Boehme, Jacob (JB), **60-3** and n, 91n, 105, **120-1**, 122, 155f, 162, 191, 193f, 206, 270, 317 ; *Aurora*, 60f, 126n, 163f, 309, 317 ; love and lust in, 126 and n ; personal emblem of, 54
' Borealis race ', 64
Borgia, Cesare, 105
Bowles, William Lisle, 76, 89, 305 ; ' heart and fancy of ', 61 and n ; moralizing of, 139
Boyer, James, 47
Bracy, 187-8, 191, 193-4, 262
Brahmans, 266, **312**
Brandl, A., 345
Breeze, 158, 329, etc.
Bristol, 46, 51, 77 and n, 82, 114, 253 and n, 318, 332. *See also* Coleridge, S. T. *Life, and* Estlin, J. P.
Bristol Library, (BB), 106, 107f, 119n, 128, 242n, 253n, 255, 326, 333, 341
Brocken, 123-4 and n
Browne medal, 84
Bruce, James, *Travels* (BT), 63, 69, 111, 125, 237, 252
Brucker, J. J., *Historia . . . Philosophiae*, 108
Bryant, Jacob, *Analysis* (BA), 66, 69, 213, 217-18 and n, 263n, 338 ; *Observations* (BO), 219 ; *Plagues* (BOP), 219

INDEX

INDEX

INDEX

INDEX

Wordsworth, Christopher, 76, 308, 325
Wordsworth, Christopher, *Chancellor of Salisbury Cathedral*, 314, 325
Wordsworth, Dorothy (WL, WDJ), 42, 147, 201, 238, 278, 308, 334, 344
Wordsworth, William (WL, WP), 17, 20-3, 25, 29, 40, 42, 93-5, 114, 133, 146f, 201, 238, 249-50, 263n, 278, 280, 286f, 290, 294, 317, 333f ; *Borderers*, 114 ; *Excursion*, 280 ; *Prelude* (WPR), 18, 21, 93, 146n, 175, 180, 257, 284, 309, 325 ; Coleridge's criticism of, 240 ; comparison with Coleridge, 280-6 and nn ; 'egotistical sublime', 39, 280 ; on nature, 21, 282 and n. *See also: Lyrical Ballads*
'World ', 34, 326. *See also* Mammon
Wrath, **120-1**, 157, 161, 215, 242
'Wrath-fire', 121, 156

Xanadu, 216, 217 and n, 221

Yeats, W. B., 24-5, 107, 143, 203
Yule, H., 331

Zeus, 262, 266
Zodiac, 50, 223
Zohars, 209